The Development
and Practice
of Electronic Music

The Development and Practice of Electronic Music

Editors

JON H. APPLETON
Dartmouth College

RONALD C. PERERA
Smith College

Authors

Otto Luening
Columbia University

A. Wayne Slawson
University of Pittsburgh

Gustav Ciamaga
University of Toronto

Joel Chadabe
State University of New York at Albany

John E. Rogers
University of New Hampshire

Gordon Mumma

PRENTICE-HALL, INC., Englewood Cliffs, New Jersey

Library of Congress Cataloging in Publication Data

APPLETON, JON H   date   comp.

    The development and practice of electronic music.

    Bibliography: p.
    Discography: p.
    CONTENTS: Luening, O. Origins.—Slawson, A.W.
Sound, electronics, and hearing.—Ciamaga, G. The tape
studio. [etc.]
    1. Electronic music—History and criticism.
I. PERERA, RONALD, joint comp. II. Title.
ML3817.A66   789.9   74-12478
ISBN 0-13-207605-5

PRENTICE-HALL INTERNATIONAL, INC., London
PRENTICE-HALL OF AUSTRALIA, PTY. LTD., Sydney
PRENTICE-HALL OF CANADA, LTD., Toronto
PRENTICE-HALL OF INDIA PRIVATE LIMITED, New Delhi
PRENTICE-HALL OF JAPAN, INC., Tokyo

Contents

v

Preface

This book is intended for three groups of readers: the layman with an interest in electronic music, the student working in the field, and the musician who wishes to broaden his knowledge of the art outside his own specialty. Until recently it has been difficult for the reader to gain a comprehensive view of the field of electronic music because the literature has been either too general or too specialized. The initial articles which appeared in the popular press usually focused on the aesthetic implications of electronic music at the expense of describing how the music was produced.

Composers writing about their own works responded by elaborating theories of compositional technique which in retrospect often appear to be justifications of their work rather than explications of techniques used in its production. Throughout the 1950s many critics felt that there was something wrong about using machines to create music, and in turn many composers often gave the impression that traditional musical means and materials had no place in contemporary music.

Since the development and practice of electronic music has been largely tied to technological innovation, it is not surprising that much of the literature has been highly specialized. Articles about new circuits or mechanical devices useful to the production of electronic music were written by engineers. Composers attempted to write about problems that required a knowledge of electronics or psychoacoustics which they did not possess.

In the last decade it has been common for composers to receive the training necessary to handle these problems, and today it is not unusual for a young composer to have competence in computer programming or to be able to design electronic equipment. Also the field has become large enough to accommodate engineers who specialize in the needs of composers and performers. In the last three years at least a dozen books about electronic music have appeared in which for the first time, the authors have attempted to offer a comprehensive view. Electronic music evolves continuously as technology evolves. New media appear, merge into one another (multimedia, intermedia), are transformed, refined, superseded. To write about the present is already to write history since the state of the art changes not by decades, but by days and hours. Perhaps because of the very speed of change we lose a sense of where we have come from—which "new" ideas are actually old ones transistorized or digitized.

To put recent history in perspective with a past already rich in experimental musical ideas the editors called upon Otto Luening to trace the course of experimental music from ancient to modern times. His history is the first chapter of this book. In the quarter century since electronic music first became widely known, a few major trends have emerged distinctly. The editors have focused on four of these, choosing a roughly chronological order. The efforts of the Cologne pioneers in "pure" electronic music (*elektronische musik*) and the research of the Paris group into *musique concrète* can be seen to have merged into what the editors view as *tape studio* music, that is, music made from oscillator or microphone sources by techniques of processing, mixing, and editing with apparatus that is mostly manually controlled. The techniques of the tape studio are discussed fully in Chapter 3 by Gustav Ciamaga.

A second generation in electronic music production is represented by the devices known as voltage-controlled synthesizers, which first appeared commercially in the mid 1960s. The background, operation and compositional implications of the synthesizer are considered in Chapter 4 by Joel Chadabe. The high-speed digital computer gave rise to a third generation in electronic music: a music whose sounds are merely *calculated* as discrete level changes and then made audible by converting numerical values first into electrical values and then, through a loudspeaker, into air pressure values. With a computer and associated equipment the composer can design a "synthesizer" on paper. His studio is never made obsolete since he can rebuild his entire system merely by writing a new program. Several programs for computer-generated music have been invented in the last few years, some highly specialized, others generalized. In Chapter 5 John Rogers discusses how one major music-generating program works and how a composer might use the program to make a piece.

Paralleling the developments in the electronic music studio, whether of the tape, synthesizer or computer variety, there has been remarkable innovation in the art of "real-time" or live-electronic music techniques. Live-electronic musicians have been highly imaginative in incorporating new technologies like video and laser into their work, and their efforts often involve collaborations between visual and plastic artists, filmmakers and engineers. Gordon Mumma details the development and practice of live-electronic music in Chapter 6.

It is impossible to understand how electronic music systems operate without some degree of understanding of electronics and acoustics. For this reason Wayne Slawson's chapter on sound, electronics, and hearing has been made the second chapter of the book. From the beginning it was the editors' conception that each chapter should be the work of a specialist in one area of the field who was also a composer, and that the writing should be directed not at the technically trained person but at the general reader. While the chapters were organized so that they could be read independently of each other, the reader will find that Chapter 2 lays important technical groundwork for the concepts presented in Chapters 3–6. Photographs and inserts have been chosen to draw as broad a picture as possible of the diversity of studios, synthesizers, and composers in the field of electronic music, and the selective bibliography and discography will guide the reader in further research or in building a representative library.

The theory advanced a few years ago by Leonard B. Meyer that a period of stasis in the evolution of musical style would shortly arrive has not proven to be correct. Innovation is still the prime force in new music, but composers continue to absorb the techniques of the past. Thus electronic music—which, according to its first European and American practitioners, meant the end of performance—is now becoming a performance art. Many of those who thought the first synthesizer would replace the tape studio still find it necessary to splice tape and to use natural sound sources. The early predictions that the use of digital computers would do away with the need for tape studios, synthesizers, and even the composer himself have been revised. It appears that in the future electronic music will integrate all of these approaches, as seen in the recent development of hybrid systems. These systems consist of computer-driven synthesizers (which also have the capability of imitating natural sound sources) that are portable, and that can be used in live performance settings, with or without conventional musical instruments.

The future will no doubt see these hybrid systems become as accessible to the layman as the piano in terms of cost and ease of use. Such electronic music systems could have an even more profound influence on our musical culture by making it possible to eliminate the distinction between creative and performance skills, as is the case in many other cultures, and thereby making it possible for anyone to assume interchangeably the roles of composer, performer, and listener. As hypothetical as this may seem, this book testifies to the rapidity with which hypothesis can become reality.

Jon H. Appleton
Dartmouth College

Ronald C. Perera
Smith College

The Development
and Practice
of Electronic Music

1

Origins

OTTO LUENING

Each chapter in this book represents a fragment of a more comprehensive history that could be written a hundred years from now. The technological aspects of music have concerned theorists and composers for many centuries. After reading the following chapter, one must admit that it is not the idea of electronic music that is new, but rather the means to realize the dreams of such diverse figures as the Roman architect Vitruvius, the sixteenth-century English philosopher and scientist Francis Bacon, and Beethoven's contemporary Johann Maelzel.

Otto Luening, together with Vladimir Ussachevsky, was the first American composer to systematically explore what was formerly called "tape music" in the United States. His account of the history of electronic music becomes personal when he describes his meeting with Ferruccio Busoni in 1917. Both Luening and Gordon Mumma (the author of the last chapter in this book) present "histories" of how electronic music developed in the United States, yet at times, it is hard to believe that they are talking about the same subject. Together, they represent an approximation of the evolution of electronic music in the last thirty years. They give us an insight that can only be provided by innovative composers who have been in the midst of all that has happened to music in the recent past.

Otto Luening was born in Milwaukee, Wisconsin in 1900. He heard about electronic sound as a possible compositional tool in 1918 from Ferruccio Busoni, with whom he was studying in Zurich. Luening's career has been distinguished by his diverse activities as flutist, opera conductor, and accompanist. He is one of the Directors of the Columbia-Princeton Electronic Music Center, a former member of the Julliard School faculty, and Professor Emeritus at Columbia University, where he taught composition and conducted opera for twenty-five years. He is a member of the National Institute of Arts and Letters, and was for many years a Trustee of the American Academy in Rome and on the Educational Advisory Board of the Guggenheim Foundation.

Luening's more than three hundred works in all categories include

1

twenty-two compositions with electronic sound, eleven of these produced in collaboration with Vladimir Ussachevsky.

Electronic music is a generic term describing music that uses electronically generated sound or sound modified by electronic means, which may or may not be accompanied by live voices or musical instruments, and which may be delivered live or through speakers.

Alongside the history of accepted and established styles of music, one can trace a long line of experiments that were sometimes unsuccessful, sometimes eventually successful, and sometimes incorporated into the mainstream of music only after a long period of time. Composers and theoreticians with advanced pioneering ideas and accomplishments run like a thread through the history of music; the advanced musician of today has not been alone in his search for new horizons. The historical record contradicts the premise that everything was invented yesterday, thus setting the contemporary scene in the proper perspective without in any way detracting from its importance.

Studies in sound and sound transmission began in antiquity. In their book, *Man's World of Sound,* J. R. Pierce and E. E. David mention that Sanskrit grammarians of the third and fourth centuries B.C., notably Panini, showed the relationship between the sounds of language and the position of the mouth, an experiment that anyone can conduct by opening and closing the mouth as if yawning and tapping the side of the cheek.

In the seventeenth century, the relationships between tongue and lip positions in producing voice sounds were more precisely systematized, and, soon after, drawings of these mouth positions were made. In the nineteenth century, Alexander Melville Bell, the father of Alexander Graham Bell, developed this concept until it became known as "visible speech." The experiments of the two Bells showed conclusively that they understood clearly the relationship between the vocal tract and the sound produced. This research later became a basis for much of the work they did in developing the telephone. In 1865 Alexander Graham Bell conceived the idea of transmitting speech by electric waves. Ten years later, the principle of reproduction and transmission of sound became clear to him while he was experimenting with a telegraph. In 1876 he was able to transmit a complete sentence; his assistant heard him say quite clearly, "Watson, come here; I want you." He organized the Bell Telephone Company in 1877, and through his Volta Laboratory in Washington, D.C., he produced the first successful phonograph record; the photophone, which transmitted speech by light rays; the audiometer; and other inventions, including the flat and cylindrical wax recorders for phonographs.

Interest in sound transmission has continued at the Bell Telephone Laboratories, resulting in inventions such as the Vocoder in the 1930s, an instrument that has strongly influenced the development of electronic music since 1948. Recently, at the Bell Labs, Max Mathews has used a computer to program vocal sounds, and has simulated vocal sounds in the form of song and even choral experiments. Others are now developing this type of sound production.

However, the transmission of sound occupied the minds of men long before the invention of the telephone. Vitruvius, the Roman architect and engineer for Augustus, wrote about the acoustics of theaters in *The Ten Books of Architecture:* "Hence the ancient architects . . . by means of the canonical theory of the mathematicians and that of the musicians, endeavored to make every voice uttered on the stage come with greater clearness and sweetness to the ears of the audience."

In the eighteenth century the Russian professor Kratzenstein produced vowel sounds from tubes to which he fixed a vibrating reed, controlled by air from a bellows. Abbé Mical, a Parisian, and Ritter von Kempelen, a Hungarian, built speaking machines. Properly run, they produced intelligible words and sentences, though they lacked the quality of the human voice.

The development of instrumental sound is equally ancient. In the fifth and sixth centuries B.C., the Greek philosopher and religious teacher Pythagoras discovered the numerical ratios corresponding to the principal intervals of the musical scale. Because of his religious inclinations, he associated these ratios with what he called "harmony of the spheres." He applied these arithmetic ratios to string lengths and to the number of sound vibrations that were produced in this fashion.

In his book, *Genesis of a Music,* Harry Partch states that acoustical studies began in China in approximately 2800 B.C., and that King Fang made a fifty-three tone scale within the octave. Ho Tcheng-Tin, a Chinese, anticipated our present twelve-tone scale by about thirteen centuries. Syu-ma-Ch-ien, an ancient Chinese historian, ascribed acoustical formulas for the pentatonic scale to Ling Lun, a Chinese court musician who lived about 2700 B.C. This ancient history was related by Chu-T'sai-Yu in the sixteenth century A.D., preceding the establishment of equal temperament in the West.

In his *New Atlantis* (1624), Francis Bacon wrote:

> We have also sound-houses, where we practice and demonstrate all sounds, and their generation. We have harmonies which you have not, of quarter-sounds, and lesser slides of sounds. Divers instruments of music likewise to you unknown, some sweeter than any you have; together with bells and rings that are dainty and sweet. We represent small sounds as great and deep; likewise great sounds extenuate and sharp; we make divers tremblings and warblings of sounds, which in their original are entire. We represent and imitate all articulate sounds and letters, and the voices and notes of beasts and birds. We have certain helps which set to the ear do further the hearing greatly. We have also divers strange and artificial echoes, reflecting the voice many times, and as it were tossing it: and some that give back the voice louder than it came; some shriller, and some deeper; yea, some rendering the voice differing in the letters or articulate sound from that they receive. We have also means to convey sounds in trunks and pipes, in strange lines and distances.

This is a remarkable prophecy of electronic music as it has developed in the twentieth cenutry.

E. T. A. Hoffmann (1776–1822), the German author, musician, painter, and jurist, now known chiefly as the hero of Offenbach's opera, *The Tales of Hoffmann,* wrote a story called "The Automaton." In it he wrote about the function and meaning of music and the development of all sorts of new glass and metal instruments. He stated that higher musical principles recognize the most unusual sounds in nature and make the most heterogenous bodies resonate, but that the composer needs to combine this mysterious music into a form comprehensible to the human ear. He said, further, that any attempts to produce sound from metal strips, glass threads, glass cylinders, strips of marble, and from strings vibrating and sounding in unusual ways were significant contributions to the development of music. Hoffmann said that these attempts to penetrate the deep secrets hidden everywhere in nature would only be retarded if the commercial exploitation of inventions took place before they had been perfected. In conclusion, he stated that the aim of the musician was to discover the perfect tone, one that becomes more perfect as it relates to the secret sounds of nature, some of which can still be heard on earth. He wrote that in primitive times music was filled with poetry and with the divine instinct of prophecy, and that the legend of the music of the spheres was an echo of that mysterious primeval time in which music had the power to effect communion with the supernatural. Hoffmann exerted a strong influence on the Italian composer Ferruccio Busoni, who lived well into the twentieth century.

Early technical experiments and developments are equally fascinating when we compare them to what is happening today. Don Nicola Vicentino (1511–72), the Italian composer and theorist, was a Renaissance artist who combined historical findings with creative works. He attempted to revive some of the Greek modes and other musical practices in his compositions. He also invented an "Archicembalo," a harpsichord-like instrument with six keyboards and thirty-one steps to an octave. His ideas aroused much opposition, but he influenced subsequent generations.

Another inventor, the Jesuit priest Athanasius Kircher, described in his book, *Musurgia Universalis* (1660), a mechanical device that composed music. He used numbers and arithmetic-number relationships to represent scale, rhythm and tempo relations; hence, the name "Arca Musarithmica."

Johann Quantz, C. P. E. Bach, Johann Philipp Kirnberger, Michael and Joseph Haydn, and W. A. Mozart were all interested in automatic music. Mozart wrote beautiful works for mechanical organ, works for which he made many sketches and revisions. The mechanical organ for which he composed was an artificial playing apparatus consisting of levers, wires, springs, and toothed wheels. Compositions were written for other mechanical instruments, including one in the form of a Rococo lady playing a piano, Pan blowing the flute, and two muses playing flute and piano, with small canary birds trilling in their cages; other figures in Spanish costumes played flutes. They were all machines, small and large masterworks of the mechanical art.

Abbé Delaborde constructed a "Clavecin Electrique" in Paris in 1761. The specifications for this instrument are in the Library of the American Philosophical Society in Philadelphia. One can speculate whether Benjamin Franklin, who was interested in music, had any knowledge of this instrument; he perfected the glass harmonica at about the same time, and conducted some experiments in underwater acoustics.

Beethoven's contemporary Johann Maelzel invented several mechanical instruments, including a chess player, the metronome, a mechanical trumpeter, and the "Panharmonicon" for which Beethoven composed a piece to commemorate the Battle of Vittoria.

An "Electromechanical Piano" was invented by Hipps, the director of the telegraph factory in Neuchatel, Switzerland in 1867. It used an electromagnet. Elisha Gray's "Electromusical or Electroharmonic Piano" was demonstrated in Chicago in 1876. In Philadelphia the same year, Koenig demonstrated his "Tonametric" apparatus, which divided four octaves into 670 equal parts.

In 1895 Jullian Carrillo, a Mexican composer of Indian heritage, wrote music in quarter tones and investigated other scale formations. He subdivided the octave into ninety-six intervals, constructed instruments to reproduce divisions as small as a sixteenth tone, and brought us to the threshold of some twentieth-century discoveries. He demonstrated his microtonal instruments in New York in 1926. These included an "Octavina" for eighth tones and an "Arpa Citera" for sixteenth tones. By 1929 Alois Hàba had composed an opera in quarter tones; Hans Barth, a quarter-tone concerto for piano and strings; and Iwan Wysch-Negradsky, a harmony textbook for composing with quarter tones. These and Busoni's experiments with a Harmonium in third tones were preparations for electronic instruments that were not exclusively tied to the scales in use at that time.

The technical development of instruments was highlighted by Edison's patent for the phonograph (1878), Helmholtz's book, *Sensations of Tone* (1885), the invention of the Emile Berliner telephone transmitter and disc record (1897), and the work of W. C. Sabin, P. M. Morse, Lord Rayleigh, Dayton Miller, Harvey Fletcher, and other scientists. In 1897 Berliner perfected the Berliner disc, which made phonograph records commercially feasible. To put these events in perspective, the Sioux Indians fought their last battle at Wounded Knee in 1890.

In July, 1906, *McClure's Magazine* published an article by Ray Stannard Baker entitled "New Music for an Old World . . . Dr. Thaddeus Cahill's Dynamophone—An Extraordinary Electrical Invention For Producing Scientifically Perfect Music." Excerpts from the article indicate the fascination with which the Dynamophone was received:

> Largest Musical Instrument Ever Built, ... instead of bringing the people to the music, the new method sends the new music to the people. . . . by opening a switch we may 'turn on' the music . . . . Democracy in Music . . . . Dr. Cahill's instrument, without in any way overestimating its capabilities, or suggesting that it will displace the present forms of musical art, gives us a hint of what the music of the

> future may be like. . . . the best music may be delivered at towns, villages, and even farmhouses up to a hundred miles or more from the central station. Small country churches, townhalls, schools, at present holding up no ideals of really good music, may be provided with the same high class selections that are daily produced by the most skillful players in the cities . . . . A HUNDRED INSTRUMENTS IN ONE . . . . Lord Kelvin encourages the inventor . . . . Electricity used to Produce Music . . . . Learning to Play the Dynamophone. . . . learning to play the new instrument has been like some new wonderful discovery in an unknown musical world. Here were limitless musical possibilities waiting to be utilized. The musician uses his keys and stops to build up the voices of flute or clarinet, as the artist uses his brushes for mixing color to obtain a certain hue. . . . the workmen in the shop speak of 'electric music.' In the end the public will probably choose its own name . . . . WE SHALL KEEP THE OLD WITH THE NEW. . . . but it would be absurd to say that the new instrument will even seriously interfere with the presentation of great music of any sort. It will rather add to the public interest in music and the appreciation of musical art. . . . we welcome the new with eagerness; it has a great place to fill; it may revolutionize our musical art; but, in accepting the new, we will not give up the old.

Shortly after Dr. Cahill gave a demonstration in Holyoke, Massachusetts, the celebrated Italian pianist and composer Ferruccio Busoni wrote his "Sketch of a New Aesthetic of Music." In this remarkable collection of "notes," as he called the booklet, he questioned much in the prevailing music practice and pointed out some new possibilities. He wrote that art forms last longer if they stay close to the essence of each individual species. He suggested that music is almost incorporeal (he called it "sonorous air"), almost like Nature herself. He opposed formalism, systems, and routine, but asserted that each musical motive contains within itself its "life germ," the embryo of its fully developed form, each one different from all others. He proclaimed that the creative artist does not follow laws already made, but that he makes laws. Busoni decried a too rigid adherence to existing notation, and said that the terms "consonance" and "dissonance" were too confining. He suggested an expansion of the major-minor chromatic scale and constructed 113 other scale formations within the octave.

Busoni predicted a revolution in the field of harmony. He was convinced that instrumental music had reached a dead end and that new instruments were needed; he suggested a scale of thirty-six divisions within the octave as an interesting possibility for new music. He wrote:

> Fortunately, while busy with this essay, I received from America direct and authentic intelligence which solved the problem in a simple manner. I refer to an invention by Dr. Thaddeus Cahill. He has constructed a comprehensive apparatus which makes it possible to transform an electrical current into a fixed and mathematically exact number of vibrations. As pitch depends on the number of vibrations and the apparatus may be 'set' on any number desired, the infinite gradation of the octave may be accomplished by merely moving a lever corresponding to the pointer of a quadrant . . . . Only a long and careful series

of experiments, and a continued training of the ear can render this unfamiliar material approachable and plastic for the coming generation and for Art.[1]

Edgard Varèse, in a reminiscence of Busoni, said:

In 1907, still in my early 20's, I went to Berlin, where I spent most of the next seven years, and had the good fortune of becoming (in spite of the disparity of age and importance) the friend of Ferruccio Busoni, then at the height of his fame. I had read his remarkable little book, "A New Aesthetic of Music," a milestone in my musical development, and when I came upon, "Music is born free; and to win freedom is its destiny," it was like hearing the echo of my own thought. . . . He was very much interested in the electrical instruments we began to hear about, and I remember particularly one he had read of called the "Dynamophone," invented by a Dr. Thaddeus Cahill, which I later saw demonstrated in New York. All through his writings one finds over and over again predictions about the music of the future which have since becomes true. In fact, there is hardly a development which he did not foresee, as, for instance, in this extraordinary prophecy, "I almost think that in the new great music, machines will also be necessary and will be assigned a share in it. Perhaps industry, too, will bring forth her share in the artistic ascent!"[2]

Two years after Busoni published his booklet, the Italian Marinetti published in *Le Figaro* (Paris) his "Futurist Manifesto," which called for a worldwide artists' revolt against the ossified values of the past, represented by the "Establishment." The movement spread rapidly to Germany, Russia, and Switzerland.

"The Art of Noises," compiled in 1913 by Luigi Russolo, a Futurist painter, is still of interest.[3] He suggested fixing the pitch of noise sounds, and classified them as follows: Group I—booms, thunder claps, explosions, crashes, splashes, roars; Group II—whistles, hisses, snorts; Group III—whispers, murmurs, mutterings, bustling noises, gurgles; Group IV—screams, screeches, rustlings, buzzes, cracklings, sounds by friction; Group V—noises obtained by percussions or metals, wood, stone, and terra-cotta; Group VI—voices of animals and men, shouts, shrieks, groans, howls, laughs, wheezes, and sobs. Russolo implemented his catalogue of noises by building a whole collection of noise-making instruments. As Varèse saluted Busoni, so did Pierre Schaeffer acknowledge Russolo, calling him the originator of the concept of noise montage, which was developed at the Centre d'Étude of the Radiodiffusion Télévision Française by mid-century.

Futurism became Dadaism when Tristan Tzara coined the term in 1916

---

[1] Ferruccio Busoni, *Sketch of a New Aesthetic of Music* (New York: G. Schirmer, 1911), p. 33.

[2] *Columbia University Forum* (Spring, 1966), 20.

[3] Nicolas Slonimsky, *Music Since 1900* (New York: Charles Scribner's Sons, 1971), pp. 1298–1302.

in Zurich. His recipe for making a poem still has a bearing on some of today's artistic manifestations.

> . . . cut out the single words of a newspaper article, shake well in a bag, take them out one by one and copy them down in the order in which you picked them and you will have a beautiful poem.

Between Busoni's booklet and the advent of Dadaism, Schönberg wrote his *Harmonielehre* (Universal Edition, 1911). In this important book, triadic harmony evolved systematically and logically to a system of chords built on perfect fourths. The work ends with a prophetic statement about timbre melodies. In 1913 the Paris premiere of Stravinsky's *Rite of Spring* took place. Orchestral rhythm, timbre, and dynamics were given a new dimension, and the work had a profound effect on composers and, indeed, on the art world in general.

When I met Busoni in Zurich in 1917, his views about composition had changed since 1907. He had met the German-American theorist Bernhard Ziehn in Chicago. In 1887 Ziehn had published a remarkable harmony text that developed a system of symmetrical inversion based on the old Contrarium Reversum. When Busoni met him in 1910, Ziehn was engaged in developing a system of canonical techniques.

In his Zurich years Busoni assumed that composers who showed him scores would have mastered technical problems by themselves. He expected experimentation and analysis—novelty for its own sake no longer interested him. He talked of form, not formula; he talked more often than in the past of taste, style, economy, temperament (human, not musical!), intelligence, and equipoise.

In the early twentieth century, technical developments became far more important than either artistic speculation or musical experimentation. The idea of the steel-wire recorder was developed by Valdemar Poulsen of Copenhagen around 1902. Lee De Forest, with inspired vision, thought first of the "Audion" (now called the "Triode") in 1906. This and his three hundred other patents had a decided influence on modern communications. Satie used dynamo and airplane sounds in his *Ballet Parade* (1917). In the early 20s Varèse suggested greater cooperation between composers and engineers, a point of view repeated by Carlos Chavez in his *For A New Music* (W. W. Norton & Company, Inc., 1937). Between 1906 and 1920, radio and phonograph techniques were perfected.

At the meeting of the Eighth Soviet Congress in 1920, the physicist Leon Termen demonstrated the first model of his new instrument, which later became known as the Theremin. The sounds were produced by hand movements in the air. Several composers used it in their compositions: Paschtschenko, Schillinger, Slonimski, Varèse, Martinu, Fuleihan, and Percy Grainger, a pupil of Busoni's who since 1895 had been developing a "Free Music" with eighth tones and complete rhythmic freedom of the single voices. Grainger's music was notated on graph paper, and he himself built machines for it.

Henry Cowell's tone clusters, first introduced in 1912 and made known to the wider public in the early 20s, became the starting point for a host of extensions of piano resonance, useful as sound sources, and for experimental music. Charles Ives, Leo Ornstein and George Antheil were other American experimenters of the early twentieth century.

In Germany, Joerg Mager built an electronic "Sphärophon," which was presented at the Donaueschingen Festival in 1926. Georgy Rimsky-Korsakov composed some experimental pieces for this instrument. Supported by the city of Darmstadt, Mager later developed a "Partiturophon" and a "Kaleidophon." All these useful electronic instruments were tried in theatrical productions, and though all were destroyed in World War II, Mager's example stimulated others to explore the field. In Germany in the 30s, Bruno Helberger and Peter Lertes developed an electric musical instrument. But it was the "Trautonium," introduced by its inventor, Dr. Friedrich Trautwein, that became a practical instrument used by a number of composers, including Paul Hindemith, Richard Strauss, and Werner Egk. Hindemith, in his *Craft of Musical Composition,* acknowledges his debt to Trautwein and his instrument for providing the foundation for many of the theses he expresses in his book. The Hindemith-Trautwein research team was discontinued because of World War II and was never active again. Improvements of the "Trautonium" by Oscar Sala resulted in the "Mixtur-Trautonium," a very brilliant instrument which Sala plays and for which he composes with skill. The German composers Henze, Orff, Erbse, and others have also composed for this instrument.

In 1916 Cowell thought of controlling cross-rhythms with a keyboard. Around 1930 he introduced his idea to Termen and paid him to construct such an instrument, which he claimed was the first "electric eye" instrument. Later Nicholas Slonimsky and Josef Schillinger used this instrument, which could produce up to sixteen rhythmic combinations in three parts, all at once if desired. In 1916 Cowell composed a quartet with rhythms in four parts that was based on the overtone series, producing rhythms across the bar lines that were perhaps not playable except by mechanical rhythmic control of the piece. Cowell composed two works for the Rhythmicon: "Rhythmicana," a concerto in four movements, and "Music for Violin and Rhythmicon."

Just preceding and during the '20s various kinds of reasearch were brought into focus. For example, Ernst Kurth published his *Grundlagen des Linearen Kontrapunkts* (1917) and other works that dealt with "musical form" in Busoni's sense of the term. In 1926 Joseph Mathias Hauer presented his theory of tropes. In France, Maurice Martenot demonstrated his Ondes Martenot in the Paris Opera on April 20, 1928. Nineteen years later, he was professor at the Paris Conservatoire, instructing classes in Ondes playing. A long list of composers have used the Ondes Martenot. For instance, in 1928 Dimitri Levidis produced a "Poème Symphonique" for solo Ondes Martenot and orchestra. Others include Honegger, Milhaud, Messiaen, Jolivet, Koechlin, and Varèse. In 1938 the inventor built a special model of the instrument after the specifications of Rabindranath Tagore and Alain Danielou for the purpose of reproducing the microtonal refinements of Hindu music.

At the 1926 Chamber Music Festival in Donaueschingen, Germany, it was suggested that recordings might be used as creative tools for musical composition. Two years later a research program was established at the Hochschule für Musik in Berlin to examine this and related problems. By 1930 Paul Hindemith and Ernst Toch had produced short montages based on phonographic speedup and slowdown, sound transposition and mixing, as well as polyrhythmic experiments. Toch produced his "Fuge aus der Geographie," a work based on four-part choral writing. Hindemith used instruments and solo voice as his sound sources. Robert Beyer, in his article, "Das Problem der Kommender Musik" (*Die Musik,* XX, No. 2 [1927–28]), expressed new ideas on space or room music but gained no significant reactions from either professionals or the public.

From the late '20s and the '30s until after World War II, many small electrical instruments were built that could imitate existing instruments. Some composers tried to introduce them, but they were not readily accepted by the public or by musicians. Such instruments included the Dynaphone (1928) and the Hellertione (1929). In 1929 A. Givelet and A. Coupleux combined oscillators with a control system that used a roll of punched paper to make the first "synthesizer." In 1928 Walter Ruttmann amused himself by manipulating sound tracks by cutting and splicing. His experiments resulted in a small score that consisted of sound effects.

In 1930 Bauhaus artists experimented with a conversion of visible or hand-drawn patterns or wave-forms into audible sounds by means of mirrors and photoelectric cells. Optical sound tracks for talking pictures were invented at about this time.

In 1935 the AEG magnetophone was invented in Germany and the Hammond electric organ was perfected in the United States. Plastic tape was invented during World War II. The working side of tape is coated with an emulsion containing microscopic metallic particles. As it passes the recording head, a fluctuating magnetic field created in response to modulated electrical signals causes the particles to align themselves in patterns. These patterns can later be made to create identical voltages in the playback head, whence they are fed to an amplifier and converted to sound.

In the late '30s and the '40s many other instruments appeared: the Sonorous Cross, an instrument something like a Theremin; the Electroacoustic Piano (Electrochord, 1936); the Novachord (1938); the Ondioline (1941); the Solovox; the Clavioline (1947); the Melochord (1949); the Electronium Pi, which was used by a number of Germans—Brehme, Degen, and Jacobi; the Multimonica; the Polychord organ; the Pianophon; the Tuttivox; the Minshall Organ; and several other electric organs.

Pierre Schaeffer, an engineer in Paris, presented a "Concert of Noises" over the French Radio in 1948. Like the Hindemith and Toch experiments of the '20s, natural and instrumental sounds were arranged in a series of montages. Schaeffer used phonographs to treat, manipulate, and play his works. In 1948 he was joined by the engineer Jacques Poullin, and they experimented with instrumental sound. Schaeffer suggested the name *musique concrète* for this music because it is made of concrete material and is organized experimentally, whereas ordinary music is created abstractly, written in symbols, and results in instrumental sounds only when it is performed. The composer Pierre Henry joined Schaeffer and they composed jointly "Symphonie pour un Homme Seul."

The first public performance of *musique concrète* was given in 1950 at the École Normale de Musique. Recordings and tapes of the program were subsequently presented in Salzburg, Austria and at the Berkshire Music Center in Lenox, Massachusetts. The same year, this new medium was used in broadcasting and in the theater. The following year, the Radiodiffusion Française organized the "Group for Research on Musique Concrète," which included a specially equipped studio for technical, acoustic, and artistic research. Schaeffer and Henry produced an opera, *Orpheus,* for concrete sounds and voice, and opened the research studio to outside composers. These included Messiaen, Boulez, Delannoy, Jolivet, Phillipot, Barraqué, Dutilleux, H. Barraud, Y. Baudrier and Hodier.

In 1952 machines for concrete music and space projection were patented. The first commercial films with concrete music and the first broadcasts of concrete music reached Holland, Demark, Switzerland, and the Koussevitsky Festival at Brandeis University in Waltham, Massachusetts. That same year, Schaeffer published his book, *A la recherche d'une musique concrète* and Andre Moles of the *National Committee for Scientific Research* joined the group.

The program notes for these early concerts best express the underlying philosophies of these pioneers. Schaeffer wrote:

> I belong to a generation which is largely torn by dualism. The cate-chism taught to men who are now middle-aged was a traditional one, traditionally absurd: spirit is opposed to matter, poetry to technique, progress to tradition, individual to the group and how much else. From all this it takes just one more step to conclude that the world is absurd, full of unbearable contradictions. Thus a violent desire to deny, to destroy one of the concepts, especially in the realm of form, where, according to Malraux, the Absolute is coined. Fashion faintheartedly approved this nihilism.
>
> If concrete music were to contribute to this movement, if, hastily adopted, stupidly understood, it had only to add its additional bellowing, its new negation, after so much smearing of the lines, denial of golden rules (such as that of the scale), I should consider myself rather unwelcome. I have the right to justify my demand, and the duty to lead possible successors to this intellectually honest work, to the extent to which I have helped to discover a new way to create sound, and the means—as yet approximate—to give it form.
>
> . . . Photography, whether the fact be denied or admitted, has completely upset painting, just as the recording of sound is about to upset music . . . . For all that, traditional music is not denied; any more than the theatre is supplanted by the cinema. Something new is added: a new art of sound. Am I wrong in still calling it music?

Messiaen had this to say:

> Music, in the harmonic sense of the word, has now attained its limit. The composers of the twentieth cenury will not go beyond it. We must wait at least two hundred years for a renewal in this direction. On the other hand, the other elements of music (especially rhythmic ones which have been forgotten for so long: duration, timbre, attack, intensity) are nowadays restored to a position of honor.

The complete Schaeffer-Henry opera, *Orpheus,* was performed at the Donaueschingen Festival in Germany in 1953. The outraged audience and press were so vociferous that international attention was soon focused on the new music and its composers. Since then the Group for Research on Musique Concrète has developed its workshops and study groups, produced much music for broadcast, concert, and theater, built a concert hall to perform the music, and trained and introduced many French composers—as well as those of other nationalities—to the public. Schaeffer and his colleagues have taken out many patents, and the work of the Group for Research has become internationally famous.

Several years before his death in 1960, Werner Meyer-Eppler supplied me with a list of the important dates in the development of electronic music in Germany, along with an urgent request to keep the record straight by publishing it at an appropriate time. Meyer-Eppler was an eminent German physicist and director of the Institute of Phonetics at Bonn University. In 1948 Homer W. Dudley from the Bell Telephone Laboratories demonstrated for Meyer-Eppler the Vocoder, a composite device consisting of an analyzer and an artificial voice. This instrument and *The Mathematical Theory of Communication* (1949) by Claude Shannon and Warren Weaver made a strong impression on Meyer-Eppler. He used a tape of the Vocoder to illustrate his lecture, "Developmental Possibilities of Sound," given at the Northwest German Music Academy in Detmold in 1949. During the lecture Robert Beyer of the Northwest German Radio, Cologne, took notice of the new possibilities of producing sound. Beyer was known as the author of the previously mentioned article, "The Problem of the Coming Music."

After the Detmold meeting, it was decided to prepare lectures on "electronic music" for the International Summer School for New Music in Darmstadt. These lectures were to be in the form of a report about known electronic instruments and the process of speech synthesis as stated in Meyer-Eppler's book, *Electronic Tone Generation, Electronic Music, and Synthetic Speech* (Bonn, 1949). The term "electronic music" was therefore used to describe any kind of music that could be produced by electronic instruments. Two lectures by Beyer and one by Meyer-Eppler on "The World of Sound of Electronic Music" were presented at the International Summer School for New Music in Darmstadt in August, 1950. Among those attending were Edgard Varèse and Herbert Eimert.

In 1951 Meyer-Eppler made systematic examinations and produced models of synthetic sounds, which led to the conclusion that previous limitations of sound production could be considerably reduced. He used a "Melochord," invented by H. Bode, and an AEG tape recorder to conduct his experiments. He presented these samples (with demonstrations) in a lecture, "Possibilities of Electronic Sound Production," in July at the International Summer School for New Music at Darmstadt. Schaeffer attended the lecture. Under the same auspices, Beyer discussed "Music and Technology" and Eimert lectured on "Music on the Borderline." At the Tonmeister meeting in Detmold in October, Meyer-Eppler lectured on "Sound Experiments," enhancing his comments with examples of sound; the demonstrations were received with reservations by some of the attending composers and with great enthusiasm by others. The term "authentic composition" was coined. Fritz Enkel, technical director of the Northwest German Radio, Colonge, was present.

On October 18, 1951, a program of music called "The World of Sound of Electronic Music" was broadcast over the Cologne radio station. It was a forum with Beyer, Eimert, and Meyer-Eppler participating, the last providing examples of sound. On the same day, a committee consisting of those gentlemen, Enkel, Schulz, and a few others from the technical department of the Cologne radio resolved "to follow the process suggested by Dr. Meyer-Eppler to compose directly onto magnetic tape" and to begin the work at the Cologne radio station. This resolution provided the impetus for the creation of an electronic studio in the Cologne radio station. In December of that year Meyer-Eppler lectured on "New Methods of Electronic Tone Generation" for an audience of about a thousand at a meeting of technical and scientific societies at the House of Technique in Essen.

In collaboration with Meyer-Eppler at the Institute of Phonetics at Bonn University in 1952, Bruno Maderna produced his "Musica su due Dimensioni" and performed it at the Darmstadt Summer School before an audience that included Pierre Boulez, Karel Goeyvaerts, Bengt Hambraeus, Giselher Klebe, Gottfried Michael Koenig, and Karlheinz Stockhausen. The program stated that the work was for flute, percussion, and loudspeaker; Maderna wrote:

> 'Musica su due Dimensioni' is a first attempt to combine the past possibilities of mechanical instrumental music with the new possibilities of electronic tone generation as presented by Dr. Meyer-Eppler in the Darmstadt Summer School for New Music in 1951.

In December, 1952 Meyer-Eppler lectured at a technical Hochschule in Aachen on "Authentic Compositions." Samples of sound and models of sounds were presented, but no actual compositions were played. Nevertheless, Eimert in his article, "Electronic Music—a New World of Sound," had this to say:

> The idea of infinite tonal material is an age-old music dream. At the beginning of our century Busoni and Schönberg occupied themselves with such "free compositional flight" . . . . They were stopped at the border of instrumental mechanism, Busoni with his splitting of his tonal materials [Eimert neglected to mention Busoni's description of Cahill's "Dynamaphone" and electric-sound production as one way out of the dilemma!], and Schönberg with his tone-color melodies. But both saw

the problem in its present-day importance, even though Busoni said, "For a generation it will not be possible of solution." The technical solution today, thanks to electronic production of sound, is no longer a doubtful quantity . . . . It is also not a matter of fantasies about the future. The first problem is rather just as concrete as it is difficult. It is simply: "Begin!"

In 1953 Eimert and Beyer produced the first compositions that used only electronically generated sounds; they received technical assistance from Enkel, Bierhals, and Schütz. Eimert and Meyer-Eppler presented samples of this program at the International Summer School in Darmstadt in July of that year; Meyer-Eppler then lectured at the International Acoustical Congress in Delft, The Netherlands, while Eimert spoke at the Premiere Decade Internationale de Musique Experimentale in Paris.

The Cologne radio presented a public concert in a small hall on October 19, 1954 as part of the series, "Music of Our Time," using only electronically generated sounds by Stockhausen, Goeyvaerts, Pousseur, Gredinger, and Eimert. The new pieces used strict serial technique. In spite of the previous concerts, attempts were later made to represent these works as the first truly electronic compositions anywhere. In 1956, under the same auspices, a similar concert took place, featuring works by Hambraeus, Koenig, Heiss, Klebe, Stockhausen, and Křenek. In contrast with earlier performances, it presented "space music" that was fed through five separate channels and through groups of speakers distributed throughout the hall. Stockhausen joined the ranks of the lecturers who now spread the gospel to new cities and other European countries.

Excerpts from reviews of the Conference on Electronics and Concrete Music over Radio Basel in May, 1955 give a good indication of how these compositions were received:

Just as this development necessarily had to come about and could not be stopped, it will be impossible to do anything against this new machine in the future. The innovators will not bypass any of the unlimited possibilities in their experiments; prominent critics and aesthetes will praise the product of "progress" and will say profound things about it. The public will not want to appear stupid and the snobs will be happy and enthused. A time, perhaps decades, of strange music and music practice is ahead of us, no question about that. Of course, in the process good minds of quality will emerge and . . . geniuses will impart to the matter something like sense and form . . . . Thus music leaves the realm of man with its thousands of physical restrictions and enters the fantastic realm of technical omnipotence. . . . The works . . . offered acceptable sonority, nothing new, and were uninteresting and weak . . . . In the "Concrète" noise art one could, if one followed it with good will, find nothing but barefaced nonsense occasionally thrown together with a great degree of refinement . . . . But let us not insult the animal that cannot laugh and let us talk more correctly about human seriousness, the seriousness of the charlatan!—*Volksrecht*

It is now up to the artist, to the composer, to derive creatively from the inner laws of this novel music a new musical theory, new music aesthetics. As in every art, here, too, the creatively shaping mind has the last ruling word.—*Schweizerische Illustrierte Zeitung.*

The reviewer of the *Landchaftler* reported the remarks of H. Stuckenschmitt:

> For two days, a new world of music has opened to us; its sounds and sonorities put us through all degrees of intellectual and sensuous disquiet. Amazement and fright, admiration and resistance, skepticism and positive responses alternate within us. We ask ourselves whether truly this is the beginning of a new world or whether perhaps the world, whether our cultural world, is about to perish. There are people who earnestly and seriously fear this, where music becomes the slave of the machine, or, where, if you will, technical progress takes hold of art.

The newspaper critic added:

> The sounds range all the way from muted snoring to a howling storm, from the twittering of birds to the chatter of machine guns. But it can hardly be said that this has anything to do with music, all the less so since the poverty of musical thought was manifested with striking impressiveness. Perhaps the matter is as . . . Stuckenschmitt said on another occasion, "The oftener we encounter these sonorous phenomena, the more they fascinate us. The initial resistance, the negative experience, gives way to curiosity and interest: the experience becomes positive. We recognize the new sounds as artistic components of our world, this technicized world, that has reshaped our lives in all its parts; already a young generation is at work to organize the form into great works of art."

The newspaper reviewer ended his remarks by saying: "Whether this electronic music of the future has a future will in all probability be decided by its further development."

The development of electronic music in the United States took quite a different turn from the path followed in Europe. Henry Brant experimented with directional sound in this country before similar music was produced in Europe. But it was Vladimir Ussachevsky who gave the first public demonstration of tape music at his Composers Forum on May 9, 1952 in McMillin Theatre at Columbia University, shortly before Meyer-Eppler's lectures at the Summer School in Darmstadt. His experiments in electronic music were independent of those in Europe. His equipment consisted of an Ampex 400 tape recorder, a borrowed Magnachord, and, later, a device designed by the young engineer, Peter Mauzey, to create feedback, a form of reverberation. Some of the other extremely limited equipment he eventually used was borrowed or purchased with his own money. The Forum attracted a great deal of attention; Henry Cowell wrote in the *Musical Quarterly* (October, 1952): "Ussachevsky is now in the process of incorporating some of these sounds into a composition. The pitfalls are many; we wish him well."

At this point, the story of electronic music in the United States becomes in part a personal narrative. I invited Ussachevsky to present his experiments at the Bennington, Vermont Composers Conference, where I was in charge of composition, in August, 1952. My own involvement in the medium began when I worked with Busoni in Zurich in 1918 and read his "A Sketch of a New Aesthetic of Music." In 1949, in the introduction to Harry Partch's book, *Genesis of a Music*,[4] I predicted that Partch's forty-three-tone scale and the sounds from the many instruments he had built could be used in conjunction with electronic and other scientific developments in sound, and that one might expect a strange and beautiful music to result. Partch himself wrote:

> Spontaneity of execution is the essence of music vitally connected to the human body, through the mouth, the ears, and the emotions. Spontaneity does not necessarily imply any inconstancy of execution; it is almost always present when a piece of music is performed, with almost no deviations, as it was conceived and the same every time. That this ideal is possible only with a very few performers is very evident, and that it is actually on the threshold of a new age as a result of greater (electronic) tonal means requiring only one or a very few performers is also very evident. Let some seventh son of a seventh son say that it will one day cross the threshold! . . . Until the electronic engineer has been educated into becoming a good husband, the carrying of his bride Music over the threshold augurs no good. The affiance has a body of well-tested and exciting dynamics, but the suitor-engineer, with an obsession for maintaining "level" in his nervous fingers, twirls them into electromagnetic oblivion in the flick of any eyelash. Perhaps some of the old lady's habits do need changing, but not by a nascent, dial-twirling, prospective young husband who gives no notice.[5]

At Bennington, Ussachevsky, at the controls of the Ampex, conducted a series of experiments with flute, violin, clarinet, piano, and vocal sounds. With earphones and a flute, I began developing my first tape-recorder composition. Most of these early works were improvised, though we soon developed various kinds of notational shorthand. We were invited by Oliver Daniel to produce a group of works for the Leopold Stokowski concert at the Museum of Modern Art in New York under the auspices of the American Composers Alliance and Broadcast Music, Inc. We transported our equipment in Ussachevsky's car to Henry Cowell's house in Woodstock, New York, where we spent two weeks. With a borrowed portable tape recorder, an oversized wooden speaker, and old carpeting to deaden sound we went to work. Using a flute as the sound source, I developed two impressionistic, virtuoso pieces, "Fantasy in Space" and "Low Speed." The latter was an exotic composition that took the flute below its natural range, but with certain acoustic combinations and the help of Mauzey's reverberation box, the flute was made to sound like a strange new instrument. I also began work on an "Invention" based on a twelve-tone row with complex contrapuntal combinations. Ussachevsky began work on an eight-minute composition that used piano as the primary sound source; transformed by simple devices, the piano in turn sounded like deep-toned gongs

---

4 (Madison, Wisc.: University of Wisconsin Press), 1949.
5 *Ibid.*, p. 44.

and bells, tone clusters on an organ, and a gamelan orchestra with metallic crescendos organized into an expressive whole.

This primitive laboratory was brought to Ussachevsky's living room in New York City, where we completed the compositions. With more borrowed equipment we added the final touch to our works in the studio of the basement of Arturo Toscanini's Riverdale home, at the invitation of David Sarser, the Maestro's sound engineer. The concert took place at the Museum of Modern Art on October 28, 1952. It was the first public concert of tape-recorder music in the United States. Ussachevsky's "Sonic Contours" and my "Low Speed," "Invention," and "Fantasy in Space" were on the program. Jay Harrison wrote in the *New York Herald Tribune:*

> It has been a long time in coming, but music and the machine are now wed . . . . The result is as nothing encountered before. It is the music of fevered dreams, of sensations called back from a dim past. It is the sound of echo . . . . It is vaporous, tantalizing, cushioned. It is in the room and yet not part of it. It is something entirely new. And genesis cannot be described.

Nat Hentoff in *Downbeat* predicted a breakthrough into pop music and Luciano Berio reviewed the concert for the Italian press.

The program was broadcast over WNYC in New York and WGBH in Boston. We were then invited to give a live interview demonstration on Dave Garroway's news program, *Today,* on NBC television. We were met at the studio by a member of the Musicians Local 802, who asked if I had a union card. I said, "No, but if any flutist in the union can improvise the program, I will be glad to have him take over." That settled the matter. A crew of eight engineers tried to connect Mauzey's little box, but it would not work. Five minutes before the telecast, Mauzey was finally allowed to operate his machine. After Garroway's introduction, I improvised sequences for the tape recorder. Ussachevsky then and there put them through electronic transformations.

In April, 1953 Radiodiffusion Française in Paris included "tape music," as our contribution was called, in their Festival. It was introduced to the Paris listeners by Bernard Blin. Broadcast Music, Inc. sent Ussachevsky to represent us. Our contributions, stemming from a desire to extend the resonances of existing instruments, were different from the European compositions. That same summer, Stokowski commissioned us to make a two-and-a-half-minute piece for his CBS program, *Twentieth Century Concert Hall.* The resulting composition, *Incantation* was produced in the Ussachevsky living room. For sound sources we used woodwind instruments, voice, bell sonorities, and piano. A program of "Music in the Making" at Cooper Union under the partial patronage of the Music Performance Trust Fund and the Musicians Union established good relations with the union. The fact that the conductor, Broekman, announced that this concert probably signalled the eventual end of live music did not seem to detract from the audience's genuine interest.

In late 1953, after receiving a commission from the Louisville Orchestra and a Faculty Grant from Barnard College, I persuaded Ussachevsky to produce a joint composition to test the feasibility of combining the new medium with a symphony orchestra. We were obliged to cover some of the expenses with our own funds, a repeated necessity for several years. The Rockefeller Foundation became interested in the Louisville project, and they purchased a machine for us. Our collaboration in this composition ("Rhapsodic Variations") was described by Howard Shanet:

> The nature and degree of their collaboration vary from one composition to another . . . . In general they work quite independently, the collaboration usually taking the form of criticism and suggestions offered to each by each other at frequent stages along the road.

Sometimes we would actually exchange or borrow materials from each other. In our pieces from this period, we not only mixed the new sonorities with the timbres of the symphony orchestra, but also devised a system of notation that would enable the conductor to follow the tape recorder and that would be acceptable for copyright in the United States. "Rhapsodic Variations," programmed on March 20, 1954 by the Louisville Orchestra, is believed to be the first performance of tape-recorder music with symphony orchestra anywhere. Recordings of our earliest music were released in 1954–55.

Our mobile laboratory, together with a projector, was next moved to the MacDowell Colony, where we composed a score for the ballet, *Of Identity*, commissioned by the American Mime Theatre. A new assignment came from Alfred Wallenstein and the Los Angeles Philharmonic Orchestra, and we produced "A Poem of Cycles and Bells," an orchestral paraphrase of our two early pieces, "Fantasy in Space" and "Sonic Contours." The transcription proved to be a post-graduate course in notation and ear training for the composers. This work was performed repeatedly in Los Angeles and elsewhere.

During this same period other private electronic-music studios were founded in the United States. The commercial studio of Louis and Bebe Barron produced electronic-sound scores for films such as "The Bells of Atlantis," first screened at the Venice Festival in the autumn of 1952, and "Jazz of Lights," "Forbidden Planet," and other films shown in this country and abroad. The Barrons depended on electronic-sound generators as their only sound source. They were in a sense preceded by Orson Welles, Luis Bunuel, and other motion picture directors who made extra-musical sounds into tape loops. Street noises and sounds made by the characters in action served as a primitive and natural source of musique concrète. John Cage and his colleagues established a bank of sounds in a private studio in the Bowery. In his selection and arrangement of material Cage was influenced by the philosophy of chance, based on the *I Ching* or *Book of Changes*. In 1954 Cage's "Williams Mix" (with eight loudspeakers) was first performed at the Donaueschingen Festival, where it made a strong impression. Edgard Varèse worked in his private studio in Greenwich Village, assisted by Ann McMillan. His composition, "Déserts," was first performed in Paris at the Concert de L'Orchestre National under the direction of Hermann Scherchen, and over Radiodiffusion Television Française on December 2, 1954. This work, combining live and electronic sounds, was received with much interest and was repeated in other European centers and later, in the United States, where it was ultimately recorded. Varèse's "Déserts" continued to attract attention here and in Europe, and he planned his "Poeme Electronique" (1958) for the Philips Radio Exhibition at the Brussels Exposition. This composition used four hundred loudspeakers accompanied by a series of projected images chosen by Le Corbusier. It was heard daily by an audience of fifteen or sixteen thousand persons for six months. The reactions ranged from terror, anger, and stunned awe to amusement and wild enthusiasm. Varèse called his work "organized sound."

In general, universities were not yet interested in electronic music at this time; exceptions were the University of Illinois, where work with computers was being done under the direction of Hiller and Isaacson, and the University of Toronto, where Hugh Le Caine, sponsored by the Canadian Research Council, was doing significant work. Commercial radio stations did not seem interested in setting up studios and research programs like those in Europe, so Ussachevsky and I decided that university sponsorship would best help electronic music to develop in the United States. We wrote a report for the Rockefeller Foundation on the state of experimental music in Europe and the United States, including recommendations about the best program to be followed here.

Our studio in the Ussachevsky living room was moved to my apartment. We then reported to President Kirk of Columbia University that unless we could have space on the campus, our whole program would be seriously jeopardized. Soon afterwards, we were provided with suitable quarters—the charming "Charles Adams" house, located on campus at the site of the former Bloomingdale Insane Asylum, now the site of Ferris Booth Hall. There we completed an abstract sound score for Orson Welles' production of *King Lear*.

In 1955 RCA demonstrated the Olson-Belar Sound Synthesizer. Alfred Wallenstein, the eminent conductor, spent three days studying this machine and reported to a gathering of engineers that if properly supervised it could add a new dimension to the art of music. A recording on which existing instruments were imitated was released. Davidson Taylor, director of the School of Arts at Columbia University, suggested that we try to obtain the synthesizer on loan. Ussachevsky wanted very much to pursue this possibility, and I wrote to several RCA executives. We heard that Professor Milton Babbitt of Princeton University, who had been preoccupied with electronic music since the late '30s, was also interested in working with this machine. In the course of discussing the possible future of electronic music, Babbitt, Ussachevsky, and I suggested first, to the Rockefeller Foundation, the formation of a University Council for Electronic Music comprising representatives from those institutions that had begun working in the field. Our report to the Rockefeller Foundation included a detailed description of the equipment and personnel needed for a representative center in the United States. It asked for technical assistants, electronic equipment, space and materials available to other composers free of charge, and a system consisting of a control console and nineteen loudspeakers for public concerts. A grant of $175,000 over a period of five years was made to Columbia and Princeton. Our application was approved with the recommendation that we procure the RCA synthesizer. In January, 1959 the Columbia-Princeton Electronic Music Center, under the direction of Professors Luening and Ussachevsky of Columbia and Professors Babbitt and Sessions of Princeton, was formed, with Ussachevsky acting as chairman. As soon as possible we invited other composers to work at the Center. These included Michiko Toyama from Japan, Bülent Arel from Turkey, Mario Davidovsky from Argentina, Halim El-Dabh from Egypt, and Charles Wuorinen from Columbia University, soon followed by many other distinguished composers from this country and abroad. Varèse revised the electronic part of "Déserts" in the Center, and for a while worked there regularly. Our policy was to invite highly qualified composers and, thus, to establish standards of accomplishment.

The Columbia-Princeton Electronic Music Center gave its two initial concerts at McMillin Theatre, Columbia University, on May 9 and 10, 1961. The programs included an introduction by Jacques Barzun, "Electronic Study No. 1" (Davidovsky), "Leiyla and the Poet" (El-Dabh), "Creation-Prologue" (Ussachevsky), "Composition for Synthesizer" (Babbitt), "Stereo Electronic Music No. 1" (Arel), "Gargoyles for Violin Solo and Synthesized Sound" (Luening), and "Symphonia Sacra" (Wuorinen).

Much of the daily press wrote favorably of the concert; many magazines reported that it was historically significant. There was, however, strong opposition from one paper, the *New York Herald Tribune*. Its leading music critic (and our Columbia colleague), Paul Henry Lang, sent an assistant to review the concert. Then Lang wrote an article under the resounding headline, "Dictatorship of the Tube," in which he hinted that young composers interested in tape music had lost their bearings. Lang received some vitriolic letters about his statements, but also some support. Long debates about whether to answer the attack finally resulted in a letter from Jacques Barzun to Lang, published in the *Herald Tribune* on May 28, 1961. Lang responded with a second article, "Music and Musicians: the Chaos Machine." Barzun's letter had said:

> Your second-hand report of what I am supposed to have said in opening the concert of electronic music at Columbia University shows again how hard it is to insinuate a fresh notion into the mind even of the judicious and the interested. The thought-cliché on the given subject is automatically substituted for the unfamiliar idea . . . It is because audiences and critics approach the new in the self-indulgent mood of a political crowd at a rally—hostile or infatuated—that the history of artistic change is such a sorry spectacle of fighting in the dark.

Lang's response expressed the fear that the machine had taken over. He wrote yet another article, "Electronic Game: Its Ground Rules," stating "Since electronic music will figure in the news more and more, perhaps we should examine the premises from which it proceeds." He described the American contributions as ". . . a harmless pastime, although actually the one legitimate facet of electronic music, for eventually these new tonal resources will be harnessed, and . . . will undoubtedly prove useful."

During the period from 1961 to 1968, the medium expanded considerably in many directions. Most important was its acceptance by popular composers and by the primary and secondary school systems. By 1968 a public record of these accomplishments was available. That year, the *International Electronic Music Catalogue,* compiled by Le Groupe de Recherches Musicales de l'Office de Radiodiffusion-Television Française and the Independent Electronic Music Center, Inc. in the United States listed 5,140 compositions in the new medium. We can readily assume that since then, several thousand more have been produced. The same catalogue listed 556 studios in 39 countries. Most of these were either professional or academic studios. Some were affiliated with radio stations, universities, or conservatories, some with junior and senior high schools. The list does not include all private or commercial installations.

From 1960 to 1970, more than 225 compositions by more than 60 composers from 11 countries were produced at the Columbia-Princeton Electronic Music Center. Of these, 60 works by 21 composers have been recorded on commercial discs. There has been a similar expansion in the other studios, now far too extensive to describe in detail. Three recent Pulitzer Prizes in music were awarded for works that use electronic sound: "String Quartet with Electronic Sounds" by Leon Kirchner, "Time's Encomium" by Charles Wuorinen, and "Synchronism No. 6" by Mario Davidovsky.

Other directions are already being explored and will undoubtedly lead somewhere, though it is difficult to predict exactly where. In 1971 Orcus Research in Kansas City published a book entitled *Bio-Music,* by Manfred Eaton. Bio-music is a term used by Orcus Research to describe a class of electronic systems that

> use biological potentials in feedback loops to induce powerful, predictable, repeatable, physiological/psychological states, which can be elegantly controlled in real time. . . . the hallucinogenic powers of electronic sensory feedback systems can be controlled and guided with a precision utterly impossible with chemical methods.

Perhaps now is the time to extend the warning that Busoni included in "A New Aesthetic of Music" in 1907; when he wrote that a long period of ear training would be necessary to make the new sounds useful for artistic purposes. It seems that if we develop a sense of responsibility and have a deep desire to bring human satisfaction to large numbers of individuals, our visions will become penetrating enough to draw on the greatness of the past, add to it our new findings, and move forward into a future that even now promises beautiful new experiences as yet undreamed of.

2

Sound, Electronics, and Hearing

A. WAYNE SLAWSON

What is resonance, formant, modulation? Why do we hear the way we do? How is electrical energy converted into the sound-pressure varia- tions we call music? Composers, performers, and listeners deal every day with phenomena that they may understand only intuitively, or not at all, even though electronic technology—especially the technology of recording—is part of the very fabric of twentieth-century musical culture.

For the composer of electronic music, a deeper understanding is vital. Commercial electronic-music systems reflect the musical bias of their designers, who are engineers. There is a certain kind of music easily produced on each instrument, and we have already learned to identify some cliches as the "Buchla sound," the "Moog sound," and so forth. Where we once heard that electronic music would usher in an era of unlimited new sonic possibilities, we now hear the criticism that the sound repertory of electronic music is de- pressingly small. The composer who comes to the electronic studio without the theoretical background to make independent decisions may be trapped in that small sound world, limited to what he can produce by trial and error and random knob manipulation.

In this chapter Wayne Slawson presents the communication chain, *which links the composer's musical intention to the listener's ear through the medium of sound. Sound and the measurement of sound are discussed in de- tail, with an especially interesting explanation of the phenomenon of reso- nance. The Fourier theorem is presented, with an explanation of the spectra of basic waveforms used in electronic music. There is also an introduction to the acoustics of speech. The second part of the chapter is devoted to transdu- cers—those links in the chain whereby sound is transformed into electrical signal, and vice versa—and to electronics. The function of loudspeakers and microphones is considered and, then, one by one, the function of electronic devices such as amplifiers, filters, and oscillators. The third section is devoted to hearing: the structure of the ear, the "place theory" and "volley theory" of frequency analysis, and the principal kinds of psychoacoustic measurements of loudness, pitch, timbre, and sound localization.*

A. Wayne Slawson, Associate Professor of Music at the University of Pittsburgh, received his A.B. in mathematics and his A.M. in music from the University of Michigan, where he studied composition with Ross Lee Finney and Leslie Bassett. He took his Ph.D. in psychology (psychoacoustics) at Harvard with S. S. Stevens. Since then, his career has been divided between teaching, composing, and research in computer synthesis of speech, a field in which he has contributed several articles to scientific journals. He has been a post-doctoral fellow at M.I.T. and the Royal Institute of Technology in Stockholm, a member of the technical staff of the Mitre Corporation, a visiting composer and researcher at the Electronic Music Studio Foundation, Stockholm, and an Assistant Professor of Music Theory at Yale University. His compositions include works for conventional instruments as well as synthesized and computer-generated sound. His piece, Wishful Thinking about Winter, *for computer-synthesized tape, has been recorded.*

No orchestration text has a chapter analogous to this one. Yet the instruments of the orchestra are complex acoustic devices that have been investigated extensively by a small but devoted band of physicists. Why are their results of only peripheral interest to practicing musicians, and why, conversely, are the technical and scientific fundamentals of electronic music considered, nearly universally, to be an essential part of a composer's training? Is it because the instruments of the orchestra are designed solely for the purpose of producing music, whereas those employed in the production of electronic music were originally designed for something else? I suspect that the question is not so easily answered. In fact, composers who write for performing instruments might well improve their craft by a knowledge of the physics of those instruments. On the other hand, there are some composers of electronic music who have only rudimentary and confused notions of the technical details underlying their productions.

Perhaps the answer lies more in the way electronic devices are used to make music. There is something more fundamental and basic about the composer's relationship to the sounds produced in the studio, by the synthesizer, or by the computer. The orchestrator is presented with his palette ready-made; the composer of electronic music must manufacture his own paint. The purpose of this chapter is to provide the composer with a technical foundation for that demanding task.

A Communication System

Electronic music can be considered a communication between the consciousness of the composer and the consciousness of the listener. The communication is accomplished by means of a system comprising several stages. Certain of these stages we understand in some detail, but most of them are beyond our present state of knowledge. The topics discussed in this chapter concern links in the system that are relatively well-understood, yet even here a good deal of uncertainty is encountered. Let us begin by tracing through the components of the system.

The beginning of this system of communication is one of its most mysterious links. We know next to nothing about what goes on in the minds of composers at the conceptual stages of composition. We have the writings of composers themselves, but these are mostly quite impressionistic and too personal to provide useful generalizations. I think we can say that a composer in the process of composition has in mind a musical *intention*. Weaknesses or strengths in his compositional skills and in later links of the communication system inevitably modify the composer's original intention.

Realization of a composer's intention is achieved through, and limited by, his craft. A composer's craft is a set of skills, of which some are quite specific and others, more general and hard to describe. In this book we are attempting primarily to strengthen the more explicit, technical side of the next link in our communication system, the composer's *compositional and technical skills*.

Let me try to distinguish between these two kinds of skills. We can learn something from Morley's *Plaine and Easie Introduction to Practicall Musicke*, from Rameau's *Traite d'Harmonie*, and from Hindemith's *Craft of Musical Composition*, but not all of any one of these great works by composers is useful to us today. The aspects of these works that do not apply to our music today— details of notation, harmony, melodic direction—constituted the technical skills of the period. What I am suggesting is that even this book may soon be out of date. Though some of it will be superseded quite properly as the art and technique of electronic music evolves, I think that, to the degree to which technique advances, some of the technical skills we are trying to impart will slip over into the compositional category and become of more lasting value.

There are several distinguishable means of producing electronic music, and these *sound-generation systems* are the first mechanical and electronic stages in our communication system. They are not merely passive links. Each different kind of system demands somewhat different technical skills, which in turn limit the composer's compositional skills and intentions.

Though often considered part of sound generation, the loudspeakers and earphones that convert the electronic results of the sound-generation system into the sounds that we hear are common to all sound-generation systems, and will be assigned a separate link in our communication chain. Microphones belong in this link as well, even though they work in the opposite direction. In electronic music they are involved only occasionally in our composer-to-listener communication system. This chapter will provide a brief glimpse into the fundamentals of *electroacoustic conversion devices*, along with a discussion of some of their limitations.

Sound itself, the next link in our communication chain, is the common stuff of all music. The science of sound—acoustics—is a well-developed and active branch of physics. Though many of the results of acoustic research are of little relevance to electronic music, there are many others, particularly in the field of elementary acoustics, that are important in themselves and that embody fundamental ideas.

The ear and the parts of the nervous system that process auditory information are called the *auditory system*. This is the next link in our chain. Far more than a passive converter of sound to electrochemical nerve impulses, the ear is a very complex analyzer of sound. Its analysis emphasizes certain aspects of sound and seems to ignore others. While much is known about the auditory system, I doubt if any psychologist or physiologist studying it would claim that he had a complete understanding. In particular, we cannot be very sure about how the ear processes the kinds of complicated sounds that are attractive to most composers.

Our chain does not end with the auditory system, however. We listen to music in quite different ways, depending on our *listening skills and attitudes*. In contrast with the functioning of the auditory system, which is usually taken to be biologically determined, these skills and attitudes are considered *mainly* to be learned. Anything as complicated as a skill or an attitude is a result both of learning and of a biologically determined predisposition. The learned portion, which we can affect, is worth examining further.

Like the composer's skills, those of the listener have both a technical aspect, which is dependent on the style and period of the music, and a more general aspect, which is the same no matter what the music is. Most of us find the great works of the tonal period more enjoyable when we learn to listen to the structural hierarchies of harmony and melody that characterize it. If we learn the principles of *cantus firmus* composition and the characteristics of the church modes, we can listen to the great works of Josquin des Pres and his contemporaries with new understanding. The music of Schönberg and his school in our own century is heard with far greater insight after we have learned the principles of twelve-tone composition and can hear the row in its various transformations. These techniques of listening parallel those of composition that are peculiar to a certain time or school of composers.

The more general mode of listening often follows and depends upon technical listening skills, but it is to be distinguished from them. All music has something in common, and we can develop skills in recognizing these common properties. These more general skills are of particular concern to us in electronic music because in music where the techniques are new, we have only this general mode of listening to help us. I think we try to hear a certain complexity of structure in all music. We categorize on many levels, based upon similarities within different aspects of the music. The multi-layered, contrapuntal nature of some music complicates this categorization, but it can be made by a careful listener. Included in this hierarchical categorization is listening for gesture. Gesture suggests movement of some sort; a static gesture suggests the potential for movement. Of course, brief gestures become parts of longer ones and we build hierarchies of gesture. When we listen to any music, we look for categorical and gestural hierarchies.

I have included the attitude of the listener in this part of the communication system because it often affects the way we listen. An attitude toward listening that is conditioned too much by the technical aspects of a particular style or period tends to obstruct the more general listening mode that permits us to approach new music. But, attitudes are also learned and, to an extent, they are subject to our conscious control. We can try to prevent the fame or obscurity of the composer, the opinions of our friends, perhaps the initial repugnance we may feel toward a particular sound, from diminishing our listening skills; the common experience of learning to like a piece to which we were initially indifferent suggests that we should do this.

I believe that the goal of this communication system and the reason for its existence is *musical understanding by the listener*. The composer of electronic music has something to say, which, by its nature, is expressible only through the communication system we have traced. Each link in the chain both supports and limits the message. This chapter is aimed at increasing the composer's knowledge about the parts of the system, so that his skills will support rather than limit what he has to say. I shall be introducing principles of acoustics, and using them to develop certain fundamental ideas that apply in both the acoustic and the electrical realm. I shall discuss briefly how electrical signals are converted into sound. Finally, I shall trace the sound into the human auditory system, in order to explore the auditory basis for important musical phenomena.

SOUND

Tiny, rapid movements of molecules of air to and fro lead to what we call sound. If the movements are too rapid and very regular, we cannot hear them; we call this *ultrasound*. If they are too slow, or to be more exact, all in one direction for a long time, we may experience them in some way—we feel a gentle breeze, for example—but we do not call what we experience sound. If the movement is too large, as in the neighborhood of a jet plane taking off, we avoid the sound or remain in its vicinity at the peril of damaging our ears. If the movement is too small—a condition seldom, if ever, realized—we say that we are experiencing silence or the absence of sound. It is our ears that define the ranges of rapidity and degree of movement of air molecules that we call sound. We shall discuss hearing a bit later, but for the moment let us concentrate on the air movements themselves. We will be dealing with the branch of physics called acoustics.

Measures of Sound

Let us begin by defining the three common measures of these air-particle movements: particle *displacement,* particle *velocity,* and *pressure.* Displacement is the distance a particle moves from its equilibrium position, which is the point in space where the particle is "at rest" with respect to the particles around it. Arbitrarily, a displacement to the right of equilibrium is considered a positive displacement; to its left, a negative displacement. Particle velocity is simply the change in displacement of the particle with time. When the particle is not moving with respect to the equilibrium position, it has zero particle velocity. When it is moving to the right, we say—again arbitrarily—that it has a positve particle velocity, and when moving to the left, a negative particle velocity. Pressure is somewhat more difficult to define rigorously. It is the result of forces that the particles in a gas exert on one another. Only a vacuum has zero pressure, so acousticians take for the equilibrium or "zero" pressure ordinary atmospheric pressure. Pressures greater than equilibrium, called *condensations* or simply *compressions,* are designated positive pressure. Those less than equilibrium, called *rarefactions* or *decompressions,* are considered negative, but only with respect to the equilibrium pressure. There is no such thing as a negative absolute pressure.

As a matter of fact, the acoustician is not especially interested in absolute measures of anything. He is more concerned with relatively small, fast variations in displacement, velocity, and pressure, with respect to equilibrium. He leaves the long-term variations to the meteorologists or atmospheric physicists. Although the names of the acoustical measures suggest that we must be concerned with particles of air, the acoustician ordinarily can treat air as if it were continuous. Only those interested in ultrasound need worry about the "graininess" of the air.

Clearly, the three measures of sound are not independent. If a particle moves to the right of equilibrium, it must have some (positive) velocity to get there, and since it is then closer to the next particle to the right, there must be a (positive) change in pressure. The three measures are closely interrelated, but the ways in which they interrelate depend upon whether or not the air is enclosed within a container of some sort. Let us begin by examining the case where the sound is not enclosed, or is enclosed in a container so large that its exact size and shape has no bearing on our analysis.

Wave Motion: Sound Propagation in Open Air

In order to carry out the analysis for air in three-dimensional space, we must utilize fairly sophisticated mathematics. But the essentials of what happens can be gleaned from a much simplified, one-dimensional model of the air. Let us imagine that the ball, the diamond, the square, and the arrowhead in Fig. 1 are particles of air. They are only four of many more particles that extend indefinitely out of the picture beyond the arrowhead. The springs between them represent the pressure on the particles. At the left, a piston is attached to the ball by a spring. All the springs are equally stiff and all the particles have equal mass. The top line, where time equals minus 1, represents the "air" in equilibrium. None of the particles has been displaced from its "at rest" position; none of them is moving, and the "pressure" is everywhere equal to its equilibrium value.

At time 0, the second line of Fig. 1, some outside force has suddenly moved the piston to the right. At successive "snapshots" of the air particles,

TIME

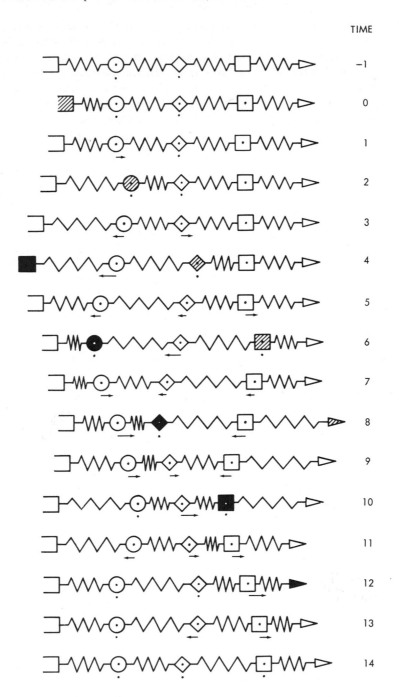

FIGURE 1.   The propagation of a disturbance through a model of the air consisting of springs and masses.

we see the piston moving gradually back toward the left until it reaches an extreme position at time 4. It then reverses direction, moving back to the right to the extreme position at time 8 and, finally, back to the position it started with before any force was applied. Let us see what effect these movements of the piston have on the air particles.

At time 0, the ball has not had time to be affected by the sudden movement of the piston. The energy from that movement is being stored by the spring. By time 1, however, the energy has been converted suddenly into kicking the ball to the right. Its velocity is represented by the small arrow just below it. Even as the ball begins to move to the right, the "pressure" in the spring between the piston and the ball begins to drop because the piston is already moving back toward the left. The ball continues to the right because it now has momentum that cannot be converted into "stored" energy instantaneously. But the spring between the ball and the diamond is compressed by the movement of the ball, and, in addition, the spring to the left of the ball is beginning to stretch beyond equilibrium as the piston moves farther to the left. The combination of the forces on either side of the ball finally bring it to a halt at time 2. With the spring to its right pushing and the spring to its left pulling, the ball at time 3 starts to move back to the left. It passes its original position, moving at high speed to the left at time 4. Here, with the springs on both sides of the ball equally stretched and, thus, cancelling each other, the ball continues to the left. It is slowed and finally halted at time 6 by the compressed spring on its left and the stretched spring on its right. The imbalance of tensions in the springs then forces the ball back toward the right again.

Let us leave the ball for a moment and look at the diamond. The spring to its left was compressed at time 2. The compression was a sudden one, so it begins to move only at time 3, reaching a maximum right deflection at time 4. There it is stopped by a compressed spring on the right and a stretched spring on the left. Now a short time previously the ball was in exactly this situation —halted with a compressed spring to the right and a stretched spring to the left. Glancing ahead to the square at time 6 and the arrowhead at time 8, we find the same conditions. With the piston supplying the original force, the ball, the diamond, the square, and the arrowhead are successively deflected suddenly to the right, where their motion is halted by the combinations of compressed and stretched springs around them. The piston and the particles are crosshatched at those positions. Similarly, the farthest left position, where the piston and the particles are filled, seems to march consecutively left to right from one particle to the next every two units of time. A careful look at the successive particles will reveal that every position of the piston has its counterpart in the particles at some later time. It is not the particles that are moving steadily to the right but, rather, the pattern of movements of the particles. The phenomenon is called *wave motion,* and its most essential characteristic is that a pattern of movements is *propagated without change of form.* It is through this characteristic of wave motion in the air that a sound made by a voice or musical instrument or loudspeaker can be heard essentially unaltered by a listener sitting across the room.

The Waveforms

Some additional fundamental concepts can be derived from our model of wave motion. Suppose we record the velocity of just the ball at each instant of time pictured in Fig. 1. The points at the top of Figure 2 are the result. If we make the reasonable assumption that velocity will change fairly smoothly between the points recorded, we can draw the curve connecting the points. This curve is called the *velocity waveform*. An analogous set of points recording displacement with respect to time is also plotted in Fig. 2. The curve joining these points is called the *displacement waveform*. Representing the pressure in Fig. 1 is the force on the springs. We can also plot an analogy to the *pressure waveform* at the ball by averaging the force on the springs on each side. The result is the third curve in Fig. 2.

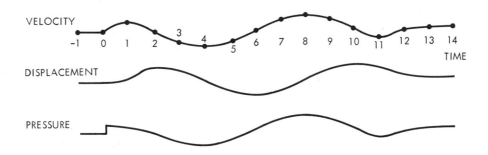

FIGURE 2.   Velocity, displacement, and "pressure" waveforms for the ball in Figure 1.

We should always keep in mind that a waveform is a record of what happens at some point in space as time elapses. Since we have "propagation without change of form," the waveform also represents the spatial distribution of pressure, velocity, and displacement at a single instant of time. We can derive from our waveforms in Fig. 2 the relations among the three different measures of sound. After a fairly complicated beginning, the pressure and velocity waveforms seem to change together. A positive pressure is accompanied by a positive velocity, and so forth. The displacement waveform, on the other hand, drags along two time units behind those of the velocity and pressure. The velocity and pressure are said to be *in phase*, while the displacement is *out of phase* with the velocity and pressure. They can be said to *lead* the displacement, or, conversely, the displacement *lags* behind the velocity and pressure.

A Simple Mechanical Oscillator

By now all of us have heard sine waves (sinusoids), but they are actually a comparatively recent phenomenon. They were rarely heard before the invention of the vacuum-tube amplifier. As a theoretical concept, however, the sinusoid is as old as Newtonian physics. Most high-school geometry books notwithstanding, a sinusoid can be honestly defined only by setting up and solving the so-called equation of motion of a simple *oscillator*. The sine and cosine waveforms *are* the solutions of that equation. We will not go through the process of solving the equation—Newton invented the calculus to do it— but we can select certain simple oscillators, and by carefully observing their motions, we can discover several fundamental facts about their behavior.

A mass on a spring, a pendulum, a bottle with a narrow neck—in fact, any system in which the forces restoring a mass to its equilibrium position are in proportion to its distance away from equilibrium—are approximations of oscillators. They are only approximations because a true simple oscillator has no friction and the restoring forces must be exactly proportional to displacement, a condition no real spring or pendulum can satisfy. But for the sake of argument, let us imagine a mass on a "frictionless" spring attached to the outside of a spacecraft far enough away from the Earth so that the effects of gravity are negligible. We will find that the mass is moving back and forth, alternately compressing and stretching the spring. A brief glimpse of its displacement waveform is given in Fig. 3. Since the spring is frictionless, the motion will go on indefinitely. Fig. 3 is all we need, however, because the motion is repetitive. During the time called T in the figure, the mass goes through a complete *cycle* from its zero position to its point of maximum displacement to the right, back past zero to its maximum left displacement, and finally back to zero. From this point the motion begins to repeat. The time T is called the *period* of oscillation. The reciprocal of the period, the number of cycles or

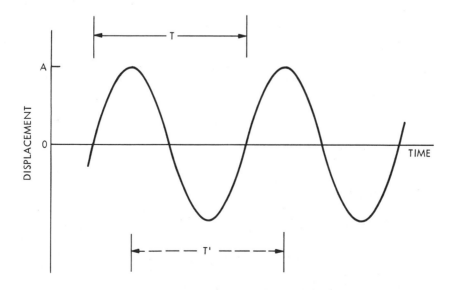

FIGURE 3.   The displacement waveform of the mass in an ideal, frictionless oscillator.

periods in a second, is called the *frequency*. The unit of frequency is the Hertz (or Hz): one cycle per second is equal to one Hz.

In Fig. 3 the period of the waveform has been measured between positive-going zero crossings of the wave. In so doing we have traced out one cycle of a *sine wave*. If, instead, we had measured the period from successive peaks of the waveform, we would have the period of T′ and a *cosine wave*. T and T′ are equal, and the cosine is simply one-quarter cycle out of phase with the sine wave. Because they are so similar, it is sometimes convenient to call them both sinusoids.

The maximum distance that the mass travels away from the equilibrium point, A in Fig. 3, is called the *amplitude* of the wave. In our mass-spring system, the amplitude was chosen arbitrarily. It is entirely controlled, in this frictionless "ideal" case, by the way the system began vibrating. Once we have specified the amplitude, the frequency (or period), and the phase, we have specified the sinusoid completely. In many cases the phase of a sinusoid is unimportant; if the position of the sinusoid in time is arbitrary, its complete description consists only of its amplitude and frequency.

An Acoustic Analogy: The Helmholtz Resonator

The first of our containers for sound, a direct analogy to the mass-spring resonator, is the *Helmholtz resonator,* named after one of the greatest of nineteenth-century scientists. It is the familiar narrow-necked bottle, which can be sounded by blowing gently across the opening in the neck. Helmholtz pointed out that the neck in the bottle constricts the flow of air so that just the air within the neck moves in and out of the bottle more or less as a unit. This "plug" of air is analogous to the mass. The air within the bottle, which is alternately compressed and decompressed as the plug moves in and out, is analogous to the spring. The farther the "mass" moves away from its equilibrium position in the neck, the greater is the restoring force on it from the air in the bottle proper. If we could keep track of a particle of air in the neck, we would find that its displacement waveform is just like that of the mass in Fig. 3.

The Resonator with Friction and a Driving Force

But real springs are not frictionless, and the air in bottles does not constantly oscillate. In more realistic masses and springs, losses of energy due to frictional forces cause the amplitude of motion gradually to decrease to negligibly small amplitudes, if not to zero. Let us bring our mass-spring system back to earth and place it on a table. Then, let us attach the spring to a piston. The piston will supply what is known as a *driving force,* and the drag of the mass on the table will be the main source of friction. A physicist would set up the more complicated equation of motion and use its solution to predict how the mass would move in response to various driving forces. He would then do experiments to see if his predictions were correct. Fig. 4 illustrates our mass and spring and the results of three of the physicist's experiments.

First, let us drive our model with a sinusoid at a low frequency (Experiment 1). The top curve in Fig. 4A is the displacement waveform of the piston, and the curve just under it is the displacement waveform of the mass. Though the peaks and troughs of the curves do not quite coincide, they are equally separated in time. The mass, therefore, vibrates with the same frequency as

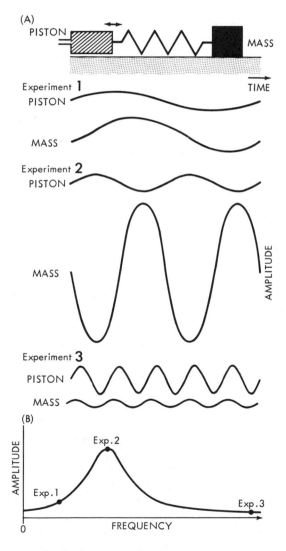

FIGURE 4. The response of a resonator to driving forces of different frequencies. (A) The waveforms of the piston supplying the driving force and the mass. (B) The resulting resonance curve.

the driving force, but it lags a bit in phase. The amplitude of the mass is slightly greater than the amplitude of the piston. At low frequencies we can observe that the spring stretches only slightly, so the mass and the piston move almost together.

The next experiment (Experiment 2) is a very special one. This time, the frequency of the piston is set to that of the mass and spring that were oscillating freely in our hypothetical frictionless spacecraft. The amplitude of the piston is the same as it was in the first case, but the amplitude of the mass is now very great indeed. It vibrates at the same frequency as the piston, but now it is exactly one-half cycle out of phase—the peaks correspond with the troughs, and vice versa. This special condition is called *resonance,* the frequency is called the *resonance frequency,* and the mass and spring are called a *resonant system* or simply a *resonator.* We shall return often to the phenomenon of resonance, for it is used in nearly every source of musical sound, whether electronic or instrumental. An oscillator, for example, can be thought of as a resonator whose frictional losses are negligible.

Now let us see what happens when the frequency of the driving piston is greater than the resonance frequency (Experiment 3). The piston is given the same amplitude as in the other two experiments, but its frequency is higher. The mass again vibrates at the same frequency as the piston, but now with a smaller amplitude. It seems to have a slight phase lead over the piston, but actually it has fallen nearly an entire cycle behind. At still higher driving frequencies, the motion of the mass will have still smaller amplitudes, but what motion it has will be at the frequency of the piston. We can state as an unequivocal rule that *a resonator may react with an amplitude different from that of the driving force, but never with a different frequency.* Fig. 4B is a kind of summary of the response of the resonator at *any* frequency. The curve is called a *resonance curve,* and on it are indicated the results of the three experiments. We shall return to these curves a little later.

An important question about the resonator that we have ignored so far is how its resonance frequency is determined in the first place. The answer is simple with the mass-spring system. A stiffer spring or a lighter mass will cause the resonance frequency to increase; a more elastic spring or a heavier mass will cause it to decrease. The question is a bit more difficult in the case of the narrow-necked bottle, but in general, increasing the volume or lengthening or narrowing the neck lowers the resonance frequency, while a shorter or wider neck or a smaller volume will increase the resonance frequency. Helmholtz's exact prediction of the resonance frequency need not concern us, because we want to delve into the principles of resonance rather than the properties of any single resonator. The principle here is that the resonance frequency depends on the properties of the physical resonator itself and not on the force that excites the resonator into vibration.

At first glance, it would seem that our model for illustrating wave motion (Fig. 1) should also be a resonating system. Would not the springs, which represent pressure, and the masses, which represent particles of air, tend to favor those frequencies that are close to the spring-mass resonance? We have

seen in Fig. 4 that the motions of a driver are drastically altered in a resonator, but in wave motion the motions of the driver are "propagated without
change of form." Evidently, air, or any other medium that supports wave
motion, does not exhibit resonance. The "springiness" of air and its mass have
a marked effect on the propagation velocity—the "speed of sound." Stiffer
springs and lighter masses increase the speed. The essential difference between the resonator and the elastic medium is that the latter is extended indefinitely (to the right in Fig. 1) and no wave is reflected from the end of the
spring-mass chain. We can set up resonance in the water in a bathtub, but in a
good-sized lake our splashing is propagated away and the waves die out on a
distant shore.

An Impulsive Driving Force

Our next topic is by far the most conceptually difficult of any we will cover in
this chapter, but it is also among the most important for understanding electronic-music production. Let us begin with a further experiment on our mass-
spring system. Suppose that, instead of driving it with a sinusoid, we move the
piston back and forth suddenly in what is called an impulse. Then let us
repeat the impulsive excitation at a very low rate. The motion of the mass
pictured in Fig. 5 is now quite different from its response to a low-frequency
sinusoidal excitation. The mass moves repetitively, reaching a maximum displacement slightly after each impulse of the piston; but between impulses, the
mass and spring vibrate with the approximate frequency of the resonance
system itself. Our physical intuition about the system may not be violated by
this motion, but our "unequivocal rule"—that no frequencies come out of a
resonator that do not go into it—apparently is, for the mass seems to be vibrating at a frequency higher than the repetition rate of the piston's impulses. If
we are to preserve our rule, we can only conclude that the piston is somehow
driving the resonator *at the higher frequencies.* Fourier analysis, a mathe-

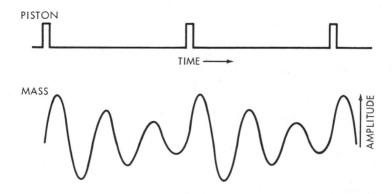

FIGURE 5.   The response of the resonator to an impulsive driving force.

matical tool of very widespread applicability, tells us that, indeed, the impulse waveform *contains* frequencies at or near the resonance frequency of our spring-mass system. Let us leave the resonator for a while and concentrate on the frequency content of various complex—that is to say, non-sinusoidal—waveforms as given by Fourier analysis.

Fourier Analysis

Fourier's theorem establishes that any physically realizable, *periodic* waveform is equal to the sum of a series of sinusoidal waveforms, called *components,* whose frequencies are *harmonically* related. The most important condition in this statement of mathematical truth is that the waveform must be periodic—it may be very complicated indeed between repetitions, but it must repeat exactly. If the theorem were limited to an assertion that periodic waveforms are made up of sinusoids, that in itself would be an important simplification. But Fourier's theorem further states that the frequencies of the sinusoidal components are in a certain relation to one another. Given the first member of the series of sinusoids—its frequency is equal to the repetition rate of the complex waveform—the subsequent members of the series are integral (whole-number) multiples of that frequency. If, for example, the impulse wave in Fig. 5 were at a repetition rate of 150 pulses per second (pps), the first member of the equivalent sinusoidal series would have a frequency of 150 cycles per second. The second sinusoid would be at 300 cycles per second; the third, at 450; the fourth, at 600; and so on. Although the members of the Fourier series may be called *partials* or *overtones,* these terms are often applied to the resonances in certain kinds of resonators. To avoid ambiguity, the sinusoids in a Fourier series should be called *harmonics.* They are numbered consecutively, starting with the lowest-frequency sinusoid, which is called the first harmonic or the *fundamental.*

Now whereas the frequencies of the harmonics are determined by the repetition rate of a complex wave, the amplitudes and relative phases of the harmonics are determined by its shape. *Fourier analysis* is the process of calculating these amplitudes and phases. And the results of the calculation—a list, a picture, or a formula specifying the amplitudes and phases of the harmonics—is called the *frequency spectrum* or simply the *spectrum.* Fourier's theorem states that the complex waveform is equal to the sum of its harmonics. We can verify any Fourier analysis simply by adding the components. This inverse Fourier analysis is called *Fourier synthesis.*

Fourier Synthesis

Fig. 6A depicts a *square wave* and its frequency spectrum. The vertical lines in the spectrum represent the harmonics. Notice that the even harmonics (two, four, six, etc.) are missing, and that the odd harmonics regularly decrease in amplitude as they increase in frequency. The odd harmonics never actually reach zero amplitude, so we cannot add all of them, but we can take the first

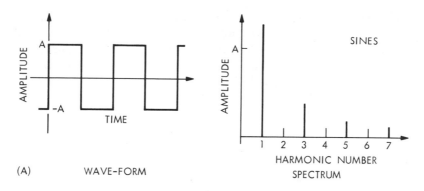

(A)   WAVE-FORM

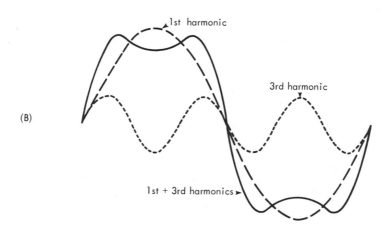

(B)

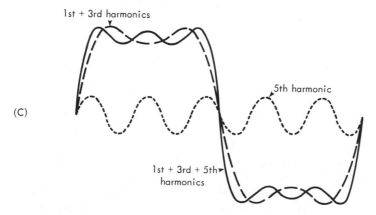

(C)

FIGURE 6.   Fourier analysis and synthesis. (A) The waveform and Fourier spectrum of a square wave. (B, C) The contributions of the first three and the first five harmonics, respectively.

few and guess at the effects of the higher harmonics. We have done just that in Figs. 6B and 6C. The first and third harmonics are drawn as dotted lines in Fig. 6B, and their sum is the solid curve. Fig. 6C shows the sum of the first, third, and fifth harmonics. We can see how with each added harmonic, the sides of the sum steepen, and the "ripple" at the top and bottom of the sum approaches the straight line of the original waveform.

Some Common Fourier Spectra

The frequency spectra of several of the waveforms most commonly encountered in electronic music are presented in Fig. 7. Here, the horizontal axis is the frequency, and the actual period of the waveform is specified. The phase relations between the harmonics are given by the indication "sines" or "cosines" and by the direction of the lines representing the harmonics—a line below the horizontal axis means a minus sine or cosine. The comparative amplitudes of the waveform and of the spectra can be compared by reference to the "A" in both graphs.

The *triangular wave* (Fig. 7A) has a spectrum containing only odd harmonics. Its shape is not very different from that of a sine wave, so we are not surprised to see that the fundamental contains nearly all of the energy. On the other hand, the *sawtooth* (Fig. 7B) is made up of both odd and even harmonics, the higher harmonics containing relatively more energy. Fig. 7C illustrates a different sort of square wave, in which zero time is placed at the middle of the square. Its spectrum apparently differs from that of the square wave in Fig. 6. A closer look will confirm that the waveform of Fig. 7C can be derived by "sliding" the square wave of Fig. 6 to the left one-quarter cycle. If we then slide our synthesis attempts (Figs. 6B and 6C) to the left by the same amount, we find that the components *become* cosines that alternate between plus and minus. But before we dismiss Fig. 7C as a distinction without a difference, let us compare it with the *rectangular pulses* whose spectra are given in Figs. 7D, 7E, and 7F.

Unlike the square wave, which is at its maximum value for exactly one-half of the total period, the rectangular pulse is "on"—or up—for a briefer time than it is "off"—or down. (In what follows, it is convenient to refer to a single pulse, but we really mean the repeated pulse or *pulse train*.) The pulse in Fig. 7D is on for one-third of the total cycle, or $\frac{1}{150}$th second. Its spectrum has a first and second harmonic, but not a third one; a fourth and fifth, but not a sixth. If we narrow our pulse still further until it is only one-sixth of a cycle wide (Fig. 7E), we find that the spectrum contains the first five harmonics, but not the sixth. If our spectrum were extended to include still higher harmonics, we would find that harmonics seven through eleven were present, but that harmonic twelve was zero. Beginning with the square wave of Fig. 7C—a special case of the rectangular pulse—we can see a rule emerging. The square wave is "on" one-half of the time; its missing harmonics are the second and all multiples of the second. In the "one-third cycle" pulse, the third harmonic and all of its multiples are zero. The sixth, twelfth, eigh-

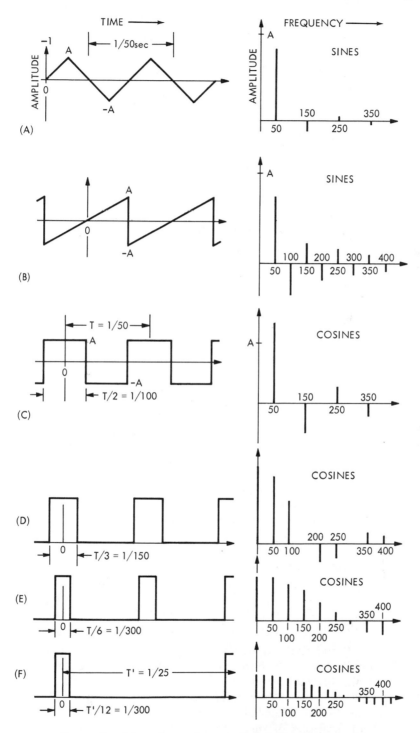

FIGURE 7.   Selected waveforms and their Fourier spectra.

teenth, etc., harmonics of the pulse that is on one-sixth of the time are zero. Let us define the *duty cycle* of a rectangular pulse as the proportion of the total cycle during which the amplitude is maximum. Then the reciprocal of the duty cycle is the number of the harmonic, all of whose multiples are missing from the spectrum.

Let us apply this rule to the pulse in Fig. 7F. In absolute duration the pulse is the same as it was in Fig. 7E, but the total period has been doubled—and, therefore, the frequency halved—and the duty cycle is now $\frac{1}{12}$th. A glance at the spectrum will verify that it is indeed the twelfth harmonic that is missing. Now if we look at the spectra of Fig. 7E and 7F in terms of frequency instead of harmonic number, we notice that the same *frequency* (300 Hz) is zero in the spectra of both. This is because the pulses in both cases have the same absolute duration. We can make a further rule: The spectrum of a rectangular pulse is zero at frequencies equal to all multiples of the reciprocal of the pulse's duration, without regard to the repetition rate of the pulse.

There is a further important concept exemplified in Fig. 7. The triangle, sawtooth, and square waves in that figure are all equally distributed about the zero line. The equilibrium value neither increases nor decreases over the long run; all increases above "zero" are matched by equal decreases below the equilibrium. This is not the case with the last three waveforms in Fig. 7, in which there are no negative values of the waveform at all. The impulses are all positive-going. Over the long run we would expect a net positive contribution from the waveform, and our zero line in the figures would represent a pressure below the actual "average" position or pressure. This positive contribution is often called the *DC component* of a waveform. The term DC stands for direct current—the kind that is produced by a battery. The sinusoidal harmonics are referred to as the AC, or alternating current, components of the wave. They "alternate" equally between plus and minus values and, therefore, cannot contribute to a change in the long-run average of the waveform.

The Impulsed Resonator Revisited

With our concept of the frequency spectrum firmly in hand, let us return once again to the simple resonator—a mass on a spring. It may seem as if we are not getting anywhere, but in fact we can now see resonance systems in an entirely new light. We can combine our knowledge of the spectrum of narrow rectangular pulses with our observations of the behavior of the resonator in response to sinusoidal excitation, in order to account for the complicated motion of the mass in Fig. 5.

Fig. 8A illustrates the spectrum of a train of pulses—like those in Fig. 5—whose duty cycle is about $\frac{1}{20}$th. Only the first eleven harmonics are given, but we can imagine them gradually decreasing in amplitude to the right beyond our graph until they reach zero at the twentieth harmonic. For the sake of concreteness we have chosen a repetition rate of fifty pps and an amplitude of

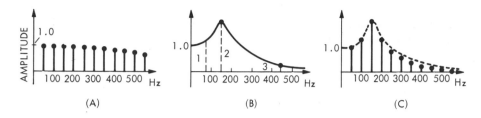

FIGURE 8.   (A) Fourier spectrum of a train of narrow pulses. (B) Resonance curve. (C) Spectrum of the response of a resonator to the pulse train.

one for the first harmonic. Fig. 8B depicts the *resonance curve* of the spring-mass resonator.

Now, let us connect our pulsing piston to the spring-mass resonator. The waveform of the motion is the complex one shown in Fig. 5. But the *spectrum* of that motion, illustrated in Fig. 8, is easier to understand. It is as if each of the harmonics of the pulse spectrum were exciting the resonator independently. The first few harmonics almost meet the resonance curve because they are nearly equal in amplitude. Then, as we would expect, the higher harmonics, which are lower in amplitude, begin to fall below the resonance curve. In summary, we can say that the *source* of energy—the piston—determines the frequencies of the harmonics, but that their amplitudes (and phases) are determined in part by the source and in part by the resonator. Before we go on to consider more complicated resonators, it is well to introduce synonyms for the resonance curve. It is sometimes called a *frequency-response* curve or a *spectrum envelope*.

A short passage in Stockhausen's *Kontakte* exemplifies the independent control of source and resonance. This passage occurs about seventeen minutes into the piece, near the beginning of the second side of the Studio-reihe Neuer Musik recording, WER 60009. A buzz-like source at a medium pitch is gradually slowed down, and the pitch falls. As the pitch becomes very low we begin to discern the individual pulses. In the meantime, a kind of melody is played with the resonance system excited by that source. Stockhausen has described this passage in detail in *Perspectives of New Music*, 1 (1962).

Acoustics of Speech

We are now prepared for an introduction to that most flexible and complex of resonance systems, the human voice. Our leap well beyond the simple spring-mass resonator is simplified by the fact that all resonances react in about the same way to acoustic excitation. They shape the excitation according to their resonance curves. Reluctantly, I will have to leave out an account of *how* our vocal tracts produce speech. We will be more concerned with *what* sounds they produce.

The vocal mechanism is divided functionally into two parts. The first is made up of the vocal cords and their associated nerves and muscle. They are the *source* of acoustic energy for most speech sounds. The other part, the vocal tract itself, consisting of the throat and mouth cavities, is a complex multiple-resonance system. Like the spectrum of the pulsed resonator in Fig. 8, the spectrum of a speech sound is the result of the interaction between the source spectrum and the spectrum envelope of the resonance system. Generally, we can say that the intensity and pitch of speech is determined by the sources; the color or timbre of speech—most of its phonetic or "linguistic" aspects—by the resonances of the vocal tract. Consonants demand a movement of the vocal structures, which produces a pattern of resonances that changes with time. The vowels on the other hand can be produced by a stationary vocal tract, which results in a stationary pattern of resonances.

The Vocal Tract

The acoustics of vowels were the subject of a concentrated research effort in the '40s and early '50s, culminating in the work of two Bell Laboratories scientists, G. A. Peterson and H. L. Barney. Table I is derived from the results of their research. The first three resonances of the vowels in a variety of English words are given for both men and children. They are labeled "F1," "F2," and "F3," in reference to a traditional term for the resonances in the vocal tract—*formant*. The six words in the table each contain one vowel and are ordered according to a certain pattern. From "heed" to "hod," the first resonance in the vowels rises in frequency; from "hod" to "who'd," it falls. Over all the vowels from "heed" to "who'd," the second resonance, F2, generally decreases in frequency. Although the children's resonances are proportionately higher in frequency than the men's, the same pattern is followed. The frequency of the third resonance changes fairly little from one vowel to the next, except in the case of "heed." Here, F3 is higher in order to "get out of the way" of the high F2.

TABLE I. Average resonance frequencies of the vowels of men and children. (Adapted from Peterson & Barney)

		heed	head	had	hod	haw'd	who'd
	F1	270	530	660	730	570	300
Men	F2	2290	1840	1720	1090	840	870
	F3	3010	2480	2410	2440	2410	2240
	F1	370	690	1010	1030	680	430
Children	F2	3200	2610	2320	1370	1060	1170
	F3	3730	3570	3320	3170	3180	3260

Adapted from G. E. Peterson and H. L. Barney, "Control Methods Used in a Study of the Vowels," *Journal of the Acoustical Society of America,* XXIV (1952), 175–84. Used by permission.

The acoustics of the consonants are too complicated to introduce in this chapter, but one can derive certain of them rather directly from the vowels. The "y" sound in "you" consists of a sort of quick slide (about $\frac{1}{20}$th of a second in duration) from the resonance frequencies of the vowel in "heed" to those of "who'd." The "w" in "we" is a slide in the reverse direction. Further slides of this sort can be produced between the other vowels. Some of them are not consonants in English, but all of them can, I believe, be exploited musically.

The Vocal Energy Source

Having considered the resonance system in speech, let us turn to the manner in which that system is excited. In certain speech sounds the vocal tract is excited by small explosions, hisses, and clicks—sounds that have *continuous spectra* with "harmonics" that can be regarded as being packed so closely together that they excite the resonances at *all* frequencies. Most of the time, however, the source of acoustical energy is the vibration of the vocal cords. Whereas the frequencies of the various vocal resonances are determined by the overall shape of the vocal tract and cannot be independently varied, the vocal cord excitation is controlled quite separately from the mouth and throat. Sentence stress is a result primarily of changes in the fundamental frequency of the vocal source. If this frequency were not independently controllable, the subtle changes of meaning in the "same" sentence arising from different stress patterns would be impossible.

Singing depends strongly on separate control of the two parts of the vocal mechanism. If the source were strongly coupled to the resonance system, as it is in most wind instruments, the fundamental frequencies would be determined by the sung vowels. Of course, in nearly all singing, different vowels are sung at the same fundamental frequency, and the same vowel is sung at different fundamental frequencies.

It has been said by some composers that speech is the most complex and interesting of musical sounds. Berio's *Visage* and Stockhausen's *Gesang der Jüngling* and *Stimmung,* among many other works, are testimony to that interest. In fact, it is possible that our ears are especially well-suited to respond to speech sounds. I have been more specific about this elsewhere[1], and I shall briefly consider the perception of speech when we discuss the auditory system in a later section of this chapter. But whether or not one finds speech sounds themselves musically interesting, a knowledge of the resonance frequencies of the vowels can often provide at least a start in reducing an imagined sound to its acoustic reality. It is knowledge that every composer of electronic music should have, and it may even suggest new dimensions to the composer of instrumental and vocal music.

[1] A. W. Slawson, "Vowel Quality and Musical Timbre as Functions of Spectrum Envelope and Fundamental Frequency," *Journal of the Acoustical Society of America,* XLIII (1968), 87–101.

TRANSDUCERS AND ELECTRONICS

Obviously, loudspeakers or earphones are required in the presentation of electronic music. But they are an integral part of the composition process as well. The possibility of hearing partial results at any stage of composition is surely one of the greatest attractions to composers of electronic music. These devices and the microphone are called *electroacoustic transducers*. They *transduce* (i.e., convert) electrical signals into sound, or, in the case of the microphone, sound into electrical signals. Their operation depends upon the fact that changes in electrical current or voltage always exert mechanical forces proportional to those changes.

Loudspeakers and Earphones

Given this physical fact, it is possible to design an electrical circuit that has as an element a device designed to use those *electromechanical* forces to create disturbances in the air. If, for example, the piston in Fig. 1 were wrapped with a coil of wire and placed between the poles of a magnet, it could be made to move back and forth in response to changes in the electrical current through the coil. In the examples of the various resonators, our heretofore hypothetical driving force could be realized in this and similar other ways by an electrical circuit.

Much has been written about the theory and technique of loudspeaker and earphone design. Loudspeakers are the more difficult problem, and nearly everything we say about them can be applied to earphones. The design goal is simply stated: the ideal speaker is capable of producing at all audible frequencies an intense sound that is exactly proportional to the input electrical signal. Needless to say, no speaker attains this ideal. Each new design, while reducing certain inaccuracies, seems to introduce some new problem that tends to offset its advantages. Elegant solutions are rare and complicated ones are invariably expensive. Commonly, loudspeakers are sold with two or more "pistons" in a single cabinet, each piston designed to reproduce a different range of frequencies. The individual components in these speaker "systems" need not satisfy very high standards at all frequencies, and their price can be kept relatively low. So-called acoustic-suspension speakers are rather inefficient, but they often reproduce sound more accurately than the more efficient loudspeakers with horns attached. Speakers that sound a bit "dry" are likely to be better in reproducing electronic music. A "rich" sound, which may attract one to a particular speaker at first, is likely to be the result of prominent peaks in the frequency response caused by resonances. These speakers are particularly undesirable in an electronic-music studio because they give their own coloring to sounds whose "color" the composer wants to control carefully himself.

The space that is to be filled with sound is a critical factor in selecting loudspeakers. In small, reverberant rooms almost any speaker will produce a sound of adequate intensity. But in large, draperied, and carpeted rooms, or outdoors, large and more efficient speakers are required. Presentations of electronic music are easily spoiled by loudspeakers that are perfectly adequate in a small room, but are incapable of filling a large hall. Efficient loudspeakers used in a larger hall, combined with the longer reverberation time in the hall, will have a marked effect on electronic music composed in a small studio with small loudspeakers. With experience, composers learn to compensate for these differences. In general, the music must have more time to "breathe" in large halls than is required in the studio. An occasional trial run in a large hall with efficient loudspeakers can be helpful at various stages of composition. Much electronic music is intended for presentation in the home, of course, where there are different problems from those discussed here.

Microphones

Microphones can be divided into two classes, the *omnidirectional* and the *cardiod,* or directional. Omnidirectional microphones are used in recording environments where all of the sources of sound present are to be recorded. The microphone responds no matter how it may be oriented with respect to the sound sources. Cardiod microphones, conversely, are most sensitive to sounds coming from the direction in which they are pointed. These microphones are used when certain sources in a field of sound are to be eliminated. In concert hall recordings, for example, cardiod microphones may be used to reduce audience noise or to emphasize certain instruments. Cardiod microphones are also available with a high directivity, where the ratio between the "straight-ahead" response and the response to one side and to the rear is very large. With these highly directional microphones, it is possible to pick up rather faint sounds from a specific source because all other sounds outside of a narrow "beam" directly in front of the microphone are eliminated. While omnidirectional microphones are used quite frequently for interviews and recording studio work, they and the highly directional microphones are special-purpose devices. For the recording of sounds to be used in concrete music, a rather "broad-beam" cardiod is probably a good compromise.

An Electroacoustic Analogy

Having traced sound back from the air into the loudspeakers that produce it, let us consider the electrical signals that drive the loudspeakers. An understanding of the details of electrical circuits demands time consuming study. For those interested, I recommend the detailed but well-written texts cited in the bibliography. But in composing electronic music, it is more important to know *what* circuits do than *how* they do it. And *what* they do is remarkably similar to what the mechanical and acoustic systems that we have been studying do. Everything we have said about resonance and Fourier analysis, for example, can be translated into the electrical realm by using a set of analogies between electrical quantities and acoustic quantities.

Ordinarily, these analogies are applied in the other direction. Electrical analysis appeals to physicists and engineers because they find it easier to deal with electrical circuits than with mechanical or acoustic systems. For acoustic systems, they usually define *voltage* as the electrical analog to pressure, and electrical *current* as the analog to velocity (strictly speaking, "volume velocity," which acts like particle velocity). Once these definitions are made, analogies are implied between electrical *inductance* and the elasticity of air or a spring, between electrical *capacitance* and mass, and between electrical *resistance* and viscosity or friction.

An Electrical Resonator

Suppose we actually construct an electrical analogy to our mass-spring, or Helmholtz resonators out of inductors, capacitors, and resistors. If we have chosen proper values for these circuit elements, the electrical resonator will have the same resonance curve as the mechanical or acoustic resonators. The resonance curve will be expressed in terms of voltage or current, of course, but in principle, that voltage can be translated directly into force on a piston and, finally, into pressure in the air through the use of an electroacoustic transducer. Apparently, electrical analogies are more than simply a means of studying acoustic systems. The analogous circuits connected to loudspeakers can actually be used to imitate the function of the acoustic systems.

The mechanical vibrations of the phonograph needle in the record groove are converted (by another kind of mechano-electrical transducer) into electrical signals that, when amplified and connected to loudspeakers, imitate the recorded sounds. What is less familiar is the possibility in the electrical realm of *generating,* as opposed to reproducing, the behavior of acoustic systems. It is this capacity of electrical systems to be *models* of acoustic and mechanical systems that makes electronic music possible. In composing electronic music we often deal with the electrical model exclusively, without regard to the realizability of the acoustic system being modeled. Indeed, going beyond what it is possible to produce with mechanical or acoustic devices is surely one of the strengths of electronic music. But what we are doing in the "unrealistic" electrical system is not different in principle from what we are doing in the acoustic system. The fundamental notions about resonance, the facts about Fourier analysis and synthesis, the ways in which sources interact with resonators—all these apply to electrical systems as well. The differences—with few exceptions—are only in degree. Let us examine some of them.

Advantages of Electrical Systems

First of all, we need not be concerned with wave propagation in electrical circuits. The propagation velocity of electricity is so great that in electrical circuits designed to operate at audible frequencies, we can assume that currents flow instantaneously through a wire. In general, the length of the wire or the physical size of the circuit makes no difference. On the other hand, the size and shape of a concert hall and the localization of sound in space are critically affected by the relatively slow speed of sound. Another important advantage of the electrical model over the acoustic system being modeled is the relative size of the "circuit elements." Physically large mechanical devices such as double basses, tubas, and thirty-two-foot organ pipes are necessary to produce the low frequencies. But these frequencies can be generated electrically with the use of almost microscopic elements.

Because propagation is essentially instantaneous and circuits can be small in size, a complex system of electrical resonances can be built whose frequencies can be changed fairly easily. Resonances can be changed in mechanical musical instruments as well. In fact, much of the effort in designing instruments lies in making these changes—which are associated with changes in pitch—as easy as possible. There remain resonances in musical instruments—usually those associated with tone color—that are fixed or only clumsily changeable. Only our speech organs are capable of subtle variation in these kinds of resonances. The recent success of electrical speech synthesizers in imitating the sounds of speech suggests how flexible electrical resonance systems can be. The *band-pass filter*, which consists of a number of electrical resonances, is designed to reject all frequencies except those within a certain "band," whose upper and lower frequencies can be set with the turn of a knob. A rough mechanical analogy in the double-reed family, for example, would be a crank of some sort that would change the mouthpiece of an oboe continuously to that of a bassoon!

Amplifiers

We have said very little about the *intensity* of sound aside from the effects of resonances on the amplitudes of sound sources. If we were dealing with the design of musical instruments, however, intensity would be of prime concern. The various resonances of the violin box are set carefully so as to increase the intensities of the open strings. We do not have this concern in electronic music because we can easily set an electronic signal to essentially any amplitude by using an *amplifier*. Originally based on the vacuum tube and now on the transistor, the amplifier functions by mutiplying any signal entering it by a factor called the *gain* of the amplifier. Instead of a laborious, exacting "tuning" of the "air" and "wood" resonances of a violin, we simply turn the gain or volume control on an amplifier to increase the intensity of the sound. The gain of certain kinds of amplifiers can be controlled by another electrical circuit, as in the "voltage-controlled" amplifiers discussed in Chapter 4. I shall return to the question of intensity when I discuss hearing, but for the moment it is enough to say that in electronic music, the control of intensity is not a problem.

The Electronic Oscillator

There are many different kinds of amplifiers, each with its own purpose, but there is one that is of utmost importance in electronic music. It is one in which the output is connected back into the input of the amplifier—a connection called, appropriately enough, *feedback.* The signal builds up in amplitude, not indefinitely but to a controlled level. The waveform that comes from this amplifier-without-an-input is controlled by its internal resonances. This *electronic oscillator* is like our mass-spring oscillator except that it has an internal energy source that enables it to compensate for "frictional" losses. Knobs control the level and frequency of these oscillators, or the frequency can be controlled electrically, as in the "voltage-controlled oscillator." Feedback is used in nearly all audio amplifiers to extend the range of frequencies amplified, but this is *negative feedback;* that is, the gain in the feedback circuit is less than one. When the amplifier has *positive feedback,* it becomes an oscillator.

Noise and Hum

Another special kind of amplifier is the *noise generator,* in which the random motions of the electrons in a vacuum tube or transistor are amplified. Like the oscillator, it has no input. The spectrum of noise signals differs somewhat from one type of noise generator to another, but for all practical purposes noise has energy at all audible frequencies. One such spectrum could be drawn as a horizontal line at a height above the frequency axis equal to the amplitude of the noise with all the space under the line filled in.

Unfortunately, noise can have its ordinary pejorative meaning in electronic music as well as anywhere else. Every time a signal is amplified some of the electron noise that is so useful in noise generators is amplified with it. Even more noise is passed on every time a sound is recorded on magnetic tape. Various schemes have been devised to reduce this buildup of noise, but it cannot be eliminated altogether. The simplest means of avoiding noise is to minimize the number of times signals are amplified or recorded.

Another common problem of amplifiers is *hum,* the drone whose fundamental is the B-flat below cello C. Hum can be heard in all sorts of audio equipment that is poorly designed or needs repair. The elimination of hum, which is the 60 Hz of American power lines, is often a complex and tedious task, best left to experts. The musician's job is to recognize hum for what it is and to complain!

THE EAR

We now know how sound travels through the air, and we have gained insight into the fundamentals of resonance. Moving backward in the musical communication system, we have discussed the behavior of loudspeakers and microphones. We have seen how the concepts in acoustics can be applied in the electrical realm, and why the amplifier makes the electrical models of acoustic systems easy to manipulate. Everything we have discussed so far has been independent of the listener. It is time now to move ahead two links in the communication chain to the auditory system. Though there remains much that is unknown about our ears, the work of sensory psychologists and physiologists has met with a degree of success. Some basic facts have been established, and from them we can guess about the more complicated ways our ears function.

Anatomy and Physiology

The ear itself can be thought of as a complex and specialized microphone. Its basic function is to convert acoustic energy into the electrochemical signals of the nervous system. For convenience, physiologists have divided our ears into three parts: the outer ear, the middle ear, and the inner ear. Each contributes to the basic function of electroacoustic transduction.

The Outer and Middle Ears

The outer ear consists of a projection of cartilage called the *auricle,* and the *auditory meatus,* the tunnel leading into the sides of our heads. (See Fig. 9.) The auricle acts as a sort of inverse horn, collecting sound waves and directing them into the meatus. The meatus in turn leads the sound through the heavy bony structures that protect the middle and inner ears. Like all tubes, the

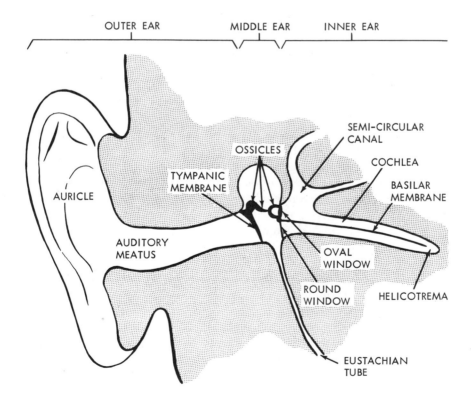

FIGURE 9.   Anatomy of the ear.

meatus has resonances that color the sound. The main resonance is a bit over 2000 Hz and is quite "flat," so it has little effect on sounds below that frequency.

The boundary between the outer and middle ears is the *tympanic membrane,* or eardrum. It acts like the diaphragm of a microphone, moving in and out in response to increased and decreased pressure in the meatus. These motions are transmitted through a set of three bony structures callled the *ossicles* to the *oval window,* which, along with the *round window,* is the boundary between the middle and inner ears. The air in the middle ear is kept at approximately atmospheric pressure by means of the *eustachian tube,* which connects to the mouth.

Functions of the Middle Ear

The middle-ear mechanisms seem to have two main functions. At "normal" sound intensities, the eardrum and ossicles convert relatively large *displacements* of the eardrum into relatively large *forces* at the oval window. The other function of the middle ear is protective. Muscles attached to the eardrum and the ossicles increase the tension in the tympanic membrane in response to intense sounds; thus, its displacement amplitude is reduced and a smaller force is transmitted to the oval window. At very high intensities, the ossicles begin to move in an abnormal manner so that the large displacements of the eardrum are dispersed in "waste motion" and never reach the oval window. The frequency response of the external and middle ears combined is fairly flat up to 2400 Hz, and then falls off rapidly. Studies have suggested that the resonance we would expect to find at that frequency is in the eardrum.

The Inner Ear

The inner ear contains the nerve endings of the auditory nerve. They are distributed along the *basilar membrane,* which increases in width as it runs down the *cochlea* from the oval window to the *helicotrema.* As suggested by its name, the cochlea is coiled in man and the higher animals, but the coiling seems to have little or no effect on hearing. For the sake of clarity it is straightened out in Figs. 9 and 10. Included in the inner ear is the *semicircular canal,* the organ of balance.

Sounds impressed upon the oval window in the form of mechanical vibrations set up a wave in the fluid that fills the cochlea. This wave travels down the cochlea in somewhat the same manner as a wave travels through the air. The important difference here is the changing width of the basilar membrane. The changing width means that the stiffness of the membrane also changes—it is stiffer at its narrower portion and more elastic at the broader end. This change in stiffness along the basilar membrane causes the traveling wave to rise to a maximum amplitude at different places depending on the frequency of the wave. High frequencies reach a maximum at the narrower, stiffer end nearest the oval window, and low frequencies, at the broader, more elastic end

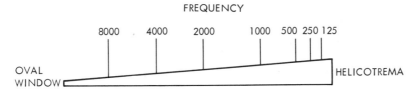

FIGURE 10. The relation between frequency and the place of maximal stimulation of the basilar membrane.

nearest the helicotrema. The distribution of these frequencies is diagrammed in Fig. 10. This much has been established mainly by the remarkable experiments conducted directly upon the basilar membranes of cadavers by Nobel laureate Georg von Békésy.

The Place Theory of Frequency Analysis

The place theory, originally proposed by von Helmholtz, is a theory of how the ear detects sounds of different frequencies. The reasoning is roughly as follows. Since the endings of the neurons, which taken together make up the auditory nerve, are distributed along the basilar membrane, different neurons are maximally excited by different frequencies. A kind of Fourier analysis is performed. When a complex sound enters the inner ear, the mechanical properties of the basilar membrane cause the component frequencies separately to excite neurons at different positions along the membrane. These neurons, maintaining their identity, excite others higher in the auditory nervous system until finally the components are separately "reported" to the cortex of the brain. The process of inhibition operating throughout the auditory pathways seems actually to "sharpen" the neural signals. The components are clearly distinguished in the brain—the high frequencies exciting regions farthest into the "temporal fold" on the side of the brain, the low frequencies stimulating regions nearer the surface of the brain. The details of this theoretical description remain somewhat in doubt, with the degree of uncertainty increasing as we trace the signals from the primary neurons in the cochlea to the brain. And we understand almost nothing about how the brain "uses" the information available at the cortex to give us pitch sensations.

The place theory of pitch—as it is cometimes called—is supported by Békésy's experiments and by a number of studies of the auditory neural pathways in higher animals. It is not unchallenged, however. In particular, its range of applicability seems open to question.

The Volley Theory

Another mechanism of frequency detection, which is said sometimes to contradict the place theory, is almost entirely neural in origin. Measurements in the auditory nerve show that individual nerve firings can occur *in synchrony* with frequencies of sound up to about 400 Hz. E. G. Wever, the major proponent of the volley theory, has shown that the synchronous nerve firings in the auditory nerve as a whole can follow frequencies as high as 5000 Hz. Whenever a waveform rises to a peak of amplitude, a "volley" of nerve firings is set off. The determination of frequency, according to this theory, would be accomplished by an unspecified neural center that acts as a sort of volley counter.

At very low frequencies of a pulse train in which we perceive individual pulses, our intuition strongly suggests that the nervous system must "follow"— that is, "fire in synchrony with"—each individual pulse. It is much less intuitively persuasive that our nervous system "follows" the train of pulses as it rises in repetition rate until we hear it as a pitched sound. Yet a great deal of evidence supports the view that such synchrony between sound and neural responses occurs, evidently throughout a range that includes the fundamental frequencies in most music.

Proponents of the volley theory do not deny that the place theory describes frequency detection at the higher frequencies. The disagreement concerns the determination of where on the scale of frequencies the volley principle leaves off and the place mechanism begins. There may not even be such a point, for it has been suggested that hearing may consist of two processes that operate independently of each other and at overlaping ranges of frequency. W. H. Huggins has proposed such a dual-process theory in an undeservedly obscure study of speech perception. We shall see how this theory of hearing can also be of explanatory value in the perception of music. Several books on the physiology of hearing, representing various levels of sophistication are cited in the bibliography, and may be consulted for more detailed information.

Psychoacoustics

Having sketched the anatomy and physiology of the auditory system, let us turn now to the results of experiments in which the entire auditory system and the abilities of man to count and to answer questions are exploited. These experiments are within the old but relatively unfamiliar branch of psychology called *psychophysics,* or, more specifically, *psychoacoustics.* The aim of a psychoacoustic experiment is to answer a question about the relation between the physical parameters of a sound, called the *stimulus,* and the auditory sensations it produces in the listener. Since there is no way of making direct physical measurements of sensation, the psychophysicist must ask the listener carefully phrased questions about what he hears. His answers, the *responses,* are the data upon which the experimental results depend.

In all of these experiments a clear distinction is maintained between acoustic quantities and "psychological" qualities. Thus frequency, intensity or amplitude, waveform or spectrum, and phase are all properties of sounds, while loudness, pitch, timbre, and apparent position in space are so-called attributes or dimensions of auditory sensations. Perhaps the central fact of psychoacoustics is that there is no simple relation between any of the acoustic and the sensory dimensions. For example, loudness has been found to be a complex function of frequency and spectrum as well as of intensity. Psychoacoustics, then, may be considered a functional study of hearing. It is an approach that complements the work of physiologists, and in a sense it provides them with problems to solve. Let us see what it can tell us about what and how we hear.

The Limits of Hearing

Near the beginning of this chapter I suggested that there are limits to our hearing capacity that may be defined in terms of what we can now recognize as frequency and intensity. Fig. 11 portrays that world of sound more specifically. Though there may be some controversy about the exact borders of this "auditory area," there is little doubt about the general shape or even the actual values plotted, if they are taken as approximations. The borders of the area are called thresholds; the upper border is the *threshold of feeling,* and the lower one, the *absolute threshold.* The actual values vary from person to person, and vary depending on the methods of measurement. The most common interpersonal variation is a raising of the absolute threshold at high frequencies

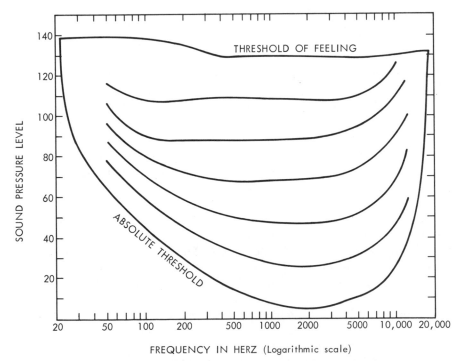

FIGURE 11. The auditory area. The curves within the area, called "equal loudness contours," are the approximate loci of tones that sound equally loud. Adapted from Stanley S. Stevens, and H. Davis, *Hearing* (New York: John Wiley & Sons, Inc. 1938).

with advancing age. This hearing loss is usually limited to frequencies above the ordinary range of musical pitches and involves the loss only of some of the higher harmonics of sounds. Because of the extreme ranges often employed in electronic music, however, audibility can be expected to vary somewhat depending on age.

Intensity and Decibels

Quantitative measurement of one important physical parameter of sound, its intensity, has been ignored so far because we have been able to speak about relative amplitude up to this point. Now, in discussing the auditory area we must refer to absolute quantities. The complication in intensity or amplitude measurement—"intensity" is usually used by psychophysicists as a generic term for the various amplitude measurements—does not result from any difficulties of measuring devices. Rather, it stems from the fact that the ear is far more sensitive to changes in pressure at low amplitudes than at high amplitudes. *Weber's Law,* which can be experimentally verified for a wide range of intensities above threshold, states the matter more exactly: *sensitivity* to changes in intensity is proportional to the intensity. Coupled with Weber's Law is the enormous range of intensities to which the ear is sensitive. At the frequencies of greatest sensitivity, the ratio of pressures between the absolute threshold and the threshold of feeling is on the order of one million to one! If the vertical axis of Fig. 11 were a *linear* scale, nearly all the sounds we hear would be crowded near the lower threshold. The use of the logarithmic *decibel* (or dB) scale serves better to distribute the sounds we can differentiate within the auditory area.

Expressed in decibels, the intensity of a sound is simply twenty times the logarithm of the ratio between its pressure (or voltage) and a reference pressure (or voltage). From the properties of logarithms it follows that a *ratio* of pressure is expressed as a *difference* in decibels. A few examples are presented in Table II. Since a value on a decibel scale represents a ratio between two numbers, the value must always be accompanied by the reference level. One might encounter an intensity expressed as "12 dB re 1 dyne/cm^2," for example. This means that the sound pressure is twelve decibels above one dyne per square centimeter, or four dynes/cm^2. In two cases the units of measurement specify the reference level by definition. The *sensation level* (SL) is the intensity in decibels above the absolute threshold. One should realize that although the SL is useful in certain contexts, it cannot be converted easily to pressure measurements, because the threshold is at different pressures at different frequencies. Perhaps the most widely used measurement of intensity is the *sound pressure level* (SPL). The reference level here is a pressure of 0.0002 dynes/cm^2, which represents the intensity at which an average listener can just barely detect a 1000-Hz tone. To give a rough impression of the actual intensities of sounds, Stevens and Davis have estimated that the loudest thunder is 120 dB SPL, an ordinary conversation is about 60, and the softest whisper is below 20. This enormous range of intensities can be compared to that of the best tape recorders, in which the ratio between the noises of tape and amplifier and the most intense signal that can be faithfully recorded—the *signal-to-noise ratio*—is only about 60 dB.

TABLE II. Pressure ratios and decibels.

Pressure ratio	dB difference
2:1	6 dB
4:1	12 dB
8:1	18 dB
1:16	−24 dB
10:1	20 dB
1:1,000,000	−120 dB

Having traced the limits of the world of sound, let us turn our attention to various phenomena of musical interest within that world. We shall begin with the sensations of pitch.

Pitch

Concern with the relation between our perception of *pitch* and the physically measurable parameters of sound has a long history. Early work in this area suffered from a lack of adequate control of the stimulus and, occasionally, from rather confused theoretical preconceptions about the relationship between mathematics and music. As the electronic oscillator was perfected, however, an easily controlled source of pure sinusoids was made available. This meant that our sense of hearing could be investigated in a manner analogous to our investigation of the behavior of a resonator. Instead of measuring the motion of the mass in response to a sinusoidal source, we ask a listener to tell us something about what he hears. When we ask about the pitch of a sinusoid, we immediately find that our auditory systems are much more complicated than the simple resonator.

The Mel Scale

To be specific, suppose we present a sine wave to a listener and then ask him to set another sine-wave oscillator to a pitch "one-half" that of the original tone. To a musician, of course, the concept of "one-half" pitch has little or no meaning. He is trained to deal with intervals that have essentially non-numerical identities. In particular, the pitches in one octave are very closely related to the "equivalent" pitches in another: octave equivalence is an important principle in Western music. In spite of the strangeness of the task, and aided perhaps by the rather indefinite "interval pitch" of a sine wave, non-musicians and an occasional musician are consistently able to make such settings. Repeated settings in which different frequencies were used as reference points permitted the psychoacoustician S. S. Stevens to draw a function relating frequency to "pitch" (or perhaps "distance pitch" would be a more accurate description). Fig. 12 shows one of these functions. The scale of pitch is given in units called *mels*. A frequency of 1000 Hz is arbitrarily given a "pitch" of 1000 mels.

Now the task of setting an oscillator to "one-half the pitch" of another seems so strange to a musician that even though he may admit the consistency of the "mel scale," he is likely to remain uninterested until the usefulness of the scale is demonstrated. Psychologists reacted at first with a great deal of criticism. But when Stevens showed that the mel scale was correlated with up to seven different independent measures—both physiological and psychophysical and including the place of maximal amplitude along the basilar membrane—most sensory psychologists, followed by the American Standards Organization, became convinced of its validity. It remains to interpret the scale in terms of musical perception.

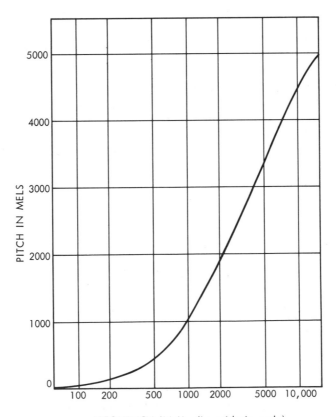

FIGURE 12.   The mel scale as a function of frequency. Adapted from Stevens and Davis, *Hearing*.

Let us hypothesize quite simply that the high-to-low aspect of musical pitch may be governed by the mel scale. Even this simple hypothesis presents problems, however. Because it is not a logarithmic scale, it does not correspond to the piano keyboard, which is tuned roughly according to a logarithmic scale. It would follow from the mel scale that any given musical interval—a major third or a fifth, for example—increases in size as the pitch rises. This contradicts musical theory, which holds that all intervals of the same kind are of equal "size" no matter where they may appear within the range of musical pitches. Evidently, the mel scale and, therefore, the distribution of stimuli along the basilar membrane have only a vague relation to our ideas about how musical pitch functions in Western music.

Interval Pitch

Present-day psychophysicists have little to say about our sense of interval. There have been in the past several attempts to represent graphically the notion of pitch class. These attempts have not added to our knowledge of what I shall call interval pitch; rather, they are attempts to account for it. A recent demonstration of the "circular" aspect of pitch perception, though hardly needed by the practicing composer, is dramatic and convincing. With the aid of a computer, Roger Shepard synthesized a sound whose pitch rose up and up stepwise and yet never seemed to get any higher in pitch. The trick is to excite what amounts to a very broad resonance with a complex tone made of sine waves tuned an octave apart that cover much of the range of audible pitches. The sine waves move up stepwise and as they do, the broad resonance causes the higher tones to fall below our thresholds of hearing. As the higher tones disappear, they are "replaced" by new tones at the bottom of the scale, which are not noticed at first because they are below the threshold. The sliding, loud, pedal-like chord in Region IV of Stockhausen's *Hymnen* and the apparent upward glissandi in Risset's *Mutations* are musical applications of this technique.

The mel scale was built using pure sinusoids, yet music consists almost entirely of complex sounds. And it is in music that we exploit interval pitch. It may be that wave-shape, and, thus, the presence or absence of harmonics, affects our sense of interval. The generalization would be that interval pitch is weak in pure sinusoids, but stronger in sounds with harmonics. It is not clear how the harmonics would improve our interval perception, but it may have something to do with their being used by our ears to "reinforce" the fundamental frequency. The pitch of a complex sound seems to be a bit more definite than the pitch of a sinusoid. This effect of harmonics on the perception of the fundamental is dramatically emphasized by "the case of the missing fundamental." It is possible to filter away the fundamental and lower harmonics of a sound without changing its perceived pitch. The lowest of the thirty-two-foot pipes in the organ provide a more familiar example of this phenomenon. The fundamental frequencies of these sounds are too weak to be heard, and they must be inferred by the ear from the higher harmonics.

The relation of the pitches in a musical scale to the harmonic series hardly provides an explanation for our perception either of pitch intervals or —except perhaps in an historical sense—of the musical scales themselves. The scales of the last two or three centuries have resulted from a patching and filling of the "natural" scales strictly in response to musical necessity. Quite clearly, the mel scale and its associated place theory also have nothing to say about the distinctive qualities of the musical intervals. On the other hand, the interaction between the fundamentals and harmonics of two simultaneous sounds separated by a given frequency ratio could result in a characteristic temporal pattern of nerve firings. Though the volley principle says little about how frequency is actually analyzed, it provides the kind of process that could underlie the well-established equating, in Western music at least, of musical intervals of the same kind, no matter what their absolute pitch.

Consonance and Dissonance

Though few present-day psychologists have dealt with musical intervals directly, some have written about the related issue of consonance and dissonance. In every case that I know of, the psychological studies have been based on a conception that is quite different from the musical one. From medieval times up to the twentieth century, musicians classified intervals as *either* consonant *or* dissonant; there was no such thing as a *degree* of consonance or dissonance. Until the twentieth century the distinction was an important one, for it governed the permissible succession of sounds. But with such an arbitrary concept—and, indeed, with one that changed with musical styles—we are unlikely to find it based upon the kind of biologically determined relationships that most psychoacousticians require.

What psychologists have studied is a perceptual continuum that they have called a consonance-to-dissonance scale. Ordinarily, this scale is considered to be the same as a "pleasant-to-unpleasant" or a "smooth-to-rough" scale. The results of such scaling experiments that use, say, two-tone intervals as stimuli, are compared to the predictions of "roughness" based on some physical measurement of the stimulus. In some cases reasonable agreement is found between the perceptual scale and the physical measurement. It is quite clear that these scales have little to do with traditional notions of musical consonance or dissonance—typically, the perfect fourth is judged more "consonant" than the major third. But the changing concepts of the musical meaning of dissonance in our own time make the research of more than passing interest.

Beats, Modulation, and Combination Tones

When two sinusoids are slightly mis-tuned, we hear a waxing and waning of the sound, which repeats at a rate equal to the difference in frequency between the two sounds. These slow variations in the sound are called *beats*. In some of the theories of dissonance—the psychologists' kind, that is—the amount and frequency of beating between the harmonics of the notes in a chord are said to determine the degree of dissonance. The beating of harmonics may have something to do with the distinctive character of musical intervals, but there cannot be a very *sensitive* relation. The "equal-tempered" scale actually departs markedly from exactly equal temperament. A piano tuned by an expert so as to include these departures is preferred by listeners over one tuned "perfectly" with the aid of frequency-measuring devices. The mis-tunings would result in quite different beat frequencies, particularly among the higher partials, of intervals of the same kind. Beats can be controlled easily with electronic instruments, and they play an important role in certain electronic pieces.

Beats are only one phenomenon within the broader topic of *modulation*. Whenever some parameter of a signal is varied by some other signal, the first signal is said to be modulated by the second. If the amplitude of the first signal is varied, the modulation is called *amplitude modulation;* if it is the frequency that is modulated, it is called *frequency modulation*. The effect of modulation is to produce a mixture of signals that consists of a central signal and signals at frequencies above and below the central signal. These *sidebands* are separated from the central signal by a frequency equal to the rate of modulation. An entire chapter of Stevens and Davis's book is devoted to the auditory effects of modulation. I heartily recommend it, especially to those composers who would like to understand in detail the effects of the "voltage-controlled" devices in modern synthesizers.

Another source of "additional" sounds is the *nonlinearity* of the transmission of sound through the middle ear. Nonlinearity means, in this case, that the eardrum and ossicles do not transmit sound to the inner ear strictly in proportion to its amplitude. At low amplitudes the sound is transmitted faithfully, but at high amplitudes the mechanical vibrations at the oval window have a lower amplitude than the sound itself. As the amplitude rises, the middle ear increasingly blunts the peaks of the waveform. The effect of this nonlinearity is to create *aural harmonics* in sinusoids and *combination tones* in mixtures of two or more sinusoids or complex sounds. These "subjective tones," as they were once called, can beat with each other. When the frequencies of combination tones are equal to the difference between the components of the two sounds, they are called *difference tones;* when equal to the sums of components, *summation tones*. As the amplitudes of the original sounds increase, the aural harmonics themselves become intense enough to produce secondary and tertiary combination tones. The marked change in tone quality that we hear as a sound increases in intensity is due in part to this protective nonlinearity in the ear.

Musical Timbre

Musical *timbre* is perhaps the most interesting auditory phenomenon for composers of electronic music. At the same time, it is the least understood and most complicated topic in psychoacoustics. In part, the problem is one of definition. The American Standards Association defines timbre as any change in a tone that cannot be accounted for by pitch and loudness. But this makes timbre a catchall that must be refined if it is to be useful to composers.

Let us examine for a moment the somewhat narrower view that timbre is what differs in the sounds of different musical instruments playing the same note. In most of the recent work on the timbre of musical instruments, researchers have found it useful to divide timbre into *steady-state* and *transient* phenomena. The attack and release portions of a note are the transients; the held portion in between, the steady-state. With only the steady-state to go by, a listener often confuses the sounds of different musical instruments. Identifications are much more reliable if the attack is heard as well. In the best of these studies, analyses of the sounds of a musical instrument have been applied in fairly successful attempts to synthesize the instrumental sounds electronically. Backus provides a very good overview of this research in his *Acoustical Foundations of Music.* But aside from the vague assertion that steady-state timbre is a function of the relative intensities of the harmonics in a sound, the research has led to no general conclusions that would relate a perceptual description of sound to its acoustical properties.

Though the narrower view of musical timbre may be of help in doing research, there remain many changes in electronic sounds in particular that cannot be accounted for by pitch or loudness; for these changes, the categories, steady-state and transient, seem inappropriate. J. K. Randall has asked how, for example, one would treat controlled changes in vibrato under the rubric of timbre. He would give up the concept of timbre entirely, but I think there is value in it that can be preserved by an approach derived from the ways sounds are produced in nature. W. H. Huggins has put the matter in the following way:

> Many of the sounds heard in everyday life come about because of "something" happening to some physical object or structure. To decribe these sounds, it is helpful to think of the "something" happening as being an excitation which is modified and transformed into the sound signal by an intervening physical system. The form of this transformation is determined by the *structural* properties of the physical system and . . . it follows simple physical laws, which do not change with time. The excitation, on the other hand, may obey no simple law and may be quite random and unpredictable. The temporal properties of the sound are thus largely attributable to the excitation and are primarily characterized by the dates [i.e., the points in time], (and perhaps also the intensities) of the various "somethings" that happen.[2]

Huggins goes on to suggest that, when listening to "meaningful" sounds, we try to identify both the "something" that supplies the original acoustic energy, and the physical object that shapes the energy through its characteristic set of resonances. In the human voice, the "something" is the buzzing of the vocal cords that is modified by the "intervening physical system," the vocal tract. Huggins's paper proceeds to describe a mechanism by which the ear may analyze the resonance frequencies. In contrast with the place theory of pitch, Huggins's theory is, rather, a place theory of resonance frequency detection or,

2 W. H. Huggins, "A Phase Principle for Complex-Frequency Analysis and Its Implications in Auditory Theory," *Journal of the Acoustical Society of America,* XXIV (1952), 582–89.

as applied to music, a *place theory of timbre*. The *pitch* in this class of "meaningful" sounds comes from the excitation, and would logically be analyzed by an entirely different process, such as volleys of nerve firings, which seems capable of staying in synchrony with fundamental frequencies throughout the musical range. If the mechanism of frequency analysis given by the varying width of the basilar membrane is devoted to analysis of the structural aspect of the sound, then the mel scale, which is the psychoacoustic correlate of that mechanism, would pertain more closely to what musicians call timbre or "color" than to pitch.

How can we apply this auditory theory, which is based so strongly on the way certain sounds are produced, to the timbre of "non-meaningful" musical sounds? In some ways, the sounds of many musical instruments are problematic because their excitation and their resonance systems are connected in such a way that the resonances *control* the excitation. The fundamental frequency in these instruments is close or equal to one of the resonances, and if my interpretation of Huggins's ideas is correct, pitch and timbre would apparently be confounded. This would not happen, however, if the ear mistakenly treated the excitation as if it were independent of the resonance system, ignored the resonance controlling the excitation, and treated the higher resonances as cues to the structural aspects of the sound that give it its timbre. This artificial division of the sound wave could be the way we perceive the pitch and color of other "unnatural" sounds as well.

A different problem is presented by the human voice. In the utterance of vowels the resonance system changes relatively little, but it changes quite drastically with respect to time when consonants are vocalized. The important points here are the speed of the changing resonances and the kind of information that the auditory system requires from those changes. Our knowledge about the perception of consonants is so limited that we cannot even guess about the second point. But we can estimate the time scale involved from the durations of those changes. The sweep of the resonances from a consonantal "locus" to that of a vowel is seldom less than thirty milliseconds for any given consonant. The theoretical implications of these facts demand that Huggins's resonance analyzers deal not only with a static resonance system, but with one that changes in time—albeit relatively slowly. Huggins meets this demand in his article by showing that such changes can be followed by the resonance analyzers he proposes. Since the theory covers more than the steady-state, transients that are identified with relatively slowly changing resonance systems —the attacks of certain musical instruments, for example—can be treated as aspects of timbre.

Is there any direct psychoacoustic evidence that supports this two-part theory of hearing? It would consist of research showing that timbre varies more strongly as a function of resonance frequencies than as a function of the relative intensities of the harmonics. One could ask whether the first of these alternatives results in the smallest variation in timbre when, for example, the pitch is changed. Given the sound whose spectrum is illustrated in Fig. 13, let us raise the fundamental frequency by an octave and ask which of the

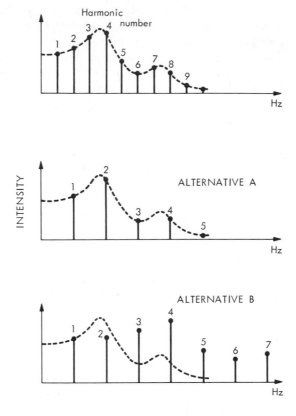

FIGURE 13. Alternative predictions of invariance in timbre under octave increases in fundamental frequency. Alternative A is the prediction of the "fixed-pitch" or formant theory; alternative B, that of the "relative-pitch" or overtone theory.

alternative spectra, A or B, results in the smallest difference in timbre. The results of my own research dealing with sounds like those in Fig. 13 showed unequivocally that preserving fixed resonances (alternative A) led to smaller differences in timbre than preserving the intensities of the harmonics relative to each other. Had alternative B resulted in the smaller differences, we would have had to conclude that a sound is relatively little affected by the resonances that shape its spectrum, and that the shape of the excitation waveform alone determines timbre. Only a single frequency analyzer, albeit a very complicated one, would have had to be postulated. The experimental evidence favored the first alternative, however, and therefore strongly supported the view that pitch and timbre are analyzed through separate, independent processes.

In certain manipulations of sounds, as in the controlled vibrato discussed by Randall, timbre defined as the effects of a relatively time-invariant resonance system may not play an important role. But nearly all sounds have timbre. Even if sounds are generated artificially, they may be processed by the ear as if—they may *sound* as if—they are the product of a resonating body struck by some kind of excitation. We miss an immense and largely untraveled world of great beauty if we ignore or fail to control this aspect of sound. For those who would experiment, I suggest the vowels whose resonances are given in Table I as a good starting point.

Loudness

Suppose we are faced with the practical task of producing a crescendo that sounds linear—that is, one that changes in loudness at about the same rate throughout its duration—in a computer-synthesis system. For simplicity's sake, let's assume that we wish to control only intensity, holding the other parameters of the sound constant. From our discussion of decibels and logarithms, one would suspect that a linear increase of intensity over time would not produce a linear increase in loudness. But what about an exponential change of intensity over time? This would be expected to result in a linear loudness change if, as suggested by the decibel scale, loudness were proportional to the logarithm of intensity. Is there some other function of time that will do better?

The results of psychoacoustic experiments on the loudness of sounds with unchanging intensities can predict the answer to these questions. In one such experiment, a refinement of the fractionation method (which produced the mel scale) was applied to loudness. Listeners were asked to give numerical estimates of the loudness of a series of sounds that differed in intensity. Any numbers could be used, but having chosen a number to represent the loudness of the first sound, the listener was to give numbers that were proportional to the loudnesses of the following sounds, using the first number as a reference. It is not hard to understand why this and other such experimental methods, developed primarily by S. S. Stevens at the Harvard Laboratory of Psychophysics, are called "direct" methods. The responses of the listeners *are* the direct answers to the experimental question, "How loud are sounds of these intensities?" Stevens's generalization about the results of these experiments is now widely accepted: Loudness grows with sound pressure according to a power function whose exponent is approximately ⅔. Fig. 14 illustrates this relation, including linear and logarithmic functions for comparison. To get a "linear" crescendo we must simply cancel out the nonlinearity of the ear. Stevens's power law predicts, and experiments confirm, that increasing intensity as a function of time to the ³⁄₂ *power* results in the "ideal" growth of loudness over time.[3]

We cannot say, based upon the "power law," how the various dynamic markings in music for performance relate to intensity, but we can give the intensity that corresponds to any *numerical* operation on loudness. Tripling or halving loudness, for example, can be accomplished by finding the appropriate values on the loudness axis in Fig. 14 and reading off the intensity values. Even though the dynamic marks in notated music have the weight of tra-

---

[3] See L. E. Marks and A. W. Slawson, "Direct Test of the Power Function for Loudness," *Science,* CLIV (1966), 1036–37.

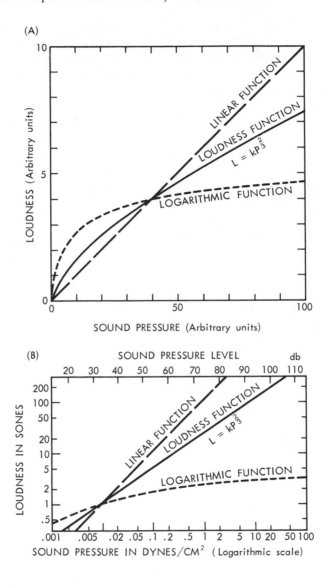

FIGURE 14.   The growth of loudness with intensity. The heavy curves represent the loudness of a 3000-Hz tone as a function of sound pressure. The dotted curves are the linear and logarithmic functions for comparison. In (A) the scales are linear and in arbitrary units. In (B) the scales are logarithmic with sound pressure on the lower scale and sound pressure level (dB re 0.0002 dynes/cm²) on the upper. The three functions cross at the proposed new 3000-Hz reference of 32 dB SPL and one sone (a measurement of loudness). A power function with an exponent of ⅔, the relation between loudness and intensity, is represented by a straight line in log-log coordinates whose slope is ⅔. S. S. Stevens, "Perceived Level of Noise by Mark VII and dB(E)" *Journal of the Acoustical Society of America*, **LI**, (1972) 575–602. Used by permission.

dition behind them, I have the feeling that this kind of numerical control of loudness may be more useful in electronic music. It better represents the continuity of loudness gradations that the composer usually intends.

Many other parameters of sound affect loudness. If, for example, a sinusoid at a fixed intensity is changed markedly in frequency, there is likely to be a change in loudness. This kind of change can be seen in Fig. 11. The curves in this figure that lie between the upper and lower threshold curves are called *equal-loudness contours*. One of these curves represents the frequency and intensity combinations that result in the same loudness. Since the curves are not horizontal lines, loudness must change with frequency. Notice that the curves give no indication of the *relative* loudnesses among the various equal loudness contours. In the middle ranges of frequency, loudness obeys the ⅔ power law and the contours could have been drawn so that their separation represented equal ratios of loudness. At low and high frequencies, however, we are simply not sure enough of the loudness-intensity relationship to draw the curves accurately. Research is still being conducted to determine improved equal-loudness contours because of their importance in the complicated task of calculating the loudness of various noises.[4]

Spectrum envelope is also an important factor in the loudness of a sound. The research on equal-loudness contours is helpful in determining the spectrum for noisy sounds, but in the case of periodic sounds difficulties crop up. An unpublished study of my own suggests a rule for vowel-like sounds: sounds with a first resonance higher than 500 Hz seem to be louder than those of equal intensity with lower first resonances. The rule is complicated by a certain lack of agreement about the proper method of measuring intensity in vowel-like sounds, so it must be applied with caution. Needless to say, the topic demands much more research.

Masking

The capacity of one sound to drown out another, a capacity particularly well-known to all orchestrators, is called *masking*. The generalization to be made here is that sounds containing low frequencies are better maskers than those containing high frequencies. This is not an absolute rule, of course. It means simply that the high frequencies in a mixture of sounds must be relatively more intense to be heard. If sounds are separated in frequency, their masking effects upon one another are decreased; but the tendency of low frquencies to mask high ones is merely lessened by frequency separation. A recent study suggests that masking is particularly effective when the masking sound is within a critical band of the masked sound. Among the implications of this study is that masking is associated with the place of stimulation on the basilar membrane. In a simplistic sense, one would indeed expect low frequencies, which maximally stimulate areas farther from the oval window, to interfere with high frequencies, whose locus is closer to the oval window.

---

[4] See Stevens, "Perceived Level of Noise by Mark VII and dB(E)."

Localizing Sound in Space

Our ears are very good at detecting where a sound is coming from. In order to localize a sound source, however, we are forced by an accident of physics to depend upon two different processes. The complication is due to the fact that the *wavelength* (the distance a sound wave travels during one cycle) of a sound in the middle-frequencies of the audible range is approximately equal to the width of the human head.

The wavelength of low-frequency sounds is significantly greater than the width of the head. The sound can "wash around" the head easily, like an ocean wave around a small post. Both ears receive about the same *intensity* of sound, even if the source of the low-frequency sound is to one side. However, there is a difference in the *time* at which, say, the peak pressure arrives at the two ears. The arrival time, or phase, difference is due to the difference in the distances from the source to each of the ears when the source is not "straight ahead." Psychoacoustic studies show that we are just capable of localizing a 100-Hz sinusoid to within three degrees of arc; this implies that the ears make use of time differences of less than one ten-thousandth of a second! Since low-frequency sound waves move around either the front or back of our heads with equal ease, there is no way of determining the front-back position of the sound source. Experiments confirm that at low frequencies we are seldom able to tell whether a sound is coming from in front of us or behind us.

As a sound rises in frequency, however, the phase differences between the two ears begin to take up a significant fraction of the period of the waveform. At about 2000 Hz a sound source located ninety degrees to one side produces a complete reversal of phase in the two ears. When the pressure increases in one ear, it decreases in the other, and vice versa. There is no way for our auditory system to determine which ear is nearest to the sound. Localization on the basis of phase differences begins to break down at 1000 Hz, and steadily worsens at higher frequencies.

Fortunately, another means of localizing sound is available at higher frequencies. As frequency increases (and the speed of propagation remains constant), the wavelength of sound becomes shorter. Thus, at frequencies above, say, 4000 Hz the wavelength is less than the width of our heads. The pressure is changing so fast that there is not enough time for the sound to wash around what is now effectively a very large object. The head forms a "sound shadow" so that the *intensity* in the ear nearest the source is significantly greater than that in the far ear. At high frequencies these intensity differences make it possible to localize sound sources about as well as at low frequencies. Since at high frequencies the auricle or pinna of the outer ear favors sound coming from the front, we are capable of accurately distinguishing front sources from back sources. Between 2000 Hz and 4000 Hz—where, incidentally, our ears are most sensitive to sound—neither phase nor intensity differences can be used by the ears, and our capacity to localize is considerably weaker.

All of the preceding applies only to sinusoids. Because most of the sounds we hear are complex, they contain frequencies outside the range where localization is weak. Psychoacoustic experiments confirm that in the middle range, complex sounds are localized considerably better than sinusoids. Speech sounds, much of whose energy is in the middle range, are probably localized on the basis of phase differences in the low-frequency components.

In electronic music that incorporates multiple sound sources, the location of an apparent sound source can be problematic. It is fairly easy to control intensity differences between two speakers; thus, for sounds with high-frequency components, the sound can be "placed" in space or moved without great difficulty. In sinusoids below, say, 1000 Hz, intensity differences must be considerably greater for localization to be effective. In very low sinusoids the spatial position would have to be simulated by small phase differences between two speakers. In the classical studio and the synthesizer, control of phase differences such as these are difficult or impossible, but computers equipped for stereo synthesis can be programmed to produce them.

Conclusion

Many important topics in the fields of acoustics, electroacoustics, and psychoacoustics have been slighted or ignored in this brief account. In particular, I have skimmed over wave motion, and have avoided altogether a treatment of standing waves in tubes. Though these and other matters are interesting and of central importance in, for example, studies of musical instruments, they are of less concern to composers of electronic music. Moreover, they are not absolutely necessary to the development of the theme that runs through the chapter. That theme was introduced with the discussion of mechanical resonators excited by an external source. The workings of loudspeakers and oscillators were seen to depend upon resonance. The frequency analyzing mechanism of the inner ear is a particularly complicated resonance system. The two-part theory of pitch and timbre perception derives from a conception of sound produced by a resonator excited by an independent source. No single phenomenon is more basic to the production of electronic music than that of resonance. I hope a foundation for at least an intuitive grasp of its fundamental principles is provided in this chapter.

My aim has been to present general principles—some, such as the treatment of musical timbre, rather speculative in nature—that may suggest new musical possibilities explorable primarily through the use of electronic devices. I have tried not to prescribe or restrict. My own experience suggests that scientific and technical knowledge opens musical doors. If the facts and theories presented here can be thoroughly mastered, then they—like any other compositional skill—will become a part of the discipline that serves to free the musical imagination.

3

The Tape Studio

GUSTAV CIAMAGA

At this writing the tape studio still represents the most prevalent approach to the composition of electronic music around the world. It served as the basis for an aesthetic developed by French composers in the late '40s and continues to dominate the thinking of these same composers today.

Although the addition of synthesizers to tape studios has expanded the resources of many composers, the multiple techniques for the storage, retrieval, and transformation of sonic material through the use of tape recorders has had a profound effect on the many "styles" of music we hear today. Many of the techniques used by composers of electronic music are used in the production of phonograph recordings of traditional instrumental music as well as rock and popular forms.

Gustav Ciamaga begins by carefully differentiating the early Cologne and Paris "schools" of electronic and concrete music, then takes the reader on a step-by-step tour of a typical "classic" studio at the end of the '50s and the beginning of the '60s. Sound generators, sound modifiers, and devices for the mixing, recording, and reproduction of sound are considered in turn. He follows this with a comparative survey of five of the most internationally important tape studios and discusses a representative musical work produced in each. Finally, he considers electronic-music notation and the teaching of electronic music.

Mr. Ciamaga, a composer, is Professor of Music at the University of Toronto and Director of its Electronic Music Studio. He has written several articles on the design of electronic music systems, and was invited to the 1970 UNESCO Conference on Music and Technology, at which he presented a paper on "The Training of the Composer in the Use of New Technological Means."

He was born in London, Ontario in 1930. He completed his undergraduate studies at the University of Toronto, and did graduate work in composition and musicology at Brandeis University.

INTRODUCTION

The *tape studio* (or electronic music studio, as it is sometimes called) is a collection of electrical and electronic equipment used by composers in the production of electronic music. The methods employed in realizing an electronic composition in the tape studio are intrinsically dependent on the possibilities arising from the medium of tape recording, and can be distinguished from the alternate methods of the *voltage-controlled synthesizer* (Chapter 4) and the *computer* (Chapter 5), even though these also rely on recording and share a common theoretical basis: musical sound as electrical signal. Although the creative output of a tape studio is *tape music,* this term was originally used to distinguish the pioneer American compositions composed in the early '50s from the contemporaneous schools of *musique concrète* (Paris) and *elektronische Musik* (Cologne). These distinctions were to lose much of their original significance early in the history of electronic music, and we now refer to all electronic music produced in a tape studio as tape music.

The first studios for electronic music were established in European broadcasting stations and, later, in music departments of North American and European universities. To suggest that all tape music is produced in institutional studios would be inaccurate, for composers have worked independently in such diverse environments as a spartan cabin at MacDowell colony (Ussachevsky and Luening, *A Poem in Cycles and Bells*), and a kitchen in a private home (Takemitsu, *Water Music*). Nevertheless, the institution can bear the sometimes considerable expense required to maintain an elaborate facility, and —a factor often ignored—the European radio stations and North American universities have been, and still are, favorably disposed to experimental music of all periods.

From their earliest beginnings, the methods and equipment of the tape studio have reflected the changing electronic technology. To distinguish the contemporary tape studio, which assimilated voltage-controlled equipment and synthesizers, from their earlier counterparts, writers and composers venerate the earlier studios and methods with the expression *classic*—e.g., the *classic studio*. The expression is useful but also misleading, for it might imply that the primary techniques developed in the first decade are outmoded. Numerous compositions from contemporary tape studios still employ classic equipment and techniques, and any declaration of their demise is premature.

At the outset, it must be stated that the methods employed and the results obtained by a composer in a tape studio (or for that matter wih a synthesizer or computer) are only *alternatives* to the normal modes of musical composition and performance, and should not be construed as either being superior to or replacing conventional music making. At one time, it was fashionable to point out the limitations of musical instruments and to show how electronic resources overcame these limitations. For example, the duration of a trumpet sound is limited by the available breath of the player whereas an electronic sound from an oscillator can sound for an indefinite length of time; or, traditional musical instruments only operate in the framework of equal temperament whereas electronic music devices can create other systems of tuning; and so forth. The arguments are pointless, for electronic music also has its own set of limitations, which the composer learns to respect in the same way as he has learned to respect those of musical instruments.

The composer is often attracted to the electronic music studio because it offers him direct or intimate control over the parameters that constitute a sound event—*frequency, spectrum, intensity, envelope,* and *duration*—and the mode of *succession* from such a sound event to the following event. Because the composer is working in the domain of sound as electrical signal, he can instantly verify his intentions as he hears the sound emanate from a loudspeaker. Each parameter is associated with the devices and techniques of the tape studio and suggests to the composer distinct creative possibilities. For example:

1. *Frequency*: oscillators may be tuned precisely to any frequency in the audio spectrum, or prerecorded sounds can be transposed to new regions.
2. *Spectrum*: a spectrum can be created synthetically by oscillators or by a pre-existent spectrum altered by filtering.
3. *Intensity*: the loudness of a sound can be varied continuously over a range of more than forty db, or a discrete dynamic profile (envelope) can be created for the sound.
4. *Duration*: the duration of a signal can be shortened or lengthened by a variety of methods, but more importantly, the duration can be calculated precisely by measuring the magnetic tape in centimeters or inches.
5. *Succession*: the succession may be ordered precisely by cutting and splicing the tape(s), and may be presented in one or more layers of sound. Once the succession of chosen sound events representing the composition is recorded, each "performance" of the composition will be identical.

The creative potential of the tape studio would hardly have been possible had it not been for the perfection of magnetic tape recording (ca. 1948–50). We sometimes focus our attention unduly on the "new" sound resources of electronic music (sine waves, white noise, concrete sounds), and neglect the medium of magnetic tape, which allows these sounds to be brought into the domain of musical composition. Most of the sound sources and modifiers used by the first composers of electronic music already existed, but it remained for the invention of the tape recorder to release and suggest new creative applications for these devices. The importance of the tape recorder for electronic composition can be stated as follows:

1. It makes possible a permanent acoustic record of any available sound or any electrically derived variant of that sound.
2. The recorder provides a means of transposing the sound material to different registers, thus obtaining new pitch locations and, possibly, new timbres.
3. The acoustic record in its unique form, magnetic tape, can be acted upon to order a musical continuity.
4. The electroacoustic transmission (i.e., amplifer/loudspeaker) of the completed composition from magnetic tape is direct and does not require an intermediary performer.

In Chapter 1, Otto Luening traced the course of the experimental music that culminated at the middle of the twentieth century with the emergence of the first schools and studios of electronic music. During the first years of experimentation, general procedures of electronic composition were established whereby the composer selected the acoustic material, submitted it to various transformations, and then ordered the resulting material. The initial step, the choice of acoustic material (which could be electronic or non-electronic in origin) characterized the electronic compositions of the early period, for the subsequent steps of treatment and organization were common to all tape composition. A historical resumé of the "schools" of Paris and Cologne, and their production techniques, will help make this clear.

The school of *musique concrète* (Pierre Schaeffer and Pierre Henry) began in Paris in 1948. After their initial experiments, Schaeffer chose to name the new art *musique concrète* to differentiate it from normal music, *musique abstraite*. In the former, the music is made directly on tape with real (concrete) sounds; in *musique abstraite,* the music is created abstractly in the composer's mind, written down in the form of a score, and then played.

Musique concrète begins with raw sound material, *non-electronic in origin,* which has been recorded on tape via a microphone. The identity of the sounds or sound objects (*objets sonores*) is transformed by a variety of means and is recorded; these newly transformed sounds on tape are juxtaposed through cutting and splicing (*montage*) to form a musical continuity. When a polyphonic texture is desired, two or more of these continuities are superimposed (*mixage*) by playing the tapes synchronously and recording the resultant mixture.

The range of raw sound material exploited for *musique concrète* is vast and can be categorized as the *sounds of our environment*[1] (e.g., dripping water faucets, jet planes, machine sounds, etc.); *vocal sounds* (e.g., breathing, speaking, singing, etc.); and the *sounds of musical instruments.* In the compositions of the Paris school, the sound of a musical instrument need not emanate from the normal mode of execution associated with that instrument; that is, a tam-tam may be played with a bow, and so forth. The characteristics of the acoustical sound source in its isolated form, the *objet sonore,* have been the subject of intensive study by Schaeffer and his associates. The last section of Schaeffer's *A la recherche d'une musique concrète* (Paris, 1952), contains a preliminary sketch for a *solfège concret,* that is, a sol-fa for perceiving and classifying the sound objects of *musique concrète.* These first principles of solfège were to be expanded in Schaeffer's exhaustive study, *Traité des objets musicaux* (Paris, 1966). The essence of Schaeffer's theories is summarized in the recorded commentary and sound examples accompanying the *Traité.* These remarkably informative recordings are required listening for all composers and musicians.

Shortly after the first concrete compositions appeared, a group of composers and scientists at Cologne (Herbert Eimert, Karlheinz Stockhausen, Robert Beyer, and Werner Meyer-Eppler) began formulating a second ap-

---

[1] These sounds are sometimes referred to as "noises"; this term should be avoided because, like "dissonance," it is open to subjective interpretation.

proach to composing with electronic means, *elektronische Musik*. Their approach begins with *electronic sound sources,* which provide the raw material for further processing. With sine-wave, pulse, and white-noise generators as the basic sound material, the composer creates complex spectra through additive synthesis (superimposing sine waves), subtractive synthesis (filtering the signal output of white-noise or pulse generators), or ring modulation (displacement of an existing spectrum), and the results are recorded on tape. Unlike a concrete sound, which has a preexistent dynamic profile or envelope, the electronic source signal is uniform in amplitude and requires planned regulation of its intensity during or after the above-mentioned processes. At this point, the remaining procedures are identical to *musique concrète;* the electronic sounds are further modified if so desired, cut and spliced to form the continuity, then synchronized and recorded.

Whereas the Paris school borrowed traditional structural forms and used programmatic titles to suggest unity for their musical montages, the Cologne school proclaimed an intellectual and theoretical affinity with the Viennese "twelve-tone" school, particularly Webern. The original notions embodied in the twelve-tone compositions of Webern were extended to include the serial ordering of all parameters, as in Stockhausen's first electronic studies, *Studie I* and *Studie II,* in which the parameters of pitch, timbre, intensity, and duration are serially ordered.[2] When Stockhausen's *Gesang der Jünglinge* (1955–56) included a boy's voice, speaking and singing along with electronic sounds, Cologne's claim to the exclusive use of electronic sounds was eroded.[3] From that point on, we can say that no basic conceptual difference existed between the schools of Paris and Cologne.

In the resumé of the Paris and Cologne schools, the first and last steps of the production methods were described. It remains now to mention briefly the intermediate step, the treatment or transformation of the acoustic source material. The transformations of the material affect one or more parameters of the sound, and are accomplished with specific apparatus or techniques arising from tape recording. Some of the possibilities have already been alluded to (p. 70); the actual apparatus and its applications will be described in fuller detail in the next section. The possible transformations are numerous and need not be systematically applied in the course of the composition, for the composer learns to "imagine" transformations and uses only those that seem promising.

THE EQUIPMENT OF THE TAPE STUDIO

A perusal of the *Répertoire International des Musiques Expérimentales* (Paris, 1962), a publication that appeared before the general availability of synthesizers, gives us a good picture of the actual instrumentation of a classic

---

2 Some early Paris compositions, notably those of Messiaen (*Timbres-Durées*) and Philippot (*Etude I*), employ serialism.

3 The early American school claimed no preference for source material, and the same can be said for the studios established in the '50s—Tokyo, Milan, Eindhoven, and others.

tape studio at the end of the '50s and the beginning of the '60s. The twenty international studios surveyed by this publication reported on the compositions produced in their studios, and also supplied lists of equipment according to a scheme that is still useful:

1. Sound generators
2. Devices for tranformation or modification of sound
3. Equipment for the mixing, recording, and reproduction of sound.

All studios surveyed for this publication had essentially similar equipment; some had pieces of unique equipment. The actual quantity and types of equipment found in some studios might seem modest by today's standards, and yet Stockhausen was able to produce his *Gesang der Jünglinge* (Cologne, 1955–56) with the prerecorded sounds of a boy's voice, a small number of generators and modifiers, the usual recording equipment, and unlimited inspiration.

The Milan studio is fairly typical of studios during the period following the appearance of the *Répertoire*.

The Equipment of the Milan Studio (ca. 1960)

Sound generators:
   9 sine-wave oscillators
   1 white-noise generator
   1 pulse generator

Sound modifiers:
    reverberation units (chamber, tape, and plate)
    octave filter
    high-pass filter (6 cutoff frequencies)
    low-pass filter (6 cutoff frequencies)
    variable band-pass filter
    third-octave filter
    spectrum analyzer
    modulators (ring, amplitude, etc.)
    variable tape-speed unit
    Springer time regulator
    amplitude filter

Recording and reproduction equipment:
    microphones
    mixing console
    amplifiers and loudspeakers for four-channel monitoring
   4 mono tape recorders (7.5/15 ips)
   2 mono   "   "   (30 ips)
   2 two-channel recorders (7.5/15 ips)
   2 four-channel recorders (7.5 ips)

Before proceeding to a detailed description of equipment for tape studios, it should be reiterated that the contemporary studio—and this includes many of the studios in the *Répertoire*—contains not only the equipment associated with the earliest tape music, but also voltage-controlled equipment and/or synthesizers as they are described elsewhere in this book. As to the description of the equipment itself, it will follow the threefold scheme noted above: sound generators, sound modifiers, and equipment for mixing, recording, and reproducing sound. This scheme is not perfect, for some pieces of equipment, such as the tape recorder, can be assigned to more than one category. In other cases, a piece of equipment will not fit any category exactly—the microphone and the keyboard are examples—and this will be noted when the piece of equipment is described.

At times, it has been found convenient to compare the equipment of the tape studio to that found in a synthesizer; the author is assuming that more readers will have seen or used a synthesizer than a classic tape studio. In general, the equipment described is commercially available, though specific manufacturer's names are not always included. In some instances, unique equipment of unusual interest will be described.

Sound Generators

The usual list of sound generators for the production of electronic music includes sine, triangular, square, sawtooth and pulse wave-form generators, and a white-noise source. Though a well-equipped studio contains all of these sound sources, tape music—particularly before the advent of the synthesizer—has relied extensively on sine-wave oscillators, pulse generators, and white noise.

In retrospect, one of the contributions of the earliest tape music is the expansion of the musical sound palette by the inclusion of sine waves and white noise. These two "colors," which have no direct equivalents in traditional musical instruments, represent the extremes of the sound spectrum; the sine wave is the purest and simplest sound found in this spectrum, and white noise, the most complex.

Sine-wave Oscillators

The sine-wave oscillator employed in tape studios is the type often used in laboratory work, and bears little resemblance to the generators of sine waves in synthesizers. (In some synthesizers, the sine wave is derived from another wave-form, triangular, which has been generated by the primary oscillator, sawtooth.) The laboratory sine-wave oscillator has been designed to generate the waveform directly and does so with greater purity of waveform and better amplitude and frequency stability. On the other hand, it is not voltage-controlled and, consequently, must be tuned manually over its usual ranges of 10–100 Hz, 100–1 kHz, 1–10 kHz, and 10–100 kHz.

The designers of voltage-controlled equipment for synthesizers argue that purity of waveform is not essential to the listener or composer. This is not true; one need only to aurally imagine Stockhausen's *Studie II* realized with five voltage-controlled "sine" generators where the so-called "sine" has a trace of harmonic content.[4] *Studie II* has a sound vocabulary based on inharmonic orderings of five sine-wave partials, and any harmonic distortion would spoil the compositional plan and its intended aural effect.

This combining of multiple sine-wave frequencies to form unusual spectra or *tone mixtures* is referred to as additive synthesis and is a feature of tape music produced in the studio. The technique demands a bank of oscillators, though in the earliest pieces from Cologne, recourse was made to multiple recording techniques to achieve a multiple sine-wave mixture. Most tape studios have at least six sine-wave oscillators, and larger banks are not uncommon.

Another requisite for additive synthesis with sine-wave oscillators is a *frequency counter,* an instrument used as an aid in accurately tuning the oscillator to the desired frequency. Sine-wave oscillators have a calibrated dial that visually indicates the tuned frequency, but these markings are approximate and for critical work a frequency counter is essential.

White-noise Generators

The output of a white-noise generator is rarely used in its raw form but, rather, is subjected to selective filtering. Because of the polyphonic filters employed in tape studios, composers can create white-noise mixtures analogous to the sine-wave mixtures noted above.

Pulse generators

In the early writings and scores of European electronic music, such as Koenig's *Essay* (1957), one reads of pulse or impulse generators. Once again, these are precision scientific instruments adapted for compositional practice. The pulse generator can be described as a variable-frequency, variable-width, rectangular-wave generator operating in the sub-audio frequency range. The dials for tuning frequency and width of pulse have been calibrated to laboratory standards. In electronic composition they are used as sound sources or, in conjunction with other apparatus as timing devices.

Microphones

The microphone is discussed here as a sound source because it provides, when used with recording apparatus, a permanent record of acoustic sound material not of electronic origin. Assuming that literally any sound is suitable material for tape composition, one must first transmit it to tape, and the microphone is the intermediary that makes this possible.

The composer working in the tape studio has access to a variety of microphones, either of the traditional "air" type, or the "contact" type that is

---

[4] Voltage-controlled generators exhibiting sine-wave purity and good frequency stability are available as commercial units intended for critical laboratory work, and are known as *function generators.* The circuitry employed in these is elaborate and costly and is not normally found in synthesizers.

attached directly to a vibrating sound body. (See Chapter 6.) Of the former type, the most popular microphones for studio use are designated as *dynamic, ribbon,* or *condenser,* terms denoting either the active element or the electrical principle upon which they operate. A further distinction is made according to the microphone's pattern of directionality, that is, its sensitivity to the regions around its active elements. (See Chapter 2.)

The dynamic, ribbon, and condenser microphones all have advocates who defend their choices on evidence that is often subjective. Assuming that the chosen microphone is a *professional* instrument and is used properly, one would be hard pressed to detect aurally the actual type used in a recording. The limiting factor in achieving a good recording is not necessarily the type of microphone used, but one or more of the following:

1. *Improper placement of the microphone in relation to the sound source.* The microphone has a specified field of sensitivity. It would be folly to place the sound source at the extremes of this field unless, of course, the effect of a distant signal is deliberately sought. A common mistake is to have the sound source in an unfavorable position, to record it normally, and then to try to boost the signal level of this recording in succeeding treatments or transformations. This has the effect of raising the signal level *and* any accompanying noise on the tape. The recorded sound should be thought of as a primary sound generator and like its counterpart, the wave generator, it should possess optimum specifications.

2. *Unsuitable environment for recording.* Some rooms have poor acoustics, which no amount of microphone selection or placement can overcome. Particular care must be taken when the microphone is placed in the proximity of tape recorders, air conditioners, and other unwanted sound sources.

3. *Poor microphone pre-amplifiers.* The signal level from the microphone is small and must be amplified 40 to 60 dB before it is useful. The microphone pre-amplifier, either a separate unit or one in the tape recorder itself, should provide this amplification with low noise and negligible distortion.

It is often stated that good microphone technique can only be acquired through trial and error; the author agrees but also suggests that much can be learned from listening and by imitation. The "concrete" compositions of the Paris school are exemplary models of microphone and recording technique.

Special Sound Generators

The following unique and unusual generators have been developed for major studios:

1. *Harmonic Tone Generator* (University of Illinois).[5] A monophonic keyboard instrument based on the principle of additive synthesis. Six sine-wave oscillators, locked in phase and representing the fundamental and five harmonic partials, are tuned by voltage control. The amplitude and envelope

---

[5] J. W. Beauchamp, "Additive Synthesis of Harmonic Musical Tones," *Journal of the Audio Engineering Society,* XIV (1966), 333–42.

of *any* partial can be preset. This feature allows a simulation of the transient properties associated with instrumental tones.

2. *Variable-Function Generator* (University of Utrecht).[6] This complex instrument can be described for convenience as a *sequencer* (see Chapter 4) with one hundred positions, each position having a programming potentiometer. The potentiometers are set to discrete DC voltage levels, which represent the arbitrary waveform. The sequencer is then cycled by a timing generator, and the outputs of the potentiometers are summed and filtered. The resultant waveform will have a frequency equal to the time taken to complete one reading of the sequence. (The basic procedure is not unlike that used in generating waveforms with a computer; see Chapter 5).

3. *Sonde* (University of Toronto).[7] This instrument was designed by Hugh Le Caine of the National Research Council, Ottawa. A small group of fixed-frequency oscillators (30), arranged in a 10×20 matrix, is used to derive 200 sine waves whose frequencies are spaced at 5-Hz intervals from 5 to 1 kHz. In the model built for the Toronto studio, each frequency is routed to a key of a touch-sensitive, polyphonic keyboard.

Devices for Transformation or Modification of Sound

The primary types of studio equipment in this second category are *reverberation devices, filters* and *equalizers,* and *modulators.*

Reverberation Devices

Any sound produced in an enclosed space is enhanced by the reverberant nature of that space. The listener at a given location in this space hears a composite signal made up of the original sound and delayed reflections of that sound. The acoustician defines this phenomenon as *reverberation time,* that is, the time required for a sound to fade away to one-millionth (60 dB) of its original intensity. In a traditional concert hall the reverberation time is approximately 1.5 to 2 seconds.

Though the terms *reverberation* and *echo* are interchanged indiscriminately, *echo* is a perceptible repetition of a reflected sound; but to be heard as an echo, the reflected sound must follow the original sound by 20 milliseconds or more. In electronic music studios, echo effects are easily produced with the aid of a tape recorder and will be discussed in the section on tape recorders. Reverberation, on the other hand, can be simulated by a variety of artificial means, some of which will be discussed in the present section. In studio parlance the term *reverberation* is often abbreviated to *reverb.* In the following description the two forms of the term will be interchanged freely.

1. *Reverberation* or *echo chamber.* The reverberation chamber is an iso-

6 S. Tempelaars, "A Double Variable Function Generator," *Electronic Music Reports,* No. 2 (1970), 13–31.

7 H. Le Caine and G. Ciamaga, "The Sonde: A New Approach to Multiple Sine Wave Generation," *JAES,* XVIII (1970), 536–39.

lated room having "bright" acoustics. At one end of the room is a loudspeaker; at the other end, a microphone. The signal to be processed is sent to the loudspeaker, and the reflections from the wall of the chamber are picked up by the microphone and routed back to a mixer for further treatment or recording.

Although the reverberation chamber has a long history, it is doubtful that anyone at the present time would want to go to the effort and expense of building one. Very few reverb chambers from past years can give the quality of performance and flexibility offered by a reverberation plate. A composer having access to an empty concert hall can easily duplicate the effect of a reverb chamber, probably with better results.

2. *Spring reverb*. The spring reverb is the least expensive device for artificial reverberation. It consists of an input transducer (the driver) coupled to a transmission line of coiled spring; at the other end of the spring is another transducer (the pickup device). The sound is propagated down this transmission line in approximately 28 to 33 milliseconds, and at the other end it is reflected back again to repeat the cycle. The time it takes for the sound to decay is similar to the reverb time of a concert hall (1.5 to 2 seconds). The overall effect approximates the reverberant sound of a small room with two parallel walls.

This simple device has a multitude of faults:

1. It is prone to a "twanginess" when excited by short bursts of sound.
2. The spring exhibits an uneven frequency response, though this can be partially corrected by equalizing its output signal.
3. It has an "unnatural" quality due to the regularity of its reflections.
4. Some listeners detect a slight shift in frequency when the input signal is compared with the reverb output.
5. The signal loss through the line may be considerable, and recovery amplifiers must be designed carefully to maintain a good signal-to-noise ratio.
6. If not properly mounted, it is prone to feedback "howl" or to excitation of the spring by external vibrations. (In this mode it behaves as a sound source and not a modifier.)

In defense of the spring reverb, one can cite the virtues of small size, simplicity, and low cost.

3. *Reverberation plate*. Most of the large tape studios make use of the commerical reverberation plate known as the EMT 140. This plate is built to professional standards, is costly, and offers superior reverberation effects. It consists of a large sheet of specially treated steel (1 × 2 meters) that is suspended by its four corners in a frame. Mounted on this sheet are two transducers. One of these drives (vibrates) the plate in a manner analogous to the vibration of a paper cone in a moving-coil loudspeaker; the other transducer acts as a contact microphone, picking up the vibrations of the plate. The maximum reverberation time is about 5 seconds. This can be reduced to as little as a half-second by gradually increasing the pressure of a fiberglas "blanket" that is held alongside the plate. The damping action can be motorized and operated by remote con-

trol from the mixing desk. In an alternate version of the plate, a second pickup
device is attached for stereo effects.

The newest reverb units simulate the effect of a delay line by using solid-
state components. The basic idea is not new, but its application to audio
technology holds much promise for the future. At the time of this writing, the
author is unaware of any tape studios using these units.

In the presentation of concert music, reverberation varies from hall to hall;
there is little that we can do about it, and its presence is taken for granted.
In an electronic composition, however, the presence or absence of reverberation is a *compositional choice* that must be carefully considered. Of all the
modifiers for electronic music, reverb is probably the most abused. One can
argue that all sound material derived from electronic sources is "dry" and
"lifeless"—that is, it lacks reverb—and should therefore be enhanced. The
addition of reverberation to an electronic sound does correct this fault, but
there is no reason why some sounds cannot be left dry so that those treated
with reverb can, by contrast, stand in even greater relief.

In studio practice, the sound from the reverb unit is rarely used directly;
rather, it is mixed or blended in various proportions with the original signal.
The most flexible arrangement for this blending, shown in Fig. 1, employs a
two-input mixer (see p. 88). One potentiometer (pot or volume control) sets
the level of the direct signal; the second pot, the level of the reverberated
signal. At the output of the mixer the combined signals are present.

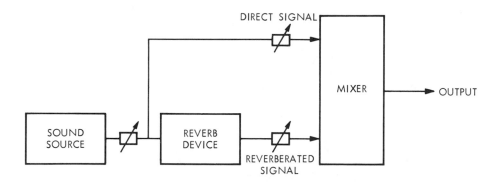

Figure 1.

Depending on the settings of the potentiometers, the output can consist entirely of the dry signal or the reverberated signal, or any intermediate combination of the two qualities. By simultaneously decreasing the level of the
original signal and gradually increasing the level of the reverberated signal,
it is possible to suggest the effect of a sound receding into the distance. If, in
addition, the reverb time is changed simultaneously (this is only possible with

the commerical reverb plate), one can also suggest a variable acoustic space for the receding sound.

Filters and Equalizers

This section deals with filters and equalizers as separate components or modules used in a studio to modify or transform sound material. (Filters and equalizers are also used in other studio equipment: the so-called crossover network in a loudspeaker is a filter; the recording and playback circuitry of tape recorders incorporates equalizers.)

A *filter* can be defined as a passive or active network that is used to attenuate portions of the audio spectrum. The distinction between active and passive is not aurally apparent to the listener; rather, it refers to elements utilized in the design of the filter. (A passive filter contains only inductors, capacitors, and resistors; an active filter also incorporates amplifiers.) An *equalizer* is similar to a filter, but in addition to attenuating, it can also amplify or emphasize selected frequency bands.

In the simplest terms, a filter or equalizer alters the frequency spectrum by exaggerating some frequencies at the expense of others. We can state that *filters* are used to *eliminate* undesired frequencies, whereas *equalizers* are used to *correct* for irregularities (or even regularities) in the spectrum.

Although filters and equalizers can be designed to operate at a single frequency or upon a single band of frequencies, it is more common in studio composition to employ *continuously variable* units that have been calibrated for the entire audio spectrum, and banks of *fixed* units, each unit covering a specific portion of the spectrum. These two types of units are represented in tape studios by the *variable band-pass filter* and the *fixed-filter bank,* respectively.

1. *Variable band-pass filter.* (Fig. 2) A unit providing the normal modes of low-pass, high-pass, and band-pass filtering. The operation of this filter is similar to that described in the chapter on synthesizers. The studio type, however, differs in the following respects:

1. It is manually tuned and not voltage-controlled.
2. It has calibrated dials (high-pass, low-pass) for setting the frequency of cutoff. The ranges normally covered are often the same as for the laboratory-type sine oscillator, i.e., 10—100 Hz, 100—1 kHz, etc.
3. It has steeper attenuation slopes than most band-pass filters supplied with synthesizers. In the unit shown in Fig. 2, the attenuation rate is 24 dB per octave.

2. *Fixed-filter banks.* These are sets of fixed filters on a common chassis having a common input; there are individual outputs for each filter and either a common or mixed output. Each filter passes a specific portion of the spectrum. Because each output is available separately, the term *polyphonic filter* is sometimes used to describe the fixed-filter bank.

FIGURE 2.   Kron-Hite filter.

In the following diagram of a typical fixed-filter bank (Fig. 3), the passes are arranged in octaves. Other arrangements that are commonly employed are half-octaves and third-octaves. Not shown in the diagram is the simple mixing network used to derive the common output; also not shown are the usual volume controls at the output of each filter. Depending on the setting of its volume control, each fixed filter functions as either a band-pass or band-reject filter. By adjusting the volume controls at either end of the spectrum, the bank also functions as a simple high- or low-pass filter.

The *fixed-filter* bank can either be obtained as a complete unit or assembled from commerical modules, which are available in different frequencies and bandwidths. Of the completely pre-assembled types, the most popular unit found in tape studios is the third-octave filter of Albiswerk, Zurich. The *Albis filter* comprises two separate units. The principal unit covers the middle of the audio frequency spectrum (90 to 6 kHz); an auxiliary unit covers the extreme

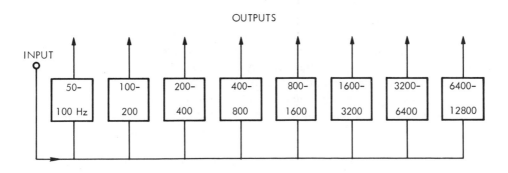

FIGURE 3.   Octave filter.

low and high ends of the spectrum (30 to 80 Hz and 7 to 19 kHz, respectively). Its third-octave filters are controlled by vertical potentiometers (sliders or faders) that are calibrated in decibels of attenuation. The physical arrangement of these sliders gives a visual, graphic representation of the spectrum modification taking place. (See Fig. 4.) The Albis filter is extremely flexible because it can perform all modes of filtering and even equalization. It is no longer manufactured, but comparable units from other companies are available.

3. *Equalizers.* The equalizer as a specific piece of equipment is not found in all studios, for its function can be duplicated by a fixed-filter bank. Equalizer circuitry and the practical presentation of that circuitry is somewhat similar to that of filters. The main difference is that an equalizer's potentiometers (for a given frequency or band) are calibrated in decibels of *boost* (amplification) and *cut* (attenuation) from a reference point of 0 dB. Depending on the manufacturer, a maximum boost or cut of 12 dB is typical.

4. *Spectrum analyzer.* The *spectrum* or *wave analyzer* is a test instrument normally used for analyzing the component frequencies of a sound. Its behavior is that of an extremely sensitive, calibrated *frequency-selective amplifier.* When a component of the spectrum, presented to its input, is the same frequency as that indicated by the dial, a dB meter is deflected. Some of the early European studios used these instruments in the manner of filters by taking an audio output at the amplifier itself.[8] The effect is similar to that of a *resonating filter* as described in Chapter 4, that is, a very narrow band-pass filter with extreme attenuation outside of the pass-band.

Ring Modulators and Frequency Shifters

Modulators are devices having two inputs and one output. The second input, called a *control* signal, acts upon the *program* signal presented to the first input—that is, it modulates the program. Of the many types of modulators, three are important to tape music studios; the *ring modulator* and the *frequency shifter,* which will be described presently; and the *amplitude modulator,*[9] which is described in the next section.

1. *Ring modulators.* This most drastic of transformation devices, which can "denature" the original sound beyond recognition, was used by all tape studios of the '50s, but for some reason was not exploited in this same period, as far as the author can determine, by the Paris school. The ring modulator continues to be popular and is found as a module in almost all synthesizers. For our purposes, it can be defined as a transformation device whose output signal consists of the sum and difference frequencies of the applied inputs, i.e., $f2 + f1$ and $f2 - f1$. If $f1$ is a sine wave of 100 Hz and $f2$ a sine wave of 200 Hz, the output of the ring modulator is a signal consisting of 300 Hz (200 + 100) and 100 Hz (200−100). If in this simple example the program ($f1$) was a

8 This is not available on all analyzers.
9 Strictly speaking, the ring modulator is a species of amplitude modulator.

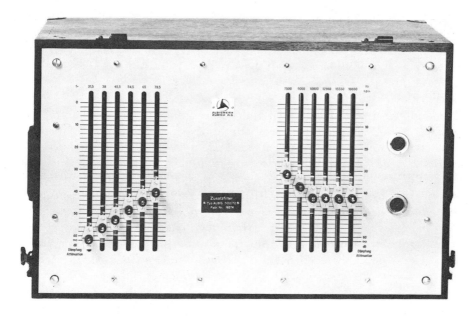

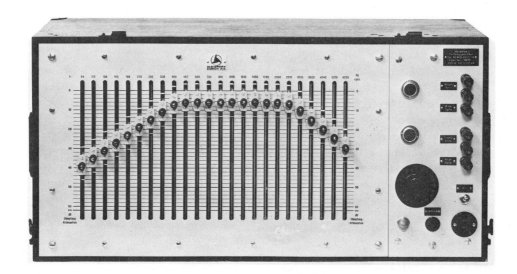

FIGURE 4. Albis filter.

waveform having a harmonic spectrum (for instance, a sawtooth), then the output would be more complex, for it would contain the sum and difference frequencies for all the component partials of the spectrum.

The description above represents the theoretical ideal and assumes a perfectly balanced modulator circuit. In actuality, the original frequencies (f1 and f2) also appear in the output, but at a lower amplitude. The quality of the ring modulator is judged by its ability to suppress the original signals. Typically, it is the control signal (sometimes called the *carrier*) that is troublesome, and in professional ring modulators it will be suppressed 60 dB below the signal level of the output.

Various circuits have been employed for ring modulators. The earliest models found in tape studios used a diode bridge with or without transformer coupling. Additional circuits, called *gates* or *squelch,* were often added to the basic circuit to suppress the carrier signal when the program input was absent or silent. Much of this early circuitry has been replaced by *multipliers,* modules originally intended for analog computers. These multipliers not only perform ring modulation close to the theoretical ideal, but can also be used as DC voltage multipliers with a voltage-controlled synthesizer.

The general tendency of the ring modulator is to produce complex spectra containing harmonic and inharmonic ordering of partials. Some writers describe this effect as "clangorous"—an apt term, for the spectra of struck bells, gongs, etc. are composed of similar harmonic and inharmonic orderings. In tape compositions, particularly in those of the '50s, the ring modulator is used not only to obtain these complex sounds but also as a simple *gating* device. In this second application, the control signal is a pulse generator gating the program at periodic intervals.[10]

The ring modulator's main features can also be construed as its weaknesses: 1) There is always a degree of unpredictability that might not be desirable; and 2) the complex sounds it produces can become too "rich" or too similar, and bore the listener.

2. *Frequency shifter.* The *frequency shifter* (also known as a tone shifter, single side-band modulator, or *Klangumwandler*), is a transformation device that shifts all the frequency components contained in the program signal either upward or downward by a fixed increment. It can be likened to a ring modulator, where only the sum (or difference) frequencies remain in the output. The complex circuitry of the frequency shifter contains modulators and a demodulator, and in contemporary versions, at least three multipliers are employed.[11] For convenience, we will describe it as a modulator having a program input, but with the customary control input *represented* by an internal oscillator that effects the frequency shift. The "shift" oscillator is tuned manually and has an excursion of 8 kHz, calibrated as −4 kHz to 0 (zero) to +4 kHz; in other words, it is possible to shift the program down or up over the range of 4 kHz.[12]

It is important to stress that the frequency shifter is not a device for "transposition" in the sense in which that term is used in music. Shifting a

10 Other applications of the ring modulator to composition can be found in H. Bode, "The Multiplier-type Ring Modulator," *Electronic Music Review,* No. 1 (Jan., 1967), 9–15.

11 H. Bode and R. Moog, "A High-accuracy Frequency Shifter for Professional Audio Applications," *JAES,* XX (1972), 453–58.

12 The maximum possible frequency shift depends on the design. The 8 kHz chosen for this example is average.

program frequency of 100 Hz (f1) by +100 Hz (shift frequency) results in a transposition of an octave: 200 Hz; but if f1 is, for example, a square wave, all the partials of f1 will also be shifted by sf, and a new spectrum no longer resembling the square wave results. (The output in this example would be a waveform containing 200, 400, 600, 800 Hz, etc.) Frequency shifting involves addition by a fixed increment; musical transposition implies multiplication by a constant ratio.

The setting of the shift oscillator determines the general aural effect. With zero shift we hear the original program unaltered. With simple sound sources and small frequency shifts, we hear nearly the original signal but at a slightly different pitch. For large shifts, there is not only a change in pitch but also the characteristic denaturing of the spectrum caused by displacing frequency components from their proper harmonic order. For tones shifted up, the components are crowded together; for tones shifted down, the component frequencies are spread out.

The important feature of the frequency shifter is that the aural effect of the denaturing does not seem as excessive as it is with the ring modulator; that is, the shifted sounds, depending on the amount of shift, bear a familial resemblance to the original sound. Their value as modifiers of simple electronic sounds is not great. It is only when we employ natural (concrete) sounds in a composition and have the option of contrasting them with their frequency-shifted equivalents that we gain a powerful compositional tool. Listen, for example, to Ussachevsky's *Of Wood and Brass.*

Keyboards and Electronic Switching Devices

In the period preceding the commercial availability of voltage-controlled synthesizers, tape studios often included devices that initiated a single event or group of sound events without recourse to general recording and splicing techniques. This species of equipment includes the *keyboard, envelope shaper, electronic switch,* and *amplitude filter.* Strictly speaking, this class of equipment does not fit the original category of sound modifiers. Though some of the devices do modify sounds, they are presented here as a group because they share the common function of "releasing" a preexistent signal.

1. *Keyboards.* Many studios have adapted keyboards, usually from electronic organs, for electronic composition. The application of such a keyboard is easily described; assuming a keyboard with twelve keys, we have in effect a twelve-input *mixer* (see p. 88). With this mixer it is possible to initiate or "play" twelve different signal sources (e.g., oscillators) melodically *or* polyphonically. This elementary device, with a long history of usefulness in traditional music, does not adapt immediately to electronic music, for its simple keying action might produce transient "clicks" at the moment of pressing or releasing the key.

Organ manufacturers employ various techniques for masking these transient clicks. Of the many possible solutions, the one employed in Baldwin keyboards is successful, and these are favored for studio use.[13] The Baldwin keys are in effect, variable resistors (volume controls), so that when a key is depressed the sound emerges gradually. Not only is the transient click masked, but it is also possible to introduce a degree of touch sensitivity whereby the loudness is proportional to finger pressure. The previous analogy to an audio mixer becomes even more apt because each key is, in effect, a mixing pot.

One might argue that there is nothing unique about a keybord connected to oscillators: if the sound sources are wave-form generators, why not employ an electronic organ? (Some of the first studios, such as the one in Cologne, had electronic keyboard instruments, but these were literally abandoned.) On the contrary, some new ideas do emerge from this adaptation. The oscillators routed to the keyboard need not be tuned in equal temperament; in fact, the signal sources need not be oscillators, but may be any audio signal source in the studio, tape outputs, filter outputs, etc. At the University of Toronto studio, twenty-four outputs from the Albis third-octave filter can be connected to a Baldwin-type keyboard. The resulting "instrument" is still useful today, for no voltage-controlled filter/keyboard combination can duplicate its polyphonic effects.

2. *Electronic switching devices.* In the above description, the key and its electrical element, the potentiometer, respond to manual control. Electronic devices that are similar to the key but respond primarily to control voltages are the *gate* and the *amplitude modulator.* The *gate* is simply an electronic switch having two states, on or off. (The term gate is used incorrectly by some synthesizer manufacturers to denote a balanced-amplitude modulator that is used as a voltage-controlled amplifier.) An *amplitude modulator* is a voltage-controlled amplifier that produces an output proportional to the magnitude of its control signal. Both amplitude modulators and gates are employed in devices associated with the tape studio.

a. *Envelope shaper.* It is often naively assumed that the balanced-amplitude modulator, when used as a voltage-controlled amplifier, is a product of synthesizer technology. These devices were previously used in electronic organs, the radio and recording industry, and even the early tape studios. (Similarly, we forget that voltage-controlled oscillators and filters were used long before the appearance of electronic-music systems.) In tape studios a voltage-controlled amplifier is often preceded by a transient generator, a device that produces variable ramp voltages corresponding to envelopes. This combination of transient generator and voltage-controlled amplifier is referred to as an *envelope shaper.* (See also Chapter 4.) The timing pulses that initiate an envelope are presented from a push button or pulse generator.

b. *Electronic switch.* The *electronic switch* provides yet another example of an electronic music device originally intended for laboratory work. As a test instrument, it is used for observing two simultaneous signals on an oscilloscope; as an audio device, its output is monitored aurally rather than visually.

---

[13] A description of the Baldwin keyboard can be found in A. Douglas, *The Electronic Musical Instrument Manual* (London, 1968), pp. 323–28. Hugh Le Caine has also designed and described touch sensitive keys. See *EMR*, No. 4 (1967), 24.

The Columbia-Princeton studio seems to have been the first to pioneer its usage as an audio device, and many North American studios have followed their example.

The electronic switch has two inputs and two outputs, but only one output is *on* or sounding at a time. A built-in square-wave generator alternately switches the inputs at a given speed, depending on its frequency setting. Typically, this can vary over a range of once or less per second to several thousand times a second. The switching circuit employs two *gates* (Fig. 5). When one gate is *on* the other is *off*. The outputs can be combined into one channel, or can be left as two separate channels for monitoring or further processing.

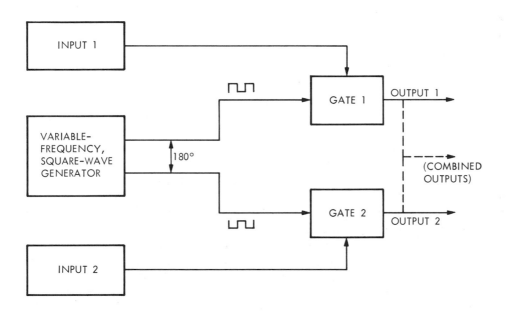

FIGURE 5. Electronic switch.

The aural effect of the electronic switch varies according to the original signal sources and the frequency of alteration. If the sources are oscillators tuned to different frequencies and alternated at slow rates (6 Hz), the aural effect resembles a musical trill or tremolo. If the frequency of alternation exceeds 20 Hz, a complex tone mixture that gives an effect not unlike a ring modulator is formed.

The basic idea embodied in the electronic switch can be realized by patching together modules of a synthesizer. Additional effects are then obtained by replacing the square-wave generator with a sine or triangular generator and/or replacing the gates with envelope shapers.

c. *Amplitude filter*. In 1955, Lietti of the Milan studio described the device that appears in the complete list of Milan equipment as an *amplitude filter*.[14] The amplitude filter is a modulator in which the control input receives the *same* signal as the program input. When the signal at the control input reaches a certain amplitude or threshold, which is adjustable, this portion of the program signal will be present at the output. The device is described as a "filter" because it "passes" only parts of the "amplitude spectrum" and suppresses the rest.

The most famous application of this device to electronic composition is Pousseur's *Scambi* (1957). This composition, and others by Ligeti and Koenig, illustrate that not all pieces of this period relied on rigorous serial technique but, rather, drew upon the unpredictabilities inherent in some electronic devices. The basic source material for *Scambi* is derived from white noise "filtered" by a frequency-selective amplifier (see p. 82). These very narrow bands of white noise, with their inherent random amplitude, are then processed by an amplitude filter. The resultant random material serves as the basis of Pousseur's composition.[15]

Equipment for Mixing, Recording, and Reproducing Sound

This section describes the devices used for interconnecting and mixing all of the studio equipment, and the equipment used in the recording and reproduction of sound material at any stage of the compositional process. Matters arising from or related to the equipment will also be discussed.

The subject matter properly belongs to the domain of broadcasting and recording, where the practices have been codified and described in the extensive literature of audio engineering. The following description can only summarize the essential details.

1. *Patch panel*. Fig. 6 illustrates a group of devices connected together as they might be used in the production of sound material for a composition. The sources, the modifier, and the other devices in this chain are interconnected (patched) with patch cords—lengths of audio cable having connectors at each end. (The entire configuration is sometimes referred to as a patch.) Rather than connecting the individual units directly, which would involve patch cords of varying lengths, it is normal practice to bring the inputs and outputs of all studio equipment to a common location known as the *patch panel*.

The patch panel consists of an array or field of jack-receptacles representing the inputs and outputs of the equipment found in the studio. It occupies comparatively little space and offers the convenience of patching at one location with short patch cords. On the patch panel are also rows of uncommitted jacks, arranged in groups and connected in parallel, known as *multiples*. These can be used to create a multiple input or output for any

[14] A. Lietti, "Soppressore di Disturbi a Selezione d'Ampiezza," *Elettronica*, V (Sept.–Oct., 1955), 1 ff.

[15] *Scambi* is described in *Gravesaner Blätter*, IV, No. 13 (1959), 36–48.

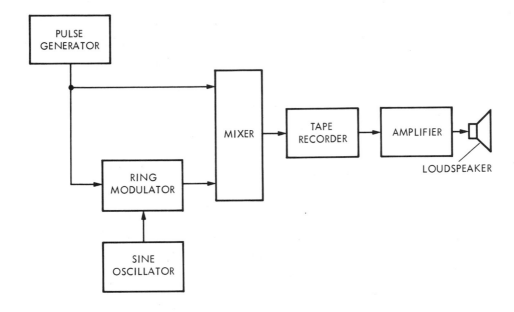

FIGURE 6.

device. For example, in the above diagram, one can see that the pulse genera-tor is routed to the ring modulator *and* mixer. To derive a second output for the pulse generator we would patch it to a multiple; a second cord would be connected from the multiple to the ring modulator, and a third cord from the multiple to the mixer (Fig. 7).

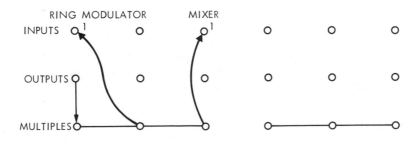

FIGURE 7.

Assuming for the purposes of illustration a patch panel limited only to the devices found in Fig. 6, the complete connections of the patch panel would appear as in Fig. 8.

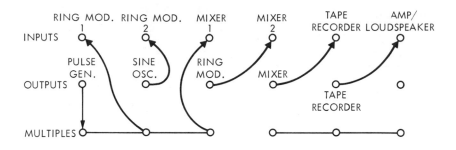

FIGURE 8.

This example is simple; in practice, the patching would be more complex. Many designers have attempted to simplify patching and patchboards, particularly the visual aspects, but in the end any solution seems just as complicated. The normal patch panel is still the easiest to comprehend, for the act of patching each device in turn is deliberative and ultimately based on the composer's understanding of each device. If the final sound at the loudspeaker is not what the composer anticipated, or if there is *no* sound, he can retrace the individual patches in the chain to determine the fault.

2. *Audio sound mixer.* An *audio sound mixer* is a device that combines two or more separate signals into one or more composite signals. It is a network designed so that one can change the amplitude level of any of the original audio signal sources without affecting the level (or frequency characteristics) of the other signals in the network.

The mixer consists of several inputs, each associated with a potentiometer (rotary pot or vertical fader) and one or more outputs, depending on the design of the mixer. In studio practice the inputs and outputs are located at the patch panel, and the mixing pots, on a desk close to the patch panel. The composer thus has, within arm's length, access to and control of much of the studio's equipment.

Mixers can be purchased completely assembled, or they may be constructed by the user from components and modules. The second course is more practical, for the completely assembled mixer is often designed to be used with several microphones. Rarely does a tape studio require the microphone pre-amplifiers that are built into these mixers as a matter of course. The basic mixing circuits appear to be simple, but their component pots and mixing amplifiers must be of high quality and must demonstrate superior reliability.

Mixers are designated by the maximum number of inputs and outputs available. A simple mono mixer might be *4-in / 1-out.* A stereo mixer, *4 + 4-in / 2-out.* Connecting the two outputs of this stereo mixer (for instance, in a multiple on the patch board) would offer the additional possibility of *8-in / 1-out.* (See Fig. 9.)

The "ideal" studio mixer has 8 (or even more) inputs and at least 4 out-

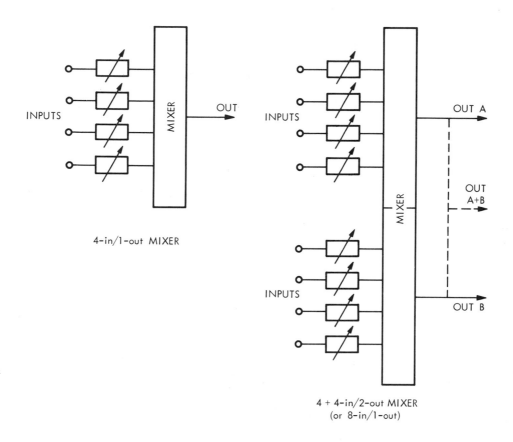

INPUTS

MIXER

OUT

4-in/1-out MIXER

INPUTS

MIXER

OUT A

OUT A+B

INPUTS

OUT B

4 + 4-in/2-out MIXER
(or 8-in/1-out)

FIGURE 9.

puts. For each *input* there is a push-button-switch array that selects any one output or any combination of the 4 outputs. The resultant 15 choices of output for each input offer great flexibility in the routing and mixing of signals. (See Fig. 10.)

A variant of this idea is the *matrix mixer,* which has a potentiometer for every input/output combination. For the ideal mixer in Fig. 10 (*8-in* to *any-of-4-out*), there would have to be 32 pots. This number of pots would be almost impossible to control manually, and the matrix mixer is usually limited to *4-in* to *any-of-4-out* (i.e., 16 pots).

For every mixer output channel there is usually an additional pot or master fader. Many situations call for presetting the input pots to a proper level and working with the master faders. Another useful feature often included is a VU meter (see p. 98) for each output channel.[16]

[16] For details of mixing circuitry, see J. Seawright, "Fundamental Concepts of Electronic Music Mixers, *EMR*, No. 4 (1967), 14–19.

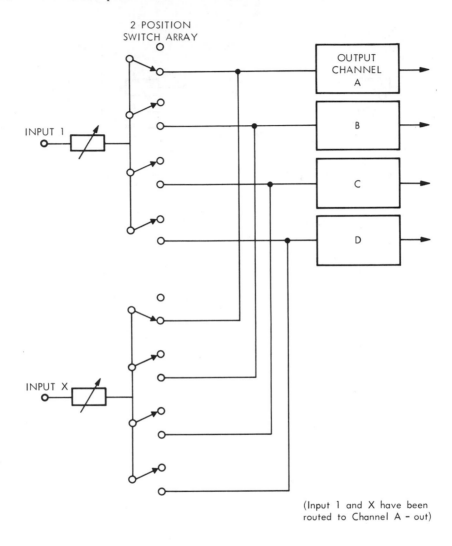

2 POSITION
SWITCH ARRAY

OUTPUT
CHANNEL
A

INPUT 1

INPUT X

(Input 1 and X have been
routed to Channel A – out)

FIGURE 10.   Multi-input/to any or all of 4-out mixer.

A complete catalogue of mixing techniques used by the composer in the tape studio would span the range from simple summing of multiple sources (e.g., sine-wave oscillators), to the structuring of complex sound events, to the final assembly (mix) of the tape composition itself. An essential aspect of tape-music technique is the composer's liberty to withhold the stereophony and antiphony of his composition until the final mix. Too often, composers ignore the potential of creative mixing. For example, if the composition is in two or four channels, one can almost predict that each channel will proceed independently for the entire piece and that no event will ever be sounded *simultaneously* in all available channels.

The knowledgeable tape composer uses the mixer in the final assembly of the composition to mediate between the monophonic, stereophonic, and antiphonal effects that are possible. He does this by assembling one or more tapes that contain the measured sound events and silences of the composition arranged in sequence. These tapes are played on machines that can be started together; the sound outputs of the synchronized tapes are fed to a mixer (e.g., the "ideal" mixer previously described), and in turn to a two- or four-channel recording machine. The composer *now* determines *at the mixer* the location(s) and desired loudness of the sound events. The procedure sounds laborious and fussy, but within this technique lies the spirit of all good tape composition: accurate and creative control of sound, time, and acoustic space.

3. *The tape recorder.* The magnetic tape recorder is fundamental to all genres of electronic music. Its capability of recording and reproducing sound information make it essential to all composition, whether realized with tape-studio equipment or with synthesizers or computers. It is equally important to live-electronic music, in which it is often a member of the ensemble.

As a recorder and reproducer it belongs to the final category of the scheme proposed for studio equipment. But as will be described subsequently, the tape recorder can function as a sound modifier or transformation device. Furthermore, when we record any sound, at any stage in the production of a composition, the tape recording itself becomes the *representative* of the original sound and can be assigned to the first category—that is, sound source.

All electronic music studios rely on professional tape recorders, the maximum number and type (mono or stereo, record/play or play only) being variable. For example, some European studios favor the use of:

4 mono recorders
2 stereo (i.e., half track, two-channel) recorders
1 or 2 multi-track (i.e., four-channel) recorders

The mono and stereo recorders are used in the preparation of the material, the stereo or multi-track machines for the final mix.

North American studios, on the other hand, probably have few or no mono machines and rely on stereo recorders for the preparation of the material. A typical North American studio might have:

2 stereo "recorders" (play only)
2 stereo recorders (normal record/play)
1 or 2 multi-track recorders

As any stereo machine can be used as a monophonic recorder/reproducer, the difference between the two lists is not great.

The minimum number of recorders that is recommended for studio composition is three—two stereo recorders (record/play) and one stereo "recorder" (play only).

Any large group of machines should be activated from a central location (remote-control panel), so that any tape-transport (or record/play electronics) can be started or stopped synchronously or independently.

The description of the tape recorder that follows begins with a discussion of its two main components, the *tape-transport* and the *record/play* electronics. The subsequent sections discuss magnetic tape, splicing, and the techniques used in composing with a tape recorder.

a. *Tape-transport.* The tape-transports of professional recorders are similar, varying only in such details as tape guides, idlers, and tension arms. Fig. 11 shows a typical *tape-transport* or deck, as it is sometimes called. The tape leaves the supply reel A, and passes the idler B and the erase head, record head, and playback head—C, D, and E, respectively. The tape is pulled along by the pinch action of the rubber puck F and the rotating capstan G. The tape then moves past another idler H to the take-up reel I.

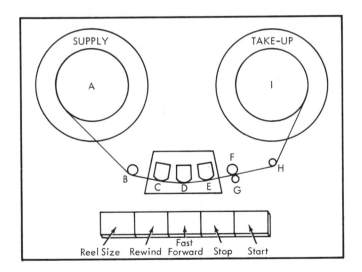

FIGURE 11.

A transport of this type employs three motors: a *capstan motor* (coupled to the capstan G), which pulls the tape past the heads at a constant speed, and *supply* and *take-up motors* (coupled to spindles and platforms at A and I), which tense and wind the tape. The modes of operation (*stop, start, rewind, fast forward*) are activated by a group of switches on the lower part of the deck.

Other details and specifications relevant to the transport include:

i. *Tape speed.* The capstan motor provides two possible speeds, usually 7.5 and 15 ips (inches per second). Some professional machines offer 15 and 30 ips; most "home" machines have 3.75 and 7.5 ips. The faster speeds are preferred in studio work, and recordings made at 15 or 30 ips have the advantages of ease of editing, lower "wow and flutter," superior frequency response, improved signal-to-noise ratio (see p. 97), and less apparent tape "drop-outs." "Wow and flutter" is a term describing periodic variations in speed and amplitude not present in the original sound. Drop-outs are small faults in the tape coating. The slower speed of 7.5 ips is adequate for less critical work, and offers greater tape economy because less tape is used.

ii. *Number of heads.* The three heads on a transport are the *erase head,* which neutralizes any magnetic pattern on the moving tape by exposing it to a strong magnetic field; the *record head,* which magnetizes the special emulsion on the tape in a series of patterns; and the *playback head,* which "reads" the patterns on the tape. When the machine is recording, the erase and record head are active; when the machine is reproducing, only the playback head is active. During the recording process, the playback head can be optionally activated to *monitor* the quality of the recording a split second after it passes the record head.

iii. *Width of tape.* Most tape transports are engineered specifically for one width of tape, either ¼″ or ½″. Tape of ¼″ width is used on single- (mono) and dual- (stereo) track recorders and ½″ tape on four-track (four-channel) recorders.

iv. *Number of tracks.* The heads are constructed in configurations to erase, record, or reproduce one or more *tracks* of information. There is no end to the confusion that has resulted from the inconsistent terminology used to describe these configurations. The following table and diagrams hopefully clarify the situation.

MODE	HEAD CONFIGURATION	MAXIMUM CAPABILITY
mono	full-track half-track	one channel
stereo	half-track quarter-track	two channel
multi-track	four-track	four channels

Mono, full-track,

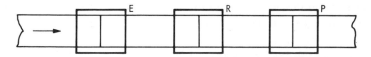

is a professional format employing the full width of the tape.
   Mono, half-track,

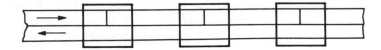

is used primarily for "home" machines. Only half of the tape width is used in recording. To use the other half, the tape must be turned over.

Stereo, half-track,

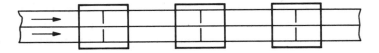

is a professional format that divides the tape into two halves and allows two independent channels of information to be recorded simultaneously. If desired, only one track need be used at a time. This allows the composer to reproduce one track while recording on the opposite track.

Stereo, quarter-track,

is the stereo counterpart of the mono, half-track head. For reasons of economy, the two tracks are arranged to allow two channels of recording in one direction and, by turning the tape over, two channels in the other direction. It is often referred to mistakenly as four-track, but only two tracks are operative at one time. For several years it has been the most popular format for "home" recorders. For studio work, the half-track stereo version is preferred not only for editing but also for the better fidelity it offers.

Multi-track,

The most popular multi-track configuration for studio work is four tracks on $\frac{1}{2}''$ tape. As with the half-track stereo format, independent recording and playback of any channel is possible.

In response to the recent interest in "quadraphonics," manufacturers are offering machines with the four-track format on $\frac{1}{4}''$ tape. Their price is considerably less than a professional $\frac{1}{2}''$ tape recorder, but the quality of performance is not comparable.

v. *Reel size.* The physical size of the deck and, to a degree, the capabilities of the motors determine the maximum size of reel that can be employed. All professional machines can handle reels 10.5″ or smaller in diameter. The 10.5″ reel allows the maximum recording time and is essential for the playback of extended compositions. The smaller reels—5″ and 7″ (see p. 99)—are convenient and easier to handle when working with shorter sections. To compensate for the variable "load" presented by the quantity of tape on reels of different diameters, the transport has a *reel-size switch* to electrically correct the supply and take-up tension.

b. *Record/Play electronics.* The heads of the recorder are electromagnets, which are made from a core of magnetic material around which a coil of wire is wound. The core is solid except for a thin *gap* which the tape must pass. These *electromagnets* are placed in circuits that prepare, process, and generate the various signals of the recording and playing process. The circuits employed are collectively known as the *record/play electronics;* they consist of an *erase oscillator, record amplifier,* and *playback amplifier.*

i. *Erase oscillator.* The *erase oscillator* provides erase current for the erase head and, sometimes, bias current for the recording head. To ensure complete erasure of any signal previously recorded, the alternating current from the erase oscillator (typically 60 kHz) is of sufficient magnitude to saturate the magnetic coating when it reaches the middle of the gap in the erase head. Then, as the tape leaves the center of the gap, the magnetizing force progressively diminishes to zero leaving the coating demagnetized or "clean."

ii. *Record amplifier.* The audio signal to be recorded is prepared by the *record amplifier* before it can be applied to the record head. The circuitry for this includes a *pre-amplifier, equalizer,* and a current source to provide *bias.*

Pre-amplifier. If the audio signal to be recorded—for instance, a direct microphone signal—is of insufficient amplitude for recording, it is increased to the appropriate level with a *pre-amplifier.*

Equalizer. One of the inherent limitations of the recording process is that it is frequency-dependent; that is, high and low frequencies are attenuated. *Equalizer* circuits are therefore incorporated in the record amplifier (and later in the playback amplifier) to compensate for these irregularities in amplitude and to increase the *signal-to-noise-ratio* (the ratio between the loudest, undistorted tone recorded and reproduced by a recorder, and the noise induced by the recording process itself).

Bias. When the tape passes the gap of the record head, the audio signal is transferred to the emulsion of the tape in the form of magnetic patterns. To eliminate the distortion inherent in this process, a high-frequency alternating current called *bias* is mixed with the audio current. Because the bias is of a comparatively high frequency (100 kHz), it does not leave its own pattern of magnetization on the tape.

iii. *Playback amplifier.* When the recorded tape is brought into contact with the gap in the play head, the magnetic patterns are interpreted as alternating voltages. Because these voltages vary in amplitude according to frequency, an equalizer is incorporated in the playback amplifier to correct the frequency response. The signal is then amplified to a level sufficient to drive a power amplifier-loudspeaker combination at listening level.

The record/play electronics are housed in one or more metal cabinets (one for each channel) close to the transport. The front panel of the cabinet always provides controls (potentiometers) for record and playback level and a *VU meter*. The *VU meter* indicates the relative levels of the sound being recorded or reproduced and is calibrated in decibels, −20 to +3 dB. The zero dB mark represents the maximum signal level that can be recorded without introducing distortion. The rear panel of the cabinet provides for the audio inputs and outputs, and the cables from the heads.

The usual performance specifications of the record/play electronics (frequency response, distortion, etc.) will not be discussed here. The standards set by manufacturers are high, and no professional recorder is sold unless it can meet these standards. In fact, the figures of performance quoted are often conservative, and machines exceed these figures easily in normal usage. But to maintain this high level of performance, the tape recorder requires more attention than other apparatus; not surprisingly, all studios service their recorders regularly.

Though the tape transport of the tape recorder has changed little since the beginnings of the tape studio, magnetic tape has been improved measurably and the record/play circuits now employ transistors. In spite of the high level of technology, the most troublesome aspect of recording is still *tape hiss*. This is background noise inevitably engendered by the recording process itself, and resembles filtered white noise. In the recording industry, the problem of tape hiss and other unwanted noises is overcome by the use of audio noise-reduction systems, of which the *Dolby system* is justly the most famous.[17] The Dolby system does reduce noise effectively, but whether it can be used efficiently in tape studios, at all stages of an electronic composition, is still open to debate.

Other problems encountered in recording often stem from the composer's misunderstanding of the recorder's capabilities. Two practical examples among many will be given.

First, the electronics of the recorder and the available emulsions can easily cope with the "normal" sounds presented to them. These sounds rarely have *fundamental* frequencies below 40 Hz or above 5 kHz, and although their accompanying partials extend to the limits of hearing, their amplitude diminishes progressively. On the other hand, some electronic sound sources operate over the entire audio spectrum at any amplitude. The recorder easily records and reproduces a 1-kHz sine wave at zero db on the VU meter; but if the composer tries to record an easily obtainable 10-kHz sine or square wave at the same amplitude level, he might be disappointed by the resultant distortion of the waveform. This is not the machine's fault and the specifications quoted by the manufacturer are honest. But the flat, undistorted response from

17 R. M. Dolby, "Noise Reduction in Electronic Music," *EMR*, No. 6 (1968), 33–37.

50 to 15 kHz claimed by the manufacturer is obtained at a recording level 20 dB below zero dB!

Second, the VU meter's ballistics—the ability of its "needle" or pointer to follow information at the exact time it is presented—can cause problems. The fast attack-transients possible in electronic music can easily fool the meter, for they are completed before the pointer can give an accurate indication of the amplitude level. (European recorders sometimes provide a second meter, the familiar beam indicator tube—"magic eye"—which gives more instantaneous readings of the program material.)

c. *Magnetic recording tape.* Magnetic recording tape is the familiar ribbon of *polyester* or *acetate* backing to which an emulsion of fine and uniform magnetic material has been bonded. The *polyester* type is extremely durable, comparatively expensive, and is recommended for archival permanence; its one disadvantage is that it can be stretched when subjected to the strain of sudden stops and starts on the recorder. *Acetate* tape is less expensive and durable, resists stretching, and tends to break cleanly under strain. Most often, these breaks can be rejoined with splicing tape. If the transport of a recorder is properly adjusted for reel size and tape thickness, there is no reason why stretching or breaking should occur at all. Assuming a common emulsion, there is no audible difference between acetate and polyester tapes. Newer tapes that are being developed combine the best features of both.

Although tape is manufactured in three thicknesses—1.5 mil, 1 mil, and .5 mil—the *1.5 mil* (.0015″) is preferred because of its strength and its lower tendency to "print-through."[18] The packaged tape is offered on reels of various diameters, of which the 7″ (1200 ft., plastic reel) and 10.5″ (2500 ft., aluminum or fiberglas reel or bulk on 'NAB' hub) are the most popular for studio work. When shorter lengths of tape are required, these are spooled on to 5″ and 7″ *low-torque* reels. These low-torque reels have a center core or hub 2.75″ and 4″ in diameter, respectively (compared with the 1.75″ and 2.25″ centers of normal 5- and 7-inch reels), and present a more ideal load or match for the tape-transport assembly.

In addition to backing, thickness, and reel size, tape manufacturers offer a choice of emulsions that claim "low noise," "low print," "high output," etc. As tape is obviously so fundamental to electronic composition, only the finest emulsions should be chosen. A tape designated as "master recording" usually embodies one or more of the above features (low noise, etc.) and will be found suitable for electronic music if the *bias* electronics of the recorder have been adjusted and matched to the characteristics of the tape.

Most of the above considerations pertain to all widths of tape. With the wider formats such as ½″, however, there is less choice in reel diameters, the 10″ (metal) reel being standard.

d. *Tape cutting and splicing.* The task of cutting and splicing tapes at various stages of the compositional process is eased considerably by using a professional *splicing block* and the *splicing tape* intended for it. Of the many

---

[18] Print-through is an effect whereby the recorded signal is transferred to adjacent layers of tape.

different splicing blocks available, there is only one suitable for efficient cutting and splicing. This is an aluminum block (Fig. 12) about 6″ long, 1″ wide, and ⅜″ high, which is placed in a convenient location near the head assembly. The top of the block has a milled groove that accepts and holds a tape of ¼″ width snugly. (Similar models are available for ½″ and wider tape.) To guide the razor blade that does the cutting, two cutting slots are provided: one for 45° splices (for gradual transitions) and one for 90° splices (abrupt transitions). In addition to being a cutting aid, the block is a jig for holding pieces of tape when splicing.

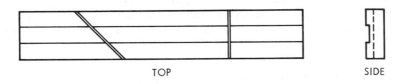

TOP   SIDE

FIGURE 12.

The manner in which a splicing block is used can best be illustrated by describing a typical task—"editing" a tape, that is, removing an unwanted sound event.

With the recorder in playback mode, the tape is advanced until the beginning of the sound is heard and the machine is stopped. The tape is now moved manually (one hand on each reel), "rocking" the tape across the playback head until the exact beginning of the sound is located. The back of the tape is carefully marked with a "grease pencil" at the center of the playback head. The tape is advanced to the end of the sound and the marking procedure is repeated. The tape is then carefully lifted out of the head assembly and placed in the block with the first cue mark matching the 45° slot. A single-edge razor blade is inserted into the slot and the cut is made, using the slot as a guide. The second cue mark is cut in the same way. The unwanted piece of tape is removed and the two ends to be spliced are carefully butted together in the block. A short piece of splicing tape is placed on the joint and pressed firmly in place. This basic technique is also used in making loops, joining sounds, joining sounds to silence (tape to leader tape), and so forth.

A certain amount of care and cleanliness must be exercised at the different stages of cutting and splicing. The grease pencil should not mark the tape head itself or the emulsion side of the tape. The razor blade should be demagnetized, for it might add an unexpected click at the point of the cut. The emulsion side of the tape should not come in contact with greasy fingers or oil on the machine.

In the early writings on electronic music, it was suggested that attacks and decays could be obtained by the angle of cutting and even by removing the emulsion from the tape. These methods are more interesting than practical, for any envelope obtained in this way can be duplicated more simply by using an envelope shaper.

The *leader tape* used at the beginning and end of compositions and within the composition to represent timed silences is available in two forms, plastic and paper. Electronic composers prefer the paper type because it is virtually noise-free. Plastic leader tape is less predictable: although in theory it is noiseless, it has a tendency to pick up static which is then read by the playback head.

The *splicing tape* used specifically with the above mentioned block is $\frac{7}{32}''$ wide—a fraction smaller than $\frac{1}{4}''$ tape—and this eases its placement into the groove of the block. The special adhesive used is pressure-sensitive and should not "ooze" if the spliced tape is stored under conditions of proper temperature and humidity. Spliced joints made with this adhesive tape are ostensibly permanent but can be taken apart if done carefully.

e. *Multi-track recording.* In the section on mixers (p. 88), a procedure was described whereby the outputs of several playback machines were synchronized, mixed, and recorded *simultaneously* on four tracks of a stereo recorder. The end product was a complete section of a composition with the amplitude and location of sounds "frozen" on the tape.

In another procedure involving a multi-track recorder, the individual tracks are recorded *separately* on four channels as follows. After the first track has been recorded, the tape is rewound to a cue mark at the beginning of the tape. The tape is played and while the first track is sounding, the second track is recording additional material. The tape is again rewound and the procedure is repeated until all tracks have been filled. At this point, the complete four-track tape could be reduced to (recorded on) one or two tracks of another machine, or even presented to a second four-channel machine for a final mix.

As an aid to multi-track recording in which the tracks are recorded and synchronized on successive passes, several manufacturers offer a feature known as *sel-sync*. When one track is playing and a second is recording, there is a natural time lag due to the distance separating the record and playback head. The sel-sync feature overcomes this lag by allowing one or more tracks of the record head to function in playback mode while the remaining tracks on the same head remain in record mode. The sel-sync is actuated by a switch that disconnects the necessary circuits and routes the record head(s) to the playback amplifier(s).

The commercial recording industry currently favors the eight- and sixteen-track format for multi-track recording. From a distance, these machines hold a fascination for the electronic composer restricted to four channels. Currently, however, the expense of these machines and their associated hardware mitigates against their use in most electronic-music studios. If the aim of the composer is multi-channel presentations of his completed compositions, it is probably more practical to present a four-track tape through a multiple speaker system in a concert hall. [19] The necessary control equipment might require the composer to assume the guise of a visible "performer." This idea partially offsets the criticism that there is nothing to "see" in concert-hall presentations of electronic music.

Some thoughts on multi-track recording: An electronic composition should not be entirely dependent for its effect on the number of tracks employed. If it has something to say, it will do so even through a single 3″ loudspeaker in a transistor radio. The number of tracks do not make a better composition, they only enhance it.

f. *Fixed- and variable-speed transposition.* In addition to its normal function of recording and reproducing, the tape recorder can be used for transforming sound. The most common technique of transformation associated with the tape recorder is obviously transposition by "octave"—that is, switching between the two fixed speeds of the capstan motor. With the aid of two recorders, it is possible to further extend these octave transpositions. Assume that the information has been originally recorded at 15 ips and is now played on a machine at 7.5 ips. A second machine records the output of the first recorder, but at 15 ips. The resultant recording, when played at 7.5 ips, is the original material transposed two octaves down. The reverse of this (transposition two octaves up) is, of course, also possible.

The use of the term "octave transposition" is misleading, for only the frequency components of the original sound are transposed an octave. And although the harmonic ratios remain the same, the resulting change in the quality we call "timbre" might be severe. The octave transposition also affects the original durations, which are either doubled or halved, and in the process the attacks, decays, and reverb time of the original sound are lengthened or shortened.

Some undesirable effects can also appear when this transposition technique is used. If the original recording contains a 60-Hz "hum," that hum will be more offensive if transposed up an octave. Similarly, preexistent tape hiss that is just bearable at normal speed will be more obvious when transposed down one octave.

The octave-transposition feature of a tape recorder can be useful, but it is often desirable to transpose prerecorded material at fixed intervals of less than an octave, or even gradually and continuously in the manner of a glissando. To do so, we place the recorder under *variable-speed control.*

Virtually all professional recorders (and most semiprofessional ones) can be used for variable-speed transposition. Under normal circumstances the capstan motor, which operates at fixed speeds, is connected to line voltage (60 Hz, 120 v). If we disconnect this motor from the line voltage and substitute a source of variable frequency (30–120 Hz), and similar voltage and power, the speed of the motor can be changed continuously over a distance of two octaves. Fig. 13 illustrates the components employed:

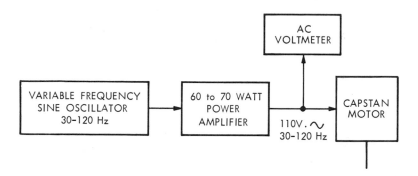

<figure>FIGURE 13.</figure>

The oscillator should exhibit frequency stability and uniform amplitude, and should have an output level sufficient to drive the power amplifier to full output. The power amplifier is usually a vacuum-tube amplifier (transistor types are not always suitable) that has an output-tap (sometimes indicated "70 v.") to properly match the capstan motor. It should deliver its output continuously over the frequency range of the oscillator.

The oscillator's frequency range (30–120 Hz) allows an octave transposition, down or up, from the fixed normal speed, represented by 60 hz. (For example, if the fixed speed is 15 ips, the recorder would operate from 7.5 ips to 30 ips). In practice, depending on the specific power amplifier and motor combination, the useful range is limited to 45–90 Hz—in other words, about a half-octave on each side of the fixed speed. The AC voltmeter shown in the diagram is connected across the output of the amplifier and gives a visual indication of the 110 to 115 volts that should be present for proper operation.

Instead of assembling the above configuration, some studios resort to commercial units designed for the same purpose. The newest of these units use transistors, and position the variable-frequency oscillator on the same chassis.

When using variable speed, it is customary to begin with prerecorded material and to vary its speed on a machine in playback mode. (It will be found that rapid glides or changes are not possible because there is a time lag between the setting of the oscillator and the settling time of the motor as it changes to its new speed.) A second machine records the newly transposed material for future playback at fixed speed. A second method begins with direct sound material, such as a tone mixture from a bank of oscillators, which is presented to the input of a recorder-amplifier. During the recording, the speed of the recording machine is varied. Upon playback at a fixed speed, we hear the effects that were executed in the recording. This method is not as practical as it might seem, for actual speed changes cannot be monitored with any certainty until playback at fixed speed.

g. *Tape loops.* A *tape loop* is a length of prerecorded sound material with its ends spliced to make an endless loop. The sound material may be a sustained signal or one or more discrete sound events. The shortest possible loop depends on the length and width of the recorder's head assembly; the longest can be almost any practical length. Great care is taken in splicing the loop and in all further handling of it. If it is anticipated that the loop will receive much use, an identical version is made as a spare.

The method used to adapt the tape loop to the recorder varies from one machine to another, depending on the physical layout and operational features of the transport. At best, the results only approximate the performance of the machine in its normal reel-to-reel operation, and some studios turn to specially designed loop-players (see p. 107). The principal problem is to maintain tension at the playback head without introducing points of friction and drag in the path that the loop follows.

For short loops, a heavy, smooth, cylindrical object placed on the deck will provide the necessary tension for proper performance (Fig. 14). (This solution is only possible if the deck is not tilted, but is reasonably horizontal.) For longer loops, it is possible to use one or more microphone stands to provide the necessary tension (Fig. 15).

The purpose of the tape loop in electronic music is practical and functional:

1. It allows continuous repetition of the sound without constant rewinding of the tape.
2. During the repetitions, the material can be subjected to various sound modifications as a test of its possibilities for composition.

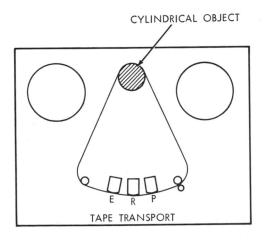

FIGURE 14.

3. If the sound material is already useful, the loop can be used in the manner of an *ostinato*.

The ostinato (along with reverberation and tape echo) is one of the most abused effects in electronic composition. The skillful tape composer masks the ostinato effect when it intrudes by varying its speed, amplitude, timbre, etc., and by introducing "rests" to break up the periodicity. By using constant modification and particularly long loops, the ostinato may not even be apparent.

h. *Tape echo effects*. With the aid of one or two tape recorders and by varying a few basic patches, the tape composer can generate many echo effects. In the following description only the basic configurations will be shown; all others are variants of these.[20]

The simplest echo effect requires a two channel-recorder. The signal is recorded, *monitored* by the playback head, and sent back to the *lower* track of the record head. When the completed tape is reproduced in two channels, the original signal is heard followed by its echo. The length of time delay depends on the distance between the two heads, and on the tape speed. For a typical professional recorder playing at 15 ips, the delay is approximately 100 milliseconds.

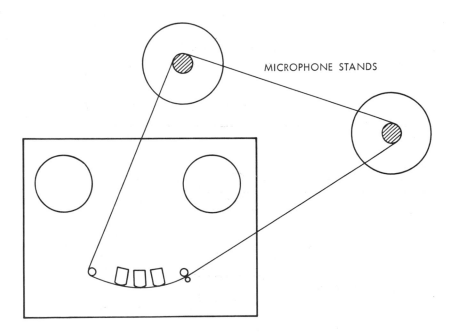

MICROPHONE STANDS

FIGURE 15.

[20] For a detailed study of tape echo effects, see A. Strange, *Electronic Music*, pp. 89–95.

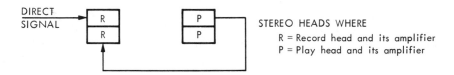

FIGURE 16.   Single echo effect.

The second basic echo effect is best realized with a mixer, for this allows the recording and playback settings to be preset and enables the effect to be monitored while it is in progress. The signal is recorded, monitored by the playback head, and sent back to the record head, at which point the process is repeated. The delay is once more dependent on tape speed and the distance separating the heads. The number of repetitions and their amplitude is a function of the gain settings at the mixer. If the mixing pot for the playback signal is turned down, there is no echo, only the direct signal. As this pot is turned up, the number of repetitions and their amplitude increase until a point is reached where the feedback signal overloads the recording amplifier and "noise" prevails.

The third effect is based on the first two, but is taken to the point of musical canons or rounds at the unison by means of extended delay. The signal paths are identical to those in Figs. 16 and 17, but the tape passes the record head and its amplifier on one machine and the playback head and its

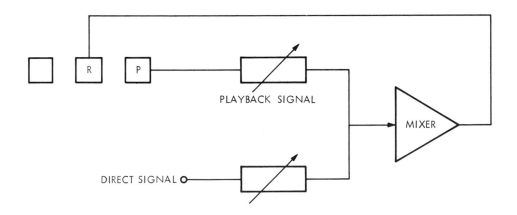

FIGURE 17.   Feedback echo effect.

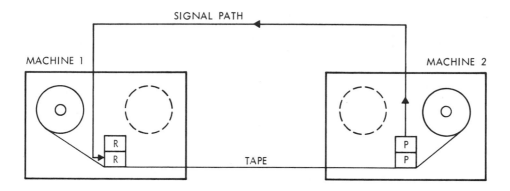

FIGURE 18. Single echo effect with extended delay.

amplifier on an identical, second machine. The machines are any convenient distance from each other (Figs. 18 and 19). The delay time at 7.5 ips will be about 1.5 seconds for every foot (12″) of distance separating the record and play heads. The mechanical execution of the above varies, depending on the machine. In any case, both machines must be started and stopped together.

i. *Special-purpose tape recorders.* Since the beginnings of electronic music, studios have either used commercial machines or built special-purpose units to obtain the special effects possible with magnetic tape.

i. *Loop players.* Scattered throughout the world are machines of various designs meant exclusively for playing loops. One particularly interesting unit, designed by G. Close for the Brandeis University studio, accepts four loops, each having its own mono-head, playback amplifier and variable-speed capstan motor. The speed of each motor can be independently varied over a three-octave range. It is also possible to use only one loop and run it past all four heads for reiterative echo effects.

ii. *Morphophone.* This is a loop device for recording and playing invented by Poullin and Moles for the Paris studio. In addition to an erase head, record head, and ten playback heads, there is an adjustable filter in each playback amplifier for special timbre effects.

iii. *Phonogène.* This is an invention of Pierre Schaeffer on which it is possible to transpose a loop in twelve discrete steps (i.e., equal temperament) from a keyboard. (A two-speed motor offers an octave transposition of these steps.) The keyboard in effect selects one of twelve capstans, each of a different diameter but all running at the same speed. Another model of the Phonogène allows continuously variable speed.

iv. *Le Caine Multi-track Recorder.* This machine is a variable-speed playback unit for up to ten (two-track) tape reels and/or loops, designed by Hugh Le Caine and used in several Canadian studios. The machine's variable-speed

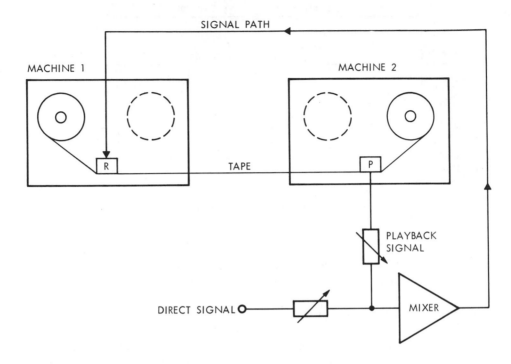

FIGURE 19.   Feedback echo effect with extended delay.

motor responds to control voltages presented from a three-octave keyboard that may be preset to any tuning system. A glide strip offers glissando effects. Basically, there are two modes of working with this machine: first, as a transposing device for prerecorded tapes; and second, as a machine for synchronizing tapes at fixed speeds. The latter mode is particularly accurate because all tapes run on a common capstan.

v. *Tape echo or "reverb" units.* These are commercial tape decks having an erase head, record head, and several playback heads, around which a closed loop of tape is transported. The play heads are not equally spaced and, thus, various delays of the recorded material are introduced. The output of the play heads is in a feedback loop with the recording amplifier, to maintain constant repetition. On expensive units the respective distances between the heads can be varied by moving the head(s) along a track. Though they are advertised as "reverberation" devices, the heads are too few to simulate the multiple and irregular reflections of reverberation, and with some material, the echo-like repetitions are readily perceived.

vi. *Springer machines.* A number of playback machines have been designed to stretch or compress the duration of prerecorded sound material without altering the original pitch. In studio jargon they are referred to as Springer machines, but this name properly belongs to the machine invented by Springer for *Telefonbau & Normalzeit* and known as the *Information rate changer* or *Pitch and tempo regulator.*

With the Springer device, which is an auxiliary to a normal tape recorder, the tape to be processed is routed past a rotating head (four heads arranged in circular fashion). The four play heads (Fig. 20) are arranged so that one is always in contact with the tape; the output is the sum of the four heads. Depending on the velocity of the rotating head, its direction of rotation, and the absolute speed of the tape, it is possible to change frequency or duration of the information without affecting the other characteristic. The range of change available is quoted as -30% and $+50\%$.

The Springer machine was originally designed to be used by radio for lengthening or shortening broadcasts. In this application it performs reasonably well. But it is doubtful that the machine will please all composers of electronic music. One characteristic of the machine that can be annoying is the "flutter" caused by phase discontinuity when the head shifts to a new section of the tape. Some composers also complain of the setup time and the awkwardness of operating two machines together. As the tape bypasses part of the main transport, it must be placed back on the main machine to be rewound safely, and so forth. Despite these criticisms, this machine, if its limita-

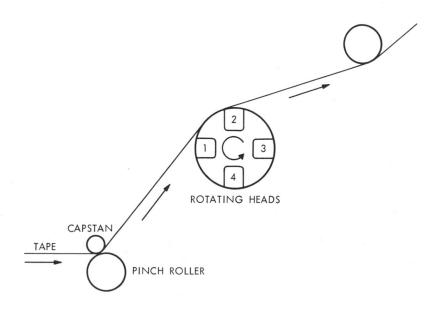

FIGURE 20.

tions are understood, can be used for a certain class of sound material. **But if** the composer is to process material that is electronic in origin, the *sequencer* and its associated hardware can more easily produce the time and pitch transposition required.

4. *Power amplifiers and loudspeakers.* The final links in any audio chain are the *power amplifier* and *loudspeaker* system.

a. *Power amplifier.* The function of the power amplifier is simple enough to describe: it receives an audio signal and amplifies it to a level of sufficient power to drive the loudspeaker system. The output signal of the amplifier should be an exact replica of the input signal; that is, it should exhibit no change except in magnitude. The principal criteria by which power amplifiers are chosen for studio use, are:

i. *Monophonic* or *stereophonic.* The choice is one of convenience. Stereo amplifiers have two identical mono amplifiers on a common chassis.

ii. *Pre-amplification.* The combined pre-amplifier/amplifier is useful but not practical. In studios, the amplifiers might be placed at remote locations, thereby negating the value of the volume controls, tone controls, etc., of the pre-amplifier.

iii. *Power output.* A unit rated at 60 watts (per channel) will suffice for both studio and concert use.

iv. *Frequency response.* It is not difficult to find units that provide the desired flat response over the entire audio spectrum.

v. *Distortion.* It is more difficult to find amplifiers that have less than .5% distortion (considered ideal) at *any* frequency and maximum power.

vi. *Input and output impedances.* The input impedance of the power amplifier should match the output impedance of the preceding tape recorder or mixer. The output impedance of the power amplifier should match the available loudspeaker system.

The specifications suggested by the above criteria can be met by some amplifiers that are designed for high-fidelity systems in the home; indeed, many tape studios use this type.

b. *Loudspeaker systems.* The principles of the loudspeaker have already been discussed in Chapter 2 of this book. There is little to add except that part of the definition just offered for an amplifier can be used to describe an ideal loudspeaker: the signal transmitted by the loudspeaker "should be an exact replica of the input signal." Unfortunately, this ideal is almost impossible to achieve, and the tape studio or composer initially selects a loudspeaker by subjective criteria.

Three general types of loudspeakers are popular for electronic music:

i. *Studio monitors.* These are systems intended for use in commercial recording and broadcasting studios. They are considered efficient and can also be used in concert halls. A loudspeaker's efficiency refers to the power needed to drive it at maximum volume. An efficient loudspeaker requires only a few watts; an inefficient loudspeaker, considerably more.

ii. *Theater loudspeakers.* These are usually too large for tape studios. They are considered extremely efficient and are obviously intended for large halls and auditoria.

iii. *Acoustic-suspension loudspeakers.* These are small, high-accuracy reproducers, considered inefficient but suitable for monitoring in the tape studio and for concerts.

The acquisition and installation of equipment for a complete tape studio —one comparable to the studio at Milan (p. 73)—represents a considerable expense. Less costly alternatives are possible and have been described by J. Seawright in the *Music Educators Journal* (November, 1968). In acquiring studio equipment, a general rule is to budget for the best tape recorders available, and only then acquire the desired sound generators and modifiers.

STUDIOS, COMPOSITIONS, SCORES, AND OTHER MATTERS

Some Important Tape Studios

It is not the purpose of this section to provide a list of all tape studios; this information can be found in the excellent compilation by Hugh Davies, "International Electronic Music Catalog" *Electronic Music Review*, Nos. 2–3 (July, 1967). The studios chosen for this discussion are commonly acknowledged to be important centers of electronic music; no further justification for their inclusion is necessary. Similarly, the compositions referred to are only selected pieces from the extensive repertoire of electronic music that has been produced over the past two decades or so.

Paris: *Groupe de Recherches Musicales* (GRM), *Service de la Recherche* (SR), *ORTF*

What is commonly referred to as the "Paris studio" is actually a department (GRM) within the Service de la Recherche (SR) of the Office de Radiodiffusion-Télévision Français (ORTF). The SR is directed by Pierre Schaeffer and includes the departments of music, film, and television. The music department, the GRM, is directed by François Bayle. The GRM is further divided into sections that deal with experimental, practical, and applied electronic composition. A permanent group of resident composers work alternately in these sections.

Although the first experiments in musique concrète were made in the late '40s, the first studio designed expressly for electronic composition was not established by the RTF until 1951. The excellent, extensive facilities of this studio have always been conducive to the production of musique concrète. In addition to the usual recording apparatus, mixing consoles, and microphones, one finds a variety of modifiers including a reverb plate, third-octave filters, a Springer time-regulator, and the special-purpose recorders noted previously (pp. 106–8), the *Morphophone* and the *Phonogène*.

The creative output from the Paris studio, both musical and written (the texts of Pierre Schaeffer), is truly prodigious and of consistently high quality. Through 1958, the important compositions are those of Schaeffer, Pierre Henry, Phillipe Arthuys, Michel Philippot, Edgard Varèse (*Déserts*, first version, 1954) and Iannis Xenakis; since 1958, the works of François Bayle, Edgardo Canton, Phillipe Carson, Luc Ferrari, François-Bernard Mâche, Ivo Malec, Guy Reibel, and Bernard Parmegiani are significant.

Pierre Schaeffer: *Etude aux objets* (1967).

This work was initially composed in 1959, revised in 1966, and the definitive version (four-channel) released in 1967. For this five-movement composition, Schaeffer chose one hundred sound objects from his vast library of recorded source material. These sounds were originally produced by musical instruments, but they rarely betray their origin. According to the composer, no electronic trickery is employed for sound transformation—just scissors, tape recorders for coyping and mixing, and simple transposition by octave as is available with any tape recorder. One of the greatest problems of electronic composition is the control of linear succession, that is, the ordering in time of disparate sound events. Schaeffer's *Etude* succeeds in presenting the listener with a meaningful continuity: the five movements in turn expose, extend, multiply, link, and finaly overlap the sound objects.

Cologne. Studio für elektronische Musik, Westdeutscher Rundfunk

The Cologne studio became operational during 1951 and was directed until 1963 by Herbert Eimert; thereafter it has been directed by Karlheinz Stockhausen. Fritz Enkel, who was the technical director in the early years and was responsible for the design of the mixing console, published a description of the studio in 1954. The instrumentation as reported by Enkel and other sources (*Répertoire* and published scores) varies somewhat, but by the end of 1960 it included:

sine-wave oscillators
white-noise source
pulse generator

ring modulator
amplitude modulator
band-pass filter
third-octave filter
octave filter
frequency-selective amplifier

Springer time-regulator
several mono recorders
four-channel recorder

One of the recorders was capable of variable speed, and could be used with special apparatus to play extended loops.

Shortly after Stockhausen succeeded Eimert as director, the studio was reconstructed and its facilities were improved and expanded. At the same time, Stockhausen turned to composing for live performers and electronic apparatus —*Mikrophonie* I (1964); *Mixtur* (1964–65); etc.—and the Cologne studio partially diverted its attention to the needs of live-electronic music.

Of the compositions realized at the Cologne studio during its first decade of operation, those of Stockhausen stand out so prominently that we tend to overlook the work of Herbert Eimert, Herbert Brün, Gottfried Michael Koenig, Mauricio Kagel, Ernst Křenek, György Ligeti, and the others who worked there during the same period.

Karlheinz Stockhausen: *Kontakte für elektronische Klange, Klavier und Schlagzeug* (1959–60).

Kontakte is often ranked as the most significant electronic composition even produced in a tape studio. Stockhausen has described all aspects of the composition in the published score, in program notes for the commercial recordings, and in articles for books and journals; the following is only a summary of the essential details.

Stockhausen began the initial experiments for this composition with the assistance of G. M. Koenig in 1958; the score and its realization were completed in 1960. The experiments dealt with synthesis of sounds, but not through the familiar technique of superimposing sine waves. The electronic sounds for *Kontakte* were made primarily with a pulse generator whose frequency and width of pulse could be varied continuously. The pulse trains were filtered with a frequency-selective amplifier, variable band-pass filter, or third-octave filter, given a dynamic shape (envelope); and recorded and synchronized with similarly generated sounds. When transposed to higher registers, the resultant synthetic timbre approximates known sounds or is heard as a variant of these sounds.

The completed composition exists in two forms: tape alone, or tape with two performers who are called upon to play various percussion instruments and piano. The tape part is conceived in four channels and the actual distribution of sounds to any of four loudspeakers has been predetermined on the tape. (In the production of the tape, Stockhausen used a *Rotations-lautsprecher,* a device in which the sound material emanating from a single loudspeaker rotates past four microphones, each connected to a separate recording amplifier on a four-track machine.) In the concert version with performers, the motion is both visual and aural: the performers move among the various instruments; the sound moves around the audience. The *contacts* indicated by the title are made among electronic and instrumental sound groups, autonomous formal structures ("moments"), and the forms of spatial movement.

Milan: Studio di Fonologia Musicale RAI

A third school of European electronic music emerged in 1955, when a studio was established at the Radio Audizioni Italiane, Milano, with Luciano Berio as its artistic director. The technical facilities were designed by Alfredo Lietti and were probably the finest in the world at the time. (The equipment of the Milan studio has been listed on p. 73.) Through 1962, the studio released works by Berio and the Italian composers Niccolo Castiglioni, Aldo Clementi, Bruno Maderna, and Luigi Nono; composers from other countries who worked at Milan include André Boucourechliev, John Cage, Henri Pousseur, and Bengt Hambraeus. The works from the Milan studio in this period show no strict allegiance to either the Paris or Cologne schools; if any generalization can be made, it is that the compositional style tends to to be more improvisatory in character.

Around 1962, when Berio's musical commitments took him from Milan, there was a temporary lull in the studio's activities. Shortly thereafter, Nono became a prominent creative force at the studio, and in 1968 the facilities were redesigned and brought up to date.

Luciano Berio: *Thema—Omaggio a Joyce* (1958).

For his *Thema* Berio restricts himself to one sound source—a woman reading a fragment from the eleventh chapter of James Joyce's novel, *Ulysses*. The recorded spoken word serves as a reference point from which Berio's musical interpretation begins. The chosen text already exhibits strong musical tendencies; Berio's setting brings out its implied polyphony and reinterprets, through transformation, its musical sounds and gestures. The techniques employed by Berio include tape cutting, third-octave filtering, superimposition of identical sounds through multitrack recording, and extreme pitch and time transpositions with a variable-speed recorder. This piece (and Stockhausen's *Gesang der Jünglinge* [1955–56] was to serve as a model for many subsequent electronic compositions that used the voice as source material.

New York: Columbia-Princeton Electronic Music Center (CPEMC), Columbia University

The official opening of the CPEMC took place in 1959, eight years after Vladimir Ussachevsky and Otto Luening created their first tape compositions. Before 1959 they had already completed some twenty-five compositions at various geographic locations, with a growing inventory of equipment. (See Chapter 1.) With its new tape-studio equipment and recently acquired RCA Synthesizer Mark II, the Center became the first adequately equipped electronic music studio in the United States. By 1969 the CPEMC had four studios, and more than sixty composers from many countries had worked there. In addition to Luening, Ussachevsky, and Milton Babbitt—all co-directors of the Center—the catalogue of the CPEMC includes works by Bülent Arel, Luciano Berio, Walter Carlos, Mario Davidovsky, Jacob Druckman, Alcides Lanza, Ilhan Mimaroğlu, Alice Shields, Pril Smiley, Edgard Varèse and Charles Wuorinen.

The four tape studios of the CPEMC are not identical, but in general they contain a central mixing console, four two-channel recorders, and one four-channel recorder. Complementing the extensive array of wave generators and modifiers are voltage-controlled modules and a complete voltage-controlled synthesizer in each studio. For multi-loudspeaker concert presentation of electronic music, the McMillin Theatre of Columbia University has been provided with a mixing panel and amplifiers for routing sound to nineteen loudspeakers.

There is no one style of composition practiced at the Center's tape studios, though some listeners think they detect a "Columbia sound"—whatever that might be. Some composers draw upon concrete source material (Ussachevsky and Mimaroğlu), and others rely on electronically generated sounds (Arel and Davidovsky). Many compositions produced at the CPEMC are meticulously crafted and provide evidence of the enormous potential offered by tape-studio techniques.

Bülent Arel: *Stereo Electronic Music No. 2* (1970).

Whereas the former piece bearing the same name (*Stereo Electronic Music No. 1* [1960]) was flamboyant and aspired to symphonic proportions, the present piece is taut and restrained. The familiar Arel thumb-prints, often imitated by other composers, can be detected: the carefully chosen clusters transposed a semitone upward, the expressive sustained envelopes chosen for these clusters, the rapid virtuoso gestures of various lengths interrupting the sustained sounds, the polyphonic layering at climaxes, and so forth. Arel is a virtuoso composer in complete control of his material. Even the well-worn effects of tape-loop ostinato, reiterative tape-head echo, and reverberation take on a new freshness in his music. The sound of *Stereo Electronic Music No. 2* are electronic in origin and are treated with filtering, ring modulation, electronic switching, and variable-speed transposition.

Utrecht: Studio voor Elektronische Muziek van de Rijksuniversiteit te Utrecht (STEM)

The electronic music facilities that were available to Dutch composers from 1955 to 1960 at the Philips research labs in Eindhoven were shifted to the Institute of Sonology at the University of Utrecht in 1960. The Utrecht studio was officially opened in 1961, and in 1964 Gottfried Michael Koenig was appointed artistic director. Since then the studio has flourished, becoming the most important center for electronic music in Europe. The activities of the studio include not only the production of electronic music but also subsidized research. The yearly seminars offered at the Institute are rigorous, and acquaint the student with historical, theoretical, and practical aspects of electronic music. A research team led by Stan Tempelaars publishes its findings on new apparatus and other related matters in the studio's journal, *Electronic Music Reports* (now incorporated into *Interface*).

The facilities of STEM for electronic composition are comprehensive, and are often based on original designs; they include "classic" studios, a voltage-controlled studio, a multi-track recording studio,. and, most recently, a computer installation. Many composers from Holland and abroad have worked at

Utrecht; from Holland: Henk Badings, Ton Bruynèl, Luctor Ponse, Dick Raaijmakers, and Peter Schat; from other countries: Konrad Boehmer, Werner Kaegi, Mauricio Kagel, and Makoto Shinohara.

> Gottfried Michael Koenig: *Terminus X* (1967).
>
> *Terminus X* is the third and final composition sharing the common title *Terminus*. *Terminus I* (Cologne, 1961–62) is the basis of *Terminus II; Terminus X* in turn develops elements from *I* and *II*. Because of the complex transmutations that take place from one composition to the next, it is possible to hear any one of these pieces as unique compositions. The entire set of pieces is interesting because it illustrates the transition from classic to voltage-controlled techniques that took place during this period.
>
> All the sounds of *Terminus X* are electronic in origin and have complex spectra resulting from the processes of modulation. The piece strives to avoid traditional musical connotations and must be heard as sound for its own sake; in the absence of an easily perceived form, Koenig offers continuous contrasts of amplitude, density, rhythmic velocity, and pitch register.

Electronic Music Scores

No score in the traditional sense is required for electronic music, as the completed composition on magnetic tape is usually invariable and does not require interpretation by a performer—that is, each "performance" is identical. Of course, the composer may prepare sketches, keep a record of "patches," and so forth during the production of a composition, but these hardly constitute a score. If a score exists for an electronic work, in all likelihood it was realized after rather than before the composition was begun. The reasons for preparing and even publishing a score are varied:

1. It can have pedagogical value; a student composer can follow the procedures and hopefully apply the knowledge gained to his own work. Often, this type of score will be detailed enough to actually reconstruct in the tape studio.

2. Copyright laws of some countries do not accept a tape as suitable evidence for registration, and a score of the electronic piece must therefore be submitted. This type of score need not be detailed, and another composer would probably have difficulty in reconstructing it exactly.

3. A score is required if the piece involves one or more instrumentalists who must synchronize with the tape. A score of this type gives cues for the entrances of the tape and/or performer(s).

4. The electronic composer has an artistic bent, and through the preparation of fanciful graphs in different colored inks feels more closely allied to the "graphic-music" movement. This type of score is usually meaningless, but provides excellent pictures for music periodicals. A secondary benefit is that it provides the composer with additional revenue beyond tape-rental fees.

The notation of scores is by no means standardized, each electronic composer having his own system of notation. The sample scores on the accompanying pages illustrate some of the methods used.

Pedagogy of Electronic Music

The university, home of so many studios, must necessarily offer instruction in electronic composition to its young composers. Ideally, this instruction should not only encompass craft but also the appropriate musical, historical, theoretical, and technical background necessary for a complete understanding of composition with electronic sounds. A suitable curriculum has been described by this writer elsewhere.[21] Even if such a program of instruction failed to produce electronic composers *per se,* there is no doubt that through the process Murray Schafer calls "ear cleaning," the student composer would acquire a new perspective on all composition not otherwise possible through traditional curricula.

From a pedagogical standpoint, this writer prefers the tape studio for teaching electronic composition. Not only does it offer a singular approach to the craft of electronic composition, it can also serve as an introduction to other available systems. The mini-synthesizers, often touted as effective teaching tools, present some beginning composers with too many options for immediate assimilation. The tape studio allows a more systematic approach through the isolation of its various components, and with this foreknowledge the synthesizer systems are easier to comprehend. Computer programs for sound generation also demand a preliminary knowledge that can be satisfied in part with practical studio experience.

Some Personal Thoughts:
Tape Studio vs. Synthesizer vs. Computer

It is all too easy to lose sight of the fact that the composer is more important than the machine or system. But granting technology its rightful place, no machine or system has been proven superior to any other despite the claims and counterclaims of designers, manufacturers, or composers. For example, it is unlikely at the present time that a composer working exclusively with synthesizers or computers could duplicate the masterpiece of studio technique, Stockhausen's *Kontakte.* Likewise, it is doubtful if a composer working with studio equipment before the '60s could successfully achieve the tonal spectra of Subotnick's *Touch,* realized with a contemporary synthesizer system; a setting of *Touch* would certainly be possible with a computer, but the programming problems would be considerable. To carry the argument to its logical conclusion, the tape studio and synthesizer lack the flexibility to replicate parts of Risset's computer composition, *Mutations.*

Ideally, the composer chooses among the available electronic music systems for their creative potential and not because of any claims for efficiency (e.g.,

21 G. Ciamaga, "The Training of the Composer in the Use of New Technological Means," in "Music and Technology," *La Revue Musicale* (Paris, 1971) pp. 143–50.

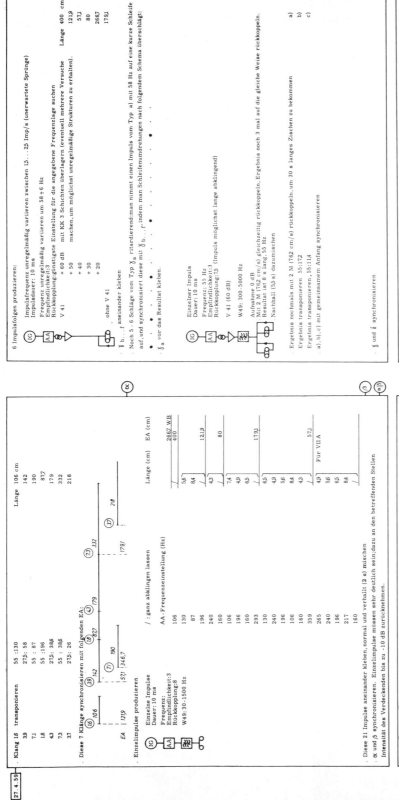

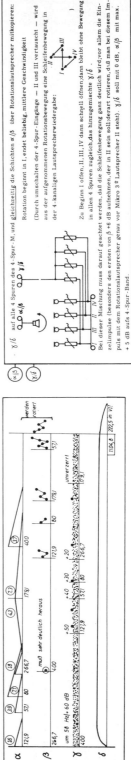

FIGURE 21. Stockhausen: Kontakte; from p. 34 of the *Realisationpartitur*. One of the most detailed scores ever published. It describes the equipment, the patch configurations, and the production techniques required to realize the composition © 1968, Universal Edition. Used by permission of the publisher. Theodore Presser Company, sole representative United States, Canada and Mexico.

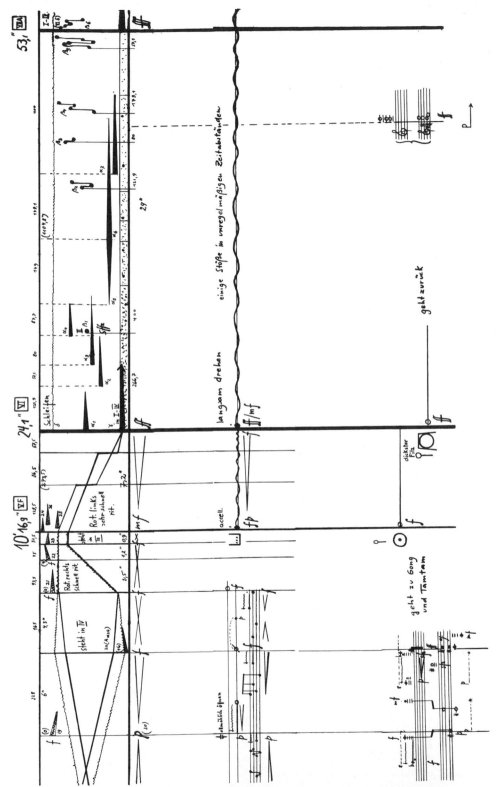

FIGURE 22. Stockhausen: *Kontakte*; from p. 12 of the *Aufführungspartitur* (performance score). A performance score for the same composition used by the two players to synchronize with the tape. The tape part is a simplified graphic representation of the electronic sounds; a stricter notation is used for the instrumental parts. The section marked VI refers to the same roman numeral in the realization score, p. 34. © 1966, Universal Edition. Used by permission of the publisher. Theodore Presser Company, sole representative, United States, Canada and Mexico.

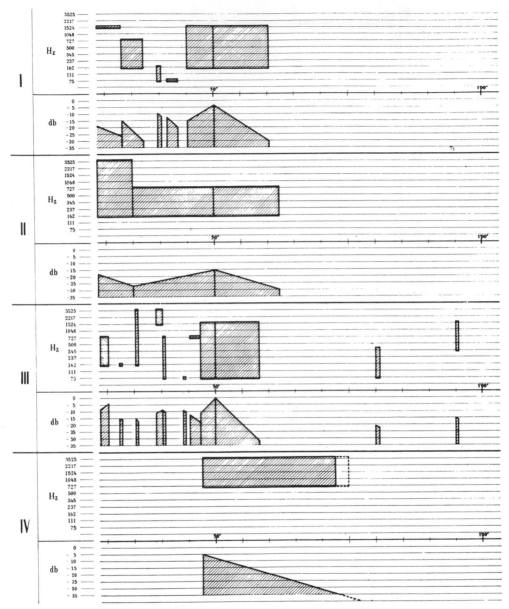

FIGURE 23. Włodzimierz Kotoński: *Etiuda na jedno uderzenie w talerz* (Study on one cymbal stroke), p. 9. This fragment of the score shows the four separate tape parts that are synchronized and mixed down to one channel to form the completed piece. As is customary, the horizontal axis indicates duration (in seconds); the vertical axis indicates pitch location in frequency (Hz) and amplitude in db. (Each frequency space represents an interval of about an augmented fourth.) The shaded rectangles indicate the bandwidths of the spectra; that is, the prerecorded signal, a cymbal stroke, has been filtered for different bandwidths and transposed to different pitch levels. The dotted lines indicate length of reverb decay. The accompanying data for the score is complete, and another composer could conceivably reconstruct this composition. Used by permission of Polskie Wydawnictwo Muzyczne, Kraków, Poland.

FIGURE 24. Mario Davidovsky: *Synchronism no. 3,* for cello and electronic sounds, p. 7. The scores for the tape operator and cellist are identical, consisting of the cello part and command "cues" for starting and stopping the tape. (In the previous Stockhausen example, the tape runs continuously.) A tape stop is automatically indicated by blank leader on the tape copy used for performance. Some of the recorded sound material (e.g., rhythmic figures) is noted throughout the score. Approximate timings required for a synchronized performance are also indicated.

121

"eliminates tedious splicing"; "no more patch cords"; "cuts composition time in half"). As Koenig has observed, most of the time spent in electronic composition rightfully deals with consideration and experiment, not with the mechanical movements of splicing tapes, setting voltages, etc. (For instrumental composition, faster pencils [voltage-controlled?] have yet to be invented.) The ideal system should deliver the composer's intentions, regardless of how long it takes.

If the various methods (tape studio, voltage-controlled synthesizer, etc.) are equally valid, and efficiency is not the primary criterion, what "personalities" do these individual systems have that appeal to the composer?

Some programs for generating sound with a computer attract the instrumental composer because they require the normal preliminary "score" (in this case, the numerical data specifying the musical intentions of the entire piece), which is a prerequisite of performance. The computer's accuracy in executing the specifications for pitch and duration exceeds the limits of perception, and in theory any sound can be synthesized, but only if the composer can provide the required data. Though many existing computer compositions have instrumental connotations, these stem from the composer's predisposition towards instrumental qualities rather than from inherent limitations in the available programs.

The voltage-controlled synthesizers, according to their manufacturers, represent the best of all worlds. They provide a keyboard for real-time performance, their hardware ostensibly replaces conventional studio apparatus, and the elementary programming devices (sequencers) are easier to address than a computer. The author feels that in trying to be all things for all composers, the designs arising from the use of voltage control are compromised; for example, the keyboard is monophonic, subtractive synthesis is the norm, *exact* repetition of programmed information is restricted by the stability of the oscillators and timing generators, and so forth. The composer who understands these limitations and can tame the abundant sound material offered by the synthesizer through the immediacy of improvisation and simple programming will not be disappointed.

The tape studio and its techniques should appeal to the composer as craftsman. The studio composer assembling pieces of tape to form an artistic whole reminds one of the mosaic craftsman who arranges pieces of glass to form a complete image. Another useful comparison, perhaps even more apt, can be drawn with the craft of cinema. The filmmaker exposes many feet of potential visual images and then edits them for the desired visual continuity. Similarly, the tape composer records many feet of potential sound images and, through splicing, arranges them in the desired aural continuity. Both crafts imply a selection process—not all source material is equally suitable—and both imply the control of succession through the accurate ordering of the time continuum.

Another attraction of the tape studio is the potentially broader base of source material available for composition. In addition to the "normal" electronic sounds common to all systems through additive and subtractive synthesis, the tape composer can draw upon the vast, yet untapped, vocabulary of concrete sounds. A concrete sound is inherently more complex and richer in nuances than one generated with electronic equipment. The tape studio composer enjoys the advantage here, for although the voltage-controlled synthesizer can process concrete sounds, its design has been optimized for electronically generated sound. Similarly, there is not enough practical analytical data for concrete sounds to take full advantage of computer synthesis.

In the final analysis, the composer must base his choice of medium not only on verbal evidence but also on the available aural evidence—the electronic compositions inspired by and realized with these systems. If the reader is willing to study the numerous electronic compositions produced over the past two decades or so, no further corroboration for any system is necessary.

Columbia-Princeton Electronic Music Center.

University of Toronto Electronic Music Studio.

Bregman Electronic Music Studio at Dartmouth College.

Studio de Fonologia, RAI—Radiotelevisione Italiana, Milan. Mixer and tape recorders.

Studio de Fonologia, RAI—Radiotelevisione Italiana, Milan. Generation and modulation equipment.

François Bayle, director of the Groupe de Recherche Musicales, Office de Radiodiffusion Télévision Française (O.R.T.F.) in their studio.

Utrecht: Studio voor Elektronische Muziek van de Rijksuniversiteit te Utrecht. Studio No. 2.

The Electronic Music Studio of the West German Radio in Cologne.

COMMENTARIES BY COMPOSERS

If the experience of electronic music is important, and I believe it is, its significance lies not in the discovery of "new" sounds but in the possibility it gives the composer of integrating a larger domain of sound phenomena into a musical thought. What has emerged from these last ten years is the suggestion that music does not constitute a category, that a dualistic conception of musical material can be overcome. Just as language is not words on the one hand and concepts on the other, but is rather a system of arbitrary symbols through which we give a certain form to our way of being in the world, so music is not always identifiable only with its conventionalized means. Verses, prosody and rhymes are no more an assurance of poetry than written notes are an assurance of music. We often seem, in fact, to discover more "poetry" in prose than in poetry itself and more "music" in speech and noise than in agreed-upon musical sounds. It is within this general perspective that THEMA (*Omaggio a Joyce*) must be approached. In it no use is made of electrically produced sounds; its only sound source is a speaking voice reading the beginning of the eleventh chapter of Joyce's *Ulysses,* as it is heard in the initial part of the piece.

A polyphonic intent characterizes the entire chapter (entitled *Sirens* and dedicated to music). Here the narrative technique was in fact suggested to Joyce by a well-known procedure of polyphonic music: the *Fuga per canonem.* The point here is not to establish the extent to which Joyce was able to transpose a typically musical fact to a literary level; this could be done only by examining the development of the whole chapter. It is possible, however, by developing Joyce's polyphonic intention, to reinterpret musically a reading of the text. Once accepted as a sound system the text can gradually be detached from its frame of vocal delivery and evaluated in terms of electro-acoustical transformational possibilities. The text is thus broken down into sound families, groups of words or syllables organized in a scale of vocal colors (from [a] to [u]) and a scale of consonants (from voiced to unvoiced), the ordering of which is determined by noise content. The extreme points of the latter scale, for instance, are constituted by the "bl" grouping (from "Blew. Blue bloom . . .") and by "s" (from the last line of this exposition, a real cadence on noise: "Pearls: when she. Liszt's rhapsodies. Hissss"). The members of these sound families are placed in environments other than their original textual contexts, the varying length of the portions of context establishing a pattern of degree of intelligibility of the text. Twice, a language other than English is used, French, from the translation by Joyce and V. Larbaud, for the phrase "Petites ripes, il picore les petites ripes d'un pouce reche, petites ripes" ("Chips, picking chips off rocky thumbnail, chips"), which serves as a modulating pattern for the transformation of continuous sounds derived from the English text, and Italian, from the translation by E. Montale et al., which allows development of periodic patterns from the rolled "r" of the words "morbida parola" ("soft word"). When highly elaborated, the vocal material is often not recognizable as such, transformations, however, are always related to the following scheme, based on three articulatory categories of the original material:

Discontinuous ⟶ Periodic ⟶ Continuous
(as in "Goodgod, he never heard inall")

Continuous ⟶ Periodic ⟶ Discontinuous
(as in sibilants)

Periodic ⟶ Continuous ⟶ Discontinuous
(as in "thnthnthn")

All transformations are accomplished by tape editing, through superimposition of identical elements with varying time relations (phase shifting, especially where Joyce is concerned with musical onomatopoeia), through wide frequency and time transpositions and through ⅓ octave filtering. Though at certain points it would have been a simple matter to extend the transformations by introducing electrically produced sounds, this was not done because the original intention was to develop a reading of Joyce's text within certain restrictions dictated by the text itself.

Finally, with THEMA I attempted to establish a new relationship between speech and music, in which a continuous metamorphosis of one into the other can be developed. Thus, through a reorganization and transformation of the phonetic and semantic elements of Joyce's text, Mr. Bloom's day in Dublin (it is 4 P.M., at the Ormond Bar) briefly takes another direction, where it is no longer possible to distinguish between word and sound, between sound and noise, between poetry and music, but where we once more become aware of the relative nature of these distinctions and of the expressive character inherent in their changing functions.

Luciano Berio
from Turnabout recording TV 34177

I've never studied music. I don't call what I do electronic music. It's *organized sound.* "Music" is like a qualitative judgment—in other words, "It's music to my ears"—but maybe not to yours; it's not really an accurate description. But *organized sound* is, because that's what I'm doing: organizing sound.

I've been to only two electronic music concerts, and I was very uncomfortable. Stravinsky described these concerts as seances, and I think he's right. Because this is *created,* not just recorded, on tape, the tape *is* the piece. Nobody can "play" it —you have to play it on a tape recorder. So, on the air, it seems to me, is a natural place for it: and on records, so people who want to can play it at home.

As I went on, the sounds began to wear off—the fascination with the sounds— and the idea of the *piece* became more important. I suppose it's something like the history of music: the first man must have picked up some non-musical thing—as I'm doing—like a rock or a hollow tube or a reed, and discovered he could make sounds with it, and that sufficed for a while. But then he discovered that if he beat on the hollow tube while somebody else blew the reed, something happened that was better than either sound. In other words, the *organization* became more important than the sounds.

I had the feeling, and I still have the feeling today, that the training I've had for what I'm doing is the best training, and if I had musical training I'm not sure it would help me; and I suspect it might hinder me. You see, I deal in a sort of chaos of sound: in *Apocalypse*, for instance, there's one little movement that has in it a cat screaming, a dime store toy that moos when you turn it upside down, doors opening and slamming shut—of course, all this is very difficult to identify in the piece now, but those are the sources. Now, there's no musical training in making music out of that.

You see, when you do this sort of thing long enough, you get so you suspect there are sounds in everything; you go around tapping things, and rapping tables. Things suggest sounds—materials that normally you wouldn't think of at all as holding sound. Because, you see, I know what I can do with them afterward. Just to record it isn't enough, it's what you do with it once you have it on tape. I mean, adhesive tape only sounds one way; the tape goes downscale as you pull it, something like a white noise glissando. I included it for the same reason I included the cymbals: I was looking for equivalent sounds, because white noise by itself isn't enough; it's only one voice, like the oscillator, and I wanted other voices; but I wanted voices that would work with it—and so, the adhesive tape and the cymbals.

It's an area, this kind of thing I'm doing, where nobody's been before—these sounds don't exist in nature. An oscillator, for instance, doesn't even make a mechanical vibration—it doesn't disturb the air unless it's played through a speaker —and it can produce fundamentals that cause overtones *inside* your head, instead of outside. And, after a while—particularly in a thing like *Quatermass*, where I'm in a—I'm lost, in a way; I'm trying to be lost, I'm trying to go into someplace I've never been, to work there—particularly with this, where the energy gets so thick, I get a little uneasy, I get the feeling sometimes that there's someone behind me. It suggests to me the effect it must have for someone else, hearing it for the first time, because I hear it for the first time at that moment. I never hear it this way in a finished piece, because that feeling is lost in the editing, where you lose all enchantment with the sounds and it sometimes gets like chopping wood. I hear it for the first time when I go in to mix, alone, and I get uneasy sometimes.

Tod Dockstader
from Owl recording ORLP—8

An electronic studio does not supply the composer with sound-material from which he merely has to make a selection. The studio rather resembles a construction kit, the components of which have no musical significance of their own. This involves the composer in working methods which greatly differ from his habitual ones. He may try to imagine sounds he has never heard before, and to produce them in the experimental phase of his work. When he assembles the finished sounds, his experience of instrumental music may come to his aid. But he might also try to put some system into the possible combinations of the building elements, to produce sounds according to this system and hope that the result of the methodic production process will have a musical meaning. In this case he also goes through an experimental phase in which he examines the question as to whether sounds that are related in the system also exhibit musical similarities.

"Terminus II" is based on systematic considerations. All sounds were derived from one original sound (the ''Urklang''); manifold transformations of the sounds led to intermediate results which were also used in the piece. The fact that the sounds succeed each other in the order in which they were produced (occasionally, it is true, in a retrograde arrangement) makes them related to one another not only musically, but technically too.

''Funktion Grün'' is also arranged systematically. Both construction and order of the sounds were calculated by a computer. For the production of the sounds in the studio, control signals were used; these signals were fixed on magnetic tape and served as an experiment with automated production forms.

Gottfried Michael Koenig
from DGG recording 137011

Concerning *Synchronisms 1–3:*
They belong to a series of short pieces wherein conventional instruments are used in conjunction with electronic sounds. The attempt here has been made to preserve the typical characteristics of the conventional instruments and of the electronic medium respectively—yet to achieve integration of both into a coherent musical texture.

In the planning and realization of these pieces, two main problems arise—namely proper synchronization (a) of rhythm and (b) of pitch. During the shorter episodes where both electronic and conventional instruments are playing, rather strict timing is adhered to. However, in the more extended episodes of this type, an element of chance is introduced to allow for the inevitable time discrepancies that develop between the live performer(s) and the constant-speed tape recorder.

To achieve pitch coherence between the conventional instruments which use the 12-tone chromatic scale and the electronic medium which is non-tempered, use is made of tonal occurrences of very high density—manifested for example by a very high speed succession of attacks, possible only in the electronic medium. Thus, in such instances—based on high speed and short duration of separate tones, it is impossible for the ear to perceive the pure pitch value of each separate event; though in reacting, it does trace so to speak a statistical curve of the density. Only in a very few instances have tempered electronic pitches been employed in the Synchronisms. Throughout all three pieces, the tape recorder has been used as an integral part of the instrumental fabric.

Mario Davidovsky
from CRI 204

In May, 1967, I composed *Prozession* for the ensemble with which I regularly go on concert tours: Fred Alings and Rolf Gehlhaar (tamtam), Johannes Fritsch (viola), Harold Bojé (elektronium), and Aloys Kontarsky (piano).

The tamtam, as in *Mikrophonie I,* is picked up with a microphone held and moved by the microphonist, and the viola has a contact microphone. These two microphones are connected to two electric filters and potentiometers which I operate during the performance. These two potentiometer outputs lead to four loud-speakers in the four corners of the hall, so that I can let the filtered sounds of each instrument wander continuously between two speakers.

A musical process is formulated in the score with methods similar to ones I had already applied in *Plus-Minus, Mikrophonie I,* and *Mikrophonie II.* The musical events are not notated in detail, but are rather variations of events taken from my earlier compositions, which the instrumentalists play from memory. The tamtam player and the microphonist refer to *Mikrophonie I,* the violist to *Gesang der Jünglinge, Kontakte,* and *Momente,* the elektronium player to *Telemusik* and *Solo,* and the pianist to *Klavierstücke I–XI* and *Kontakte.* I play the filters and potentiometers with a technique similar to that of *Mikrophonie I.*

For every event the score prescribes for each player the degree of change with which he must react, either to the previous event that he has played himself or to an event that another has played. Thus, in the moment of performance, an "aural tradition" is established between my earlier music and this *Prozession,* as well as among the players.

Since the first rehearsals, during which every player reacted mostly only to himself, continuously bringing new events into play, we have now—after several performances—become an *ensemble* in which the players react strongly to one another. Single events undergo chain reactions of imitation, transformation, and mutation, all players often binding themselves for long time spans to one musical network of feedback.

Karlheinz Stockhausen
from Candide recording CE 31001

"Lyric Variations for violin and computer" was commissioned by Paul Zukofsky in the summer of 1965; and, after three years of extensive collaboration among composer, violinist, and recording engineer, was completed in the summer of 1968. Since the violin frequently plays several parts simultaneously—and anyway since the piece was conceived as sound emanating solely from two widely separated loudspeakers—there is no distinction between a "live performance" and a "recording" of this piece: in concert, a tape-recording is played through speakers.

Variations 1–5 are for violin alone. Variations 6–10 are for computer alone; and are structurally analogous to variations 1–5 in reverse order, so that the last variation for computer alone (var. 10)—the 2-minute "jungle" of variable rates of change (which takes 9 hours to compute)—corresponds to the opening 2-minute violin melody (var. 1). Variations 11–20, for violin and computer together, are a transformation of variations 1–10; with variation 20 presenting in a quite direct way the total pitch-time configuration which the variations vary.

Throughout the computer part, I have tried to impose upon conventionally peripheral aspects of sound (vibrato, tremolo, reverberation, wave-form transformation, etc.) the same degree of elaborate structuring that I impose (and that any composer imposes) upon pitch, attack-rhythm, and duration. For this reason, the listener ought provisionally to lay aside the obsolete and vague notion of "timbre"—a bushel-basket for whatever aspects of sound we may in the past have relegated (however mistakenly) to the role of subliminally "lushing-up" pitch-production—and ought instead to follow the individual participation of such aspects in the unfolding of the piece. (For a detailed discussion of these and allied problems, see my three articles in Vol. 5, no. 2 of *Perspectives of New Music*.)

The rhythmic relations of violin to computer (and of violin to violin) is nasty enough to require, if an intolerable burden is not to be imposed on the violinist during recording, a special time-beating arrangement. We adopted the expedient of having the computer produce a set of "metronome" tapes, whose sole use was to be played to the violinist through earphones while he played his part into the microphone. All violin and computer tracks were then transferred to sprocketed film (whose 96 holes per second guarantee accuracy of synchronization to within 1/2 of 1/96 of a second), from which the final master tape was produced.

J. K. Randall
from Cardinal recording VCS—10057

Time's Encomium is the title because in this work everything depends on the absolute, not the seeming, length of events and sections. Being electronic, *Time's Encomium* has no inflective dimension. Its rhythm is always quantitative, never qualitative. Because I need time, I praise it; hence the title. Because it doesn't need me, I approach it respectfully; hence the word "encomium."

In performed music, rhythm is largely a qualitative, or accentual matter. Lengths of events are not the only determinants of their significance; the cultivated performer interprets the structure to find out its significance; then he stresses events he judges important. Thus, for good or ill, every performance involves qualitative additions to what the composer has specified; and all composers, aware or unaware, assume these inflections as a resource for making their works sound coherent.

But in a purely electronic-work like *Time's Encomium*, these resources are absent. What could take their place? In my view, only the precise temporal control that, perhaps beyond anything else, characterizes the electronic medium. By composing with a view to the proportions among absolute lengths of events—be they small (note-to-note distances) or large (overall form)—rather than to their relative "weights," one's attitude toward the meaning of musical events alters and (I believe) begins to conform to the basic nature of a medium in which sound is always reproduced, never performed. This is what I mean by the "absolute, not the seeming, length of events."

Time's Encomium was composed and realized between January 1968 and January 1969, at the Columbia-Princeton Electronic Music Center in New York. I employed primarily the RCA Synthesizer, and therefore (because of that device's characteristics) the basic materials are the twelve tempered pitch classes and pitch-derived time relations. The RCA Synthesizer—familiar through several works of Milton Babbitt—is prejudiced by its design toward 12-tone equal temperament. This may be a disadvantage if one is attempting non-tempered pitch relations; but if one accepts the limitation as a boundary condition of one's work from the start it ceases to be a problem. In the near future, however, when computer synthesis becomes widespread, the issue will disappear.

Afterwards, I made the large-scale structure of processing the synthesized material in one of the Center's analog studios. Thus the work consists of a core of synthesized music, most of which appears in Part 1, surrounded and interlarded with analog-studio transformations of that music. The synthesized can always be identified by its clarity of pitch, and the familiar, almost "instrumental" sound of its constituent events. The processed almost always contains reverberation. Thus, metaphorically, the listener stands in the midst of the synthesized music, which presents itself to him with maximal clarity; and stretching away from him, becoming more and more blurred in detail, the various transformations—from the slightly altered to the unrecognizable.

Charles Wuorinen
from Nonesuch recording H–71225

Changes was commissioned by the Serge Koussevitzky Music Foundation for performance at the Library of Congress. The texture of the composition comprises the same three elements throughout: lines, chords, and percussion; and each textural element delineates a different aspect of the composition's pitch structure. The chords play segments (3 to 6 notes) of the twelve-tone set that forms the basis of the work. In the course of the work the chords sound all 48 forms of the set. The lines play six-note segments of the set which are related to the original by rotation. The percussion duplicates the pitch-class content of the chords (i.e., the percussion linearizes the pitches of the chords).

For the computer performance I designed an 'orchestra' of 'instruments' that emphasize the different types of pitch-delineation. For the lines, a family of registral instruments was created which consist of a pulse generator (of the type used in speech synthesis) which is fed into multiple banks of filters in series. As the amplitude of the banks of filters is varied, the timbre of the note changes. Further, the center-frequency settings of the filters are changed with each chord change, so that the timbre-change itself changes as a function of the chord changes, which are themselves a function of the rate at which the lines sound all twelve tones. As the work progresses, each note in the lines incorporates more and more timbre-changes, so that at the end each note changes timbre six times. All of the 'percussion' sounds entail a timbre-change which is the result of different components decaying at different rates.

Charles Dodge
from Nonesuch recording H–71245

The vocoder used in *North American Time Capsule 1967* by Alvin Lucier was designed by Sylvania Electronics Systems to encode speech sounds into digital information bits for transmission over narrow band widths via telephone lines or radio channels. There is no written score of this work. The performers are asked to prepare material using any sounds at all that would describe to beings far from our environment, either in space or in time, the physical, spiritual, social, scientific or any other situation in which we currently find ourselves. The performers' sounds are fed into the vocoder and are modified during the performance both by the sounds acting as control signals and by the manual alteration of the vocoder components.

Alvin Lucier
from Odyssey recording 32 160156

4

The Voltage-controlled Synthesizer

JOEL CHADABE

The most important technical development in electronic music in the '60s took place in the United States: the introduction of the compact, transistorized, modular, voltage-controlled electronic-music system. Late in the decade came even smaller integrated systems especially adapted for real-time performance. By 1970 there were several hundred of these "synthesizers" in use, primarily in American colleges and universities, conservatories, schools, commercial and private studios. For the first time, electronic music entered the mainstream of popular and commercial music, and the name of engineer Robert Moog, designer of the best known synthesizer, became a household word.

The voltage-controlled synthesizer integrates most of the separate components of the tape studio into a functional system. There are today almost a dozen types of synthesizers marketed commercially, from the simplest specialized devices costing less than a thousand dollars to large, non-specialized devices containing digital memories and several of each kind of function module for generation, filtering, sequencing, etc., costing over twenty thousand dollars. In this chapter Joel Chadabe takes the reader step by step through a synthesizer system: the relevant electronic theory, the logic and design of each synthesizer module, and some ways in which a composer might approach the entire interconnected system.

Joel Chadabe received his A.B. from the University of North Carolina and did graduate work at Yale, where he studied composition with Elliott Carter. He was a participant in the Ford Foundation Artists-in-Residence program in West Berlin in 1964, and established the electronic music studio at the State University of New York at Albany, of which he is now director, in 1966. He has written articles on electronic music for magazines such as Perspectives of New Music, Melos, Electronic Music Review, *and* Musique en Jeu. *His compositions, which include works for instruments and electronic*

138

sounds, have been performed in this country, Europe, and Australia, and he has received awards from the Research Foundation of the State University of New York, the Cultural Council Foundation, and ASCAP.

INTRODUCTORY CONCEPTS

Basic Description of the System

To begin, the voltage-controlled synthesizer is not a simple object. It is a hardware system that is different in many ways from computers and from many other devices or systems that are also referred to as "synthesizers," such as the RCA Mark II Electronic Music Synthesizer.

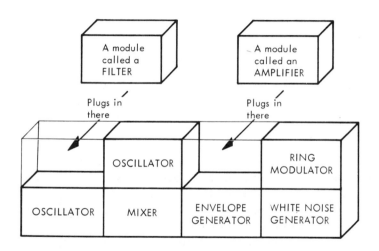

FIGURE 1.

A voltage-controlled synthesizer is a kind of musical erector set where all the different components, called *modules,* are mounted together in the same cabinet (Fig. 1). In the same way that one may buy hi-fi sets either as separate components—to be connected together as a system at home—or as integrated packages, synthesizers are either designed as modular or integrated systems. Whether they are modular or integrated depends simply on how they are to be packaged for certain applications; synthesizer "packages" may be designed to be particularly efficient as "instruments" for live performance, for example, or as educational tools, or as compositional systems.

Whatever the package, each synthesizer includes several different types of modular functions, and these different functions are interconnected and manipulated so that they perform cooperatively. They are interconnected by means of patch cords, switches, matrix switches or matrix pinboards—the particular device varies from model to model. Electricity flows through these connections, conveying information from one module to another.

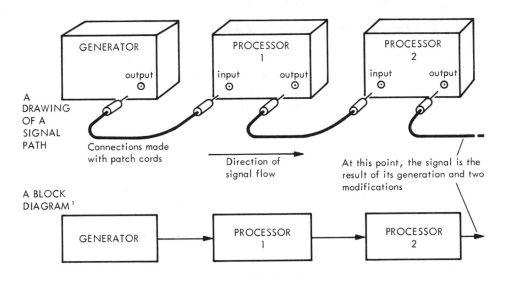

FIGURE 2.

A flow of information is called a *signal*. A *signal path* (Fig. 2) is a coherent route from a generator to a terminating point, which may pass through various modules, each of which processes the signal in some specific way. Although there are many different types of modules, and although each type has a very specific function, each module fits into one or the other of two categories: (1) a *generator,* from which the basic signal originates, or (2) a *processor,* in which the signal is in some way modified. Each successive modification further specifies the signal. Every signal is the end result of a signal path, the result of its generation and all its modifications.

Voltage and Waveforms

How does electricity convey information? Electricity is the flow of electrons through a conductor; it occurs when a *force field* is established in a conductor by the application of a voltage. *Voltage* is analogous to electrical pressure, and functions in a wire in a manner analogous to that of water pressure in a pipe (Fig. 3) or wind in a tunnel. As wind may vary in strength and change in direction, so voltage may vary in strength and change direction in a wire. Volt-

---

1 As a convention of the block diagrams in this chapter, all inputs will enter from the left, all outputs will exit from the right, and all control inputs will enter from the bottom of each block.

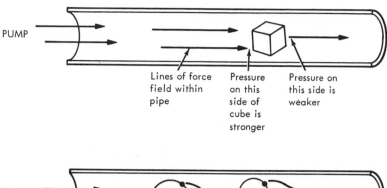

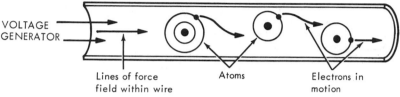

FIGURE 3.

age is measured in *volts*. Changes in voltage convey information. Voltages are categorized according to the way they change in strength and the way they change direction. There are four basic categories: (1) *AC voltages,* (2) *DC voltages,* (3) *time-variant voltages,* and (4) *random voltages.*

An *AC voltage* changes direction through a circuit periodically. One direction is graphed in positive values and the other direction is graphed in negative values (Fig. 4A). The zero-volt line is the instant of direction change. A graph in which changes in voltage are plotted vertically and time is plotted horizontally is called a *waveform. AC* waveforms are usually described in terms of *shape, frequency,* and *amplitude.* There are several standard shapes, which will be discussed later. *Frequency* is the rate of recurrence of a cycle per unit time, and is measured in *hertz* (abbreviated Hz). One Hz equals one cycle per second. *Amplitude* can be measured in several different ways: (1) the word *amplitude* usually refers to an average voltage in *either* direction; (2) the *peak-to-peak amplitude* of a waveform is the distance between its maximum positive value and its maximum negative value; and (3) *instantaneous amplitude* is the distance from the waveform curve to the zero-volt line at any instant.

A *DC voltage* is unvarying and always occurs in one direction through a circuit. It is graphed as a constant value that is either positive or negative (Fig. 4B). Because DC voltages are by definition unvarying, they cannot, strictly speaking, be considered signal voltages because a signal contains information, and information is conveyed through voltage change. But a description of AC voltage variation does not account for all the ways in which voltage may vary. What do we call, for example, the voltage that varies as in Fig. 4C, and does

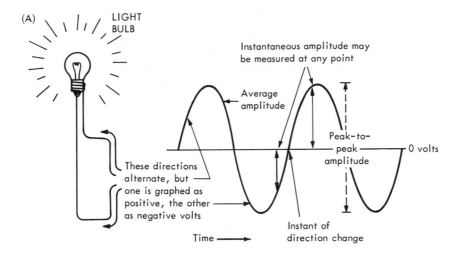

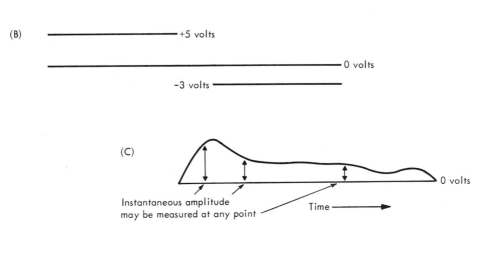

FIGURE 4.   (A) Graph of an AC waveform (sine wave). (B) Graph of a DC voltage. (C) Graph of a transient time-variant voltage. (D) Graph of a periodic time-variant voltage (sawtooth shape).

not change direction through a circuit? It cannot be called AC because it does not change direction, and it cannot be considered DC because it is not unvarying. It is sometimes referred to as "DC with an AC component," or "biased AC," or "changing DC." But for the sake of simplicity, let us designate as *time-variant voltages* (literally, voltages that vary in time) all voltages that vary but remain either positive or negative, with the understanding that this category includes nonperiodically changing voltages, as in Fig. 4C, as well as periodically changing voltages, as in Fig. 4D. A *random voltage* changes unpredictably in both directions and contains, by definition, no correlation between any one instant and any other instant.

Categorization of Signals

In a synthesizer, AC, DC, time-variant, and random voltages are generated by different modules and are used in the formation of signals. There are (1) *audio signals* and (2) *control signals,* so named because of the way they are used. A voltage applied to a loudspeaker and heard as sound is an *audio signal.* There are different types of control signals, the functions of which I shall illustrate in the following paragraphs by describing their use in controlling the intensity of a light bulb.

Using a rheostat, we can gradually alter the intensity of a light bulb. Rheostats are usually operated manually, but suppose we had a rheostat that would respond to a voltage instead of manual operation (Fig. 5A). The light intensity would then change in proportion to the voltage applied to the (voltage-controlled) rheostat, and that voltage could be called a light-intensity-control-signal or, more simply, a *control voltage* or *control signal.* Note that this type of control signal changes the light bulb's intensity continuously.

A switch turns a light on or off, and the light remains on as long as the switch is in the "on" position. The switch could be replaced by an electronic *gate,* which remains open, with the light bulb on, as long as a *gate voltage* remains positive (Fig. 5B).

Alternatively, the light might be controlled by a push-button switch, one that requires one push to turn it on and another to turn it off. In this case, it doesn't matter how long the switch is depressed since it performs its function instantaneously. This is the way a *trigger voltage* (Fig. 5C) functions. Note that the duration of a trigger voltage has no control function.

In terms of the synthesizer, these signals may be summarized as: (1) *audio signals,* which are applied to a loudspeaker, and which must be at audio frequencies to be heard; (2) *control signals,* which continuously control the activity of another module, and which may be *any* voltage except trigger voltages; and (3) control signals that are *trigger* or *gate* voltages, which may be used to turn a module *on* or *off,* to *start* or *stop* a module's operation, or to *shift* from one position to another, and which may be voltage spikes, pulses, or switches.

The next question is: What are the generators and processors that produce signals with these functions?

MODULES NORMALLY ASSOCIATED WITH AUDIO SIGNALS

The generators that are usually associated with the audio signal path are *oscillators* and *random-voltage generators,* and the processors are *mixers, amplifiers, ring modulators,* and *filters.*

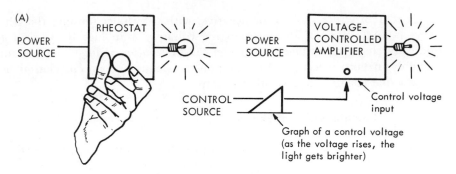

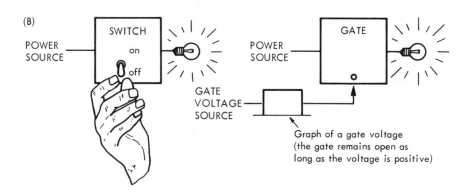

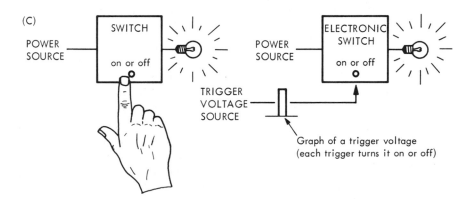

FIGURE 5.

Oscillators and Basic Waveforms

An *oscillator* is an AC waveform generator. Synthesizer oscillators are usually constructed to offer a range of frequencies that extends from between 20 Hz and about 1 cycle every 30 seconds (which are the sub-audio frequencies, useful

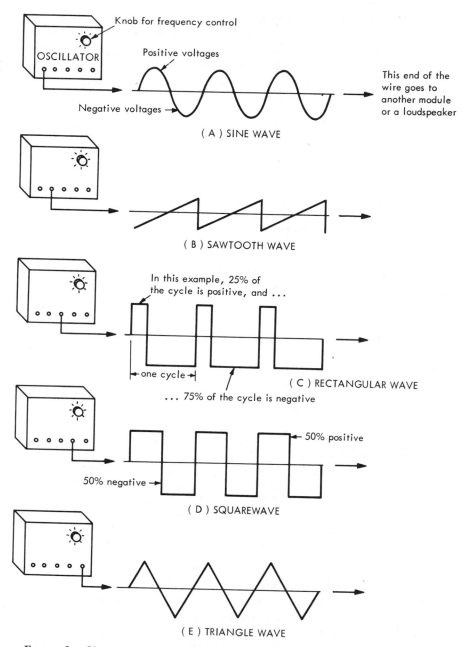

Knob for frequency control

OSCILLATOR

Positive voltages

Negative voltages

This end of the wire goes to another module or a loudspeaker

(A) SINE WAVE

(B) SAWTOOTH WAVE

In this example, 25% of the cycle is positive, and . . .

one cycle

. . . 75% of the cycle is negative

(C) RECTANGULAR WAVE

50% positive

50% negative

(D) SQUAREWAVE

(E) TRIANGLE WAVE

FIGURE 6.   Chart graphing oscillator's output voltage in standard waveforms.

as single impulses or control voltages) upward to about 20 kHz, the highest frequencies in the audio range. They usually offer *sine, sawtooth, rectangular, square* and/or *triangle waveforms* (Fig. 6), and in some models changes between waveforms are continuously variable and voltage-controllable.

A waveform, as a graph of voltage change in time, may be used as a *shape* per se. When applied to a loudspeaker cone, for example, the cone will move in and out as the voltage graph moves up and down. But any waveform may be analyzed, by Fourier analysis, as a sum of sine waves. The concept of a *spectrum* deals with the component sine waves, rather than their total. *Spectrum* may be defined as the frequencies and amplitudes of discrete sine waves and/or frequency bands as they comprise a total waveform. *Spectrum* and *waveform* are complementary ways of describing the same phenomenon.

According to Fourier analysis, *sine, sawtooth, rectangular, square,* and *triangle waveforms* are composed of the following specific spectra:

1. *Sine wave.* Cannot be further analyzed.
2. *Sawtooth wave.* Contains all harmonics in the harmonic series (sine waves that are integral multiples of a fundamental). The amplitude of each harmonic relative to the amplitude of the fundamental is the inverse of that harmonic's position in the series; for example, the amplitude of the second harmonic is one-half that of the fundamental.
3. *Rectangular wave.* Harmonic content is variable. The harmonics are in the same basic amplitude and frequency relationship as in the sawtooth spectrum, but certain harmonics are absent or attenuated, depending on the percentage of the cycle that is positive. If a cycle is 25% positive, every fourth harmonic will be missing (see Fig. 6C). If a cycle is 20% positive, every fifth harmonic will be missing.
4. *Square wave.* A rectangular wave that is 50% positive. Consequently, every second harmonic is missing, and the waveform contains only odd-numbered harmonics.
5. *Triangle wave.* Contains only odd-numbered harmonics, as does the square wave, but the amplitude of each harmonic relative to the amplitude of the fundamental is the square of the inverse of that harmonic's position in the series. For example, the third harmonic's amplitude is one-ninth that of the fundamental.

These spectra can be verified by adding sine waves (with graph paper) at the proper frequencies and relative amplitudes. If, for example, a sine wave at 100 Hz and at a certain amplitude is added to another sine wave at 200 Hz that is one-half the amplitude of the first sine wave, and to a third sine wave at 300 Hz that is one-third the amplitude of the first sine wave, etc., their sum will resemble a sawtooth waveform.

Mixers

Mixers add voltages. The output of a mixer is at every instant the sum of all the instantaneous amplitudes at its inputs. In this sense, mixing is analogous to *Fourier,* or *additive,* synthesis. If several sine waves are mixed, they will sum into one spectrum in the output from the mixer. Mixing complex signals is only an extension of that concept—all of their frequencies and amplitudes become a part of one complex spectrum, graphed as one total waveform, in the output from the mixer.

Frequency Modulation

Most of the oscillators found in synthesizers are *voltage-controlled.* A voltage-controlled module is one whose function may be controlled by an applied control voltage. The use of a control voltage to change the frequency of a voltage-controlled oscillator is called *frequency-modulation.* The output from the oscillator is the *modulated signal,* and the control voltage is the *modulating signal.* (Other terms are sometimes used: *carrier signal* instead of *modulated signal,* and *program signal* instead of *modulating signal.* It should be noted that there is no consistent terminology regarding modulation in electronic music; the terms *modulated signal* and *modulating signal* are used here because they describe the situation simply and clearly.)

Frequency modulation may have one of two results: (1) If the modulating signal is either a slow time-variant voltage or a sub-audio AC waveform, and the modulated signal is at an audio frequency, there is no perceptible timbre change in the modulated signal, which simply changes frequency in proportion to the instantaneous amplitude of the modulating signal (Fig. 7). If an AC modulating signal at a frequency of about 7 Hz is set to the minimal perceptible amplitude, it will produce a *vibrato* effect in the modulated signal. (2) If the modulating and modulated signals are at audio frequencies, the timbre of the modulated signal changes. Extra harmonics, called *sidebands,* apppear in the spectrum of the modulated signal. Sideband content is specifically determined by the frequency and amplitude relationship between the modulating and modulated signals and by their wave-shapes.

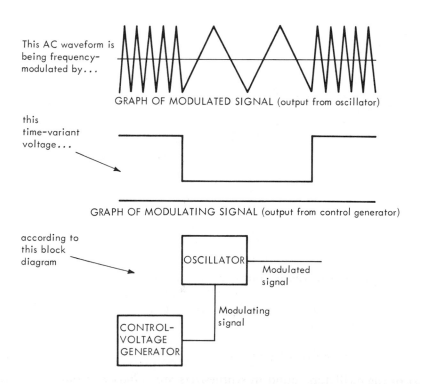

This AC waveform is being frequency-modulated by...

GRAPH OF MODULATED SIGNAL (output from oscillator)

this time-variant voltage...

GRAPH OF MODULATING SIGNAL (output from control generator)

according to this block diagram

OSCILLATOR

Modulated signal

Modulating signal

CONTROL-VOLTAGE GENERATOR

FIGURE 7.

Amplifiers, Amplitude and Balanced Modulation

Amplifiers increase voltage. The ratio of output amplitude to input amplitude is called *gain*. The use of a control voltage to vary the gain of a *voltage-controlled amplifier* is called *amplitude modulation*. The modulated signal is the signal that has been processed by the amplifier, and the modulating signal is the control voltage (Fig. 8A).

Amplitude modulation may have one of two results: (1) If the modulating signal is either a slow time-variant voltage or a sub-audio AC waveform, there is no perceptible timbre change in the modulated signal. The amplitude con-

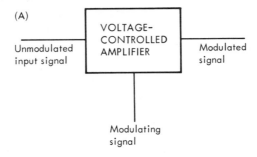

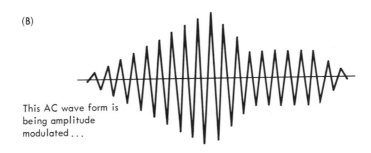

FIGURE 8.

tour of the modulated signal changes in proportion to the instantaneous amplitude of the modulating signal (Fig. 8B). If an AC-voltage modulating signal at a frequency of about 5 Hz is adjusted to the correct amplitude, it produces a *tremolo* effect in the modulated signal. (2) If the modulating signal is an audio frequency, the timbre of the modulated signal changes. Sidebands, which contain the sums and differences of all the frequency components of both inputs plus the inputs themselves, appear in the modulated spectrum.

Ring modulation is balanced amplitude modulation; that is, the modulating and modulated signals are interchangeable. Any two signals may modulate each other. The important difference between amplitude and ring modulation is that in the former at least one of the original signals is present along with the modulation sidebands, whereas in the latter both original signals are absent (which is to say, very much attenuated), leaving, for all practical purposes, just the modulation sidebands, which are the sums and differences of all the frequency components of both inputs. For this reason, ring modulation seems to abstract sounds, making them less recognizable, and it has become a standard technique for modifying non-electronic sounds. Some good examples of amplitude and ring-modulation techniques can be found in Karlheinz Stockhausen's *Telemusik* and *Hymnen*.

A *balanced modulator* functions as a ring modulator when both signals are audio frequencies, and as a voltage-controlled amplifier when the modulating signal is a time-variant voltage. A *frequency shifter,* or *single-sideband modulator,* functions as a ring modulator except that the output contains *either* the sums *or* the differences of all the frequency components of both inputs.

Random-voltage Generators

The output from a *random-voltage generator* is the least pitched and most complex spectrum available from the synthesizer. A random voltage is nonperiodic and unpredictable. Its spectrum, sine waves at infinitesimal amplitudes and at frequencies infinitely close to one another, may be called a *continuous spectrum*. The energy distribution within the spectrum may, however, be determined statistically. All frequencies in white noise, for example, have an equal probability of occurrence. There are two audio outputs from most random-voltage generators:

1. *White Noise.* Defined as equal sound energy per unit bandwidth. There will be equal sound energy between 100 and 200 Hz, for example, and between 1000 and 1100 Hz.
2. *Pink Noise.* Defined as equal sound energy per octave bandwidth. Since the ratio of frequencies for an octave is 2:1, there will be equal sound energy between 100 and 200 Hz, for example, and between 1000 and 2000 Hz.

Filters

A *filter* selectively attenuates frequencies in the spectrum of an input signal. There are usually two basic types of filters in synthesizers: (1) filters whose

(A)

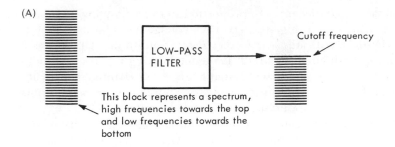

This block represents a spectrum, high frequencies towards the top and low frequencies towards the bottom

(B)

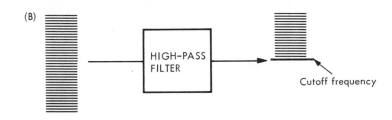

(C)

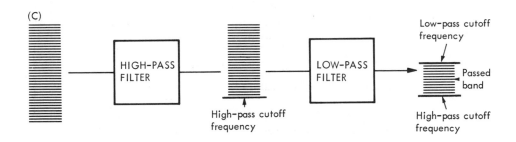

(D)

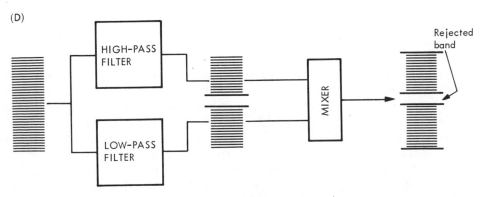

FIGURE 9.

cutoff frequency is variable and usually voltage-controlled, and (2) fixed-filter banks.

Of the variable cutoff frequency type, a *low-pass filter* attenuates frequencies *above* its cutoff frequency (Fig. 9A), and a *high-pass filter* attenuates frequencies *below* its cutoff frequency (Fig. 9B). If a low-pass and a high-pass filter are connected one after the other, their functions combine, and they become a *variable band-pass filter* (Fig. 9C). The *band,* which is the frequency range between the high-pass and low-pass cutoff frequencies, is described in terms of both its *center frequency,* which is the frequency in the center of the band, and its *bandwidth,* which is the difference between the two cutoff frequencies. If a signal is applied to both high-pass and low-pass filters simultaneously, and if they are set with their cutoff frequencies overlapping and their outputs directed through a mixer, a *band-reject* (also called *band-stop* or *notch*) *filter* (Fig. 9D) results.

Low-pass, high-pass and band-pass functions are combined in a *multimode filter,* which has one cutoff frequency control but separate outputs for each function (Fig. 10). Note that in the band-pass mode the bandwidth is not variable.

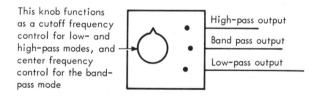

This knob functions as a cutoff frequency control for low- and high-pass modes, and center frequency control for the band-pass mode

High-pass output

Band pass output

Low-pass output

FIGURE 10.

A *fixed-filter bank* consists of several band-pass filters whose cutoff frequencies are not variable, but whose bandwidths are contiguous and collectively extend throughout the audio range. A signal is applied simultaneously to all the filters (Fig. 11), each of which passes only a narrow bandwidth. Each narrow band is then routed into an associated attenuator, so that certain bands may be eliminated from the output spectrum without affecting any of the others. The outputs from the attenuators are then mixed into a final, single output. Note that low-pass and high-pass filters alter a spectrum from above and below, while a fixed-filter bank alters it from within. If the design of a particular fixed-filter bank allows for separate outputs from each of the filters, the outputs may be passed through voltage-controlled amplifiers, rather than attenuators, before mixing, which allows for another type of automated filtering control.

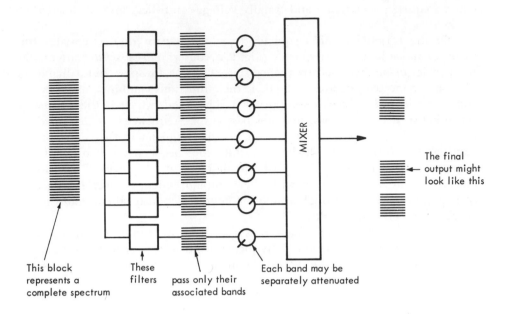

This block represents a complete spectrum

These filters

pass only their associated bands

Each band may be separately attenuated

MIXER

The final output might look like this

FIGURE 11.

A *voltage-controlled filter* is a filter whose cutoff frequency varies in proportion to the instantaneous amplitude of an applied control voltage (Fig. 12).

Processing Non-electronic Sounds

The standard technique for building sounds in a synthesizer is to combine simple signals, by mixing or modulation, into a certain complexity and then to *specify* those signals by subtracting from their spectra in a filter. This technique is known as *subtractive synthesis*. The use of non-electronic sounds, introduced into the system via a microphone, can be appealing because live sounds are usually complex before processing. Although the waveforms of live sounds can be used as frequency-modulating signals, it is a more usual procedure to process them by amplitude modulation of some kind, followed by filtering. If a sound is pitched, ring modulation can change its pitch as well as its timbre, and because the sound itself is absent from the output signal of the ring modulator, it can be made unrecognizable. Non-electronic sounds may be ring modulated, frequency shifted, amplitude modulated, combined with other sounds in a mixer, and/or filtered.

Categorization of Sounds[2]

To summarize, audio materials available from a synthesizer are: (1) waveforms, taken directly from oscillators, (2) frequency-, amplitude-, and/or ring-

[2] Based on a similar categorization done by Lejaren Hiller.

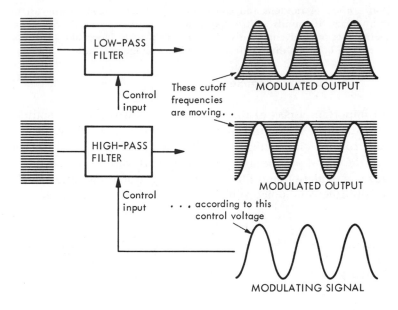

<figure><caption>Figure 12.</caption></figure>

modulated waveforms, (3) non-electronic sounds introduced, via a micro-phone, into the synthesizer for processing, (4) waveforms taken from dissimilar sources and mixed, and (5) random voltages. These signals and the sounds they produce may be categorized in a scale of spectrum types from most clearly pitched to least pitched, as follows:

1. *Harmonic spectrum.* Consists of sine waves at frequencies that are integral multiples of the lowest frequency present, which is called the "fundamental." The sounds of clearly pitched instruments—clarinets, violins, etc.—are harmonic spectra. The electronic equivalent is any of the waveforms directly available from an oscillator, which are completely periodic. For example, a properly filtered square wave can sound like a clarinet in the chalumeau register. A sawtooth wave can be made to sound like a violin.

2. *Inharmonic spectrum.* Consists of sine waves whose frequencies are not integral multiples of a fundamental and are consequently, by definition, in an in-harmonic relationship. Bells, cymbals, drums, etc. are examples of instrumental inharmonic spectra. Any frequency-, amplitude-, or ring-modulated waveforms can be inharmonic spectra. Within this category there is an immense variety of specific sounds.

3. *Ordinary noise.* A mixture of sound types consisting of some elements of a *defined* spectrum (of discrete sine waves), and some of a *continuous* spectrum (bands of sound energy), such as the sound of a car coming down the street. It could be a non-electronic sound processed with electronic sounds.

4. *Narrow-band noise.* An indefinitely pitched spectrum with a clear register placement, such as the whine of a jet engine or steam whistling out of a kettle. It can be produced by filtering white or pink noise.

5. *White noise.* A random and continuous spectrum encompassing all the audio frequencies. It sounds a little like a fountain or a waterfall. Sea sounds, with their lower-pitched energy distribution, are a little more like pink noise. This sound can be taken directly from a random-voltage generator.

Audio Signal Summary

The most important aspect of the audio signal path is that its modules define the points at which the sound may be changed. If, for example, an audio signal path consists of a voltage-controlled oscillator and a voltage-controlled filter, then the sound produced by that signal path can be varied only in terms of frequency modulation and filtering. Stated as questions (Fig. 13), the audio signal possibilities might be: Which signal source? White or pink noise? A

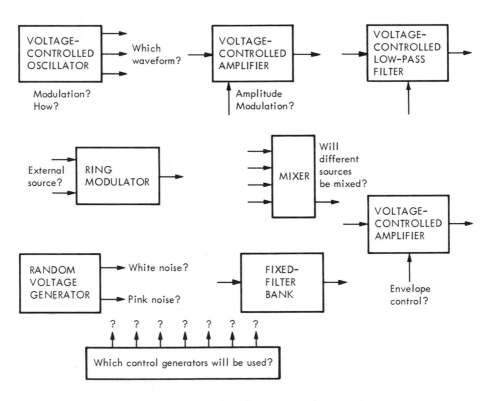

FIGURE 13.   Some possibilities for the audio signal path.

waveform from an oscillator? Which waveform? Modulated? How? Will different sources be mixed? Will non-electronic sounds be used? Which type of filtering is desired? Low-pass? High-pass? Band-pass? Band-reject? Fixed-filter bank? The logic of the arrangement of modules can be stated simply as follows:

Each step provides the material for the next operation, and each step along the signal path further specifies the signal. The settings of the modules determine their specific output and the range within which they operate in response to a control signal.

CONTROL-VOLTAGE GENERATORS

Any generator whose output can approach audio rates of change can be used with equal ease as an audio or control-voltage generator. Because of their normal wide frequency range, outputs from oscillators need no modification for either application. Random voltages are, however, somewhat special. Anything modulated with unfiltered audio-frequency noise will sound like noise. The aural effect is relatively unvarying because the ear averages the random changes. But filtered noise can be interesting as a frequency-modulating signal if the random changes are centered around the frequency band of, say, maracas. The point of filtering noise—eliminating the high-frequency components from the spectrum—is to slow down waveform changes to where they are easily perceptible. If a random voltage, intended for use as a control signal, is put through a low-pass filter so that only sub-audio frequencies remain, changes will be slowed down to the point where it is easy to differentiate between one point of the waveform and another. Some commercially available random-voltage generators have an extra output at which sub-audio random voltages are available for use as randomly changing control voltages.

If a waveform changes at audio rates, it can be used in either audio or control signals. If it changes at slower-than-audio rates, it is useful only as a control voltage. As mentioned earlier, in descriptions of frequency and amplitude modulation, audio frequency and sub-audio change rates produce different effects in the modulated signal. We can differentiate between two time scales at which changes occur: (1) the "audio-time scale," where each cycle of the modulated waveform is changed differently, and (2) the "conscious-time scale," where changes occur over a number of cycles and, thus, can be consciously perceived and remembered. Audio-time-scale changes, which occur usually in the millisecond range, can give sounds an interest, a liveliness. Conscious-time-scale changes, which generally occur over a period of seconds or minutes, are associated with changes in envelope, pitch, timbre, loudness, continuity, etc.

There are several types of time-variant voltage generators, standard with synthesizers, that are designed to be exclusively used in generating control signals in the conscious-time-scale range. Each of these generators is differently designed, but each may be characterized in terms of (1) *method of operation,* which can be (a) performance, (b) automation, or (c) automation-by-sensing; (2) *waveform change-type,* which can be (a) cyclic, (b) transient, or nonperiodic, or (c) random; and (3) *output wave-shape,* which may be (a) discrete levels, (b) curves, or (c) slopes.

Oscillators operate automatically, their output change-type is cyclic, and their output waveshape depends upon the waveform selected. Random-voltage generators operate automatically, their output change-type is random, and their output wave-shape is in curves.

Function Descriptions

A *transient* pattern is one that occurs once when triggered, and that must be triggered again to recur. The *transient generator* is often called an *envelope generator* because it is so often used in amplitude modulation, and it is primarily for that purpose that its pattern of voltages is designed. It works like this (Fig. 14): (1) when the module is turned on by a switch or a gate voltage, its output rises from zero volts to a fixed maximum level in a certain time, which is preset by the user; (2) the output then automatically falls from that maximum voltage in a certain time, which can be preset, (3) to a level at which the sustaining control is preset, and remains at that level until the module is (4) turned off, at which point the output voltage falls from the sustaining level back to zero. The time durations of the initial rise, initial fall, and final fall, and the level of the sustaining are all preset by adjusting four different knobs; during operation, they sequence from one to the other automatically. That method of operation may be considered automation by presetting, with the triggering manually performed or automated. The output waveshape consists of a slope, curves, and a discrete level. The waveform change-type is transient.

A *Schmitt Trigger Circuit* senses an input voltage, and when that voltage rises above a certain preset threshold, the circuit generates a gate voltage, the duration of which is determined by how long the input remains above the threshold (Fig. 15). If the input is periodic, the gate voltage occurs at periodic intervals. If the input is random, the gate voltage occurs at random intervals and is of random durations. A transient generator can be triggered automatically by the output of a Schmitt trigger circuit (or, for that matter, by pulses from an oscillator or by any other gate-voltage generator).

The *envelope follower* traces the envelope of an input AC or random

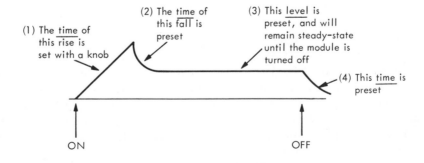

FIGURE 14.

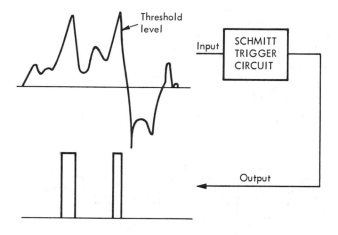

Figure 15.

signal, and converts that trace to a proportionally changing time-variant voltage. Its operation is automatic-by-sensing, its output wave-shape is usually curves, and its output change-type depends on the nature of the input signal.

The *sample-and-hold generator* senses an input signal, and at a trigger signal, it outputs a steady-state voltage that is of the same value as the input voltage at the instant of triggering. It holds that steady-state voltage until it is re-triggered. If the input is a triangle wave and if the trigger is periodic and at the right relative frequency, the output from the generator can be a staircase waveform (Fig. 16A). If the input is random and the trigger periodic, the output is a voltage that changes periodically to an unpredictable level (Fig. 16B). If the trigger is the output from a Schmitt trigger circuit that is sensing a random waveform, and if the input to the sample-and-hold generator is a random waveform, the output from the sample-and-hold generator is discrete but random levels that change at unpredictable time intervals. The sample-and-hold generator senses automatically, but it may be triggered automatically or manually. Its output-voltage wave-shape is in discrete levels, and its output change-type depends on what is being sampled.

A *ribbon controller* generates a voltage proportional to the position along a length of ribbon that is touched (Fig. 17). It is operated by performance. The output wave-shape and output change-type are determined by the performer.

A *keyboard controller* can be conceptualized as a ribbon controller that is divided into discrete steps, but some keyboards can generate more than one voltage simultaneously, and some are sensitive to velocity of key depression and to pressure. Many keyboards are designed so that they generate gate-voltage outputs synchronously with the depression of each key. *Touch-sensitive keyboards* have strips that are touched instead of keys that are depressed. Keyboards are performed and their output waveshape is discrete levels, the change-

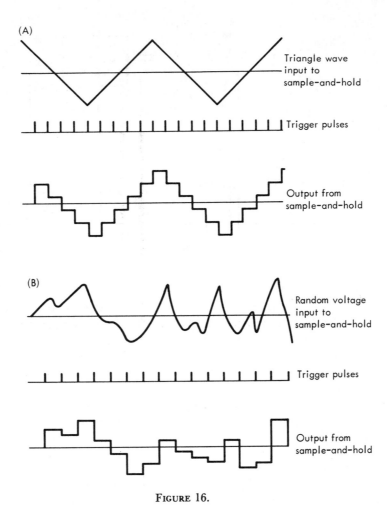

(A)

Triangle wave input to sample-and-hold

Trigger pulses

Output from sample-and-hold

(B)

Random voltage input to sample-and-hold

Trigger pulses

Output from sample-and-hold

FIGURE 16.

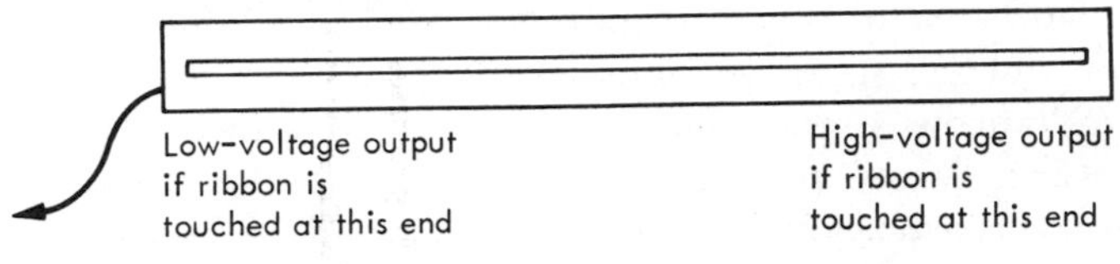

Low-voltage output if ribbon is touched at this end

High-voltage output if ribbon is touched at this end

FIGURE 17.

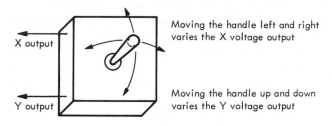

X output

Moving the handle left and right
varies the X voltage output

Y output

Moving the handle up and down
varies the Y voltage output

FIGURE 18.

type of which is determined by the performer. Some keyboards allow for these discrete levels to be smoothed out into glides between voltage levels. Because they so resemble traditional instruments, keyboards are often used to control pitch, but the output from a keyboard, like any voltage, may be used to control any voltage-controllable function.

An *X-Y controller,* or *joystick,* generates two voltages simultaneously. One voltage is determined by position of the lever on the *x*-axis, and the other voltage is determined by the lever's position on the *y*-axis (Fig. 18). Curves and slopes are far easier to perform than discrete levels.

A *sequencer* (Fig. 19) is a chain of single-stage voltage generators, each

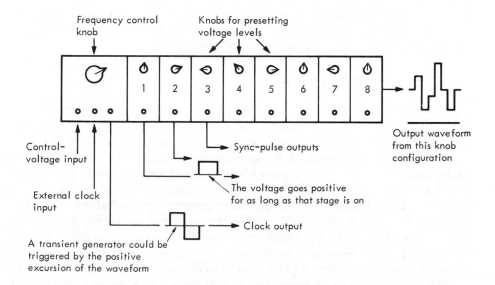

Frequency control
knob

Knobs for presetting
voltage levels

1 2 3 4 5 6 7 8

Control-
voltage input

External clock
input

A transient generator could be
triggered by the positive
excursion of the waveform

Sync-pulse outputs

The voltage goes positive
for as long as that stage is on

Clock output

Output waveform
from this knob
configuration

FIGURE 19.

of which generates one or more steady-state voltages, the levels of which are determined by presetting knobs. These stages are turned on and off in sequence. The stepping along from stage to stage is usually accomplished by a built-in *clock,* a trigger-pulse oscillator. At each trigger impulse, the previous stage is turned off and the next one on. The speed of the sequence depends upon the frequency of the pulse oscillator, which itself is usually voltage-controlled. Sequencers can be synchronized with other modules if they are designed with an external clock input (which bypasses the internal clock), a clock-pulse output, and sync-pulse outputs from each stage.

The voltage levels of the sequencer are preset, but then sequence automatically. Triggering is usually automatic. The output wave-shape is discrete levels. If the sequence is set to run through a series of voltages and then turn off, the output change-type is transient. If the sequencer cycles, the output is cyclic. Some sequencers are designed so that the stages may be actuated in any order, and in that case the change-type is performed in the sense that a group of preset discrete voltage levels is ordered.

Summary

The performance generators normally associated with synthesizers are ribbon controllers, keyboards, and joysticks. Generators that operate automatically are transient generators, sequencers, oscillators, and random-voltage generators. Generators that operate automatically-by-sensing are envelope followers, Schmitt trigger circuits, and sample-and-hold generators. There are several other generators that are available but not usually found in commercial synthesizer packages, such as *photocells,* which conduct current in proportion to light intensity; *footpedals,* which generate a voltage proportional to foot position; *paper-tape readers,* which sense pre-punched holes in paper tape; and *frequency-to-voltage converters,* which generate a time-variant voltage proportional to the frequency of an input AC voltage.

CONTROL SYSTEMS

The most important characteristic of synthesizers as systems is that complexity is generated by processing simple signals. Control voltages, like audio voltages, may be processed to produce more complex and interesting shapes than are available from any one module. Some examples of mixing control voltages are illustrated in Fig. 20: (A) the output from a keyboard is mixed with a slow sine wave; (B) several sub-audio square waves from different oscillators, at slightly different frequencies and amplitudes, are mixed, producing a far more complex shape than the simple two levels of a single square wave; and (C) two sawtooth waves are mixed together to simulate a staircase wave-form. Note that two of these resultant wave-shapes could be generated by a sequencer, sample-and-hold generator, keyboard, or ribbon controller.

Several control signals constitute a control system. A control system that

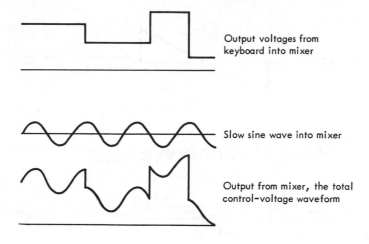

Output voltages from keyboard into mixer

Slow sine wave into mixer

Output from mixer, the total control-voltage waveform

FIGURE 20A

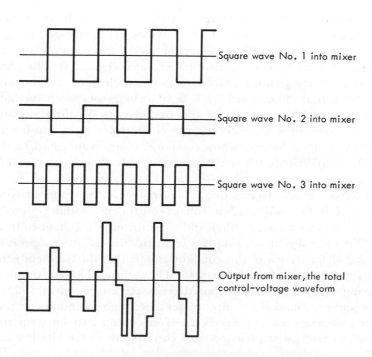

Square wave No. 1 into mixer

Square wave No. 2 into mixer

Square wave No. 3 into mixer

Output from mixer, the total control-voltage waveform

FIGURE 20B

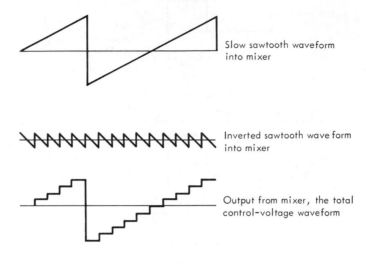

Slow sawtooth waveform
into mixer

Inverted sawtooth wave form
into mixer

Output from mixer, the total
control-voltage waveform

FIGURE 20C

directly affects some aspect of the audio signal path is a first-level control system.

In addition to mixing, however, control signals may be frequency and/or amplitude modulated. Consider these examples. (1) A voltage-controlled oscillator is modulated by another voltage-controlled oscillator, which in turn is modulated by a third voltage-controlled oscillator (Fig. 21A). The effect is that the frequency of the frequency-modulating signal changes. (2) The modulating signal is amplitude modulated by a third voltage-controlled oscillator, with the result that the amplitude of the frequency-modulating signal changes (Fig. 21B). Controllers that affect first-level control systems constitute *second-level control systems*. Systems whose component signals are coordinated in time are *synchronous*. Systems whose component signals are not coordinated in time are *asynchronous*.

Fig. 22 is a block diagram of a basic single-level synchronous system. The audio signal is the output of a voltage-controlled oscillator processed first through a voltage-controlled filter and then through a voltage-controlled amplifier. The control system is simply a keyboard and a transient generator. The identifying characteristic of this configuration is that the transient generator is triggered every time a key is depressed. These things happen simultaneously: (1) a change in pitch as the keyboard generates a new voltage; (2) a sudden brightness to the sound as the filter passes more high harmonics, as the voltage from the transient generator moves the filter's cutoff frequency up and down; and (3) an envelope with an attack that corresponds to the filtering contour.

The system can be made more complex by mixing an audio frequency and/or vibrato frequency with the keyboard voltage; and/or by using several

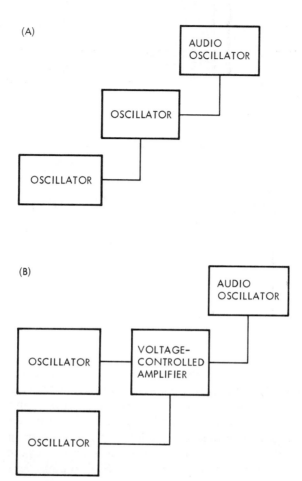

(A)

(B)

FIGURE 21.

voltage-controlled oscillators, mixed, as the audio generators; and/or by ring modulating the audio signal before it goes into the filter—using a sine wave as the other input to the ring modulator—and/or by any number of other changes, additions to, or substitutions of one control module for another. The system is defined not by the particular modules used, but by the coordination of controls. Changes occur together. It is an instrument-imitation system because the filter is always controlled by the same signal that modulates amplitude. In instrumental sounds there is always a proportional relationship between harmonic content and loudness. As an instrumental sound gets louder, it contains more high harmonics; the coordinated use of a low-pass filter and voltage-controlled amplifier simulate this relationship. Within the range of

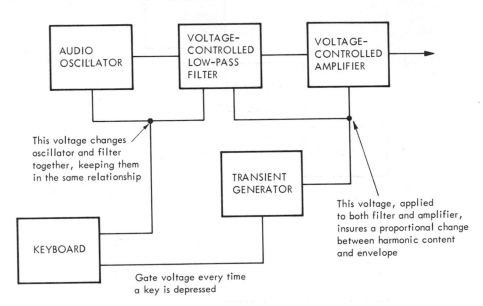

This voltage changes oscillator and filter together, keeping them in the same relationship

This voltage, applied to both filter and amplifier, insures a proportional change between harmonic content and envelope

Gate voltage every time a key is depressed

FIGURE 22.

that type of system, however, an immense variety of different specific sounds is possible. Walter Carlos's *Switched-On Bach* is an excellent example of instrument simulation with a synthesizer. If a performer wishes to imitate a particular instrumental sound, he must hear it clearly in ways that are transferable to the techniques of the equipment. He might listen for spectrum type (clearly pitched? inharmonic?), spectrum distribution (a gong or large bell has more high harmonic components than a bass drum, for example), and envelope contour (fast attack? slow? slow decay?).

Fig. 23 is a block diagram of a complex multi-level asynchronous control system. A voice is one input into a ring modulator. The other input comes from a voltage-controlled oscillator that is controlled by the output from a sample-and-hold generator that is sensing a random voltage and is triggered by a Schmitt trigger circuit that is sensing the output from an envelope follower that is sensing a tape recording of a Chopin nocturne. The oscillator changes frequency to unpredictable levels at time intervals proportional to the loudness of the nocturne. The high-pass filter is controlled by an inverted version of the same sub-audio sine wave that controls the low-pass filter. That sine wave is frequency modulated by another oscillator and amplitude modulated by a sequencer, so that the bandwidth of the variable band-pass filter connection is continuously varying. The audio signal is connected to two output amplifiers, each of which is controlled by one output from a joystick controller, so that spatial distribution between two output channels is performed.

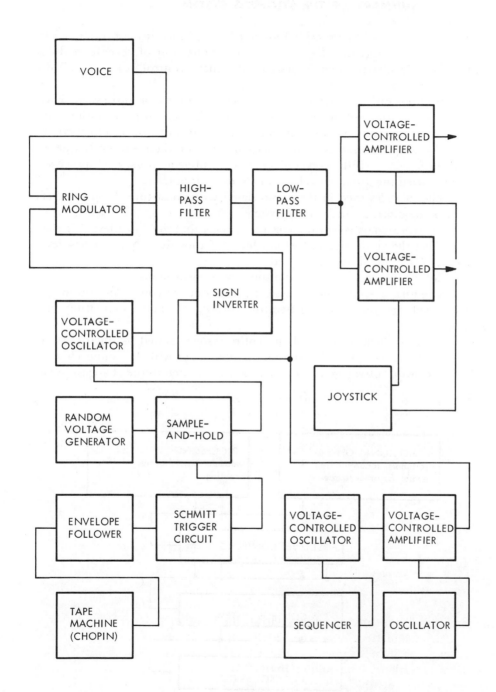

FIGURE 23.

SUMMARY OF THE SYNTHESIS SYSTEM

(1) Each module has a specific function. These functions are combined to specify a resultant signal. The coherent interconnection of several modules constitutes a signal path that is designated either "control" or "audio," depending on its use.

(2) Modules can be categorized as either generators or processors. Each generator is characterized by an output wave-shape, method of operation, and output change-type. Some generators are designed to function as either audio or control-voltage generators, and others—because of their slower frequency (or rate-of-change) capability—exclusively as control generators. Each processor has a specialized function, whereby it modifies an input.

(3) The modules used in the audio signal path constitute the parameters that can be modified by the control system.

(4) Control signals constitute control systems that are "first-level" if they directly affect the audio signal, "second level" if they directly affect first-level control signals, "third level" . . . , etc.

(5) Control systems can be synchronous or asynchronous.

(6) The final output from the system is the result of combining audio and control waveforms by various generating, processing, and modulating procedures.

Fig. 24 is a block diagram of the entire system. Stated as questions: (1) What will be the basic sound material? In what ways will the sound change? (2) Which control-voltage generators will be used to determine changes? What

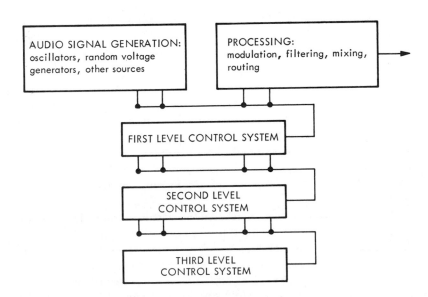

FIGURE 24.

wave-shape? What output change-type? Which changes will be automated, and which performed? (3) Which parts of the system will be synchronous, and which asynchronous?

COMMENTARY

The Mark II Electronic Music Synthesizer, designed by Harry Olsen and Herbert Belar at RCA in the '50s, was the first comprehensive electronic music system designed to produce *any* sound. Like voltage-controlled synthesizers, which it foreshadowed, it is a system based on the concept that each sound comprises several parameters (frequency, amplitude, spectrum, envelope) that are independently controllable in real time, each by a specialized electronic function. Simply stated, frequency is determined by oscillators; amplitude and envelope by amplifiers; and spectrum by filters. The idea of a sound specified in terms of separable parameters is also the point of a non-electronic musical theory, *serialism*. Milton Babbitt, in his *Three Compositions for Piano* (1947), applied pre-compositionally thought-out schemata to the organization of pitches, durations, attacks, dynamics, and other parameters, as independent variables. It is as if science and aesthetics were on parallel though independent courses. Even the control device of the RCA Mark II Electronic Music Synthesizer was easily used in conjunction with serial techniques. It was punched-paper tape—a sound must be specified before it is heard. The Columbia-Princeton Electronic Music Center eventually acquired the Mark II, and Babbitt, one of the directors of the Center, had a vehicle with which to apply serial theories to electronic music. Babbitt's *Ensembles for Synthesizer* (1964) is an excellent example of those techniques. Another is Charles Wuorinen's *Time's Encomium,* which was initially composed with the Mark II and then modified with a voltage-controlled synthesizer.

The development of the first voltage-controlled synthesizers by Robert Moog in New York, Donald Buchla in California, and Paul Ketoff in Rome was made possible by the easy availability of semiconductors and an industry-wide shift to a transistor technology in the early '60s. It was a significant step forward for musical engineering. The voltage-controlled synthesizer is a flexible and expandable system. Its modular functions may be arranged to any efficiency, and (most important) control systems are interchangeable. When it is used for performance, the performer need only choose his gesture and find the control-voltage generator that will convert that gesture to a voltage. For programming, anything from sequencers to punched-paper tape to computers is available and possible.

With systems that are marketed as separate modules, the buyer may choose and shape his own system, but manufacturers have themselves designed different integrated and sometimes rather specialized units, such as the *Electric Music Box, Mini-Moog, Sonic VI, ARP Pro Soloist, Odyssey, Electrocomp 200, EML–101,* and *Synthi AKS,* all of which have different features. To the extent that a system is structured and specialized, it is easy and efficient to operate but limited in flexibility. To the extent that it is unstructured and nonspecialized, it is unlimited in flexibility but slower and less efficient to operate.

One notable and early example of a small, compact, yet relatively non-specialized synthesizer is the *Synket,* designed by Paul Ketoff in 1964. John Eaton, a composer and performer who had been familiar with the Synket since its conception, immediately saw the possibilities in small synthesizers as performance instruments, and has been concertizing with the Synket since the first performance of his *Songs for R.P.B.* at the American Academy in Rome in 1965—the first time a synthesizer was used as a concert instrument. Since then, Eaton's compositions, particularly *Concert Piece for Synket and Orchestra, Thoughts on Rilke,* and *Blind Man's Cry,* have used the synthesizer in ensemble with traditional instruments, voices, and/or other synthesizers.

Whether one is performing in a concert hall or conducting a real-time operation in a studio, a variety of different gestures, such as changing patch cords, resetting switches, adjusting knobs, operating footpedals and keyboards, is required. The question is which aspect of which signal is to be performed. The operation of a first-level control system is analogous to the playing of traditional musical instruments. A preset timbre (analogous to the choice of instrument) is played in terms of pitch, loudness, and timing. However, a more complex and less traditional approach is possible. The first-level controls may be automated with sequencers, sample-and-hold generators, or other devices, and a second-level control system may be operated. By using the synthesizer as a semi-automated system, more changes may occur simultaneously. It is perhaps that capability—automating things to change independently and simultaneously—that most differentiates synthesizer operation techniques from traditional instrumental performances. Morton Subotnick's compositions, *Touch, The Wild Bull, Silver Apples of the Moon,* and *Sidewinder,* are all excellent examples of complex real-time system operation, with their multiplicity of activity and simultaneous but differently changing sounds. Since, as a general rule, automation is necessary to achieve real-time complexity, recent design developments applicable to synthesizers have been directed toward efficiency and flexibility in control systems.

The CEMS (Coordinated Electronic Music Studio) System is an example of a voltage-controlled system that extends automation capability to the point where an entire composition can be automated (not excluding, however, performance). Designed by the author and Robert Moog, it was installed at the Electronic Music Studio at the State University of New York at Albany in 1969. The CEMS System consists of three interrelated sub-systems: (1) audio generation and processing—a normal grouping of voltage-controlled oscillators, filters, amplifiers, mixers, and accessories; (2) continuous control-voltage generation from a bank of eight sequencers that are interconnected so that they may run synchronously, asynchronously, or in succession; and (3) a timing system consisting of a clock and decoders that read the clock and generate gate voltages or trigger pulses at preset clock readings. The first use of the system was to generate structures similar to tape music by putting several sounds in a predetermined, timed sequence *before* they were recorded on tape. Secondly, synchronous and asynchronous control signals were used to continuously modify various aspects of a complex audio system. My *Ideas of Movement at Bolton Landing* is the result of a synchronous control system, some aspects of which are performed. The third development with this system was to generate both audio and control waveforms with the sequencers, which led to a systems concept somewhat different from that of conventional synthesizers.

There are several basic operations in a system of sequencers, applicable to as few as two sequencers: (1) synchronous permutation (Fig. 25A), (2) scaling (Fig. 25B), (3) cascading (Fig. 25C), and (4) asynchronous operation. The waveforms that are put out from the sequencers can be used as independent voltages, applied to different control inputs, or mixed to create more complex and longer waveforms than are available from any one sequencer. They can be offset to fluctuate around zero volts by mixing them with a negative DC

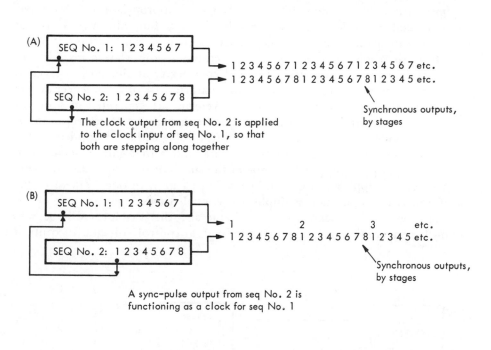

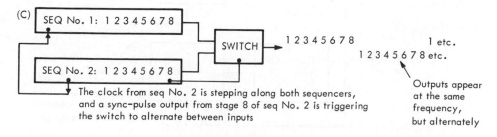

FIGURE 25.

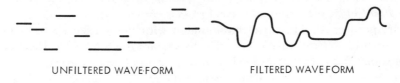

UNFILTERED WAVE-FORM   FILTERED WAVEFORM

FIGURE 26.

voltage. They can be filtered. A low-pass filter used to smooth out sharp rises and falls between discrete waveform levels is called a "smoothing filter" (Fig. 26). Filters are designed that can function in sub-audio as well as audio ranges, so that—with a filter whose frequency range is appropriate—control waveforms as well as audio waveforms can be filtered. But, although it is not always true of specific manufactured models, sequences can function at audio as well as sub-audio frequencies, and generating audio waveforms with sequencers allows for greater flexibility and complexity at the initial stages of waveform generation. The most important characteristic of a sequencer system is, however, that at whatever frequency, waveforms are generated in segments and, thus, are dynamically variable. Sequencer-generated waveforms can be amplitude modulated (Fig. 27). If the control voltage that is applied to the modulating amplifier is passed through a gate, and if that gate is opened and closed by a sync-pulse output from one of the stages of the sequencer, the control voltage will appear at the amplifier only in sync with one segment of the waveform. If that operation is duplicated enough times, each segment of the waveform will be independently controllable and the waveform will be continuously changeable according to the individual control voltages. In contrast

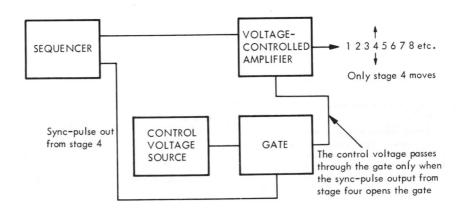

FIGURE 27.

with *additive synthesis,* which is the addition of sine waves to a total spectrum, and *subtractive synthesis,* which is the generation of the basic material that is specified in a filter, this technique is called *waveform synthesis.*

Since there is now a trend toward digital control systems, a rudimentary explanation of differences between *analog* and *digital* electronics may help clarify the principles of digital control, as well as place the synthesizer in context.

Analog electronic devices produce a voltage quantity that may be *measured.* A quantity of three volts, for example, is measured as an instantaneous amplitude of three volts. That principle is exemplified in a thermometer, which may be considered an analog measuring instrument, though not electronic. A sine-wave oscillator is an analog waveform generator that continuously produces a varying voltage in the shape of a sine wave. That voltage, changing in time in that shape, is the specialized and unique output from that circuit, and is always available on demand from that circuit. In comparison with digital circuits, analog circuits are efficient and specialized.

Digital electronic devices are constructed of switches that are either open or closed and that may be *counted.* A quantity of three volts, for example, is counted as a certain number of closed switches. These switches, called *bits,* are arranged in rows called *registers.* Registers are themselves arranged in rows, and their information can be read out in a sequential (or, in many cases, any) order. The stepping along from register to register is controlled by a clock. The information contained in the registers in the form of closed and/or open switches is converted to a voltage level, which is analog, by a *digital-to-analog converter.* When a series of registers are read out into the converter in sequence, the output from the converter is a corresponding series of voltage levels (Fig. 28). If a sine wave is to be digitally generated, it must be thought of as a series of instantaneous amplitude points, each of which is stored as a certain number of closed or open switches in a register and then converted to a corresponding voltage level. The digital generation of a sine wave is inefficient in comparison with the simplicity of taking the output from an analog sine-wave generator; but the sine-wave generator produces *only* the sine wave,

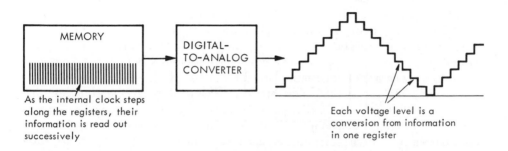

As the internal clock steps along the registers, their information is read out successively

Each voltage level is a conversion from information in one register

FIGURE 28.

whereas a digital circuit can produce *any* waveform. In comparison with most analog circuits, most digital circuits are inefficient and nonspecialized.

The principle of a series of locations from which information is read out in sequence applies to both analog sequencers and digital memories, both of which generate waveforms in segments. The primary difference between analog sequencers and digital memories is in precision of specification—as against precision of output. The audio output from a digital system is analog and, as such, is as subject to imprecision as any analog system. But information may be read into digital systems as a series of numbers, and information is "read into" analog sequencers by turning knobs. A series of numbers is inherently more precise than a series of knob settings. For the composer, the difference is a question: How does the composer want to specify compositional information?

It is a characteristic of many digital devices that information can be read in through an intermediate symbology, such as punched-paper tape or punched cards. That procedure offers the considerable advantage of providing a ready-made "score" for the composition that can be stored independent of the music. Although Emmanuel Ghent used a punched-paper tape to control a synthesizer in one of his compositions, and although the RCA Mark II Electronic Music Synthesizer, which is analog, is controlled by means of a punched-paper tape, the technique of specification through an intermediate symbology is not usual with analog equipment. Analog equipment generally offers the possibility of real-time adjustment of controls while a composition is in course.

In summary: Digital devices are more flexible than analog devices, but less efficient. Digital procedures offer the composer the opportunity to precisely specify compositional information as numbers; analog procedures offer the composer the opportunity not to specify compositional information in numbers. Digital procedures offer the possibility of an intermediate information symbology that may serve as a "score," while analog procedures offer real-time access to controls. (Although this comparison of advantages is useful, it is not, however, invariably true of every device. In certain applications, digital techniques may be more efficient than analog, and there are many unique digital or analog devices that must be considered in light of their own particular qualities.) Systems that combine digital and analog electronics are called *hybrid* systems.

Hardware aside, the most important differentiating factor among automated control systems is whether they are *memory-automation* or *process-automation* systems. The term *memory-automation* means that an automation system is used to realize what a composer has previously detailed. A composer writes a piece in a more or less traditional manner, reads the information into the system, and the system "performs," or executes, what the composer has specified. It is a use of automation as a tool to a specific end, akin to using a computer to address envelopes, or using a machine to build cars. Memory-automation is necessary because the machine is more efficient or has a greater work capability. A computer can perform a waveform in audio-time, differentiating levels far faster than a performer can play them on a keyboard.

The *Synthi Digital Sequencer 256* is an excellent example of a digital memory-automation control-voltage generator. Information can be read into a series of 256 registers by performing a keyboard (which generates two voltages —one proportional to the key pressed, the other to the pressure exerted) through an *analog-to-digital converter,* which sets the registers. At command, the information that has been stored in the registers is read out through a *digital-to-analog converter.* This process may be repeated for several channels. At command, different channels may be played back simultaneously, and the playback may be made faster or slower than the original by simply speeding up or slowing down the rate at which the registers are read out. Since each instantaneous amplitude point is stored in a separate register, one point may be changed ("edited") without affecting any others, simply by selecting that particular register and reading another voltage into it. There are many interesting features to the device that allow for synchronous and asynchronous outputs from different channels. Note that the device is designed to be most efficient for memory-automation because it stores detailed information, decided by the composer, to be played back at a later time.

The term *process-automation* refers to a technique whereby the composer decides the "rules of the game" (which define the nature of the process), and an automation system supplies information that will—as a consequence of the rules of the game—determine the details of the composition. Two different examples of process-automation may illustrate the idea. (1) A synthesizer that is automated by control voltages coming from different sensors that are sensing humidity, movement of people, smoke in the air, volume of conversation, etc., is set up in an art gallery. The details of the music are to be determined by various atmospheric conditions, which are statistically, rather than precisely, determinate in detail. The composer has decided the nature of the process, the specific types of devices used, and the parameters of the audio path that will be modulated. (2) A computer has been programmed to generate continuously a series of random voltages that are used to control various parameters of an audio signal. The composer has decided the details of the audio signal, the parameters to be modulated, the range within which the modulations are to function, and, of course, the nature of the control system itself.

The concept of process-automation may seem difficult to accept because of its implication that a composer gives up control of detailed musical decisions. But in fact, the real difference between the two approaches (the composer precisely specifies vs. the composer specifies the process, which generates details) is the difference between detailed determinacy and statistical determinacy. Statistical prediction, in both random and nonrandom processes, determines the probability with which any event (or voltage level, or voltage change) in a group of events will occur. Much of John Cage's music is process-automated, but it should be noted that Cage always chooses the material of the composition and the group of events from which a random selection is made. The *I Ching,* functioning as the process, was used to automate the composition of *Birdcage* in the Albany studio in April, 1972. Cage had previously recorded material on several tapes, and the *I Ching* was used to determine the durations and arrangements of selections from these tapes and their modulations.

In terms of musical structure, process-automated forms are not built on relationships between adjacencies, as are all other musical forms, which are linear. Tonality, for example, produces linear forms because a chord is part of a progression defined by the preceding and subsequent chords. Juxtaposition form (the basis of most tape music), where one sound is placed after or mixed with another sound, is a linear form because the effect of each event depends upon its immediate surroundings. In Stockhausen's *Telemusik,* sounds are juxtaposed according to a criteria of complementarity—short sounds are juxtaposed with long sounds, high sounds with low sounds, periodically changing sounds with nonperiodically changing sounds, etc. But if one throws dice, does any number have a direct relationship to the preceding number? In process-automation forms, each event occurs because it is generated by the rules of the process, and not because of its relationship to an adjacent event.

An unusual example of a process-automation generator is a device called *Daisy,* a voltage and trigger-pulse generator built by John Roy in collaboration with the author. Daisy generates information (rather than recording, remembering, and playing back) by the use of two pseudo-random sequencers. A *pseudo-random sequencer* is a type of shift register where the information in each bit is transferred sequentially to the next bit (something like a bucket brigade), but where one or more bits are changed as the result of a complex logic, thus making it difficult to predict exactly what state the bits will be in at any instant. The sixty-four bits of each sequencer are divided into sixteen groups of four bits each. Since four bits can have a total of sixteen aggregate configurations (Fig. 29), each group of four bits can generate sixteen numbers, each of which is convertible into voltage levels or time intervals.

0000   0001   0010   0011   0100   0101   0110   0111   1000   1001   1010
1011   1100   1101   1110   1111

FIGURE 29.

As indicated in Fig. 30, a clock is stepping along both pseudo-random sequencers. At the instant of sampling, the information in each of the four-bit groups in pseudo-random sequencer #1 is converted into analog voltage levels in the digital-to-analog converter. At the same instant, the information in each of the four-bit groups in pseudo-random sequencer #2 determines the time interval at which the programmable counter will generate a trigger pulse for each output channel. This trigger pulse is also routed as a possibility for triggering the digital-to-analog converter to sample pseudorandom sequencer #1, which would result in one of sixteen randomly selected voltage levels changing at random time intervals. The programmable counter is triggered by the output from the time-base, which consists of periodic pulses at frequencies slower than the clock. If the output from the timebase were used to trigger the digital-to-analog converter, the result would be random voltage levels changing at periodic time intervals. Though there are additional features to this device, the basic outputs are sixteen channels of trigger pulses

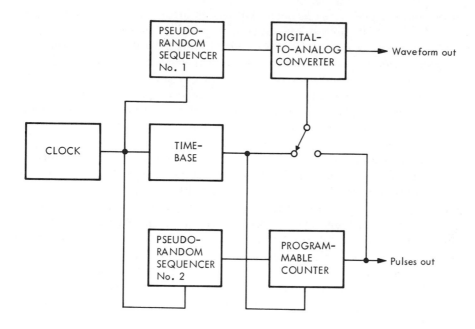

that occur at random time intervals, and sixteen channels of voltage levels, each channel a random selection of one of sixteen voltages that change at either periodic or random time intervals. The voltage levels may be made to occur within any range between zero and ten volts.

Daisy is a control-voltage generator in that its outputs do not approach audio rates of change. But Salvatore Martirano has designed and built, in collaboration with several engineers at the University of Illinois, the *Sal-Mar Construction,* a unique and complete hybrid process-automation synthesis system that approaches the complexity of a computer. Information is generated, stored, continually reassembled into groups of different lengths, and routed to a vast range of constantly changing audio parameters, which include a complex spatial distribution system. The Sal-Mar Construction is performed, but performance in this case means an interaction with an automated process by, among other things, changing the range within which the process operates, rerouting signals to control different parameters, looping certain figures in a complex periodicity, and controlling the speed of the process. It is a particularly interesting system because it was constructed *to be* a composition, and in that way it is a representation of art and technology as one. The system *is* the composition.

The most general—i.e., nonpersonal—digital waveform generator is, of course, a computer. Several studios and manufacturers in this country and in

Europe have begun to experiment with computer-controlled analog equipment. At the EMS Studio in London, a generally useful program called MUSYS was developed, and Bell Laboratories, Murray Hill, New Jersey, developed another program, GROOVE. Other experiments include the design of new synthesizers especially for computer control, such as the installation at Dartmouth College developed by Sydney Alonso and the new synthesizers of Donald Buchla. At the present time, computers are usually used as memory-automation systems, though some composers, notably Lejaren Hiller, have used them in process-automation. Like synthesizers, computers are systems of equipment that vary from model to model; many analog synthesizer functions and special-purpose digital devices designed for electronic music have parallels in computer systems. The CEMS System, for example, is conceptually akin to an analog computer. The Synthi Digital Sequencer 256 is basically a model of a digital-computer memory. Daisy, which has one type of output, is a hardwired model of a computer program. Computers are relatively general systems, made specialized by programming. General systems are relatively inefficient because they must be adapted to particular uses, but they are flexible because they can be used in many different specialized situations. Specialized systems such as Daisy or the Synthi Digital Sequencer are extremely efficient, but they are relatively inflexible because they are variable only within the range of their specialized function. In selecting a system with which to work, a composer must decide what best suits his compositional inclinations.

The identity of a sound lies in the way it changes. Even a categorization of spectrum types deals with waveform changes, from completely periodic to random. Though working procedures associated with synthesizers tend to favor the conceptualization of separate audio and control systems—whereby audio systems constitute the basic parameters that may be changed and control systems determine the ways in which they change—it is more accurate to observe that audio signals themselves embody a change-type in audio-time and that control signals, operating in both audio- and conscious-time scales, add further dimensions of change to the final signal, or sound. The problem is how to describe sounds in terms of the way they change and how to apply that information in a musically meaningful way. Traditional music theory provides an excellent language for describing diatonic pitch relationships, but it completely lacks a language for describing sounds. A clarinet sound, for example, is described as the sound that a clarinet makes. Electronic sounds cannot be described meaningfully in terms of their sources. Does "a frequency-modulated sound" bring something to mind outside of a technique? In fact, frequency modulation—and every other electronic technique—may produce a considerable variety of specific sounds. Traditional music theory deals almost exclusively with pitched sounds, but there is nothing in synthesizer or computer equipment to especially favor a composer's choice of pitched sounds; in fact, most modulation procedures produce relatively unpitched sounds. Traditional music theory has, at best, a tangential application to electronic music, and in the absence of an effective theory, we are limited in perception. What we need is a theory that will enable us to describe sounds in terms of change, and apart from their sources. Let us assume that the nature of a synthesis system is equivalent to the structure of a composition, in that one produces the other; and let us assume that theories that are applicable to technical systems are also applicable to descriptions of sound and, by extension, to compositional structures. We may then ask, quite apart from any technical consideration, questions about sound, using a borrowed vocabulary. Which aspects of a sound are changing? How are they changing—randomly, periodically, transiently? Are the changes synchronous or asynchronous? At which time-scales are changes occurring? A waveform that is periodic at an audio-time scale may change pitch randomly at a conscious-time scale, as at the opening of Subotnick's *Silver Apples of the Moon*. And conscious-time-scale changes can occur over a range of from relatively fast changes to long-term changes that become the overall form of a composition.

The Mini-Moog.

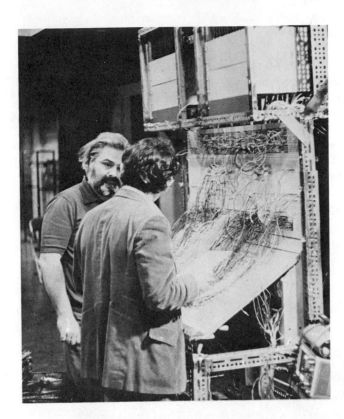

Salvatore Martirano and
the Sal-Mar Construction,
Albany, Spring, 1973

ElectroComp, model 200.

The Sonic VI.

The Electric Music Box, model 101 (small system), manufactured by Buchla Associates.

The Electric Music Box, model 200
(studio system), manufactured by
Buchla Associates.

The ARP 2600.

John Eaton with the
Synket.

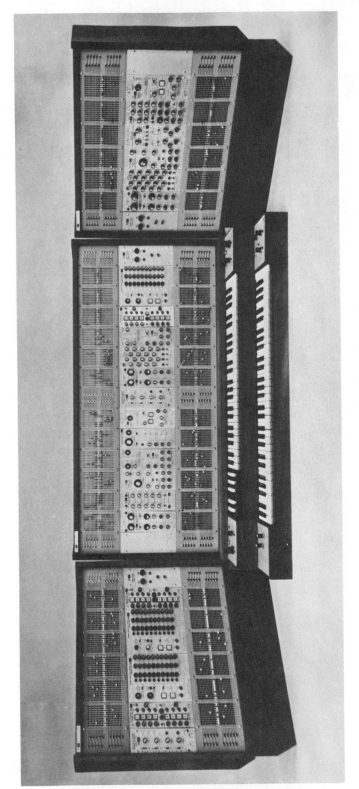

The ARP 2500 Electronic Music Synthesizer.

Moog Music Inc. Synthesizer IIIc, with two Sequencers on the right and left of the top row.

Peter Zinovieff operating the Synthi 100 at the EMS Studio in London.

Joel Chadabe operating the CEMS System, Electronic Music Studio, State University of New York at Albany.

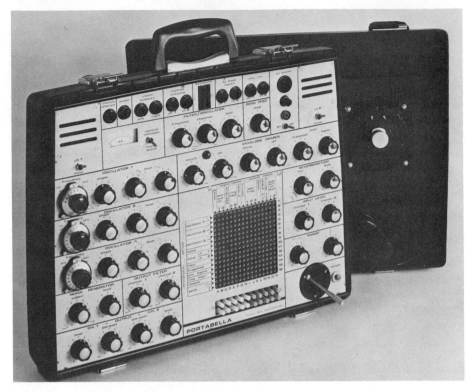

The Portabella, which contains the same instrumentation as the Synthi A.

5

The Uses of Digital Computers in Electronic Music Generation

JOHN E. ROGERS

The layman often has a fundamental misunderstanding of the role of computers in electronic music. He believes that computers are used to compose the music, to make the musical choices previously determined by the human imagination. Historically, this is partly correct because most of the musical work done with computers during the '50s took this direction. It was soon realized that a computer program to make compositional decisions was far too complicated and, in any case, had to reflect the bias of the composer or engineer who wrote the program.

The significant use of the computer in musical composition occurred when composers discovered the limitations of the tape studio for works requiring the careful control of pitched materials, and when they realized how difficult it was to synthesize complex and rapidly changing waveforms with analog synthesizers. The latter, taken for granted by composers working with acoustic instruments, became the special concern of composers using the electronic media because the pure electronic signals seemed to be lifeless and because composers were especially concerned with new timbral structures made possible by the medium.

In the following pages John Rogers explains exactly how the computer works, how it is used to control analog devices, and, finally, how it is used to actually synthesize sound and music. He assumes that the reader has no previous experience with computers, but it would be fair to say that he assumes one has read the previous chapters.

John E. Rogers was born in Dallas, Texas in 1938. He received a Bachelor of Arts in Philosophy and a Bachelor of Music in Trombone from the University of Georgia in 1960. He did graduate work at the Yale School of Music, receiving a Master of Music in Theory and Composition in 1962, and at Princeton University, where he received a Master of Fine Arts in Composition in 1965.

He is presently Director of the Electronic Music Studios at the University of New Hampshire, where he has been since 1967.

He is the author of several articles concerning serial technique and analysis, and he has composed numerous instrumental and electronic works. For the past several years he has been involved with computer-sound synthesis and electronic music in general.

INTRODUCTION

Great strides have been made in the last few years in the development of analog electronic music systems. Many of these systems are discussed in detail in other chapters of this book. Several limitations of these systems are, however, still and increasingly apparent.

The most severe limitation is in the area of types of control devices. When the power of the most advanced sequencer or keyboard controller is compared to that of even a mini-computer, this limitation is obvious. Sequencers and keyboards have at most a few hundred memory positions. Sequencers cannot, in general, address individual memory positions; they must usually move through an entire sequence to reach a designated position. Keyboard controllers have "random access" to each memory position (i.e., key), but this is coupled with a strict limitation on the number of positions available simultaneously. Digital computers have random access to at least several thousand memory positions. This access is so fast that for many of our musical purposes, we may regard all memory positions as simultaneously available. Further, digital computers usually have associated peripheral storage devices, such as tapes and discs, which allow extremely fast access to millions of storage locations.

Sequencers can be programmed in only a very limited sense. Systems that rely on expanding the number of sequencers soon demonstrate a lack of programming flexibility, and tend to create situations in which the sequencers are more in control of the final result than the user. Keyboard controllers are "programmed," if that word may be used at all in this sense, by the performer's acts. Naturally enough, the accuracy of this programming is directly proportionate to the keyboard facility and general performing skill of the user. Digital computers and their associated peripheral devices allow the user to store and execute instructions that amount to the generation of an entire composition. The requirements are that the user understand exactly what he wants and be able to specify it in a language the computer understands.

The second great limitation of present-day analog studios is the number and kind of available devices. One of the basic laws of electronic music studios is that no matter how many units of a certain kind one has, he will always need one more. Further, many units that are either necessary or highly desirable for certain musical passages (for example, versatile logic gates for control voltages; or highly accurate, continuously variable, voltage-controlled filters and oscillators) are not commonly available. The lack of units of certain kinds either rules out the possibility of certain effects or requires that elaborate solutions involving unusual uses of available devices be invented. Units used in the latter manner are, of course, no longer available for their normal tasks. This lack means that, at best, it will not be possible to realize most pieces in "real-time." It may be possible to realize the pieces one "line" or one section at a time. However, if generating one section takes many passes, each requiring complicated resettings and repatchings of most of the devices in the studio, the composer is sorely tempted not to generate the section at all, but to do something easier.

The above problems have led to a great emphasis on the multi-track tape recorder. This expansion of signal storage capability, when coupled with appropriate use of "click tracks" and mixing techniques, makes possible many desired effects. From the point of view of logical design, however, this seems an expansion at the wrong end of an electronic music generating system. It would seem much more desirable to expand the control and signal generation capabilities of the system so that desired musical passages might be generated directly. This expansion must involve digital computers as essential units in electronic music generation.

BASIC USES OF COMPUTERS IN ELECTRONIC MUSIC

There are two basic methods of using computers in electronic music generation. First, it is possible to use a computer as a "digital" control device for an "analog" studio. This method preserves many of the strengths and weaknesses of the analog devices available in a particular studio, while allowing them to be programmed in a sophisticated manner. This method of using computers may turn out to be very practical for many composers whose universities already own extensive analog electronic music systems. Recent reductions in prices of mini-computers capable of handling this task also contribute to the attractiveness of this method.

The second use of computers bypasses analog studios entirely and uses the computer to generate the sounds of a piece almost directly. This method requires a large, high-speed digital computing system such as one based around the IBM 360/65; a sound synthesis program such as MUSIC4BF or MUSIC360; and at least two channels of digital-to-analog conversion. This method not only allows complete control of musical events, but also obliterates problems concerning numbers of units available and the lack of certain kinds of devices. A "unit" is now simply a program or sub-program that may be stored in the computer and called by the user as many times as he desires. The strengths of this system seem fairly obvious. The weaknesses come not so much from the few absolute limitations of this method as from the lack of available acoustic knowledge to serve as the basis for developing programs. It is hoped that this lack may be remedied by the results of current research projects at the Bell Telephone Laboratories and elsewhere, which use the computer to analyze the sound characteristics of both electronic and acoustic instruments. A practical inconvenience in using computer sound synthesis programs is the inevitable time-delay associated with running long jobs at large computing installations.

These two uses of computers possess many similar features of design and operation. Further, the methods of solving musical problems on each type of system are not contradictory, but complementary. The most desirable electronic music generation system, then, would allow both types of computer uses. In addition, such an ideal system should probably allow for digital control of digital devices, a technique that will be mentioned at the very end of this chapter.

Digital and Analog—A Basic Problem Defined

The terms *analog* and *digital* refer not so much to characteristics of things in themselves, as to ways of representing things or ways of computing things. The basic distinction between analog and digital has to do with the way *quantity* or *magnitude* is represented and/or computed. In a *digital* representation, one *counts* a finite number of single units and uses the resulting number to represent quantity. In an *analog* representation, one physical quantity represents another "analogously."

Let's take a simple example to get a clearer idea of this difference. Suppose we have a number of items and we want to represent their quantity or magnitude. One way to do this would be by counting; this is the digital method. The basic problem of this method is what quantity to count as a single unit. Suppose we count one item as one unit; we will then encounter difficulty when we try to represent fractional numbers of items accurately. To get around this difficulty, we might decide to use a fractional division of the item as one unit. Theoretically, we could keep reducing the size of our counting unit until we reached the atomic or molecular level, or even beyond. In actuality, the counting unit is usually somewhere between the two extremes of the item itself and its atomic weight.

Digital or counting methods of representation of quantity possess many powerful features: they are absolutely precise, so that there is never a doubt about the number that is being presented; they may be made extremely accurate; and they may be applied to almost any type of event.

Another method of measuring the quantity or magnitude of our items is by weighing them. To do this, we put the items on a scale. The position of the pointer on the scale varies directly with the weight of the items. We now have a measurement by analogy; one magnitude (pointer position) varies analogously with another (weight of items). One should not be confused by the fact that the readout on the scale is digital.

Sometimes it is difficult to specify the exact position of the pointer on the scale. This reflects a difficulty often encountered in analog methods: they tend not to be precise. Further, the accuracy of representation of the physical quantity is limited by the accuracy of the physical mechanism performing the analogy. This accuracy is high in analog computers. It is often said that *analog* methods are better suited to representations of *continuous* phenomena, while digital methods are better suited to those phenomena consisting of *discrete parts*. There is some truth in this rather simplistic statement. But at a fundamental level we cannot say with authority whether nature itself is continuous or made up of discrete parts. Thus, if an event that appears to be continuous is represented by enough discrete parts, its representation will also appear to be continuous.

This does not mean, of course, that digital methods automatically provide the best representations for all events. This point must be decided by referring to the particular event and by considering the number of digits necessary to represent the event in time and magnitude, and the type of use intended for this particular representation.

Consider the envelope shown in Fig. 1. This square-edged waveform is typical of digital representations.

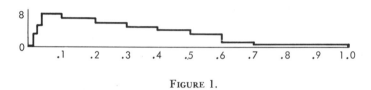

FIGURE 1.

If the smooth envelope of Fig. 2 is desired, it will be necessary either to expand gigantically the number of digits used (see later discussion of digital representations of sound waves) or generate the wave analogically.

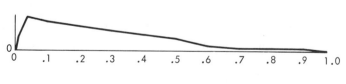

FIGURE 2.

Further, even if we expanded the number of numbers greatly, this of itself would not help us generate the wave in an electronic music studio or with real musical instruments. Neither of these categories of devices will accept numbers as control information; they are not digital devices, but analog ones.

The envelope of Fig. 2, which is a greatly oversimplified approximation of a piano's, could be generated in an analog electronic music studio by the "patch" shown in Fig. 3.

The following timing diagram shows the individual responses and final interaction of the devices in Fig. 3. The amplitude changes of the devices are

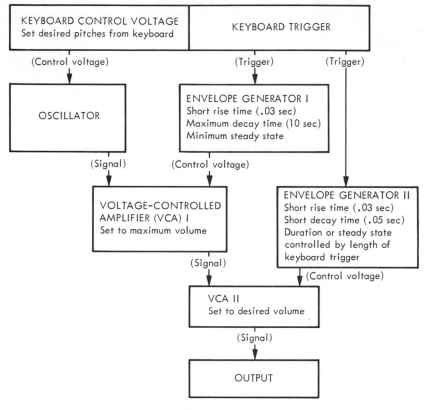

plotted against time. The duration of the keyboard trigger is assumed to be three seconds. The frequency and timbre of the note are not considered in the timing diagram.

There are at least two senses in which the previous process was an analog one. First, the envelope was generated by using devices that produce "control voltages" analogous to the desired envelope shape. Second, the control voltages were analogous to settings on various control potentiometers. These facts illustrate the basic principle at work in the design of most analog electronic music systems: units that produce sound are themselves controlled by devices that are set analogously by the user to generate control voltages again analogous to the desired effect.

Some of the units in an analog electronic music studio also have digital aspects associated with their operation. Such a unit in the above "patch" is the keyboard trigger source. The trigger has only two states of operation, on and off. These states can be represented easily and precisely by the numbers 0 and

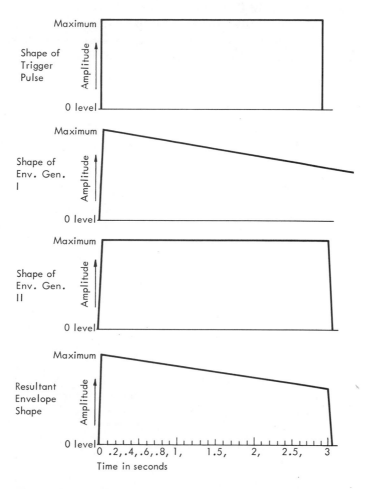

FIGURE 4.   Timing diagram for note of 3 seconds' duration.

1, where 0 indicates that the unit is off and 1 indicates that it is on. The numerical system involved in this representation is the *binary number system,* whose only numerals are 0 and 1. The state of operation of the keyboard trigger can be represented, then, by one *binary digit,* or *bit.*

Many control devices in an analog studio have both analog and digital aspects. A close examination of a "sequential voltage source" will help make this clear. For a simple case, let us consider an eight-position sequencer with the capability of one control voltage from each position. At any one instant of time, each position of the sequencer is either on or off. This means that the state of any one position may be represented by one bit. Furthermore, we may make a distinction between the positions available on the sequencer and the states of these positions. We have now made a distinction between the *address* of a value (Are we in position 1, position 2, etc.?) and the *value itself* (Is that value 0 or 1—is the state of the position on or off?). We might specify these addresses in the decimal number system—position 1, position 2, . . . position 8. We will probably find it more convenient to express these addresses in the binary number system, the same system we used to express the value of that address.

Example 1: Numerical Representations of Addresses of Sequencer Positions

Decimal Value	Binary Value
position 1	position 0001
position 2	position 0010
position 3	position 0011
position 4	position 0100
position 5	position 0101
position 6	position 0110
position 7	position 0111
position 8	position 1000

Notice that we are now expressing more information than can be contained in one bit; we need 4 bits to allow us to express a decimal value of 8. The largest decimal number that can be represented in n bits is $2^n - 1$. The largest decimal number that can be represented in 3 binary bits is thus $2^3 - 1$ or 7. The largest with 4 bits is 15.

We are now able to refer to and express the state of any one position of the sequencer by one 5-bit number. The first four bits give the address of the position; the last bit gives its state. This "coding" of information is fairly representative of typical uses of the binary number system.

Example 2: States and Addresses of Sequencer Positions

00010	position 1 off		01010	position 5 off
00011	position 1 on		01011	position 5 on
00100	position 2 off		01100	position 6 off
00101	position 2 on		01101	position 6 on
00110	position 3 off		01110	position 7 off
00111	position 3 on		01111	position 7 on
01000	position 4 off		10000	position 8 off
01001	position 4 on		10001	position 8 on

The reader will have noticed that the real control information the sequencer stores is not represented in the above scheme. This is because the control information present at each position is not a number, but a control voltage. It is set by turning a knob an analogous amount, and it controls some unit that requires an analog control. Essentially, then, the sequencer is digital with respect to time, but analog with respect to value.

Digital-to-Analog and Analog-to-Digital Conversion

Sound waves are periodic alternations in atmospheric pressure whose frequencies are between 20–20,000 Hz. These alternations may be produced by the vibrating strings, reeds, and air columns of acoustic instruments; they may also be produced by electronic instruments whose output voltages or signals cause vibrations in loudspeakers. We have seen that both the controls and signals of these electronic music instruments are analog. We have also stated as one of our purposes the use of computers to generate both control functions and the signals themselves. Yet the only computers that possess enough inherent power to perform this task are digital computers, and these computers yield numeric output, not analog voltages. Fortunately for us, a linkage between the "real," analog world and the world of digital computers is often necessary today, and devices have been developed to perform this linkage. These devices are digital-to-analog converters (DACs) and analog-to-digital converters (ADCs). An ADC changes an analog voltage into a binary number and, thus, allows us to put "analog information" into the computer. A DAC is a device that converts a binary number to an analog voltage. It allows information from the computer to affect analog devices. DACs are the more common type in most musical applications.

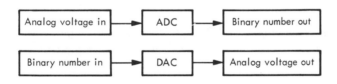

FIGURE 5.

Each separate number or *sample* that goes into a DAC or comes out of an ADC is made up of a string of bits. The number of bits determines the range of quantities or amplitudes available per sample. If each sample were 8 bits long, the converter would allow 255 ($2^8 - 1$) as a maximum amplitude, would have 256 possible amplitude levels (0–255), and would be called an 8-bit converter. A 12-bit converter would allow a maximum amplitude of 4,095, have 4,096 possible amplitude levels, and obviously produce better representations of fine differences in amplitudes.

A further aspect of the operation of a converter is how often to "sample" or "obtain a sample." The rate at which binary numbers are supplied to a DAC or obtained from an ADC is called the *sampling rate* (*SR*). The frequency of SR determines the range of frequencies that the converter can handle accurately. Both DACs and ADCs are available in a wide variety of sampling rates and ranges.

A simple "analogy" may help clarify the above. Think of an ADC as somewhat analogous to a movie camera. Both sample events which take place in time. The SR of the camera is the number of frames per second. The individual samples or "snapshots" of a motion picture are, however, analog; they are photographic representations. The individual samples of the ADC are digital; they consist of numeric information to be transferred to the computer.

Digital Representations of Sound Waves

Suppose .we have a "patch" in our analog studio, the output of which is four independent and simultaneous musical lines. Despite the polyphonic character of this passage, the actual output of the electronic music system is a single, rapidly changing voltage. When this voltage is passed through amplifiers and speakers, the ear will be able to discriminate various component frequencies and distinguish different pitches, timbres and rhythms. But for our immediate purposes, we should emphasize the principle that any number of simultaneous and independent musical events add up to only one resultant waveform.

Since the final output of the system is a rapidly changing *voltage,* it is an appropriate input to an ADC. Suppose the following is a short (.001 sec.) segment of that resultant voltage:

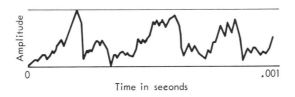

FIGURE 6.

The large number of amplitude variations in this time segment indicates the presence of high frequencies in the segment. Suppose SR is 10,000 samples per second; since the portion of time we are considering lasts $\frac{1}{1000}$ of a second, we will be able to "take ten pictures" of the wave that occurs during it. This would produce a result approximately like the following:

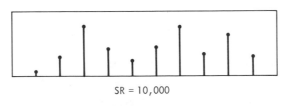

SR = 10,000

FIGURE 7.

SRs of 20,000 and 40,000 samples per second, respectively, produce the following results:

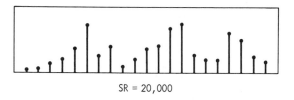

SR = 20,000

FIGURE 8.

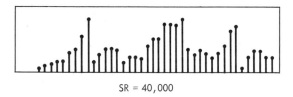

SR = 40,000

FIGURE 9.

Digital Sampling Errors

We see that higher SRs obviously produce a more accurate representation of the frequency content (i.e., shape) of the wave. But even at 40,000 samples per second, we do not have a completely true representation. If frequencies are being lost, what is happening to them? If frequencies are being added, where are they coming from? What sampling rates are appropriate for music?

Suppose we had a voltage level and it changed to another level. How many amplitude points or samples are necessary to represent this? The answer is two.

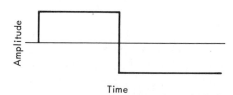

FIGURE 10.

One sample represents only a level, not a change of levels. A cycle of a periodic waveform has at least two levels. To represent this, we need two samples.

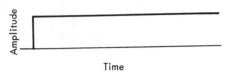

FIGURE 11.

Thus, to make possible an accurate representation of the frequency content of a changing voltage, the sampling rate must be twice as high as the highest frequency one wishes to represent. The following figure shows what happens when we attempt to represent a frequency of 6,000 Hz with an SR of 10,000:

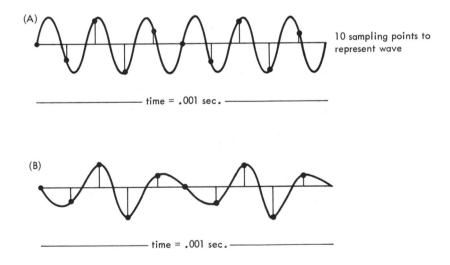

FIGURE 12.   (A) Sampling with SR Too Slow; (B) Smoothed Resultant Frequency

We see that frequencies above SR/2 are not merely lost, they are misrepresented. The resultant frequency is four somewhat misshapen cycles in .001 second, instead of six cycles. This would indicate a frequency of 4,000 cycles per second instead of 6,000. This is the problem of *foldover*, one of the basic errors that can occur in D/A and A/D conversion. All frequencies above SR/2 fold over, with reference to SR/2.

Example 3

$$\text{Foldover frequency} = \text{SR} - \text{Input frequency}$$
$$4{,}000 \qquad\qquad = 10{,}000 - 6{,}000$$

It is clear that an ADC must be prevented from receiving these upper frequencies; if it receives them, it will produce spurious output. The best way to remove these frequencies is by passing the input signal through a very sharp, low-pass filter with an upper cutoff frequency of SR/2. If we are attempting to digitize sound waves, we should have an SR of 40,000 samples per second if we define the audio range as 20–20,000 cps. If we must filter at below 20,000 cps, we will probably remove some audible components from the signal.

Spurious frequencies produced in the process of D/A conversion may also be removed by filtering. Let us take the numeric representation of the waveform shown in Fig. 9 and pass it through a DAC, noting that each of these samples represents an *instantaneous amplitude* of a sound wave. The output of the DAC would resemble the following:

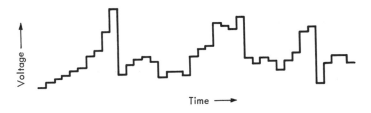

FIGURE 13.

This shows that a DAC is analog with respect to value, but remains digital with respect to time. It does not smooth out the wave, but simply retains one amplitude value until the next is presented. The square-edged waveform indicates the presence of many undesired upper partials. If the same low-pass filter as before is placed on the output of the DAC, it will remove all frequencies above SR/2. The undesired partials should fall in this range, and, thus, this filter will have the effect of smoothing the wave so that it resembles the original analog input quite closely. Since it is impossible to represent frequencies above SR/2 accurately, this filtering process should not remove any valid frequencies. If SR is 40,000, it will not be necessary to place a filter on the output of the DAC; SR/2 is 20,000 Hz., a frequency higher than the highest frequency in the audible range. In this case the ear itself is the ultimate "low-pass" filter.

The other basic conversion problem is called *quantizing error*. This error occurs when there are not enough bits available to represent the correct amplitude value. A 12-bit ADC can deal with 4,096 amplitude values. If the passage being sampled requires more values than this, it will not be a totally accurate representation. This error is not ordinarily significant in converters of 12-bit accuracy or better. One should notice that quantizing accuracy improves dramatically as the number of bits increases. A 16-bit converter, for example, could represent 65,536 discrete amplitude levels. Converters of more accuracy become progressively more difficult to build, but are now becoming available.

Quantizing errors can also occur with DACs if there are not enough bits to represent the waveform accurately. With DACs there is the further possibility of supplying too large a number to the converter. Suppose we have a 12-bit DAC, and supply it with the number 5,035. This results in the following disastrous representation, in which the number is actually reduced by 4,096, the value that the thirteenth bit should have provided. In computer terminology, this kind of error is often called *overflow*.

Example 4

decimal 5035	=	binary 1 0011 1010 1011
		the 13th, "left-most," or "high-order" bit is lost yielding
decimal 939	=	binary 0011 1010 1011
alternatively ——		decimal 5035
		decimal −4096
		decimal 939

Suppose our *sample out of range* had occurred in the following context:

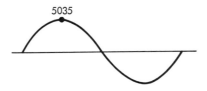

5035

FIGURE 14.

The resultant waveform would be:

4095

2047

0

FIGURE 15.

This sudden discontinuity will result at best in a click, and at worst in total distortion. This kind of error can be prevented if the user knows the values of the numbers he is using and makes sure that none of them exceed the sampling range of the D/A. Practically, this often turns out to be quite difficult, and most sound generation programs offer a rescaling feature that automatically scales all amplitudes to within the available range. This feature usually solves the problem of *samples out of range*.

Musical Uses of Digitized Analog Values

In the above, we have concentrated on sampling a sound wave with an ADC and generating a sound wave from digital samples with a DAC. In the former case, we produce input appropriate to a computer; in the latter case, the input comes from the computer. After a sound wave has been digitized, it may be altered or analyzed by computer programs. Finally, the digitized wave or another generated by the computer with the use of a sound synthesis program may be transmitted to a DAC to be converted to a series of analog voltages that trace the shape of the waveform. This process is called *computer sound generation.*

There are also many important applications of DACs and ADCs in analog studios. Consider our earlier "patch" with a keyboard control voltage source controlling the frequency of an oscillator. Digitizing the keyboard control voltages would give us an accurate, numerical representation of the voltages necessary to control the oscillator. These control voltages, once digitized, could be modified and/or analyzed by the computer. Alternatively, by using a control voltage generating program, the computer could provide a series of numbers representing the desired control voltages. These numbers could be transferred to a DAC. The analog voltage output of the DAC would be used to control the original oscillator. What we are seeing here is an example of *digital control of an analog electronic music device.* In this application, we do not need converters with fast sampling rates. The converter should be able to sample or accept a sample when it receives a trigger pulse, and it should be able to hold that sample until it receives the next pulse.

Example 5: Digitized Sound Wave

Example 6: Computer-Sound Generation

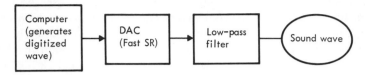

Example 7: Digitized Control Voltages

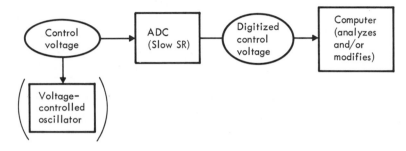

Example 8: Digital Control of an Analog Device

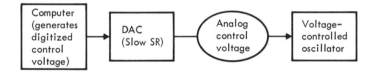

Digital and Analog Recording Devices

Sounds are usually recorded on analog tape or disk recorders. Analog tape recorders for the home are typically mono or stereo and range in speed from $1\frac{7}{8}$ to $7\frac{1}{2}$ inches per second (ips). Professional analog tape machines may record as many as sixteen different tracks and run at speeds of 15 ips or more. An analog tape recorder records a continuously varying magnetic field on tape that is called, appropriately enough, magnetic tape. When the recorded tape is played back, the magnetic charges on the tape cause electrical currents in the playback head of the tape recorder; these currents eventually produce the sounds we hear.

A digital tape recorder records digital information in the form of strings of bits. Digital tape recorders are typically either seven- or nine-track and run at speeds which allow 320,000 bits to be transmitted per second. The recording is usually done on half-inch magnetic tape. The nine-track recorder is the most common in IBM 360 installations. Of its nine tracks, only eight contain the user's information. The contents of all tracks are presented simultaneously; thus, nine tracks present 8 bits of information. This 8-bit unit is basic to the organization of the IBM 360 and is called a *byte.* The ninth bit is used as a check on the operation of the tape recorder and is called the *parity* bit. IBM 360 tapes are written at a density of 800 or 1,600 bytes per inch (bpi). Fig. 16 shows how information is written on a nine-track, 800-bpi digital tape.

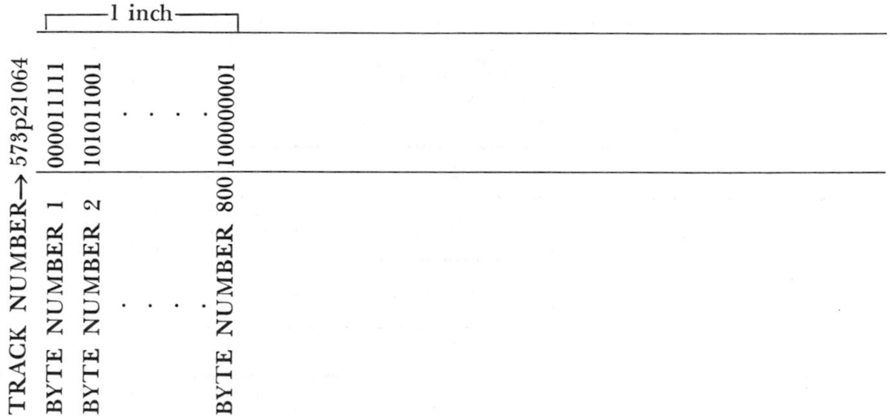
1 inch
TRACK NUMBER→ 573p21064
BYTE NUMBER 1 000011111
BYTE NUMBER 2 101011001
. . . .
BYTE NUMBER 800 100000001

FIGURE 16.

Since each byte contains 8 bits, we may store values from 0–255 in one "nine-track byte." Because we usually need more values than this, tape programming allows us to combine bytes or even parts of bytes to form larger units. The typical larger unit in IBM 360 systems consists of 4 bytes and is called the *word.* In music, we often need a 12-bit unit for transmission to a 12-bit DAC. We can easily obtain this by linking three 8-bit bytes to form two 12-bit words:

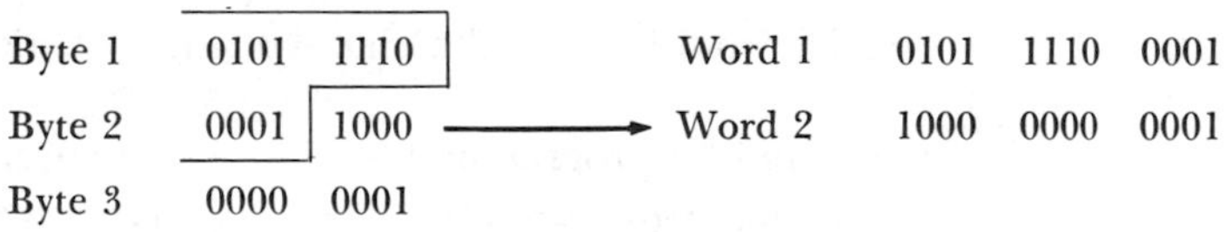
Byte 1 0101 1110
Byte 2 0001 1000
Byte 3 0000 0001
Word 1 0101 1110 0001
Word 2 1000 0000 0001

FIGURE 17.

Digital disk recording allows even more speed in the transmission and more flexibility in the handling of data.

Basic Characteristics of Digital Computers

Earlier, we pointed out that a studio sequencer is digital with respect to time, but analog with respect to value. If the value stored at each position of the sequencer were digital, we would then have a totally digital sequencer. The

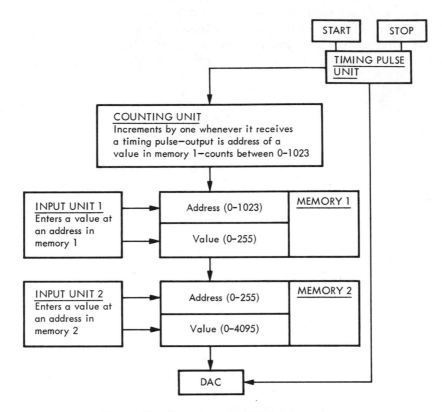

FIGURE 18.   Programmable Digital Sequencer.

characteristics of such a device would reflect the characteristics of digital computers.

Fig. 18 shows the basic plan of a programmable digital sequencer.[1] Its two main differences from an analog sequencer are these: (1) the values at each position are digital; and (2) each position may be selected by specifying its address (thus, one is no longer limited to one fixed sequence of events corresponding in length to the number of sequencer positions). The simplest form of this device requires an input unit, two separate memories, an instruction counter, and an output unit. Memory 1 is a storage area for "instructions" to the device; in our case, these instructions are simply addresses of "sequencer positions" to be selected—that is, addresses in memory 2. The values in memory 2 correspond to the control potentiometers of the analog sequencer. These

[1] This sequencer is not similar in design to the digital sequencers presently being marketed by Electronic Music Studios London, Ltd. Its design was suggested to me by Lee Morin, an undergraduate student at the University of New Hampshire.

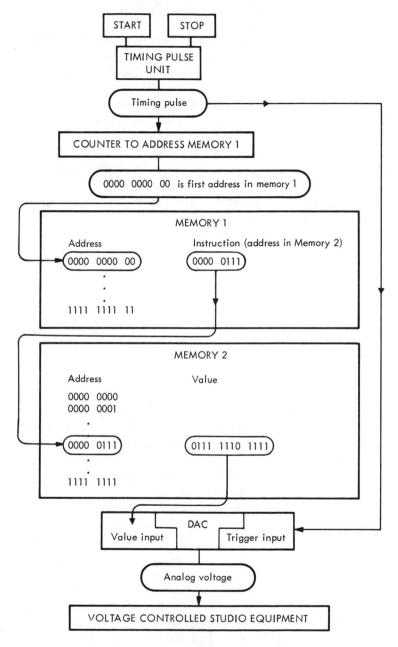

FIGURE 19.

values will be transferred to a DAC whose output will be used to control analog units in the studio.

Let us assume that 256 values may be stored with 12-bit accuracy, and that 1,024 addresses or instructions to call these values may be stored. Memory 1 should then contain 1024 positions; each position should contain a 10-bit address ($2^{10} = 1024$) and an 8-bit value ($2^8 = 256$). Memory 2 should contain 256 positions, each of which should contain an 8-bit address and a 12-bit value. In each of these cases, the "first position" in memory will have an address of binary 0. Suppose that our first memory position in memory 1 stores "position 8" (binary 0000 0111), and that position 8 in memory 2 stores decimal 2031 (binary 0111 1110 1111). Fig. 19 shows what happens when the "instruction counter" addresses the first instruction in memory 1.

The operation of the digital sequencer reveals several of the main characteristics of digital computers:

1. The capacity to accept the user's data and instructions through an *input* section; this unit is not completely defined in this case.
2. The capacity for storing the user's *data* in numeric form, in this case, in *Memory 2*.
3. The capacity for storing the user's instructions or *program* in a numeric form, in this case, in *Memory 1*.
4. The capacity for *executing* the instructions of the program sequentially, in this case, provided by the *instruction counter*.
5. The capacity for providing results to the user through an *output* section, in this case, the DAC.

The input and output sections together perform the function of allowing the device to interact with the real world; they are thus sometimes considered to be one large section called the input/output or I/O section. Typical I/O devices for digital computers are card-readers and -punches, digital tapes and disks, line printers, cathode-ray tubes, DACs and ADCs, teletypewriters, paper-tape units, and pen-and-ink plotters.

The first major change that should be made in our digital sequencer to convert it into a "real" computer is the combining of our two memories into one. In computers, both instructions and data are stored in the same memory:

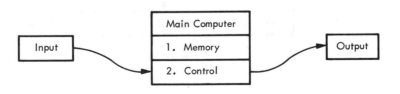

FIGURE 20.

This change necessitates a more sophisticated control unit that will allow a choice of which instruction is to be executed. Basically, most computers allow three modes of choice. The simplest mode is *sequential;* the instructions are executed one after another, as was the case with Memory 1 of our original unit. The second mode of instruction choice is called *branching.* It allows certain instructions to be skipped or *branched around.* It should also be possible to *loop* repetitively through an instruction sequence. Examples of looping and branching will be given shortly.

The control unit we have been discussing is usually called the central processing unit (CPU). It normally contains as a primary element an arithmetic logic unit (ALU). The ALU, as one would expect, performs arithmetic operations (addition, subtraction, multiplication, division, comparison, exponentiation) and logical operations. (In computer terminology, logical operations refer to shifting numbers left or right, character manipulation, and Boolian operations [AND, OR, NAND, etc.].) In order to perform these operations quickly, the ALU usually contains at least one and oftentimes several high-speed registers. There are usually separate registers for integer and for fractional or "floating-point" numbers. The speed of a computer is usually measured in terms of its cycle time, a cycle being the loading of one "word" of memory into a register in the CPU.

The following two examples make use of the power of the ALU, and exhibit branching and looping. Ex. 9 illustrates the simplest possible branching statement; the instruction at location 3 is simply skipped. Ex. 10 shows a loop to add all the numbers between 1 and 5. For convenience, addresses and values are given in the decimal rather than the binary number system, and instructions are presented in a form very close to ordinary language.

Example 9: Branching

Memory Address		Contents of Address
1		Add the values at locations 7 and 8, and store this value at location 9
2	instructions	Go to location 4
3		Multiply the value at location 9 by itself, and store the result at location 9
4		Add the value at location 6 to that at location 9, and store the result at location 9
5		Stop
6		1
7	values	10
8		12
9		0

Example 10: Looping

Memory Address		Contents of Address
1		Add value at location 6 to value at location 5, and store result at location 5
2	instructions	Add value at location 8 to value at location 6, and store result at location 6
3		Compare value at location 6 with value at location 7: if value at location 6 is smaller or the same, go to instruction at location 1; if value at location 6 is larger, go to instruction at location 4
4		Stop
5		0
6	values	1
7		5
8		1

In this program, location 5 serves as our "accumulator"; it stores in chronological order 0, 1, 3, 6, 10, 15. Location 6 serves as our counter, and location 7 defines the maximum count. When the value at location 6 exceeds the value at locations 5—that is, when the value of location 6 is 6—the program stops. The final answer is 15, the last value of location 5.

Our final programming example (see Example 11) shows a sequence of instructions that might be used in a simple music program. The program performs the following tasks:

1. Adds two given numbers and stores the result where the first number had been.
2. Compares that result with a third number.
3. Transfers the larger of the two numbers to a DAC.
4. Stops.

We see in these programs that memory contains both instructions and data. These types of information seem to be different in kind. Data appear as numbers; instructions look more like English. Actually, for the computer both instructions and data must be in numeric form, as they were in the digital sequencer example. To accomplish this, programs must exist to translate the user's instructions to numeric form. These programs, usually furnished by the manufacturer of the computer or by professional programming companies, are called *assemblers* or *compilers*. They allow the user to express instructions in forms other than numeric ones, but they will accept only very limited numbers and very stringently controlled types of instructions. The actual numbers into which these instructions are translated are called the *machine language* of the computer. Basically, there is a one-to-one correspondence between assembly-language instructions and machine code; the former are simply mnemonics for machine code. Compiler languages such as FOR-

Example 11: A More Complicated Program

Memory Address		Contents of Address
1		Add contents of address 7 to contents of address 8, and store result at address 7
2	*instructions*	Compare contents of address 7 with contents of address 9: if contents of address 7 is larger, continue sequential execution of program; if contents of address 9 is larger, skip to instruction at address 5
3		Transfer contents of address 7 to DAC 1
4		Skip to instruction at address 6
5		Transfer contents of address 9 to DAC 1
6		Stop
7	*values*	100
8		210
9		300

TRAN or ALGOL are general-purpose languages available on almost all present-day computers. They often must pass through several stages of translation before they reach machine code. For this reason they are somewhat inefficient in terms of using each computer to its best advantage. In general, the higher the level of the language, the easier it is to use, the farther it is from actual machine code, and the more computer time it takes to execute.

Since assembly languages are simply mnemonics for machine code, they are particular to each type of computer. There is thus a particular assembler for the IBM 360 series; this assembler is totally different from one for another brand of computer, say CDC, or even for another type of IBM computer, such as the 7094. Though assemblers are not always as convenient for the user, they are much more efficient for the computer. For many musical uses of the computer, assembly-language programming is an economic necessity.

The above indicates one more deficiency of our digital sequencer turned computer; it had no *instruction set* or *language*. The only way it could be programmed was by actual machine code—that is, entering instructions into the machine in the form of numbers. This type of coding might be possible with a machine at this primitive level of programming. With a large computing system, however, actual machine-language programming is almost never attempted.

Simple Programming Concepts—A Program and a Subprogram

A computer program is a set of instructions to the computer. A user's program is stored in the computer, along with his data and with various other programs that may be needed. If these programs are "called" by the user's program, they are called *sub-programs* to his *main program*. There is no absolute difference in these two types of programs. Specialized or "library" sub-programs are often supplied by the manufacturer or the installation.

Suppose the user computes sine functions very often in his program. Rather than writing out this set of instructions each time he needs to compute the function, he might use a sub-program that computes sine functions. He would *call* or *branch to* this sub-program when it was needed; it would compute the function and *return* to the main program with the needed value. Most computer installations provide a sine sub-program that users may call in this manner.

Example 12

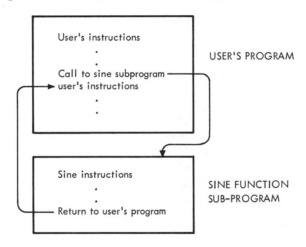

It is usually much more clear and efficient to design many sub-programs that perform particular tasks rather than writing one large program to solve all aspects of the problem. Music programs make great use of this technique.

The disadvantage of using sub-programs is that they are more time-consuming for the computer. When a program "calls" another program, it must store certain values from and certain locations in each program. With reference to the *calling program,* for example, the address of the next instruction after the call must be stored. This is called the *return address.* Without that address, the *called program* could never return to the main program. In most cases, the computer time lost by using sub-programs is more than offset by the programming or design time saved.

Large and Small Digital Computers

Today, there are two basic types of computer installations. Most readers of this text have probably seen a computer center at a university, a research center, or a large business. Such a center typically contains a large and power-ful central computer such as an IBM 360, a CDC 6600, or comparable machine. Such a computer and its associated support devices might well cost several million dollars. A computer user almost never works directly with the com-puter in this large installation.

Typically, he submits his "job" on a deck of punched computer cards to an operator who "reads" the deck into the computer through a card reader. The operating system of the computer then places the job in a "jobqueue" to wait its turn to execute. This method of job handling in a computer installa-tion is called *batch processing*. It is used in centers that have a high per-centage of jobs which require a large amount of computer storage and power.

Alternatively, a user might communicate with a large system via a re-mote terminal, such as a teletype unit. In so doing, he would share the large computer with many other users. This method of using computers, often called *time-sharing*, gives each user the illusion that his job is being processed immediately. Actually, the central computer is scanning the jobs of all the users, but its scanning rate is extremely rapid. This diffusion of the power of a large computer may make the time-sharing system inappropriate for jobs that require a large number of calculations and/or a large amount of computer storage. For this reason, it is usually impossible to run computer sound syn-thesis programs on systems that are exclusively time-sharing.[2] Time-sharing systems are ideal for short, experimental kinds of jobs, such as those typically submitted by students in undergraduate courses. Because of the variety of needs of the users of a large system, it is often necessary for a computer center to provide both time-sharing and batch-processing options.

A second type of computing system is one based on a *mini-computer*. There are many specialized applications for which a computer would be useful. Many of these require that special devices be attached to the computer or that the computer be taken from place to place. It is almost always im-possible and undesirable to use a large computer for these applications. In the past ten years, small computers have been developed that are designed for this type of usage. The PDP–8, manuafactured by Digital Equipment Corpora-tion, is centainly the most famous machine of this type.

A mini-computer can often be purchased for between $2,000 and $5,000; an entire small computing system can often be had for under $10,000. With the intense competition presently taking place among manufacturers for this small computer market, and with the spectacular advances now taking place in digital technology, we can expect small computers to drop in price while rising in power during the next few years.

---

[2] This situation is now changing. Some computer manufacturers have developed time-sharing systems on which it is possible to run short sections of MUSIC 4 type jobs. Examples of this type of system are the sound generation facilities at Colgate University and at the Artificial Intelligence Laboratory at Stanford University. The central computer in both these facilities is Digital Equipment Corporation's PDP-10.

Digital Control of an Analog Electronic Music Studio

In general, any devices in an analog studio that are controlled by control voltages may be controlled by a computer and a DAC. Any devices that produce or manipulate control voltages are normally replaced by the computer and its DACs. The important analog devices in a digitally controlled studio thus become those units devoted to signal generation, signal modification, and signal storage. These include:

1. Accurate voltage-controlled oscillators and harmonic generators.
2. Voltage-controlled filters of various types.
3. Voltage-controlled amplifiers or gates.
4. Mixers (preferably voltage-controlled).
5. Various signal-modifying devices, such as ring modulators, frequency shifters, and reverberators.
6. High-quality analog tape recorders.

Of the other traditional units in an analog studio, keyboards may still have some limited usefulness in allowing the user a "performance" option, or in giving him a convenient way to enter information into the computer. Sequencers and timing pulse units have a much reduced usefulness. Envelope generators are also less useful, though sometimes convenient, especially if they possess any voltage-controlled properties. Such units as control-voltage processors are ordinarily useful only to the extent of the instabilities of the analog units receiving the control voltages from the DACs.

The digital control system needed for this type of studio must include the items that follow:

1. A mini-computer is the basic control device. It is, strangely enough, one of the least expensive items on this list. A computer such as Digital Equipment Corporation's (DEC) PDP–8e or Texas Instrument's (TI) 980a is completely adequate. The computer should have sufficient storage capacity to allow it to be programmed in a high-level language, preferably Assembly Language. It should also have an internal clock (usually a crystal-controlled oscillator) to allow precise timing control of events.

2. The digital tape unit is the primary storage device in the system. It stores the user's programs and the control information for the generation of his piece. A fairly slow tape unit, such as DEC's DECtape, is minimally adequate for this task. A larger and faster unit that is compatible with IBM computers would offer many advantages, however.

3. A teletype unit with paper-tape reader and punch is necessary to enter information into the computer and to provide printed copies of the user's programs. Alternatively; a cathode-ray-tube (CRT)-type terminal may be preferred because of its silent operation, if there is some way of obtaining printed output. Information entered in this manner is processed by the computer and

then stored on digital tape. It is not economically feasible, and probably not a good idea in any case, to equip mini-computers with card-readers and card-punches.

4. There is usually one DAC for each analog unit to be controlled. In a moderate-sized studio, this will probably amount to over twenty DACs. The converters should be at least 12-bit accuracy. The sampling rates of the converters need not be especially fast, for the times we are considering are *note-times,* not *cycle-times,* of sound waves. Note-times are extremely slow by computer standards. The DAC must also be connected to or "interfaced with" the computer; this is not a difficult problem with most mini-computers. Units that alter the voltage level output of the DACs may be necessary if the DACs must control analog devices of essentially different types of synthesizers. These voltage alteration units are called operational amplifiers or "op-amps."

5. A digitally-controlled analog switching matrix is a kind of super patching panel into which are brought all signal and control inputs and outputs of the system. Below, we see the basic design of a 5 × 5 or 25-position matrix.

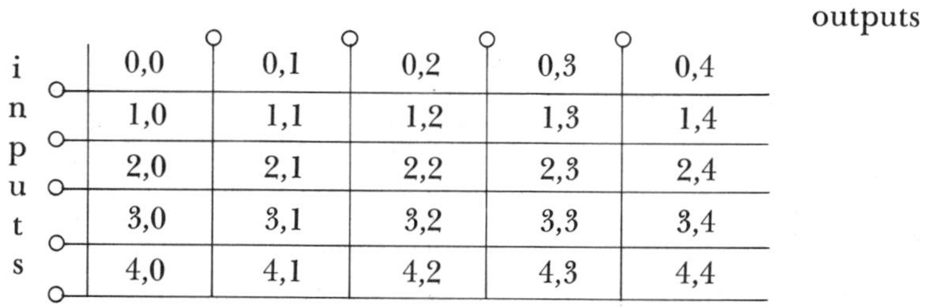

outputs

		0,0	0,1	0,2	0,3	0,4
i		1,0	1,1	1,2	1,3	1,4
n		2,0	2,1	2,2	2,3	2,4
p						
u		3,0	3,1	3,2	3,3	3,4
t						
s		4,0	4,1	4,2	4,3	4,4

FIGURE 21.

Each and every input can be connected to each and every output. Let us number both rows (inputs) and columns (outputs) from 0 to 4. We may then numerically specify the connection of each input and output: the connection of input 0 to output 0 is represented by (0,0); input 1 to output 0 by (1,0); input 4 to output 2 by (4,2); etc. Such connections might be physically accomplished by placing switches at each intersection of a row and a column. If these switches were similar to the usual control switches on synthesizers, the matrix would be extremely cumbersome to operate. There is another kind of switch, however, called a *relay.* A relay is essentially a switch that can be turned on by a trigger voltage. Since computers can output trigger voltages, computers can turn relays on and off. A digitally-controlled analog switching matrix consists of a matrix of analog inputs and outputs connected to each other by many relay switches that are turned on and off by the control computer. Each relay is given the address number indicated above. The switching matrix must contain logic circuits that decode the address furnished by the computer and that allow the relay at that address to be activated.

For most synthesizers, the matrix consists of two separate portions: one for control voltages, the other for signals. As with all switching matrices, the essential problem with this one is to provide enough positions to accommodate all devices that need to be interconnected. Thus, it will probably be necessary to place a limit on the number of possible connections of several devices. For example, since a white-noise source normally requires no input, it is a waste of positions to allow an entire row of inputs for this device. Given an economical use of positions, a switching matrix for a moderate-sized studio would probably require 30 × 30, or 900 positions.

Among the many advantages of this digitally-controlled matrix, perhaps the most impressive are:

1. General confusion is greatly reduced, as both device connection and device programming are done by computer.
2. The user can store "patches" with his program and data—the "instrument" is stored with the "score."
3. Connections of devices can be changed almost instantaneously during the course of the realization of a piece.

A digital switching matrix exactly like the one described above is not presently available. A working 10 × 10 prototype has been designed and installed at the Electronic Music Studio of the University of New Hampshire, however. Several devices somewhat similar to this, some of which contain mixing features as well, are now appearing in commericial recording studios.

An entire digital control system like the one just sketched would cost between $20,000 and $50,000. Although this figure is high, it is not beyond the reach of today's larger installations, especially when one considers the dramatic reduction in the number of multi-track analog tape recorders needed in the studio.

The idea of a digital control system might be thought of as the "player-piano" concept raised to the nth power, except that what is being controlled is not the action of a piano, but the units in an analog electronic music studio. Essentially, one uses the computer to generate control information for musical events—timing information, pitch information, timbre information, loudness information, modulation information, etc. In order to generate this information, two quite different types of computer programs are necessary.

The first program generates control information and records or "writes" it on digital magnetic tape. This program may be executed on any computer that has a digital tape drive compatible with the tape drive of the control computer. If the control computer has an IBM compatible tape drive, for instance, then a large IBM system could be used to generate the control tape. The first program should accept input in which the composer can express his musical ideas and intentions in a straightforward and natural way. The general types of information the composer must convey to the computer are (1) "patching," or instrument-definition information; and (2) musical event information—the specific "notes and rhythms" of the work.

The second type of program reads the control tape generated by the first,

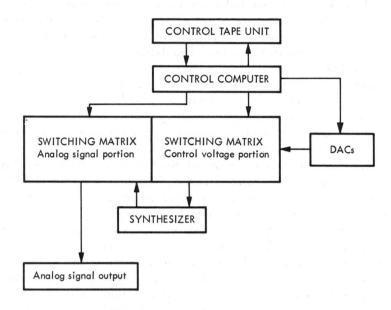

FIGURE 22.

sets up programmed patches, transfers information to DACs, and controls the timing of the musical events in accordance with the information on the tape.

In cases where the programming is of limited complexity, the computer may be used to generate the composition directly in real-time. This is possible because the computer deals with times corresponding to "musical event times." The computer can perform hundreds of thousands of operations per second, and often it will be able to compute the information for the next event in the time in which the present one is occurring. In this case we would obviously need only one large control program. This type of procedure is especially valuable in testing musical ideas. In more complicated cases the storage capacity of the computer and its digital tape unit still make possible the pre-programming and "real-time" realization of an entire musical composition. Such a feature is almost inconceivable in any other mode of electronic music generation.

A system exactly like the one described above does not presently exist in full. We have partly realized the construction of such a system at the University of New Hampshire Electronic Music Studio. A system somewhat similar to this has been designed and is now being marketed by Peter Zinovieff and Electronic Music Studios, London. This system involves a PDP–8 computer, a disk storage unit, and the Synthi 100 Synthesizer. However, the present trend of this manufacturer is away from systems of this type and toward digital control of digital devices.

A somewhat more elaborate, yet similar system is the GROOVE system developed by Bell Telephone Laboratories. This system was designed around a Honeywell DDP–224 computer and a large disk storage unit. While the system has many interesting and useful features, it has several drawbacks that make it difficult to export to another installation. The most notable of these is cost—$400,000.

Perhaps the most interesting system of this type is the digitally-controlled analog system presently being marketed by Buchla Associates. It is distinct from all other systems we have discussed in that it is intended mainly as a live-performance facility. It places a much higher emphasis on analog devices than all other systems.

The analog system is made up of Buchla System Series 200 Modules, which are also marketed separately as the Electric Music Box. The heart of the system is a Function Processing Unit that generates 64 simultaneous analog functions that are used to control the Series 200 modules. This unit is most accurately regarded as an analog computer especially designed for music. Other units in the system include a 16-input, 16-output, computer-controlled gating matrix; a medium-speed, 12-bit ADC; an analog timing pulse unit that communicates with the computer; a video display unit; a teletype unit and a second typing keyboard for entering information into the computer; a 16-bit mini-computer; a cassette digital tape unit; and a "software" or programming package. The cost of this system, which includes a sizable analog synthesizer, is $40,000–$50,000.

An Example of a Hypothetical Digitally-Controlled Analog System in Operation

One desires to realize the following passage. The instrument should resemble a piano in sound.

FIGURE 23.

The following steps will be necessary:

1. Instrument Design—A desired "patching network" of analog and digital devices is designed and a numeric coding of this "patch" is prepared for

input to the main music control program. The following gives this "patch" for the above instrument:

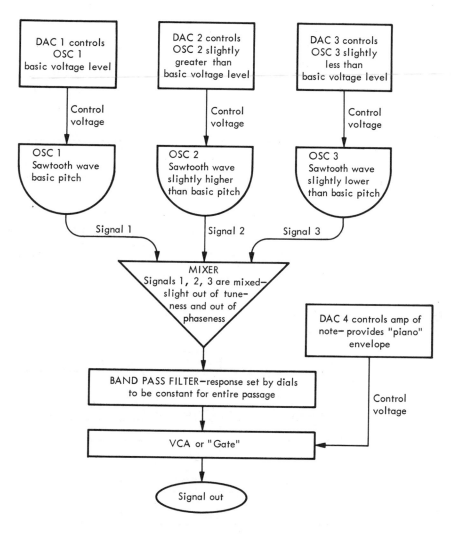

FIGURE 24.

This design reflects a number of compositional and acoustic decisions:

    a. Three oscillators are to be used to simulate the three piano strings. They will be given a complicated timbre, and will eventually be filtered.

b. Only one band-pass filter will be used, and it will be fixed for the course of the passage.

c. Only one gate will be used. This means that a "piano-type" envelope will have to be computed and sent to the gate via DAC 4. Notice the difference in this procedure and that shown in our earlier analog example, where attack generators were used in tandem to simulate a piano envelope.

2. Digital Device Programming—A program to compute inputs to various DACs is designed. This program will also be a part of the user's input to a master music-control program. Fig. 25 shows a logic "flow" diagram for the above instrument:

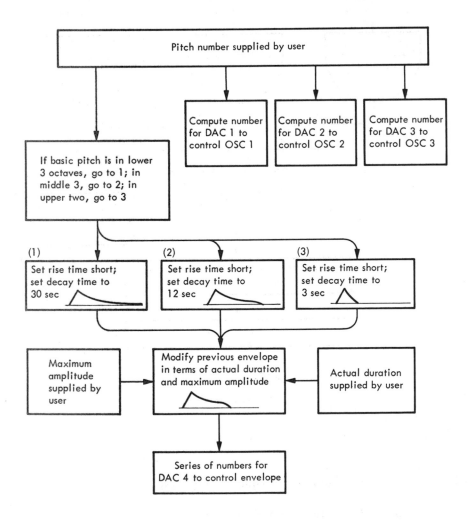

FIGURE 25.

Perhaps the most interesting aspect of the above flow chart is the manner in which the input for DAC 4 is computed. First, the basic pitch is noted, since the decay time of the note will vary with register in a manner similar to that of a piano. Frequencies in the lowest three octaves will be given decay times of 30 seconds, frequencies in the next three octaves will be given decay times of 12 seconds, and frequencies above that will be given decay times of 3 seconds. Each envelope will have a short attack time. Second, the actual duration of the note will be used to generate an envelope with a short attack time and a moderately short decay time. Finally, this second envelope will be "mapped onto" the first. Fig. 26 shows the results of the above steps for a note in the lowest three octaves whose duration is 3 seconds.

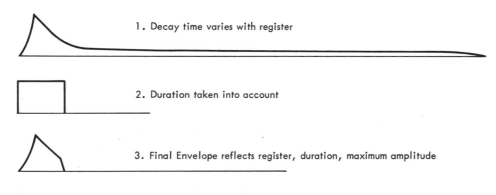

1. Decay time varies with register

2. Duration taken into account

3. Final Envelope reflects register, duration, maximum amplitude

FIGURE 26.

The above steps should result in different envelope patterns for different notes, depending on their register. These patterns are represented as a string of "binary" numbers that are transferred to DAC 4. When these numbers pass through this DAC at a high rate of speed, they should result in a control voltage that varies in a manner analogous to the desired envelope shape. It requires at least several hundred of these numbers per second to achieve a "smooth" envelope. Note the difference between this manner of control and that applied to the control of pitch; digital information for pitch is furnished only once per note. Neither of these control information speeds is so fast that we need be concerned with the types of distortions mentioned in our earlier discussion of digital sampling errors.

3. Musical Event Coding—The particular pitches, durations, timbres, and amplitudes of the piece are coded into a form acceptable to the music control program. Let us express pitch in 8VE.PC (OCTAVE-POINT-PITCH-CLASS) notation. In 8VE.PC coding, the octave of a note is represented by the part of

the number to the left of the "point," and the particular "note" or pitch-class is represented by the part of the number to the right. Octave 8 is middle *c;* the *c* above is octave 9; the *c* below is octave 7. The *c♯* above middle *c* would be 8.01; the *b* below middle *c* would be 7.11.

Rhythm requires, at the least, two pieces of information: the starting time of a note, and the duration of that note. We will express both these times in beats rather than seconds. Since the notes are legato, each will last until the next begins.

Finally, let us express amplitude in a scale where 1 represents the lowest amplitude value (similar to pp), and 6 represents the highest (similar to *ff*). Example 13 shows the coding of our musical example:

Example 13

St. Time	Duration	8VE.PC	Amplitude
1	.25	6.10	3
1.25	.25	6.03	3
1.50	.25	6.05	3
1.75	.25	6.02	3
2	1.25	6.00	3
3.25	.25	6.01	3

The information discussed in 1, 2, and 3 above (patching information, programming information, and musical event information) will be input to the main music program. This program will write a control tape for the section of music. When the control tape is played back through the control computer, the following will occur:

1. Patching information will be transferred to the digital switching matrix, which will connect the specified devices.
2. Binary numbers will be transferred to specified DACs.
3. Control voltages will come from the DACs, and will control the analog devices in the studio.
4. The piece will result.

For simplicity, I have used a simple one-voice piece as an example of the system in operation. Actually, the number of simultaneous "voices" will depend on the number of devices in the analog studio and the speed with which the digital tape drive can supply information.

COMPUTER SOUND SYNTHESIS

Computers were first used to synthesize sound in the late 1950s at Bell Telephone Laboratories in Murray Hill, N. J. Most computer sound synthesis programs in use today are based, at least in part, on "MUSIC4," the most successful of the early Bell Telephone programs written by Max Mat-

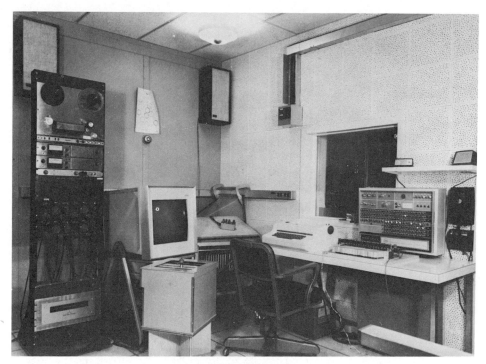

The GROOVE Facility at the Bell Telephone Laboratories.

The control console in the Elektronmusikstudion, Stockholm, Sweden.

The main studio of Electronic Music Studios, London, England.

thews and Joan Miller. The most common and versatile present-day sound synthesis programs are "MUSIC4B" (an expansion of MUSIC4, written in the assembly language of the IBM 7094 by Godfrey Winham and Hubert Howe); "MUSIC4BF" (a FORTRAN-language adaptation of MUSIC4B; one version written by Hubert Howe, the other by Godfrey Winham); "MUSIC360" (a program historically derived from MUSIC4B, but written in the assembly language of the IBM 360 series of computers by Barry Vercoe); and "MUSIC7" (a program very similar to "MUSIC360," but written in the assembly language of the XDS SIGMA7 computer by Hubert Howe). An interesting and some-what different program is described by Wayne Slawson in his article, "A Speech-Oriented Synthesizer for Computer Music."[3] Slawson's program, written in MAD (the Michigan Algorithm Decoder), relies to an extraordinary extent on the timbral analogies between vocal sounds and music. Many important recent developments have centered around the work of John Chowning and Leland Smith at Stanford University, and their programs are now becoming available throughout the country. Other computer synthesis programs include "MUSIGOL," "MUSIC5," "PERFORM," and John Clough's "TEMPO," which includes the first programming language designed especially for sound synthesis.

Other things being equal, it would be highly desirable to have a general music program that could be used with equal convenience on any computer. Such a program would have to be written in a universally available, high-level language. MUSIC4BF satisfies these conditions; it can be used on any com-puter that has a FORTRAN compiler. Unfortunately, other things are not equal. All the above programs are extremely time-consuming and, thus, ex-pensive to run; but programs written in assembly language are much faster than programs written in FORTRAN. "MUSIC360," for example, is between five to twenty-five times as fast as "MUSIC4BF." This means that five to twenty-five times as much music can be generated in the same amount of computer time. Economic factors thus make assembly-language programming almost a necessity.

It is obviously neither possible nor particularly desirable to discuss all the above programs in this chapter. Detailed reference manuals are available for each of these programs (see bibliography). We will concentrate, first, on de-scribing those features and problems that are basic to all computer sound gen-eration programs. Second, we will cover common types of "unit-generators, methods of instrument design, and score preparation for all the "MUSIC4B-type" programs. Finally, "MUSIC360" coding will be discussed in detail, and an example of an actual "MUSIC360" computer run will be analyzed.

Computer sound synthesis is the most flexible means of generating elec-tronic music. It allows the composer a control over sound generation that is limited only by his own knowledge of acoustics, music, and computer instru-ment design. Basically, anything that can be conceived accurately can be realized accurately. In this process the computer is not the control device for

---

[3] Journal of Music Theory, XIII, No. 1.

analog units; rather, it generates the specified sounds totally. The computer generates numbers, or "samples," that represent instantaneous amplitudes of sound waves. (See earlier discussion of D/A CONVERSION.) These numbers are passed through a DAC, with appropriate output filtering. When the varying voltages from the DAC are passed through an amplifier and speaker system, sound results.

Because of the almost unbelievably large number of calculations necessary in this process, it is not feasible to transfer numbers to the converter as they are being generated. This means that "real-time" generation of computer music is not presently possible since even the fastest computing systems are not fast enough to generate samples at the necessary sampling rate. Instead, a tape or disc is used to store the digital samples as they are being computed. After all the samples of the piece have been computed and stored, the entire tape or disc "record" is "played back" at a constant rate through the converter. Our earlier discussion of D/A conversion made clear that the converter ought to be able to run at an SR of 40,000 samples per second, per channel. Each sample must be of at least 12-bit accuracy, and it is highly desirable to have 16-bit accuracy. Normally, there will be one DAC for each channel, though the speed of many present-day DACs is such that one DAC is fast enough to provide information to several channels though a multiplexing technique.

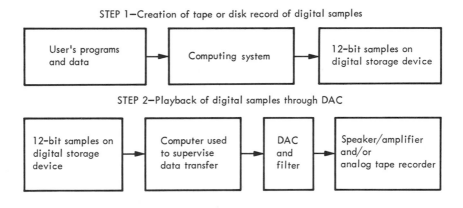

FIGURE 27.

Basic Programming Concepts in Computer Sound Synthesis

In a technical sense, the purpose of a computer sound synthesis program is to generate samples according to the composer's directions. The main sound synthesis program usually contains sub-programs called "unit generators." These units perform functions somewhat analogous to the units in an analog studio, but because they are digital they possess many advantages over their analog counterparts: they are completely compatible with one another and may be linked in any desired sequence; since all outputs and inputs are compatible, the same type of unit generator can be used to perform both signal and control functions; the units are extremely accurate, even at low frequencies; they are extremely versatile; and except for the reverberation unit, which requires a large amount of computer memory, the number of units available for the realization of a composition is almost unlimited.

Computer instrument design consists of linking together unit generators, a process conceptually similar to "patching" in an analog studio. A particular linkage is called an "instrument." Various "instruments" are combined into a user's "orchestra." In addition to an orchestra design, the user must also provide the data that "plays" the instruments. This data, which is called the "score," triggers the instruments and provides them with information by which they control various musical parameters. As will be seen, the user has great flexibility in the way he may specify data, and his manner of specification may vary with his choice of instrument design.

Frequency Generation

Given a constant SR, the number of samples per cycle determines the basic frequency in cycles per second (Hz). To take an unrealistically simple example, suppose we have 20 samples for each cycle of a wave and the SR = 100. The frequency is 5 cps (100/20 = 5).

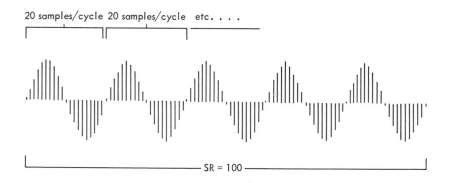

20 samples/cycle 20 samples/cycle etc. . . . .

SR = 100

FIGURE 28.

For the general case:

cps = SR/samples per cycle; therefore,
samples per cycle = SR/cps

For a desired frequency of A440 with an SR of 20,000, the number of samples per cycle is 45.4545 (20,000/440). This raises a basic problem in frequency generation inasmuch as we cannot present a fractional number of samples to the converter. Yet we cannot simply "round off" to 45 samples per cycle, for this would produce the wrong frequency. We can, however, present 45 samples for some cycles and 46 for others. Suppose that for every 2000 cycles, 909 had 46 samples per cycle and 1091 had 45. This would result in 90,909 samples for 2000 cycles, or an average of 45.4545 samples per cycle. The frequency error is distributed over a large number of cycles and is actually very minor; digital methods offer much more precise control of frequency than is possible with even the best analog equipment. Though the above is theoretically the basic technique for controlling frequency in computer synthesis, we will see shortly that the situation is somewhat more complicated in practice.

Sampling a Stored Function—Basic Frequency and Amplitude Problems

It seems logical that the individual unit generators of the program would consist of equations (sine functions, exponential functions, etc.) that, when executed, would result in the samples. However, this is not the case, and for a very good reason. Computing sine functions, to take a typical example, is quite time-consuming for the computer. If each unit generated its numerical output directly by computing equations, a music program would take days, not hours, to execute. Another method of generating these numbers must be used, yet that method must preserve the accuracy and flexibility of the more obvious one. This alternative method is called *sampling a stored function*.

For all computer music generation programs, a stored function is a table of numbers ranging between −1.0 and +1.0 This table is stored in successive locations in the computer. Waveforms and other desired shapes need be generated only once, usually at the beginning of the program. After that, needed values are simply looked up in the function table. The reason for storing values in the range of −1 to +1 is so that a given input amplitude value may be multiplied times all the values in the function and produce a result whose peak amplitude corresponds with the original amplitude value. (See later discussion of unit generator OSCIL, pp. 230, 231.) Many programs have followed the convention of using 512 locations for stored functions. There is no particular magic to this number beyond the advantage of its being a power of two ($2^9 = 512$) which makes the programming of "table look-ups" simpler, and the fact that 512 is a sufficient number of locations to store most functions accurately.

Many computer routines exist for the generation of function shapes, and many useful musical shapes can be generated quite easily. Some of these routines will be treated in detail when we discuss score preparation. Function 1 of the computer printout at the end of this chapter shows a 128-position representation of a sine tone, stored in 512 locations. If a computer "instrument" plays each successive value of this function on successive samples, the number of samples per cycle will obviously be 512. A repeating waveform may be obtained by continuously cycling the program back through the values of the function. If SR is 20,000, a frequency of slightly more than 39 cps (Hz) will be produced, since $20000/512 = 39 +$. Frequencies other than 39 Hz may be obtained by taking less or more than 512 samples per cycle. The former case requires skipping some values in the stored function; the latter requires repeating some. To obtain the correct number of samples per cycle from the stored function, the music program must obtain a sampling increment (SI). If SI is 1, all 512 values are used; if SI is 2, 256 values are used. For the general case, $SI = 512/$ samples per cycle. As before, difficulty arises when the desired frequency requires a fractional number of samples per cycle and/or a fractional sampling increment. There are two aspects to this difficulty. One concerns accuracy of frequency representation; its solution is similar to that discussed earlier. The other concerns accuracy of amplitude representation.

We have seen that A440 requires 45.4545 samples per cycle when the SR = 20,000. To produce this frequency, SI must be 11.264 (512./45.4545). We will speak of the function location that is currently furnishing the amplitude value as the *phase* (PHS). Let us begin at phase position 1. The next position is obtained by adding the sampling increment to the current phase (11.264 + 1 = 12.264). There is no function location of 12.264, and, therefore, no amplitude value is stored at such a position. There are two basic solutions to the problem of what number is to be furnished as the amplitude value for this nonexistent location. OSCIL, the simplest unit generator for frequency in MUSIC4B-type programs, uses the value at the previous position of the function while retaining the nonexistent position number for the next addition of SI. For a location of 12.264, then, OSCIL would furnish the value at location 12. The next location would be 23.528 (11.264 + 12.264). The OSCIL solution usually produces a fairly high degree of accuracy, but it can create problems if there are wide amplitude changes between adjacent function locations. The loss in quality that results when OSCIL is used as a frequency generator is called "quantization noise"; it may be heard as a slight hiss surrounding the tone.

Another unit generator, OSCILI, performs a linear interpolation between the values at the two adjacent locations. The interpolated value is proportional to the fractional part of the location.

Function Location	Value	PHS	Interpolated Value
12	.5		
13	.7		
		12.264	.5528

$(.7 - .5 = .2;\ 12.264 - 12 = .264;\ .264 * .2 = .0528;\ .5 + .0528 = .5528.)$

The OSCILI solution is obviously more accurate. For high audio quality, OSCILI must be used despite its slower time of operation.

If we continue to add SI, we will obtain, after 45 additions, a location of 507.880 (45 * 11.264 = 506.880; 506.880 + 1 = 507.880). The next addition will produce 519.144, a location greater than 512. This location must be reduced by 512 to produce a location in the function (519.144 − 512 = 7.144). Continuing this process through successive samplings of the function will result in a number of cycles being represented by 45 samples and a smaller number of cycles being represented by 46 samples. This alternation will even out to 45.4545 samples in the same manner as before, and will produce an effective frequency of A440.

It is very easy to become confused about the difference between sampling increment (SI) and sampling rate (SR). In fact, it is unfortunate that such similar terms are used to denote two totally different aspects of sound conversion. SR is associated with the process of D/A conversion; it is the number of 12-bit samples transferred to the converter every second. SI is the number of locations to skip when "sampling" an internally stored, digitized function shape. The following equations should help clarify the relations among cps, SR, SI, and 512.

$$\text{since} \quad \text{samples per cycle} = SR/cps$$
$$\text{and} \quad SI = 512/\text{samples per cycle}$$
$$\text{it must also be true that}$$
$$SI = (512./SR)/cps \qquad \text{by substitution}$$
$$\text{and}$$
$$SI = (512. * cps)/SR$$
$$cps = SR (512./SI)$$
$$SR = (cps * 512.)/SI$$

Unit Generators—Definitions and Basic Uses

Unit Name	Inputs	Flow-Chart Symbol
OSCIL	AMP, SI, F, PHS	
OSCILI	AMP, SI, F, PHS	

OSCIL and OSCILI are the basic frequency-generation units in most programs derived from MUSIC4B. For the reasons explained earlier, OSCILI produces much higher quality output and should be used for signal generation; OSCIL is more suited to control-type functions.

The output of these units consists of amplitude values. The number of amplitude values per cycle determines the frequency. The magnitude of the amplitude is determined by the "amp" input. This input is often called the "multiplier" input because it is multiplied times each successive value obtained from sampling the stored function. When the location in the function contains a value of 1 (the largest value a function can contain), the amplitude output will equal the multiplier input. The "amp" input thus determines the "peak amplitude" of the output. Frequency is determined by the sampling increment, or "SI" input. The function or "F" input simply informs the unit where the desired function shape is stored in the computer. If the F input is 1, the unit uses the first stored function; if the F input is 2, the second is used; etc. The phase input sets the position in the function from which sampling begins. Phase inputs are specified in positions 0–511 instead of 1–512. A phase of 0 indicates that sampling will begin with the "first" position in the function.

Unit Name	Inputs	Flow-Chart Symbol
PITCH/IPITCH	8VE.PC	8VE.PC
CYCLE/ICYCLE	CPS	CPS
OCTAVE/IOCTAVE	OCTAVE	OCT
PERIOD/IPERIOD	DUR	DUR

Because it is rarely convenient for the user to specify frequency as "SI," MUSIC4B-type programs include several units whose sole function is to convert various frequency representations to SI. These are "PITCH," which converts 8VE.PC to SI; "CYCLE," which converts cycles per second to SI; "OCTAVE," which converts an octave representation to SI; and "PERIOD," which converts a duration to SI. Units beginning with the letter "I" are "initialization-time" units, and may be called only once per note. We will clarify the difference between initialization and performance units in a later discussion.

OCTAVE.PC representation was discussed earlier, in connection with digital control of analog equipment. Most users who code "notes" find this mode of frequency representation very convenient. There are several cases in which it is inconvenient, however. Suppose we want a frequency modulation of a half step around a center frequency of middle c. In 8VE.PC, middle c is 8.00, and a half step is .01. But if we alternately add and subtract .01, we obtain 8.01 and 7.99. Unfortunately, in 8VE.PC, 7.99 represents the same frequency as 15.03, an extremely high note. This kind of arithmetic difficulty can be avoided by expressing frequency in CPS (Hz) or in "OCTAVE" form.

In OCTAVE representation, the number to the left of the decimal point has the same meaning as it does in 8VE.PC. The fractional number to the right of the point is a linear representation of interval. The interval of a half step is $\frac{1}{12}$ of an octave and, in this sense, would be represented by .0833; a tritone is one-half of an octave ($\frac{6}{12}$) and would be represented by .5. The above example of frequency modulation would work if the numbers involved were 8.00 for middle c and .0833 for a half step. We would obtain an FM between 7.9167 and 8.0833. In octave form, 7.9167 is lower than 8.00. Another advantage of OCTAVE representation is that it allows all frequencies to be represented fairly easily, whereas 8VE.PC allows only 12-tone equal temperament, unless modified by the user.

One purpose of "PERIOD" and "IPERIOD" is to obtain one cycle of a function per note. If the duration of the note were one second, then the frequency would be 1 cps. If the duration were 25 seconds, the frequency would be $\frac{1}{25}$ of a cycle per second. The sampling increment produced by **PERIOD** is appropriate to a frequency that is the reciprocal of the duration (1/duration). **PERIOD** thus performs the same function as **CYCLE** with an input of (1/duration).

UNIT NAME	Inputs	Flow-Chart Symbol
ENVLP	AMP, RISE, DUR, DECAY, F1, F2	

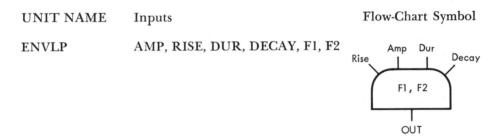

A basic unit for envelope control is "ENVLP." It allows rise and decay shapes to be determined by sampling stored functions. Its basic inputs are amplitude (in 0–2,047 units), rise time (in seconds), duration (in seconds), decay time (in seconds), function number for rise shape, and function number for decay shape. "ENVLP" has the initially confusing feature of calling for the decay function shape to be stored backwards. This is done because it makes possible the use of the same function for both rise and decay shape, thereby conserving computer storage space.

UNIT NAME	INPUTS	Flow-Chart Symbol
OUT	A, B, C, D	

A basic output unit is, appropriately, "OUT," which may receive up to four inputs. Each input gives the amplitude value that goes to a particular output channel. The first input specifies the output to CH 1; the second to CH 2; etc. Four inputs would be needed for a quadraphonic composition; two would be appropriate for stereo.

With the above unit generators as the basic components, we can construct a simple "instrument" that will allow us control of pitch, amplitude, envelope, waveshape, and duration.

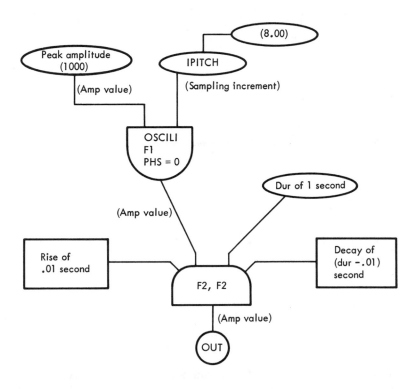

FIGURE 29.

The following is typical of the information that would be needed in order for this instrument to function:

1. Peak amplitude is specified for each note; let us assume a value of 1,000 (in a range of 0–2047) for this note.
2. Pitch is specified for each note in 8VE.PC; SI is generated by IPITCH; assume a first pitch of 8.00.
3. Function number 1 specifies the basic wave-shape for OSCILI to sample; it may be a sine wave or a sum of sine waves.
4. The rise time is constant for all notes: .01 second.
5. Duration is specified for each note; let us assume a duration of 1 second for the first note.
6. Decay time is defined as "duration-rise time" and, thus differs from note to note; in this case, decay time is .99 second.
7. Function number 2 specifies the rise shape; let us assume an exponential rise.
8. Function number 2 is sampled backwards to produce an exponential decay.

Fig. 30 shows the envelope of ENVLP applied to the output of OSCILI:

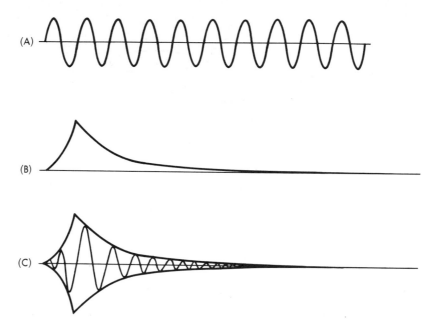

FIGURE 30.　(A) Basic Frequency. (B) Envelope. (C) Envelope applied to basic frequency.

An envelope that changed continuously during the course of the note could be obtained by using a control oscillator—an "OSCIL" would do—to modulate the amplitude input to a signal oscillator—an "OSCILI."

The following are important points in the operation of the above instrument:

1. The frequency input to OSCIL is determined by IPERIOD of the duration; if we assume a note duration of 10 seconds, IPERIOD will produce a sampling increment appropriate to a frequency of 1/10 cps. If the frequency input to OSCIL were from "ICYCLE," we would have created a general amplitude modulation instrument that could produce amplitude variations of a shape specified by F1 at a specified number of cps.
2. Function 1 is the shape of amplitude modulation. If IPERIOD is used, the shape could be a typical envelope shape such as that shown below. If ICYCLE is used to cause rapid amplitude modulations, it is advisable to change F1 to a smoother waveform, perhaps a sine wave, unless a "flutter-tongue" type of amplitude modulation is desired.

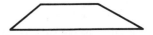

3. Note that this envelope will stretch or contract as its duration varies. This method of envelope control does not allow accurate specification of rise and decay times.

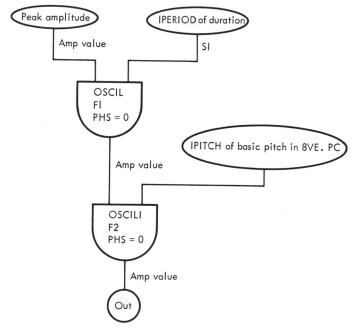

FIGURE 31.

The instrument shown in Fig. 32 provides full amplitude control with amplitude modulation, plus accurate rise and decay specification in seconds.

If OSCIL is used to control the frequency input to OSCILI, frequency modulation is the result as seen in Fig. 33.

The following are important points in the design in Fig. 33:

1. OSCIL controls the amount, speed, and shape of frequency modulation.
2. A "frequency designation" is needed for the "amplitude" input to OSCIL. This designation determines the amount or "bandwidth" of frequency modulation. In this case, the "frequency designation" is defined as .01 times the basic frequency. If the basic frequency is 1,000 cps, this input will be 10 cps.
3. The frequency of frequency modulation is determined by the frequency or "rightmost" input to OSCIL. In this design, this input is specified in CPS. Let us assume an input of 15 cps.
4. The shape of frequency modulation is determined by the function stored in F1. Let us assume this is a sine wave whose stored values will range from −1 to +1.
5. This function is sampled with an SI determined by an ICYCLE with an input of 15. Since the "amplitude" input was 10 cps, a sine curve with amplitude values between −10 and +10 will be generated 15 times per second.
6. The changing values generated by OSCIL are added to a basic frequency of

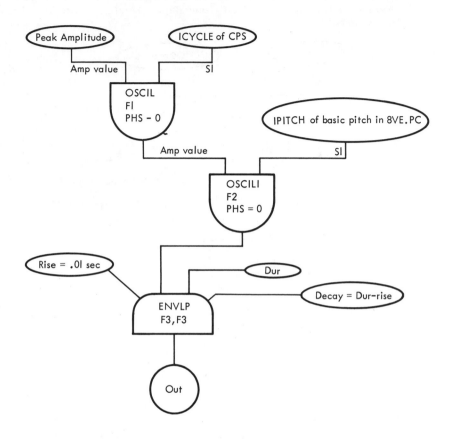

FIGURE 32.

1,000 cps on each sample. Thus, at a frequency of 15 times per second, the basic frequency will change continuously from 990 to 1010 cps.

7. This changing frequency in cps is converted to SI by CYCLE, and becomes the frequency input to OSCILI.

8. Inasmuch as the function shape in OSCIL determines the shape of frequency modulation, we have designed a general-purpose FM control unit. If the amplitude (bandwidth), frequency, and function inputs are appropriate, any FM shape, including upward and downward glissandi, may be generated.

9. It would have been more efficient for the computer to convert both frequencies in cps to sampling increments before the modification and addition steps. It is somewhat more confusing, however, to think of sampling increments being added than to think in terms of cps. At this stage of discussion, clarity rather than efficiency is the goal.

Several problems that are not immediately apparent arise when only OSCIL is available to act as an FM control unit. For this reason, most sound generation programs provide units that specialize in this task. These units, all

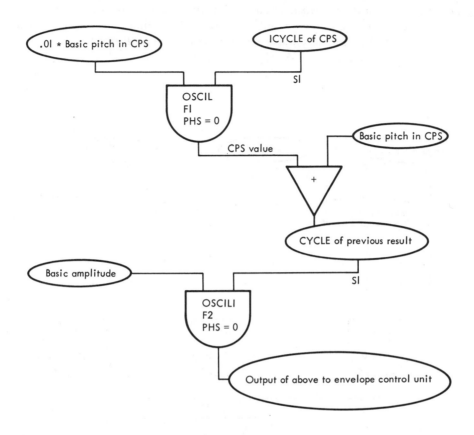

FIGURE 33.

of which are modifications of the basic design shown above, have names such as VPITCH (variable frequency generator with inputs in 8VE.PC) and VOC-TAVE (variable frequency generator with inputs in OCTAVE form).

One of the most striking differences between analog and computer sound synthesis is the manner in which different waveforms are generated. Usually available in analog studios are oscillators that produce sine waves, triangle waves, sawtooth waves, pulse waves, and square waves. Other wave-shapes are commonly produced by passing the output of the oscillator(s) through filters. This method of wave-shape production is called "substractive synthesis."

The waveform supplied to OSCILI, when OSCILI is used as an audio-signal generator, should be a sine wave or a sum of sine waves. The stored function is thus produced by "additive synthesis," and represents different harmonically related frequencies. When one stored cycle represents a large number of partials, the upper ones are less well-represented, this leads to certain problems in fidelity. Further, it will be impossible to store a wave containing nonharmonic partials since one cycle will not give a true picture of the repeating waveshape. The instrument design in Figure 34 is one way to solve both of these problems. The number of partials available is equal to the number of OSCILIs. Partials above SR/2, of course, should not be attempted. The function shape for each OSCILI is a sine wave.

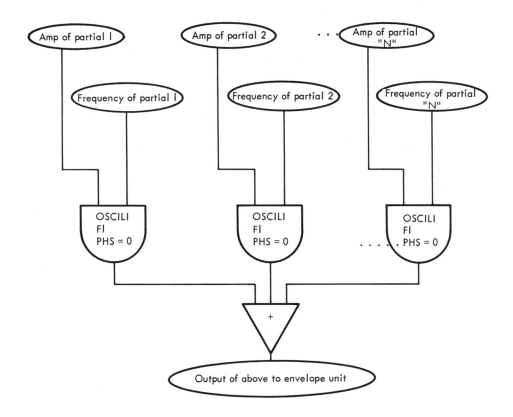

FIGURE 34.

A principle very similar to this is used in the unit generator, "FORMNT," the highest-quality audio unit in most sound-generation programs. FORMNT allows the user to specify any number of harmonic or nonharmonic partials with maximum accuracy. Its name is a computer abbreviation for *Formant,* an acoustic term for a region of frequencies resonated by a particular instrumental or vocal sound. One of the most valuable features of this unit is that it allows the user to specify characteristics of a formant filter internal to the unit. Other features of FORMNT include (1) the automatic elimination of frequencies above SR/2, thus removing the problem of foldover; and (2) an amplitude in rms (root mean square) rather than a peak value, thus making possible a more realistic relationship between designated amplitude and perceived loudness. The versatility and accuracy of this unit make it one of the slowest unit generators (that is, it requires more computer time).

UNIT GENERATOR	INPUTS	Flow-Chart Symbol
RAND	AMP	
RANDH	AMP, SI	

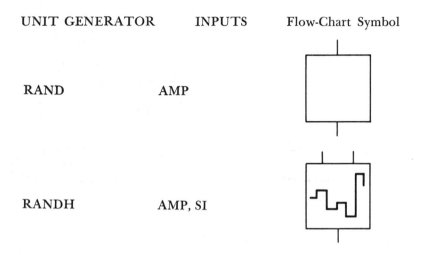

MUSIC4B-type programs typically have three or more different unit generators for producing random numbers. We will discuss two common ones: RAND, a signal generator for white noise, and RANDH, a unit more commonly used for control functions.

RAND is extremely simple. It accepts an input "AMP," and outputs white noise with the rms amplitude "AMP." An instrument that utilizes RAND is illustrated in Figure 37, following a discussion of a type of filtering that uses the unit generator, "RESON."

RANDH is more complicated in that it accepts an "SI" input as well as "AMP." RANDH generates a new random number in the range of 0 to 1 every 512/SI samples; it multiplies that random number times AMP, and outputs the result. It holds the old random number until a new one is generated, hence its name RANDH. At first, the choice of time interval for number generation might seem puzzling. The reason for this becomes clear when one realizes that one cycle of a "normal" computer oscillator's output contains 512/SI samples. Thus, RANDH generates a new random number at a time interval commensurate with "one cycle."

The instrument design in Fig. 35 uses RANDH to generate random frequency deviations within an interval defined by .05 times the basic frequency. These deviations occur five times per note.

The following are important points in this instrument design:

1. Since we want the random frequency fluctuations to be both .05 above and .05 below the given pitch, we must ask for a total interval (INT2) of twice the

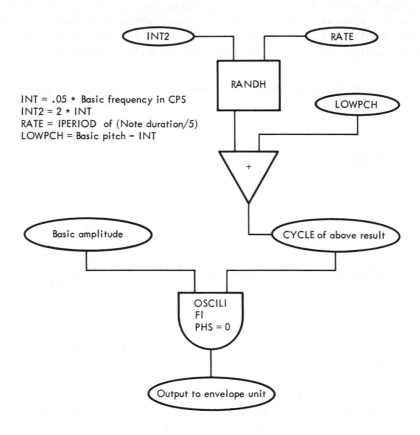

INT = .05 * Basic frequency in CPS
INT2 = 2 * INT
RATE = IPERIOD of (Note duration/5)
LOWPCH = Basic pitch − INT

FIGURE 35.

original interval. The original interval is subtracted from the basic pitch to provide the lowest pitch (LOWPCH).

2. Consider the basic pitch to be 500 cps. We desire random notes between 525 cps (500 + [.05 × 500]) and 475 cps (500 − [.05 × 500]). To do this, "INT" is calculated to be 25 cps, and "INT2," 50 cps. LOWPCH then becomes 475 (500 − 25). The output of RANDH lies between 0 and INT2, that is, between 0 and 50. The output of RANDH is added to LOWPCH, producing a random fluctuation between 475 and 525 cps.

3. Notice that the "amplitude" input to RANDH is expressed in cps. This means that the output of RANDH is a relevant number of cps and is, thus, an appropriate number to add to LOWPCH, which is also in cps. The result of this addition is the input to "CYCLE," which converts cps to the sampling increment needed by OSCILI.

4. The rate of occurrence of random pitch fluctuations is to be 5 times per note. A frequency of once per note is obtained by IPERIOD of the duration. Since sampling increment and frequency vary directly, a sampling increment appropriate to 5 times per note may be obtained either by (IPERIOD of the duration) × 5, or by IPERIOD of (duration/5).

5. I have not corrected for the fact that 25 cps below 500 is not quite the same musical interval as 25 cps above. In this particular application, the correction did not seem essential.

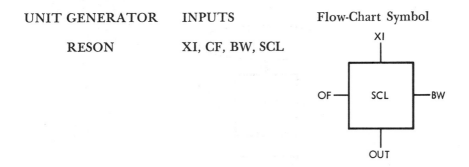

UNIT GENERATOR	INPUTS	Flow-Chart Symbol
RESON	XI, CF, BW, SCL	

"RESON" is a digital band-pass filter. Its relevant operating characteristics may vary from note to note, but do not vary during the course of any one note. Its inputs are the signal to be filtered (XI), the center frequency (CF), the bandwidth (BW), and an amplitude scaling factor (SCL). None of the latter three may vary during the course of a note; they are, thus, "initialization-time" inputs. Both CF and BW are expressed in cps. Figure 36 depicts the basic operation of a band-pass filter. Assume that the SR = 10,000; therefore, the highest available frequency is 5,000 cps.

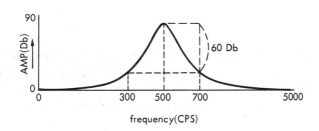

FIGURE 36.

In the settings for the above filtering, CF is 500 cps and BW is 200 cps. There are two potentially confusing aspects to these specifications. First, BW really refers to "half band-width"; it is the distance in cps on either side of the CF. Second, some signal is still present after the distance specified by BW. The signal is reduced by approximately 60 db at this point, however. The amplitude scaling factor for "RESON" is set at "1" for a normal signal and "2" for a noise.

Fig. 37 illustrates an instrument in which noise is filtered by a RESON with a CF of middle C (261 cps) and a BW of approximately one half step

(.05 × cps). This extreme filtering produces noise that has a very strong pitch center of middle C.

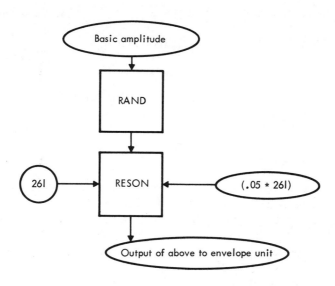

FIGURE 37.

A little reflection will show that "RESON" may be used as a "high-pass" or "low-pass" filter as well as in its band-pass mode. If CF is set at 0, BW determines the high-frequency cutoff, and the filter is low-pass. If CF is set at SR/2, BW determines the low-frequency cutoff, and the filter is high-pass.

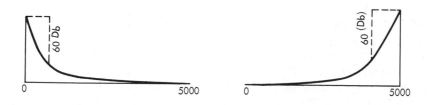

FIGURE 38.

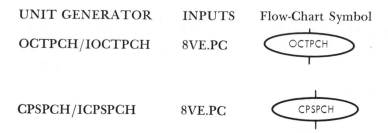

UNIT GENERATOR	INPUTS	Flow-Chart Symbol
OCTPCH/IOCTPCH	8VE.PC	OCTPCH
CPSPCH/ICPSPCH	8VE.PC	CPSPCH

There are usually many "convenience" routines for converting one form of pitch representation to another. While the user can code these routines as arithmetic statements in his orchestra, they do provide a labor-saving feature, especially in assembly-language orchestras such as those of MUSIC4B, MUSIC7, and MUSIC360. We will have occasion to use two of these routines—the ones shown immediately above—in later examples. Both accept an input in 8VE.PC. OCTPCH and IOCTPCH output a number in octave form; CPSPCH and ICPSPCH output a number in cps. The instrument design in Figure 39 illustrates the use of ICPSPCH in our previously designed noise instrument. This design allows us to express CF in 8VE.PC and to have the instrument convert that form to the cps mode needed by "RESON."

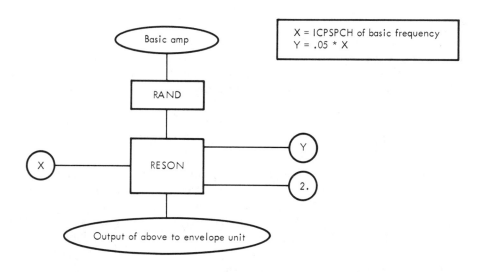

FIGURE 39.

Most computer music programs utilize many other unit generators. Among these are "VRESON," the digital filter whose characteristics may be varied during the course of a note; "BUZZ," which, among unit generators for pitch, has the output most appropriate for filtering; RANDI, an interpolating random-number generator; OSCIL1; SEGMNT; SEGMNTS; SLOPE; EXPON; LINEN; BALANCE; COMB; ALPASS; REVERB; MIXTAPE; MIX; MIXER; and CALLSUB. Information about these and other available units may be obtained by consulting the reference manual for the sound-generating program involved. Some of the "unit generators" for logical and arithmetic statements in MUSIC360 will be discussed later in this chapter.

Score Preparation

The score for a computer piece is usually a "deck" of computer cards, though some programs allow data to be entered from a terminal. These cards provide triggering and other types of information for the computer instruments. The cards themselves are normal 80-column, "Hollerith" cards with the following format:

	COL 1	COL 2–72	COL 73–80
	OP	DATA	COMMENTS

The "OP" or "operation" field tells the basic music program what kind of information is found on the rest of the card. The remainder of the card is divided into 12 "Parameter" or "P-fields" of 6 columns each. Each P-field can contain up to 6 decimal digits or 5 decimal digits plus a decimal point. If the field does not contain a decimal point, the numbers must be "right-aligned" in the field. If all the data cannot be put on one card, continuation cards may be used. The number of legal continuation cards depends on the particular kind of score card used. If the card is a continuation card, P1 contains 6 columns of information. Otherwise, P1 is shortened to 2 columns to allow for the OP and an optional NUM field.

I-Cards

I (instrument)-cards are the triggers for our instruments. Often, there will be one I-card for every attack point in the piece, though, as will be seen, the composer may define the relationship between musical event and trigger in almost any way he chooses. I-cards have an "I" punched in the operation field. All I-cards have the following types of information in the first three P-fields:

P1—number of instrument to be triggered
P2—starting time of event (in seconds or beats)
P3—duration of event (in seconds or beats)

The meaning of the remaining P-fields is defined by the composer in his instrument design. The purpose of these P-fields is to allow an input to an instrument to vary from event to event (note to note); otherwise, all values would have to remain fixed for the instrument. Consider the following clarification (Fig. 40) of the first computer instrument we designed:

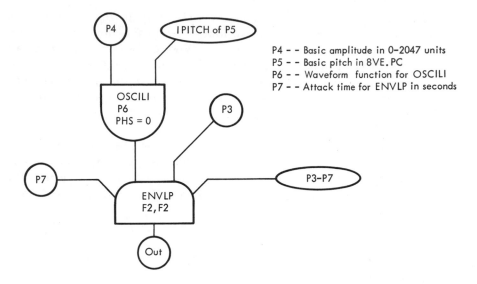

P4 - - Basic amplitude in 0–2047 units
P5 - - Basic pitch in 8VE. PC
P6 - - Waveform function for OSCILI
P7 - - Attack time for ENVLP in seconds

FIGURE 40.

The following I-card would "play" this instrument—which we will call instrument number 1—at time 0, for a duration of 1 beat, and at an amplitude of 1,000 and a pitch of middle C. The attack time would be .08 seconds, and the wave-shape function used by OSCILI would be function 5.

OP	P1	P2	P3	P4	P5	P6	P7
I	1.	0.	1.	1000.	8.00	.5	.08

F-Cards

Another important "score card" is the F-card. The F-card contains an F in the operation field, and is used to call for the generation and storage of function shapes. Most computer music programs contain a large number of sub-programs that enable the user to generate almost any conceivable function shape quite easily. In MUSIC4B-type programs, these sub-programs are named GEN01, GEN02, GEN03, . . . GEN20. The F-card calls one of these function-generating routines, provides data for it, and specifies the number of the function. This number is simply the number of the storage location in the computer for this particular function, and has no meaning aside from this. The first three P-fields of all F-cards give the following information:

P1—function number (1, 2, 3, . . . etc.)
P2—time of generation of function (usually time 0 since a function must be generated before an instrument can use it)
P3—number of function-generating sub-program to be called (1 for GEN01, 2 for GEN02, etc.)

The remaining P-fields furnish data to be used by the function-generating routine. We will now consider calls to four different function-generating routines—two that generate sines or sums of sine waves, one that generates exponential shapes, and one that generates linear ones. Printouts of all the functions we will discuss here are shown near the end of this chapter in an example of a complete computer music run. If the user places .1 after the number calling his "GEN routine," the main music program will provide a printout of the function.

Our first function is simply a sine wave. The easiest routine to use for this is one called GEN10 in all MUSIC4B-type programs. (It has this name simply because it happened to be the tenth sub-program designed to generate functions.) This routine computes sums of sine waves. The meaning of the P-fields from P4 on is defined for GEN10 as:

P4—amplitude of partial 1
P5—amplitude of partial 2
P_n—amplitude of partial $_n$-3

The following card will generate a sine wave as F1:

OP	P1	P2	P3	P4
F	1.	0.	10.1	1.

The following card would generate four harmonically-related partials. The relative amplitudes of partials 1–4 are 4, 1, 2, 3.

OP	P1	P2	P3	P4	P5	P6	P7
F	3.	0.	10.1	4.	1.	2.	3.

Both of the above functions would be appropriate ones to be sampled by the OSCILI of our instrument in Figure 40.

The next shape we will generate is the first half-cycle of a sine wave, a function that is often very useful for control purposes. We cannot use GEN10 for this because it assumes harmonic or integral partial numbers. "GEN09" is the appropriate function-generating routine for this task. It accepts inputs for partial number, relative amplitude of partial, and phase. GEN09 makes the following uses of the fields from P4 on:

P4, P7, P10, etc.—   partial number
P5, P8, P11, etc.—   amplitude of partial
P6, P9, P12, etc.—   phase of partial

Partial numbers may be specified in any order. Fractional partial numbers (nonharmonic partials) are legal, though GEN09 is not normally the best routine available to generate sums of nonharmonic partials because it cannot be used with "FORMNT," the only unit generator that generates nonharmonic sounds directly. The following card would generate our half-cycle sine curve:

OP	P1	P2	P3	P4	P5	P6
F	7.	0.	9.1	.5	1.	0.

GEN07 generates linear shapes and GEN05, exponential ones. Both make the same uses of the fields from P4 on. Remember that functions are stored in 512 locations. These routines allow you to specify the type of shape that will be drawn over a specified number of locations.

A function shape that rises linearly from 0 to 1 over 512 locations is specified as follows:

OP	P1	P2	P3	P4	P5	P6
F	8.	0.	7.1	0.	512.	1.

One sees that P4 and P6 represent amplitudes 1 and 2, and that P5 gives the number of locations over which amplitude 1 changes to amplitude 2. An exponential function cannot accept a zero value. We can generate an exponential rise from .001 to 1 over 512 locations by using GEN05.

OP	P1	P2	P3	P4	P5	P6
F	6.	0.	5.1	.001	512.	1.

Either of the above functions would be appropriate functions for "ENVLP." A linear decay is generated by the following card:

OP	P1	P2	P3	P4	P5	P6
F	10.	0.	7.1	1.	512.	0.

More complicated shapes can be easily drawn by keeping in mind the following relationships:

P4, P6, P8, etc.— Amplitude 1, amplitude 2, amplitude 3, etc.

P5, P7, etc.   — Number of function locations between amplitudes 1 and 2; number of function locations between amplitudes 2 and 3; etc. The sum of the number of locations—that is, the sum of the numbers in odd-numbered P-fields from P5 on—is normally 512. Otherwise, the function shape is incomplete. (This is sometimes desirable, of course.)

A function shape with a linear rise from 0 to 1 over the first half of the function (256 locations) and a linear decay over the second half is specified as follows:

OP	P1	P2	P3	P4	P5	P6	P7	P8
F	11.	0.	7.1	0.	256.	1.	256.	0.

Finally, an exponential shape that rises from 1 to 1,000 over 64 locations and that descends from 1,000 to 1 over 256 locations requires the specifications shown next. The last 192 (512 − [256 + 64]) locations of this function are 0.

OP	P1	P2	P3	P4	P5	P6	P7	P8
F	14.	0.	5.1	1.	64.	1000.	256.	1.

Other Score Cards

There are many other different kinds of score cards. Later, we will use the "E(end)-card," which is always the last card of the score; the "S(section)-card," which may be used to divide the score into whatever sections the user finds convenient; and the F0-card, which is used to generate silence. Suppose a section of our score is the following:

OP	P1	P2	P3	P4	P5	P6	P7	P8
F	8.	0.	7.1	0.	512.	1.		
F	11.	0.	7.1	0.	256.	1.	256.	0.
F	0	2						
S								

We have generated two meaningful functions and called for one that is nonexistent. Calling for function 0 is interpreted as calling for a silence at the time of its generation—in this case, time 2. Since no notes are generated in the section between times 0 and 2, the effect is to produce 2 seconds of silence. F0-cards are often used to insure a few seconds of silence at the beginning and the ending of a piece. If this is not done, these parts may be spoiled by the noise generated when the D/A converter goes on and off.

Other important score cards are the "T-card," which specifies the manner in which the tempo is controlled; the "C-card," which allows the user to insert comments into the score without affecting the sonic output; and the "A-card" and "B-card," which allow the user to call his own A and B subroutines.

Instrument Coding

The coding presented here is in MUSIC360. MUSIC4BF, though perhaps more widely available, requires an understanding of FORTRAN. MUSIC360 can be understood, at a basic level, with only the information presented in this chapter. Further, MUSIC360 is becoming more widely available because of the proliferation of IBM 360 and 370 computers and because of the willingness of Barry Vercoe, the author of MUSIC360, to install the program in various computer centers around the country.

A call to a unit generator is made on an ORCH card. The ORCH card has four fields, which are the normal fields for coding IBM assembler-language programs. In IBM parlance, these four fields are called the *name, operation, operand,* and *comments* fields. In MUSIC360, they are more commonly referred to as the *label, command, arguments,* and *comments* fields. There is no fixed-field format in IBM assembler coding; the end of a field on a card is symbolized by a blank. Nevertheless, many MUSIC360 users find it convenient to adhere to the following field designations when typing ORCH cards:

Col 1–9	Col 10–19	Col 20–59	Col 60–71
Label	Command	Arguments	Comments

The command field contains the name of a unit generator. The arguments field contains the arguments for the unit generator, separated by commas. The label field may be blank, may contain a number, or may contain an alphabetic label. If the label field contains a number, that number is the statement label of that particular program statement. It can be used to allow program flow to pass to that statement from a program statement other than the one immediately preceding. If the label is alphabetic, it is the name of the output of the unit generator used in the statement. The purpose of naming a unit's output is to enable that output to be referred to later. It might typically be used as the input to another unit. Though the naming of the output is, in a sense, arbitrary, it is usually wise for the user to select a name that is indicative of the output's most important feature. Numeric labels may contain from 1 to 4 digits. Alphabetic labels must begin with an alphabetic character, and may contain from 1 to 7 alphabetic and/or numeric characters.

The comments field is not recognized by the assembler except for the fact that it is printed out. The user may leave it blank, or he may insert comments that help him remember the purpose of the instruction being encoded.

The following is the format of an "ORCH(orchestra)-card" showing a call to OSCILI:

Label	Command	Arguments	Comments
Note	OSCILI	AMP, SI, NF, PHS	

"Passes" of the Main Music Program and the "Calling" of the User's Orchestra

The main music program makes three "passes" over (or interpretations of) the user's score. In PASS1, the program reads, stores, and prints the user's score cards. User-written FORTRAN subroutines called "A-subroutines" may be called at the end of PASS1 to modify the user's score. Typically, these subroutines perform those types of score-card modification that are more easily done before the cards are sorted into chronological order. Inversions, transpositions, and metrical modifications are among the usual tasks of A-subroutines. The effect of these routines is shown in the PASS2 printout.

The output of PASS1, the complete user's score, is the input to PASS2. This pass sorts the score according to beginnings of events, and converts all durations into seconds. Other user-written subroutines called "B-subroutines" may be called at the end of PASS2. Since these routines are called after sorting, it is usually inconvenient to use them to perform the note- or metric-modification tasks associated with A-subroutines. The only common B-subroutine is one that automatically assigns instrument type. This routine surmounts the common mistake of calling for an instrument that is already "playing." After all the B-subroutines have been called, the PASS2 score is stored and printed.

PASS3 reads the PASS2 score and calls the user's orchestra to generate the actual amplitude samples. The output of PASS3 is stored on a digital tape or disk, from which it is eventually converted to sound. PASS3 also provides the user with a printout that shows certain important features of the samples and functions that were generated. PASS3 is by far the most time consuming pass for the computer.

In addition, the calling of the user's orchestra has three relevant temporal divisions, in order that redundant evaluations of expressions may be avoided. MUSIC4BF shows these divisions explicitly by having the user design three separate "orchestra" subroutines: subroutine INITL, subroutine SETUP, and subroutine ORCH. The user of MUSIC360 does not assign separate names to these temporal divisions, nor does he design separate subroutines for each of them. It is, nevertheless, essential for the MUSIC360 user to understand these three relevant times, for they affect the way the program operates.

Time 1—Initialization of the Orchestra

Certain features of the user's orchestra remain the same for the entire run of the job. These are the sampling rate, the number of channels, the maximum number of functions, and the maximum number of instruments. These aspects of the user's orchestra are defined in subroutine INITL in MUSIC4BF. In MUSIC360, the first three variables are defined by a DECLARE statement, which must precede the definition of the first instrument in the orchestra. The fourth variable need not be specified in MUSIC360, except in regard to individual instrument design.

Time 2—Initialization of the "Note"

Certain features of the user's orchestra change from note to note, but do not change during the course of any one note. The duration of the note, for example, could not change during the time of its own duration. It would be just as senseless to change the instrument number of the instrument while it is playing, or to change the starting time of the note after the note has started. Those aspects of the orchestra that change only once per note should be computed only once per note. Unit generators that need to be called only once per note are called "initialization" units and begin with the letter "I." Most unit generators are available in both initialization and performance versions. The unit generator that converts OCTAVE.PC to a sampling increment, for example, is available in both the PITCH (performance) and the IPITCH (initialization) forms. If the frequency remained constant over the course of the note, IPITCH could be used; if the frequency changed, as in frequency modulation, PITCH should be used. In MUSIC4BF, this part of the user's orchestra is called subroutine SETUP. In MUSIC360, both performance and initialization calls may be placed in the user's orchestra program. It is up to the user to decide which is appropriate at that point in his program. Obviously, a great deal of computer time can be wasted by a call to a performance unit when only an initialization one is needed. On the other hand, a call to an initialization unit when a performance unit is needed will produce wrong results.

Time 3—Performance of the Orchestra

Certain features of the user's orchestra must be used more than once per note, perhaps on every sample. The calls to these portions of the orchestra are essentially the "performance" of the orchestra. It is in this part of the run that the digital samples are generated and stored on tape or disk. It is obviously the most crucial part of the computer run, and it is normally the part that requires the most cpu time for the computer. In MUSIC4BF, the coding for the performance units of the orchestra is placed in subroutine ORCH.

The following shows the coding necessary to generate the call to OSCILI that occurs in the instrument diagrammed in Figure 41:

Label	Command	Arguments	Comments
PCH	IPITCH	P5	
NOTE	OSCILI	P4, PCH, P6, 0.	

Note that P-fields of I-cards are not subscripted in the argument lists for MUSIC360 unit generators. P5 is legal; P(5) is not. P6 is legal; P(6) is not. Note also that numeric values may be inserted directly in the argument list; the last argument to OSCILI is 0. Finally, note that the output of IPITCH (an initialization-time unit) is labeled "PCH" and is used as an input to the OSCILI argument list.

The following table summarizes the basic unit generators we will need in order to code both a simple and a relatively complicated orchestra:

Label	Command	Arguments
	PITCH/IPITCH	8VE.PC
	CYCLE/ICYCLE	CPS
	OCTAVE/IOCTAVE	OCTAVE
	PERIOD/IPERIOD	DURATION
	OCTPCH/IOCTPCH	8VE.PC
	CPSPCH/ICPSPCH	8VE.PC
	OSCIL	AMP,SI,F,PHS
	OSCILI	AMP,SI,F,PHS
	ENVLP	AMP,RISE,DUR,DECAY,F1,F2
	RAND	AMP
	RANDH	AMP,SI
	RESON	AMP,CF,BW,SCL
	OUT	A, B

In addition to the above units, we must also be able to make arithmetic assignment statements and carry out arithmetic operations. In MUSIC360, these functions are performed by the VAL and IVAL (initialization-time unit) statements. The formats for arithmetic assignment, addition, subtraction, multiplication, and division that use VAL and IVAL are shown below. IVAL is called only once per note, of course.

Label	Command	Arguments	Comments
X	VAL/IVAL	1	X = 1
X	VAL/IVAL	A	X = A
X	VAL/IVAL	A + B	X = A + B
X	VAL/IVAL	A − B	X = A − B
X	VAL/IVAL	A * B	X = A TIMES B
X	VAL/IVAL	A / B	X = A / B

MUSIC360 also provides a variety of statement types to facilitate transfer of program control. The "GOTO" and "IGOTO" statements cause unconditional transfer to the statement whose arithmetic label appears in the argument field of the "GOTO" statement.

Label	Command	Arguments
	GOTO/IGOTO	100

Whenever the above statement is encountered in the execution of the orchestra, the program transfers to the statement labeled "100."

Conditional transfers transfer to a labeled statement only if a particular condition is met. The transfers available in MUSIC360 are listed below. Note that the initialization form of IFGO is IIFGO. An initialization-time unit transfers only once per note.

Label	Command	Arguments
	IFGO/IIFGO	(A.EQ.B),100
	IFGO/IIFGO	(A.GT.B),100
	IFGO/IIFGO	(A.LT.B),100
	IFGO/IIFGO	(A.GE.B),100
	IFGO/IIFGO	(A.LE.B),100
	IFGO/IIFGO	(A.NE.B),100

"EQ," obviously, means "equals." "GT" and "LT" mean "greater than" and "less than," respectively. "GE" and "LE" mean "greater than or equal to" and "less than or equal to," respectively. "NE" means "not equal to." If the logical condition stated in the argument list is true, transfer occurs. In the first argument in the above table, if it is true that A = B, the program transfers execution to the statement labeled 100. In the last argument, if it is true that A and B are not equal, transfer occurs.

Sometimes it becomes necessary to transfer to a statement whose output must have an alphabetic label. This cannot be done directly in MUSIC360, in which a statement cannot have both an alphabetic and a numeric label. The purpose may be accomplished by inserting a "NULL" or "NO OPERATION" statement before the statement that must receive the alphabetic label, giving the NULL statement a numeric label, and then transferring to the NULL statement. By analogy with FORTRAN, the NULL statement in MUSIC360 is the command, "CONTINUE." Examples of its use will be seen shortly.

Another important feature of MUSIC360 orchestra coding is the use of "U-symbols." These symbols provide an alternative to labeled outputs for unit-generator calls. U1 is the name of the output of the previous unit; U2 is the name of the output of the second previous unit: etc. U-symbols are convenient at points in a job where the branching is uncomplicated or where a numeric label is needed. Alphabetic labels are often more convenient than U-symbols in complicated situations.

"REVAL" and "IREVAL" statements are used to re-evaluate a variable. Consider the error revealed by the following code (assume that P5 and P6 define pitch in 8VE.PC, that P4 defines amplitude, and that P7 defines function number):

Label	Command	Arguments
X	IPITCH	P5
Y	IPITCH	P6
	IIFGO	(P5.GT.8.00),100
X	IVAL	Y
100	OSCILI	P4,X,P7,0.

This program segment converts 8VE.PC in P5 and P6 to sampling increments. The "SI" outputs of IPITCH are labeled X and Y, respectively. If P5 is greater than 8.00, an attempt is made to re-evaluate X to Y. This attempt produces the coding error of duplicate labels: there are two statements labeled X. This is illegal because the program cannot know which one to use at any given time.

This error can be avoided by using "IREVAL." Both "IREVAL" and "REVAL" have two arguments, "A" and "B." When either IREVAL or REVAL is encountered in execution, A is re-evaluated to B. B may be a variable, a number, or an arithmetic expression (A/B is an expression, for example). The following is the corrected code for the re-evaluation attempted earlier:

Label	Command	Arguments
X	IPITCH	P5
	IIFGO	(P5.LE.8.00), 95
	IPITCH	P6
	IREVAL	X, U1
95	OSCILI	P4, X, P7, 0.

An orchestra definition begins with the command "ORCH" and ends with the command "ENDORCH." The coding of instrument number "N" begins with the command "INSTR" with the argument "N" and ends with the command "ENDIN." If, for example, the instrument is the fifth one of the orchestra, the definition begins "INSTR 5." Duplications of an instrument design may be produced by using the instrument numbers involved as arguments to the INSTR command. "INSTR 1,2," for example, means that instruments 1 and 2 are duplications of each other; likewise, "INSTR 2,6" means that instruments 2 and 6 are duplications. Duplicate instruments are necessary if one wishes to have two of the "same" instruments play at the same time.

The second command of the orchestra is usually "DECLARE." This command sets the sampling rate, the number of channels (mono, stereo, quad), and the total number of functions used.

Label	Command	Arguments
	DECLARE	SR = 10000, NCHNLS = 2, F = 10

The card that usually follows "DECLARE" is one that specifies one of the following options: "RESCALE," "RESCALE LATER," or "NOTAPE." The "RESCALE" option allows the user to have his final tape "rescaled" in proportion to the maximum value that can be accepted by the D/A converter (2,047 in the case of a 12-bit converter). This option requires two tapes—an intermediate, non-rescaled tape and a final, rescaled one. RESCALE with the argument "LATER" writes only the intermediate tape; it assumes that this tape will later be rescaled for conversion. "NOTAPE" means that no tape will be written. This option is valuable for short tests in which the user does not need to hear his output. If none of the above three commands is included with the orchestra, an unrescaled final tape is written.

The command "PSAVE" must be included in each instrument definition in the orchestra. This command has arguments that inform MUSIC360 how many P-fields of the note cards must be saved for a particular instrument. You will remember that the meanings for P1, P2, and P3 are the same for all score cards. They indicate the instrument number, the starting time, and the duration of the event. Often, neither P1 nor P2 is specifically used in the user's orchestra. If that is the case, neither need be saved in the "PSAVE" statement. Suppose the instrument uses P-fields up through P9. PSAVE would then need the arguments "(3, 9)," if P1 and P2 were not to be saved; but if P1 and P2 were used in the instrument, PSAVE would need the arguments (1, 9). The arguments to PSAVE must be enclosed in parentheses and separated by a comma.

The ORCH definition is usually preceded by a "PRINT" command with the argument "NOGEN." This is not a MUSIC360 command. It is an IBM system command that suppresses certain aspects of the printing of the MUSIC-360 ORCHESTRA. If it is not included, information which is not meaningful to most users is printed out. Another system command is contained on the "END" card, which must always follow the "ENDORCH" card that marks the end of the orchestra definition. The "END" card informs the IBM assembler that the coding for your assembly-language program, i.e., your orchestra, is complete.

Our first orchestra will contain only one instrument. It has the same structure as the instrument shown in Fig. 41.

Label	Command	Arguments
	PRINT	NOGEN
	ORCH	
	DECLARE	SR = 10000, NCHNLS = 2, F = 10
	RESCALE	
	INSTR	1
	PSAVE	(3, 7)
	IPITCH	P5
	OSCILI	P4, U1, P6, 0.
	IVAL	P3-P7
	ENVLP	U2, P7, P3, U1, 6, 6
	OUT	U1, U1
	ENDIN	
	ENDORCH	
	END	

The above instrument can play only one note at a given time because it contains only one oscillator. Suppose the musical passage to be realized required 5 notes at once. This would necessitate the creation of 5 identical instruments. If these were instruments 1–5 of the orchestra, they could be created by changing the "INSTR" card of the above orchestra to:

Label	Command	Arguments
	INSTR	1, 2, 3, 4, 5

Let us now change the above instrument design so that it will automatically modify its choice of function shape according to the pitch present in P5. Let's say that function number 1 is appropriate for all pitches above 11.00, function number 2 for all between 10.00 and 11.00, number 3 for all between 9.00 and 10.00, number 4 for all between 8.00 and 9.00, and number 5 for all below 8.00. We will place one of these numbers in the position of "P6" in the OSCILI argument list. We will name the variable representing the function number "FNUM," set its original value by means of an IVAL statement, and re-evaluate it according to the 8VE.PC number in P5. All these calculations need be done only once per note, so we will use initialization-time units.

Now P6 is available to serve some other function, as it is no longer affecting function shape. At present, we have no way of controlling channel balance. Let's make one final modification of this instrument so that a number between 0 and 1 in P6 will determine the balance between channel 1 and channel 2. If "N" is the number in P6, then "N times SIGNAL" will go into channel 1 and "(1. − N) times SIGNAL" will go into channel 2. If the number in P6 were .357, for example, then 357/1,000 of the signal would go into CH 1 and 643/1,000 would go into CH 2. The instrument design in Example 15 encompasses these changes. Note that the exponential function for ENVLP has been changed to F6 because F2 was changed to a sum of sines.

Example 15.

Label	Command	Arguments
	PRINT	NOGEN
	ORCH	
	DECLARE	SR = 10000, NCHNLS = 2, F = 10
	RESCALE	
	INSTR	1
	PSAVE	(3, 7)
FNUM	IVAL	1
	IIFGO	(P5.GE.11.00),100
	IREVAL	FNUM, 2
	IIFGO	(P5.GE.10.00),100
	IREVAL	FNUM, 3
	IIFGO	(P5.GE.9.00),100
	IREVAL	FNUM, 4
	IIFGO	(P5.GE.8.00),100
	IREVAL	FNUM, 5
100	IPITCH	P5
	OSCILI	P4,U1,FNUM,0.
	IVAL	P3-P7
SIG	ENVLP	U2, P7, P3,U1,6,6
SIG1	VAL	P6 * SIG
CH2MLT	IVAL	1. − P6
SIG2	VAL	SIG * CH2MLT
	OUT	SIG1, SIG2
	ENDIN	
	ENDORCH	
	END	

Job Submission Procedures and the Job Control Language

We now possess an orchestra of one instrument type. Shortly, we will code a score and show a printout of a deck that could be submitted for a computer run. But before we do this, we need to confront the problem of what steps are necessary to have our job run on a large IBM 360 or 370 computer. Setting up MUSIC360 so that it will run at a particular computer center is a task of considerable magnitude; it requires the aid of both systems programmers at the installation and professional programmers who understand MUSIC360. I will assume, for the purposes of this chapter, that the task of making MUSIC-360 operational has been accomplished.

At UNH, we have MUSIC360 stored, in "object" or "executable" form, on a disk in the computer center. Whenever a user wishes to run a MUSIC360 job, he types the following cards:

```
//  EXEC MUSIC360
    INCLUDE PROG(MUSIC360)
    ENTRY MAIN
```

He then inserts them at the appropriate points in his deck. These three cards generate a large number of job control statements in the job control language (JCL) of the IBM 360 operating system (OS). Most users find IBM JCL extremely confusing; thus a "catalogued procedure" for running MUSIC360 is essential.

Also to be included in the user's job deck are other JCL statements that tell the system whether the cards it is reading represent a program or the data for a .program. If the cards are a program, the operating system must be told what the coding language is. The MUSIC360 user's deck always contains an assembly-language program, his orchestra. This program must be preceded by a "//ASM.SYSIN DD *" card. If FORTRAN A and/or B subroutines are included, they must be preceded by a "//FORT.SYSIN DD *" card. The data of a MUSIC360 run is the score; it must be preceded by a "//GO.SYSIN DD *" card. If the job is creating digital tapes, these must be specified on cards beginning "//GO.FT08F001 DD UNIT = TAPE9" for a final tape and "//GO.FT09F001 DD UNIT = TAPE9" for an intermediate tape. There are only two parameters of the tape card that must concern the user. The parameter "LABEL = (2, NL)" means that this job's output is written on the second file of the tape. Proper use of this parameter allows the user to store several jobs on one tape. The other parameter, which varies is the tape number. Finally, each job must be preceded by two "JOB" cards and one "SETUP" card, which informs OS and the operator about certain characteristics of your job; each job must end with a "//" card.

Ex. 16 is the JCL needed for a run at UNH. We will assume that "RE-SCALE" is specified, causing the job to need two tapes, and that the job will take 60 minutes of CPU time.

Example 16.

```
job number  JOB  (UNH,
//   your account number),'name',MSGLEVEL=1,CLASS=E,
//   REGION=210K,TIME=60
/*SETUP  REGION=210K,TIME=60,CLASS=E
//   EXEC  MUSIC360
//ASM.SYSIN  DD  *
```

        (your ORCH cards with RESCALE specified)

```
/*
//FORT.SYSIN  DD  *
```

        (your A and B subroutines in FORTRAN)

```
/*
//LKED.SYSIN   DD   *
  INCLUDE PROG(MUSIC360)
  ENTRY MAIN
/*
//GO.FT08F001   DD   UNIT=TAPE9,DISP=(NEW,KEEP),DSN=MUZAK,
//   LABEL=(2,NL),VOL=SER=your final tape number
//GO.FT09F001   DD   UNIT=TAPE9,DISP=(NEW,KEEP),DSN=INTER,
//   LABEL=(1,NL),VOL=SER=your intermediate tape number
//GO.SYSIN   DD   *

                    (your score cards)

//
```

Ex. 17 shows an actual deck with a very simple score for a run of the previously designed orchestra at UNH:

Example 17.

```
//A0113466   JOB   (UNH,
//  L128),'ROGERS EXAMPLE',MSGLEVEL=1,CLASS=E,REGION=210K,TIME=60
/*SETUP   REGION=210K,TIME=60,CLASS=E
//   EXEC   MUSIC360
//ASM.SYSIN   DD   *
                PRINT              NOGEN
                ORCH
                DECLARE            SR = 10000, NCHNLS = 2, F = 10.
                RESCALE
                INSTR              1
                PSAVE              (3, 7)
FNUM            IVAL               1
                IIFGO              (P5.GE.11.00),100
                IREVAL             FNUM, 2
                IIFGO              (P5.GE.10.00),100
                IREVAL             FNUM, 3
                IIFGO              (P5.GE.9.00),100
                IREVAL             FNUM, 4
                IIFGO              (P5.GE.8.00), 100
                IREVAL             FNUM, 5
100             IPITCH             P5
                OSCILI             P4, U1, FNUM, 0.
                IVAL               P3 — P7
SIG             ENVLP              U2, P7, P3, U1, 6, 6
SIG1            VAL                P6 * SIG
CH2MLT          IVAL               1. — P6
SIG2            VAL                SIG * CH2MLT
                OUT                SIG1, SIG2
                ENDIN
                ENDORCH
                END
```

```
/*
//LKED.SYSIN    DD    *
  INCLUDE PROG(MUSIC360)
  ENTRY MAIN
/*
//GO.FT08F001    DD    UNIT=TAPE9,DISP=(NEW,KEEP),DSN=MUZAK,
//    LABEL=(2,NL),VOL=SER=CC0992
//GO.FT09F001    DD    UNIT=TAPE9,DISP=(NEW,KEEP),DSN=INTR,
//    LABEL=(,NL),VOL=SER=CC0995
//GO.SYSIN    DD    *
```

F 1		0	10.1	1							
F 2		0	10.1	1	5						
F 3		0	10.1	4	1	2	3				
F 4		0	10.1	7	1	2	6	3	4	5	
F 5		0	10.1	13	1	2	12	3	4	11	5
	10	7	8	9							
F 6		0	5.1	.0001	512	1					
F 0		2									
S											
I 1		1	.1	500	7.00	1	.001				
I 1		1.125	.1	500	8.01	0	.001				
I 1		1.250	.1	500	6.06	1	.001				
I 1		1.375	.1	500	9.03	0	.001				
E											
//											

Observations on Approaches to Computer Instrument Design

There are at least two radically different philosophical approaches to computer instrument design. On one hand, one might design his instrument so that one I-card would be sufficient to cause the instrument to "turn on" and perform the entire piece, or at least a substantial segment of it. This would obviously require a complicated instrument design, and a large number of P-fields would probably be required in order to supply enough data for the instrument to work correctly. It is easy to think of cases where this approach would be helpful, and our more complicated instrument in the following job is of this design.

At the other extreme, suppose that each I-card triggers only what we would normally conceive to be one note. The instrument definition would probably be simpler, but the number of I-cards would be much larger. Obviously, how one designs his instruments will depend on (1) the characteristics of the piece, and (2) the way the composer wants to think of the piece. Most instrument designs are somewhere between these two extremes.

The second of these two approaches to instrument design invites the use of user-written subroutines to modify or generate note cards. Musical passages that are clearly related to previous passages may be generated from the score cards of those passages by using A- and in some cases B-subroutines that invert, transpose, rotate, remove, rearrange, or perform some other relevant operation.

This method often saves the user much of the labor of punching score cards; more important, it may allow him to generate desired musical patterns much more easily than if he had to calculate them by hand. Since this chapter does not assume a knowledge of FORTRAN, it is not feasible to cover A and B routines here. The interested reader is referred to the reference manuals for MUSIC4 and/or MUSIC7 for a discussion of these routines.

A Final Overview of a System for Computer Sound Synthesis

The following is a summary of the steps in the design and execution of a computer-realized composition:

Preparation for Computer Run

1. A desired musical passage is envisioned.
2. An orchestra consisting of various instruments is designed; the characteristics of the orchestra are determined by the needs of the composition.
3. An orchestra definition is coded and the "ORCH" cards are punched.
4. The score is coded and the score cards are punched.
5. The user's orchestra and score cards are placed with cards that call the main music program (which is assumed to be stored on a disk in the main computer center) and with other appropriate "JCL cards," and the job is submitted.

Computer Run

6. The job is executed by the operating system of the computer, and calls the main music program—in our case, MUSIC360.
7. PASS1 of the main music program reads, optionally modifies, and stores the user's score.
8. PASS2 reads, modifies, and stores the PASS1 score.
9. PASS3 reads the PASS2 score, calls the user's orchestra, and generates the samples to be stored on digital tape or disk.

Sound Conversion

10. The digital tape or disk record is played back at a constant SR through one to four channels of filtered D/A conversion; the outputs of the DACs are recorded on analog tape.
11. The analog tape is played back on an analog tape recorder.

A COMPLETE EXAMPLE

Characteristics of the Desired Musical Passage

A) Several four-note chords are to be played. Each chord may receive multiple attacks. The chords should move from CH1 to CH2 and back to CH1, or vice versa, over the course of the note. The wave-shape of each voice of the chord may be a sine tone or a waveshape determined by our previous FNUM routine. The overall envelope shape should be a short exponential rise, a steady state portion, and a fairly long exponential decay. The envelope of the multiple attacks is a medium-short exponential attack and decay.

B) The noise equivalent of the above instrument is to be obtained by subjecting four noises to very sharp filtering, so that each noise will have the sense of a "center frequency."

C) A series of notes are to be generated with the following properties:

1. Pitch is to be random within a specified interval, with respect to a specific pitch, and within a shape that may be varied over the series of notes.

2. Rhythm is to be determined by (1) a basic duration determined by the number of notes specified in a given time period (P3 is the time period); (2) an "offset" value to be added to or subtracted from the duration obtained by (1); and (3) a shape that determines the manner in which the value of (2) is added to the duration obtained by (1).

3. Channel balance is random with respect to any one "component note."

4. Changes of pitch produced by 1 above, changes of rhythm produced by 2, and changes of channel produced by 3 must all occur at the same time.

5. The number of partials in the basic wave-shape is to be determined by the "FNUM" routine used earlier, or, alternatively, the waveshape may simply be a sine curve.

Fig. 41 is a musical score of the passage to be realized:

Orchestra Design

Three basic instrument types are needed to realize the above score. Fig. 42 is the flow chart for instrument type 1.

The meaning of the P-fields for INSTR 1 is:

P4 — Basic amplitude in 0–2,047 units.
P5 — Pitch of note 1 in 8VE.PC.
P6 — Pitch of note 2 in 8VE.PC.
P7 — Pitch of note 3 in 8VE.PC.
P8 — Pitch of note 4 in 8VE.PC.
P9 — If P9 contains a 0, chord starts in CH2, moves to CH1, and returns to CH2; if P9 contains any other number, chord starts in CH1, moves to CH2, and returns to CH1.
P10 — If P10 contains a 0, FNUM determines the function. Otherwise, a sine curve is used.
P11 — The number of attacks per note.

The instrument shown in Fig. 43 is exactly like INSTR 1 after the "add box." The following lists the meaning of the P-fields for INSTR 2:

P4 — Basic amplitude input for RAND as a white-noise generator.
P5 — Center frequency FOR RESON 1.

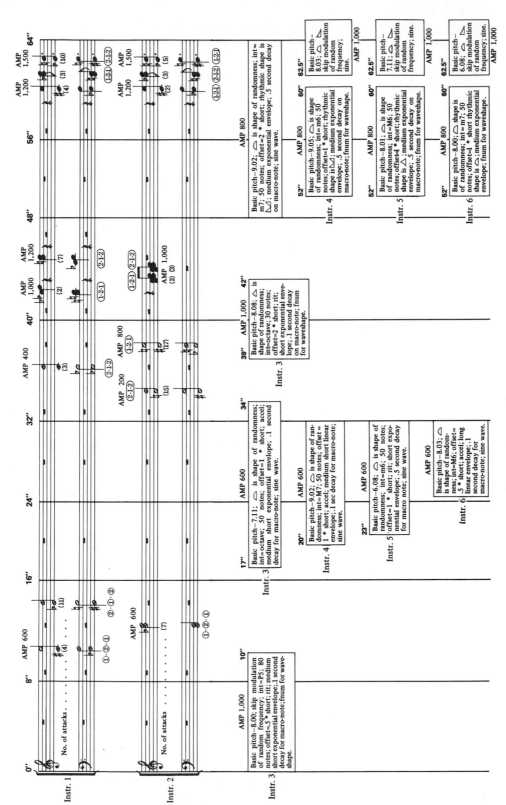

FIGURE 41. Musical Score.

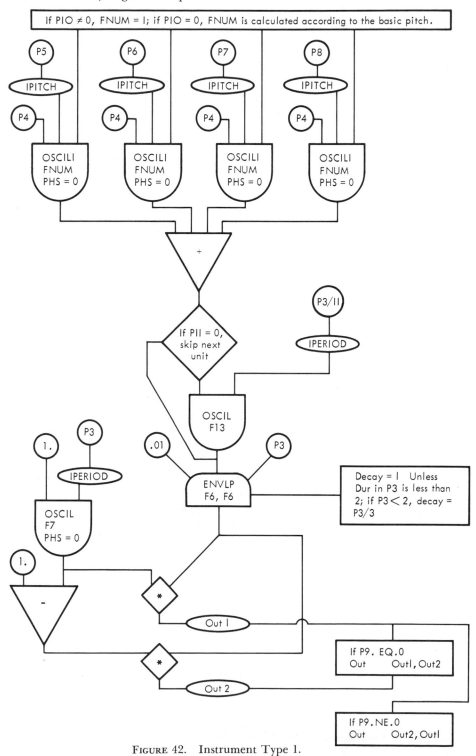

FIGURE 42. Instrument Type 1.

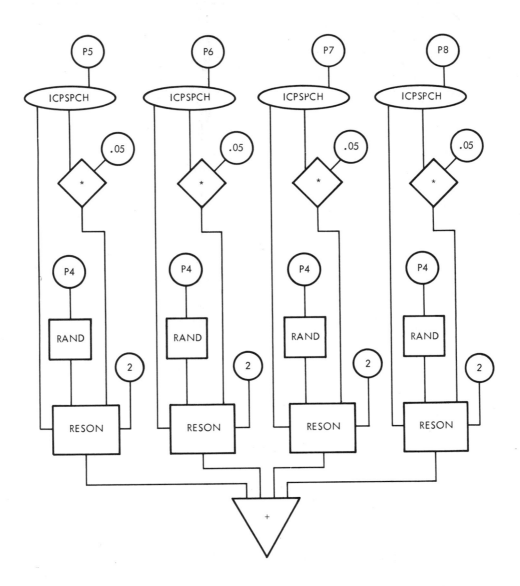

FIGURE 43.   Instrument Type 2.

P6 — Center frequency FOR RESON 2.
P7 — Center frequency FOR RESON 3.
P8 — Center frequency FOR RESON 4.
P9 — Same as for INSTR 1.
P10 — Not used in this INSTRUMENT.
P11 — Same as for INSTR 1.

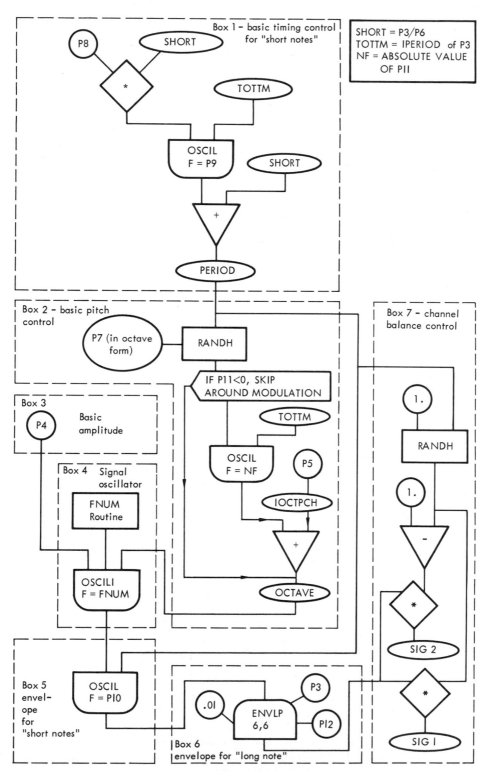

FIGURE 44.   Instrument Type 3.

Note that bandwidths for RESON are determined in the INSTR, and are all .05 times the respective CFs. Note also how ICPSPCH was used to convert 8VE.PC to the CPS mode of specification needed by RESON. Using this feature allows us to use exactly the same data for instrument type 2 that we used for instrument type 1.

Our third instrument-type is more complicated, and is typical of the level of complexity of the computer instruments used in most compositions. In designing such an instrument, it is essential to think on at least one level of organization higher than that of the unit generator. Otherwise, one becomes lost in a morass of detail. In the flow chart of Fig. 44, relevant groups of unit generators are boxed together by dotted lines. We see that these boxes reveal seven levels of structural organization. These seven levels are actually subgroups of the following:

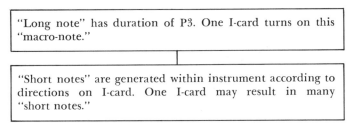

FIGURE 45.

The functions of the seven "structural boxes" in Figure 44 are summarized below:

Box. 1: This box provides basic timing control for the short notes. First, a "basic short duration" is obtained by dividing the duration of the long note (P3) by the number of notes desired (P6). For example, if P3 were 2 seconds and P6 were 10 notes, we would produce a basic duration of .2 seconds, which we will call "SHORT." P8 specifies a number to be multiplied times SHORT to obtain an offset duration to be added to (or, in the case of a negative-going function, subtracted from) SHORT. The manner in which this duration affects SHORT is controlled by the function-shape given to OSCIL #1. Suppose that P8 specifies a multiplier of .5, and that the function-shape specified is a linear rise. This means that the output of OSCIL increases from 0 to .5 over the time specified by P3. This value is added, sample by sample, to our first duration, SHORT. We see that over time P3, the durations of the "short notes" will increase from .2 to .3 seconds. These durations must be converted to sampling increments by PERIOD.

Box 2: This box controls pitch, and has three primary elements. First, a basic pitch is specified in 8VE.PC in P5. This pitch is converted to octave form by IOCTPCH since it will be modified both positively and negatively by RANDH and OSCIL #2. An interval, which defines the maximum random deviation from the basic pitch, is the "AMPLITUDE" or "BANDWIDTH" input to RANDH. It must be expressed in octave form. Suppose this interval is .5, a tritone. This means that the output of RANDH will vary randomly between 0 and .5, at a rate determined by Box 1. The output of RANDH becomes the amplitude input to OSCIL #2, whose frequency is IPERIOD of P3. Suppose the function input to this OSCIL is a sine wave. This means the output of OSCIL will be "random" numbers in the range of plus or minus .5. Randomness will be greatest at the two peaks of the sine wave (+.5, −.5). We see that this OSCIL has the effect of controlling the "shape" of randomness.

Box 3: The basic amplitude is expressed in 0–2,047 units.

Box 4: This box contains the signal oscillator, an OSCILI. It receives an AMP input from Box 3, a random frequency input determined by Boxes 1 and 2, and a function number determined by our FNUM routine. Note that FNUM has been modified to reflect the fact that the highest pitch in time P3 is now (IOCTPCH of P5) + P7.

Box 5: This box provides an envelope for the "short notes" by using an OSCIL as an envelope unit. The AMP input is the signal from OSCILI. The frequency input is the output of Box 1 in order that envelope changes will correlate with frequency changes produced by Box 2. The envelope shape may be specified in P10. Functions 9, 13, and 14 are typical envelope shapes that could be used.

Box 6: Here we have the envelope of the "macro-note." This box applies an overall envelope shape to all the notes generated in time P3. The ENVLP used here has an attack time of .01 second and a decay time specified in P12.

Box 7: This box provides a random channel balance. The time of change of channel balance must correlate with the time of "short-note" generation. The SI input to this RANDH thus comes from Box 1.

Orchestra Coding

The next step is coding the above orchestra in MUSIC360 and punching the "ORCH" cards. The ORCH coding is shown as the assembly-language step of the following computer run. Note that we have called for four of our type-3 instruments. Though each type-3 instrument generates many notes one after the other, it can play only one note at a time.

Score Coding

The score of the musical example in Figure 41 is shown as the PASS1 printout in the following job. Note that relatively few note cards are present for instruments 3, 4, 5, and 6, in proportion to the number of notes they will generate.

Job Submission

The "JCL" for this job is the same as that shown in Examples 16 and 17. Much additional JCL is generated by the operating system and by our MUSIC-360 procedure. The printing of all this JCL (several pages) is suppressed by specifying "MSGLEVEL = (0, 0)" on the job card. This printout is not meaningful to one unfamiliar with the 360 system.

Computer Run

The important parts of the computer run are noted on the printout of the run. The computer has already finished executing the job before the printout begins. This is how it is able to tell you, at the beginning of the printout, how long the job took.

The relevant divisions of the printout are as follows:

1. The first page shows the job card plus information about what happened during each of the steps of the job. The job has the following steps:
   - A) ASSEMBLY LANGUAGE (STEP /ASM)
   - B) FORTRAN   (STEP /FORT)
   - C) LINKAGE EDITOR   (STEP /LKED)
   - D) EXECUTION   (STEP /GO)
2. The remainder of the printout is a detailed record of the execution of the above steps.
   - a. STEP /ASM shows the assembling of the orchestra. Many comments on the design of each INSTRUMENT are included here. Assembly language comment cards begin with an "*".
   - b. STEP /FORT is a null step; it contains no program in this job since we are not using A- and B-subroutines. The printout of this null step is not included here.
   - c. STEP /LKED links our orchestra with the main music program and provides a "loading map" detailing this linkage. We have not included a printout of this step, as it would be meaningful only to those with substantial computer experience.
   - d. STEP /GO begins with the execution of PASS1, followed by the execution of PASS2. Many comments are included in the PASS1 SCORE, PASS1 comment cards begin with a "C." The printout of PASS3 begins with the statement, "beginning of performance," followed by the printout of 18 functions. The peak amplitudes between time spans determined by beginnings and endings of "notes" are also printed out. CH 1 amplitudes are printed to the left of CH 2 amplitudes. Finally, information on the creation of the digital tape is provided. This particular job created an intermediate tape which will be "RESCALED LATER" to a final tape.

Conversion to Sound

The final step of the job is the playback of the digital tape through a two-channel D/A converter set at SR = 10,000. At UNH this is a separate job that requires a special use of the operating system. A printout of this job is not included because it would not mean much to one unfamiliar with the details of how our converter runs.

```
//A0000015  JOB   (UNH,                                             JOB 587
// L128),'ROGERS EXAMPLE',REGION=210K,TIME=70,CLASS=F
***SETUP   GION=210K,TIME=70,CLASS=F
***LINES   20
***COPIES  5
// EXEC  MUSIC360
//ASM.SYSIN DD *
IEF142I - STEP WAS EXECUTED - COND CODE 0000
IEF373I STEP /ASM    / START 74100.0137
IEF374I STEP /ASM    / STOP  74100.0153 CPU   2MIN 49.17SEC MAIN 208K LCS    OK
INH377I STEP /ASM    / STOP  74100.0153 RC=   0      UNUSED MAIN   2K LCS    OK
IEF142I - STEP WAS EXECUTED - COND CODE 0000
IEF373I STEP /FORT   / START 74100.0153
IEF374I STEP /FORT   / STOP  74100.0157 CPU   0MIN 02.44SEC MAIN  84K LCS    OK
INH377I STEP /FORT   / STOP  74100.0157 RC=   0      UNUSED MAIN 126K LCS    OK <-----    00002010
//LKED.SYSIN DD *
IEF142I - STEP WAS EXECUTED - COND CODE 0000
IEF373I STEP /LKED   / START 74100.0157
IEF374I STEP /LKED   / STOP  74100.0159 CPU   0MIN 18.72SEC MAIN  92K LCS    OK
INH377I STEP /LKED   / STOP  74100.0159 RC=   0      UNUSED MAIN 118K LCS    OK <-----
//GO.FT09F001 DD UNIT=TAPE9,DISP=(NEW,KEEP),DSN=INTR,LABEL=(2,NL),        00002050
// VOL=SER=CC0970                                                         00002060
//GO.SYSIN DD *                                                           00002070
IEF142I - STEP WAS EXECUTED - COND CODE 0000
IEF373I STEP /GO     / START 74100.0159
IEF374I STEP /GO     / STOP  74100.0600 CPU  47MIN 26.54SEC MAIN 190K LCS   OK
INH377I STEP /GO     / STOP  74100.0600 RC=   0      UNUSED MAIN  20K LCS    OK <-----
IEF375I   JOB /A0000015/ START 74100.0137
IEF376I   JOB /A0000015/ STOP  74100.0600 CPU  50MIN 36.87SEC
```

```
LOC  OBJECT CODE    ADDR1 ADDR2  STMT    SOURCE STATEMENT

                                   1  ************************************************************
                                   2  *                                                          *
                                   3  *                                                          *
                                   4  *      HERE IS THE ASSEMBLY LANGUAGE STEP.                  *
                                   5  *                                                          *
                                   6  *                                                          *
                                   7  ************************************************************
                                   8          PRINT    NOGEN
                                   9          ORCH
                                 126          DECLARE  SR=10000,NCHNLS=2,F=20
                                 176          RESCALE  LATER

              INSTRUMENT TYPE 1
                                 182          INSTR    1
                                 219  ************************************************************
                                 220  * INSTR TYPE 1 PRODUCES A 4-NOTE CHORD.                    *
                                 221  * AMPLITUDE FOR EACH VOICE IS THE SAME AND IS EXPRESSED IN P4. *
                                 222  * PITCHES OF NOTES 1-4 ARE EXPRESSED IN 8VE.PC IN P5,P6,P7,P8. *
                                 223  * P9 GIVES 0 OR 1 TO CUE TYPE OF CHANNEL CHANGE            *
                                 224  * IF P10 IS NOT ZERO (OR BLANK), THE WAVEFORM FOR ALL THE OSCILI'S *
                                 225  * IS A SINE WAVE. IF P10 CONTAINS A ZERO, FNUM DETERMINES   *
                                 226  * THE WAVEFORM FUNCTION NUMBER.                            *
                                 227  * P11 GIVES THE NUMBER OF ATTACKS PER NOTE. P11 MAY BE ZERO. *
                                 228  * IF P11 IS ZERO, ONLY THE MAIN ENVELOPE IS APPLIED TO THE NOTE. *
                                 229  ************************************************************
                                 230          PSAVE    (3,11)
                                 244  NOTE1   IPITCH   P5              **************************
                                 271  NOTE2   IPITCH   P6              * SAMPLING   INCREMENTS  *
                                 298  NOTE3   IPITCH   P7              * FOR   FOUR  OSCILI'S.  *
                                 325  NOTE4   IPITCH   P8              **************************
                                 352  FNUM    IVAL     1               *      HERE   WE         *
                                 363          IIFGO    (P10.GT.0),100  * COMPUTE THE            *
                                 372          IIFGO    (P8.GE.11.00),100 * FUNCTION NUMBER      *
                                 382          IREVAL   FNUM,2          * BASED ON               *
                                 393          IIFGO    (P8.GE.10.00),100 * THE HIGHEST          *
                                 403          IREVAL   FNUM,3          * PITCH. THE             *
                                 414          IIFGO    (P8.GE.9.00),100 * HIGHEST PITCH         *
                                 424          IREVAL   FNUM,4          * IS ASSUMED TO BE       *
                                 435          IIFGO    (P8.GE.8.00),100 * IN P8.                *
                                 445          IREVAL   FNUM,5          **************************
                                 456  100     CONTINUE
                                 461  SIGNAL1 OSCILI   P4,NOTE1,FNUM,0. **************************
                                 483  SIGNAL2 OSCILI   P4,NOTE2,FNUM,0. * HERE ARE THE SIGNAL   *
                                 505  SIGNAL3 OSCILI   P4,NOTE3,FNUM,0. *   OSCILLATORS         *
                                 527  SIGNAL4 OSCILI   P4,NOTE4,FNUM,0. **************************
                                 549  SIGADD  VAL      SIGNAL1+SIGNAL2+SIGNAL3+SIGNAL4  * FOUR PITCHES *
                                 569  DECAY   IVAL     P3/3.           * HERE WE SET DECAY TO 1/3 *
                                 583  *                               * NOTE DURATION.         *
                                 584          IFGO     (P11.EQ.0),105  * IS THERE ONLY ONE ATTACK? *
                                 593          IIFGO    (P11.EQ.0),105  * IF SO, SKIP AROUND MULTIPLE *
                                 602  *                               * ATTACK UNIT.           *
                                 603  TME     IPERIOD  P3/P11          * DUR/NO. OF ATTACKS .   *
                                 633  *                               * CONVERTED TO SI FOR OSCIL. *
                                 634          OSCIL    SIGADD,TME,13,0 * OSCIL USED FOR REPETITIVE *
                                 656          REVAL    SIGADD,U1       * ATTACKS.               *
                                 667  105     CONTINUE                 **************************
                                 672  SIGENV  ENVLP    SIGADD,.01,P3,DECAY,6,6        * ENVELOPE *
                                 698  DURFRQ  IPERIOD  P3              **************************
                                 715  CHNFAC  OSCIL    1.,DURFRQ,7,0.  * HERE WE SET CH. BALANCE. *
                                 737  CH2OUT  VAL      SIGENV*CHNFAC   * THE OUTPUT OF OSCIL IS MUL- *
                                 751  CHNFAC1 VAL      1.-CHNFAC       * TIPLIED TIMES THE SIGNAL FOR *
                                 765  CH1OUT  VAL      SIGENV*CHNFAC1  * CH 1.  1 - THE OUTPUT OF *
                                 779          IFGO     (P9.EQ.0),101   * OSCIL IS * TIMES THE SIGNAL *
                                 788          OUT      CH1OUT,CH2OUT   * TO GET CH2. FURTHER, IF *
                                 801          GOTO     102             * P9 IS UNEQUAL TO 0, CH1 *
                                 804  101     OUT      CH2OUT,CH1OUT   * AND CH2 ARE REVERSED.  *
                                 821  ************************************************************
                                 822  102     CONTINUE
                                 827          ENDIN
```

```
                   INSTRUMENT TYPE 2

LOC  OBJECT CODE   ADDR1 ADDR2  STMT    SOURCE STATEMENT
                               845          INSTR    2
                               878  *************************************************************
                               879  *  THIS IS A NOISE VERSION OF INSTRUMENT TYPE 1.            *
                               880  *  IT WILL ACCEPT THE SAME DATA AS INSTRUMENT TYPE 1.       *
                               881  *  A SENSE OF PITCH CENTER IS OBTAINED BY PASSING A WHITE NOISE *
                               882  *  FROM RAND THROUGH FOUR DIFFERENT RESONS.  EACH RESON HAS A CF *
                               883  *  EQUAL TO THE SPECIFIED FREQUENCY, AND A BW OF APPROXIMATELY A 1/2 *
                               884  *  STEP.                                                    *
                               885  *  AMP INPUT TO RAND IS IN P4.                              *
                               886  *  CF'S 1 - 4 ARE EXPRESSED IN 8VE.PC IN P5,P6,P7,P8.       *
                               887  *  P9 SHOWS A 0 OR 1 TO CUE TYPE OF CHANNEL CHANGE.         *
                               888  *  P10 IS NOT NEEDED IN THIS INSTRUMENT, BUT NO ERROR IS PRODUCED BY *
                               889  *  PLACING A NUMBER IN P10.                                 *
                               890  *  P11 HAS THE SAME FUNCTION AS IN INSTR TYPE 1.            *
                               891  *************************************************************
                               892          PSAVE    (3,11)
                               906  AMP      RAND     P4                   *      WHITE NOISE          *
                               922  NOTE1    ICPSPCH  P5                   * HERE WE ARE CONVERTING PCH *
                               949  BW1      IVAL     U1*.05               * TO CPS FOR CF INPUT TO    *
                               963  NOTE2    ICPSPCH  P6                   * RESON, AND MULTIPLYING    *
                               990  BW2      IVAL     U1*.05               * BY .05 (APPROXIMATELY A   *
                              1004  NOTE3    ICPSPCH  P7                   * 1/2 STEP) TO OBTAIN THE   *
                              1031  BW3      IVAL     U1*.05               * BW INPUT.  SINCE FOUR CF'S *
                              1045  NOTE4    ICPSPCH  P8                   * AND 4 BW'S ARE INVOLVED,  *
                              1072  BW4      IVAL     U1*.05               * THIS MUST BE DONE 4 TIMES. *
                              1086  SIG1     RESON    AMP,NOTE1,BW1,2.,0.   ***************************
                              1110  SIG2     RESON    AMP,NOTE2,BW2,2.,0.   * HERE THE WHITE NOISE IS  *
                              1134  SIG3     RESON    AMP,NOTE3,BW3,2.,0.   *FILTERED BY 4 RESONS.     *
                              1158  SIG4     RESON    AMP,NOTE4,BW4,2.,0.   ***************************
                              1182  SIGADD   VAL      SIG1+SIG2+SIG3+SIG4
                              1202  DECAY    IVAL     P3/3.                * HERE WE SET DECAY TO 1/3  *
                              1216  *                                       NOTE DURATION.          *
                              1217  * FROM HERE ON, THE INSTR IS LIKE INSTR 1.
                              1218           IFGO     (P11.EQ.0),105       * IS THERE ONLY ONE ATTACK? *
                              1227           IIFGO    (P11.EQ.0),105       * IF SO, SKIP AROUND MULTIPLE *
                              1236  *                                       ATTACK UNIT.            *
                              1237  TME      IPERIOD  P3/P11               * DUR/NO. OF ATTACKS .      *
                              1267  *                                       CONVERTED TO SI FOR OSCIL. *
                              1268           OSCIL    SIGADD,TME,13,0      * OSCIL USED FOR REPETITIVE *
                              1290           REVAL    SIGADD,U1            * ATTACKS.                  *
                              1301  105      CONTINUE                       ***************************
                              1306  SIGENV   ENVLP    SIGADD,.01,P3,DECAY,6,6
                              1332  DURFRQ   IPERIOD  P3
                              1349  CHNFAC   OSCIL    1.,DURFRQ,7,0.
                              1371  CH2OUT   VAL      SIGENV*CHNFAC
                              1385  CHNFAC1  VAL      1.-CHNFAC
                              1399  CH1OUT   VAL      SIGENV*CHNFAC1
                              1413           IFGO     (P9.EQ.0),101
                              1422           OUT      CH1OUT,CH2OUT
                              1435           GOTO     102
                              1438  101      OUT      CH2OUT,CH1OUT
                              1455  102      CONTINUE
                              1460           ENDIN
```

```
                    INSTRUMENT TYPE 3

LOC  OBJECT CODE    ADDR1 ADDR2  STMT    SOURCE STATEMENT
                                 1478           INSTR     3,4,5,6
                                 1514   *****************************************************************
                                 1515   * HERE IS OUR 'PARTLY RANDOM' INSTRUMENT.                       *
                                 1516   * P4 SPECIFIES AMPLITUDE IN 0 - 2047 UNITS.                     *
                                 1517   * P5 SPECIFIES BASIC PITCH BEFORE RANDH HAS ANY EFFECT.         *
                                 1518   * P6 SPECIFIES THE NUMBER OF NOTES TO OCCUR WITHIN TIME SPAN P3.*
                                 1519   * P7 SPECIFIES THE INTERVAL OF "RANDOMNESS" IN OCTAVE FORM.     *
                                 1520   * P8 SPECIFIES A NUMBER (USUALLY, THOUGH NOT ALWAYS BETWEEN 0 AND 1) *
                                 1521   * TO BE MULTIPLIED TIMES THE AVERAGE DURATION (P3/P6) TO OBTAIN A *
                                 1522   * RHYTHMIC OFFSET VALUE TO ADD TO THE AVERAGE DURATION.         *
                                 1523   * P9 SPECIFIES THE FUNCTION WHICH DETERMINES THE "SHAPE OF RHYTHMIC *
                                 1524   * CHANGE" -- ACCEL, RIT, OR SOME OTHER SHAPE.                   *
                                 1525   * P10 SPECIFIES THE FUNCTION TO BE USED TO GIVE ENVELOPE SHAPE TO *
                                 1526   * THE "SHORT NOTES" PRODUCED INTERNALLY IN INSTRS 3,4,5,6.      *
                                 1527   * P11 SPECIFIES THE FUNCTION WHICH CONTROLS THE SHAPE OF "MACRO-NOTE" *
                                 1528   * RANDOM FREQUENCY MODULATION. IF THIS FUNCTION SHAPE IS SMOOTH, *
                                 1529   * SOME GLISS EFFECTS WILL BE INTRODUCED. IF THE SHAPE CONTAINS  *
                                 1530   * SHARP EDGES, ABRUPT PITCH CHANGES WILL BE INTRODUCED BUT THESE *
                                 1531   * WILL NOT NECESSARILY COINCIDE WITH BEGINNINGS OF              *
                                 1532   * "SHORT NOTES". IF P11 IS NEGATIVE, MODULATION OF THE RANDOM INT- *
                                 1533   * ERVAL IS SKIPPED. IN THIS CASE, CHANGES OF PITCH WILL BE IN THE *
                                 1534   * RANGE OF THE RANDOM INTERVAL AND WILL COINCIDE WITH THE BEGINNINGS *
                                 1535   * OF SHORT NOTES.                                               *
                                 1536   * P12 SPECIFIES THE DECAY FOR THE "MACRO-NOTE".                 *
                                 1537   * IF P13 IS A POSITIVE NUMBER, THE WAVESHAPE FUNCTION OF THIS    *
                                 1538   * INSTRUMENT IS A SINE WAVE. IF P13 IS ZERO OR BLANK, FNUM      *
                                 1539   * DETERMINES THE WAVESHAPE BASED ON THE HIGHEST PITCH IN THE     *
                                 1540   * TIME SPAN OF P3.                                              *
                                 1541   *****************************************************************
                                 1542           PSAVE     (3,13)
                                 1556   SHORT   IVAL      P3/P6               * AVERAGE DURATION OF SHORT NT*
                                 1570   TOTTM   IPERIOD   P3                  * SI FOR MACRO NOTE.          *
                                 1587           IVAL      P8*SHORT            * RHYTHMIC OFFSET             *
                                 1601           OSCIL     U1,TOTTM,P9,0.      * CONTROL FOR RHYTHMIC OFST.  *
                                 1623           VAL       ABS(U1+SHORT)       * OFFSET ADDED TO AV. VAL.    *
                                 1638   SHORTM  PERIOD    U1                  * SHORT DUR CONVERTED TO SI.  *
                                 1655   RINT    RANDH     P7,SHORTM           * RANDOM INTERVAL IN RANGE P7 *
                                 1673           IIFGO     (P11.LT.0),50       * SKIP OVER NEXT OSCIL IF NO  *
                                 1682           IFGO      (P11.LT.0),50       * MODULATIONS OF RINT DESIRED *
                                 1691   NF      IVAL      ABS(P11)            * P11 MADE POSITIVE.          *
                                 1703           OSCIL     RINT,TOTTM,NF,0.    * MODULATION APPLIED TO RINT  *
                                 1725           REVAL     RINT,U1             * OLD RINT SET EQUAL TO NEW.  *
                                 1736   50      CONTINUE
                                 1741   PC      IOCTPCH   P5                  * WE NEED PITCH IN OCT FORM   *
                                 1757           VAL       U1+RINT             * FOR ACCURATE SUBTRACTION.   *
                                 1771   SAMPIC  OCTAVE    U1                  * OCTAVE FORM TO SI.          *
                                 1793   OC      IVAL      PC+P7               * HIGHEST PCH OVER TIME P3.   *
                                 1807   FNUM    IVAL      1                   ******************************
                                 1818           IIFGO     (P13.GT.0),100      * HERE WE  COMPUTE           *
                                 1827           IIFGO     (OC.GE.11.00),100   * THE FUNCTION               *
                                 1837           IREVAL    FNUM,2              * NUMBER FOR SIGNAL OSC.     *
                                 1848           IIFGO     (OC.GE.10.00),100   * BASED ON HIGHEST PCH IN    *
                                 1858           IREVAL    FNUM,3              * TIME P3.                   *
                                 1869           IIFGO     (OC.GE.9.00),100    *                 OC IS      *
                                 1879           IREVAL    FNUM,4              *            NOW   THE       *
                                 1890           IIFGO     (OC.GE.8.00),100    * HIGHEST PITCH.             *
                                 1900           IREVAL    FNUM,5              ******************************
                                 1911   100     CONTINUE
                                 1916   NOTE    OSCILI    P4,SAMPIC,FNUM,0.   * HERE IS SIGNAL OSC.        *
                                 1938           OSCIL     NOTE,SHORTM,P10,0.  * ENVELOPE FOR SHORT NOTES.  *
                                 1960   SIG     ENVLP     U1,.01,P3,P12,6,8   * ENVELOPE FOR MACRO NOTES.  *
                                 1986   *****************************************************************
                                 1987   * NOTE THAT WE ARE USING A LINEAR DECAY ON THE MACRO NOTE.      *
                                 1988   * AN EXPONENTIAL DECAY SOMETIMES CAUSES QUANTIZATION PROBLEMS WHEN *
                                 1989   * IT IS THIS LONG.**********************************************
                                 1990   CH1MLT  RANDH     1.,SHORTM           ******************************
                                 2008   SIG1    VAL       SIG*CH1MLT          * HERE ARE THE CARDS THAT    *
                                 2022   CH2MLT  VAL       1.-CH1MLT           *              GIVE          *
                                 2036   SIG2    VAL       SIG*CH2MLT          * RANDOM CONTROL OF CH BAL.  *
                                 2050           OUT       SIG1,SIG2           * CHANGES OCCUR AT SHORTM.   *
                                 2063   300     CONTINUE
                                 2068   *****************************************************************
                                 2069           ENDIN
                                 2092           ENDORCH
                                 2385           END
```

```
C       THIS IS THE BEGINNING OF PASS1.
C       USER'S COMMENTS ARE PRINTED OUT IN PASS1, BUT NOT IN PASSES 2,3.
C
C
C       SECTION 1 GENERATES FUNCTIONS AND A BEGINNING SILENCE.
C
C       SINES AND SUMS OF SINES FOR WAVESHAPES
C
F 1         0 10.1     1
F 2         0 10.1     1     5
F 3         0 10.1     4     1     2     3
F 4         0 10.1     7     1     2     6     3     4     5
F 5         0 10.1    13     1     2    12     3     4    11     5     6
     10     7     8     9
C
C
C       FUNCTION SHAPE FOR ENVLP
C
F 6         0  5.1 .0001   512     1
C
C
C       HALF-CYCLE SINE WAVE FOR CONTROL.
C
F 7         0  9.1    .5     1     0
C
C
C       ENVELOPE FUNCTIONS.   GENO7 FOR LINEAR; GENO5 FOR EXPONENTIAL.
C
F 8         0  7.1     0   512     1
F 9         0  7.1     0    64     1   384     1    64     0
F10         0  7.1     1   512     0
F11         0  7.1     0   256     1   256     0
F12         0  7.1     1   256     0   256     1
F13         0  5.1     1    64   100   448     1
F14         0  5.1     1    64  1000   256     1
F15         0  7.1     0    64     1    32    .8   224    .8   192     0
F16         0  5.1     1    64  1000    32   800   224   800   192     1
C
C
C       THESE FUNCTIONS ARE USEFUL FOR SHAPING THE AMOUNT OF RANDOM
C       FREQUENCY MODULATION.   F17 HOLDS THE VALUE 1 EXCEPT FOR A
C       SHORT BEGINNING AND ENDING "0" SEGMENT.   F18 HOLDS 1 THRUOUT
C       AND IS THUS A "STRAIGHT-LINE".
F17         0  7.1     0    31     0     1     1   448     1     1     0
     31     0
F18         0  7.1     1   512     1
C
C
C       F 0 CARD TO GENERATE A SILENCE.
F 0         2
C
C       END SECTION 1.
C
S
C       A TEST NOTE IS GENERATED
I 1         0     2   500  8.00  8.01  8.02  8.03     0     1     1
C
C       ANOTHER SILENCE TO SEPERATE TEST NOTES FROM BODY OF PIECE.
F 0         6
C
```

```
C       END SECTION 2.
S
C
C
C       HERE ARE THE NOTE CARDS (I-CARDS) FOR THE PIECE.
C
C
C
```

CINST CNU	ST TME	DUR	AMP	PCH1	PCH2	PCH3	PCH4	CH CUE	FNUM	NO ATTKS
I 1	10	2	600	9.04	8.01	7.09	6.10	0	0	4
I 1	14	2	600	9.02	8.03	7.11	6.08	1	1	11
I 1	36	2	400	9.02	8.00	7.10	6.08	1	0	3
I 1	42	1	1000	9.04	9.03	8.02	7.11	0	1	2
I 1	44	1	1200	9.05	9.02	8.01	8.00	1	0	7
I 1	61	1	1200	9.04	8.01	7.09	6.10	1	1	4
I 1	62	.5	1200	9.05	9.01	6.11	6.07	0	1	3
I 1	62.5	1.5	1500	9.02	8.03	7.11	6.08	1	1	10

```
C
C       REMEMBER INSTR TYPE 2 IS A NOISE VERSION OF INSTR TYPE 1.
C
C
```

CINST CNU	ST TME	DUR	AMP	PCH1	PCH2	PCH3	PCH4	CH CUE	NO ATTKS
I 2	12	2	600	9.05	9.01	6.11	6.07	0	7
I 2	34	2	200	9.02	8.05	7.07	6.06	1	15
I 2	38	2	800	9.04	8.03	7.05	6.08	0	17
I 2	43	.5	1000	8.11	6.09	8.07	8.05	0	2
I 2	43.5	.5	1000	8.11	6.09	8.07	8.05	1	3
I 2	61	1	1200	9.04	8.01	7.09	6.10	0	2
I 2	62	.5	1200	9.05	9.01	6.11	6.07	1	3
I 2	62.5	1.5	1500	9.02	8.03	7.11	6.08	0	5

```
C
```

CINST CNU	ST TME	DUR	AMP	PCH	NO NOTES	RAND INT	RHY MULT	RHY FUNC	SHENV FUNC	RAND FUNC	LNOT DK

```
C
I 3      0    10   1000  8.00        80  .5833     .5      8     13     -1     .1
CSINE OR
CFNUM
        0
I 3     17    17    600  7.11        50    1        1     10     13      7     .1
        1
I 3     39     3   1000  8.08        30    1        2      8     14     11     .1
        0
I 3     48    16    800  9.02       100  .9167      2     12     16      7     .5
        1
I 4     20    12    600  9.02        50  .9167      1     10     15      7     .1
        1
I 4     52     8    800  9.05        50  .6667      1     12     13      7     .5
        0
I 4     62.5  1.5  1000  8.03        15  .9167      1     10     16     -1     .01
        1
I 5     23     9    600  6.08        50  .667       1      8     14      7     .1
        1
I 5     52     8    800  8.01        50  .75        1     11     13      7     .5
        0
I 5     62.5  1.5  1000  7.11        15  .75        1     10     13     -1     .01
        1
I 6     25     7    600  8.03        50  .75       .5     10      9      7     .1
        1
I 6     52     8    800  8.00        50  .8333      1      7     13      7     .5
```

```
        0
I  6     62.5   1.5  1000  6.08      15 .8333      1     10     13     -1    .01
        1
C
C      SILENCE AT END OF PIECE.
F 0        66
C
C
C      E CARD SIGNALS END OF SCORE.
E
```

PASS ONE EXECUTION TIME WAS   10.53   SECONDS.

SECTION NO.   1

F	1.	0.0	10.1000	1.0000	0.0	0.0	0.0	0.0	0.0	0.0	0.0
F	2.	0.0	10.1000	1.0000	5.0300	0.0	0.0	0.0	0.0	0.0	0.0
F	3.	0.0	10.1000	4.0000	1.0000	2.0000	3.0000	0.0	0.0	0.0	0.0
F	4.	0.0	10.1000	7.0000	1.0000	2.0000	6.0000	3.0000	4.0000	5.0000	0.0
F	5.	0.0	10.1000	13.0000	1.0000	2.0000	12.0000	3.0000	4.0000	11.0000	5.0000	6.0000
	10.0000	7.0000	8.0000	9.0000	0.0	0.0	0.0	0.0	0.0	0.0	0.0
F	6.	0.0	5.1000	0.0001	512.0000	1.0000	0.0	0.0	0.0	0.0	0.0
F	7.	0.0	9.1000	0.5000	1.0000	0.0	0.0	0.0	0.0	0.0	0.0
F	8.	0.0	7.1000	0.0	512.0000	1.0000	0.0	0.0	0.0	0.0	0.0
F	9.	0.0	7.1000	0.0	64.0000	1.0000	384.0000	1.0000	64.0000	0.0	0.0
F	10.	0.0	7.1000	1.0000	512.0000	0.0	0.0	0.0	0.0	0.0	0.0
F	11.	0.0	7.1000	0.0	256.0000	1.0000	256.0000	0.0	0.0	0.0	0.0
F	12.	0.0	7.1000	1.0000	256.0000	0.0	256.0000	1.0000	0.0	0.0	0.0
F	13.	0.0	5.1000	1.0000	64.0000	100.0000	448.0000	1.0000	0.0	0.0	0.0
F	14.	0.0	5.1000	1.0000	64.0000	1000.0000	256.0000	1.0000	0.0	0.0	0.0
F	15.	0.0	7.1000	0.0	64.0000	1.0000	32.0000	0.8000	224.0000	0.8000	192.0000	0.0
F	16.	0.0	5.1000	1.0000	64.0000	1000.0000	32.0000	800.0000	224.0000	800.0000	192.0000	1.0000
F	17.	0.0	7.1000	0.0	31.0000	0.0	1.0000	1.0000	448.0000	1.0000	1.0000	0.0
	31.0000	0.0	0.0	0.0	0.0	0.0	0.0	0.0	0.0	0.0	0.0
F	18.	0.0	7.1000	1.0000	512.0000	1.0000	0.0	0.0	0.0	0.0	0.0
F	0.	2.0000	0.0	0.0	0.0	0.0	0.0	0.0	0.0	0.0	0.0

SECTION NO.   2

I	1.	0.0	2.0000	500.0000	8.0000	8.0100	8.0200	8.0300	0.0	1.0000	1.0000	0.0
I	0.	6.0000	0.0	0.0	0.0	0.0	0.0	0.0	0.0	0.0	0.0

SECTION NO.   3

I	3.	0.0	10.0000	1000.0000	8.0000	80.0000	0.5833	0.5000	8.0000	13.0000	-1.0000	0.1000
	0.0	0.0	0.0	0.0	0.0	0.0	0.0	0.0	0.0	0.0	0.0
I	1.	10.0000	2.0000	600.0000	9.0400	8.0100	7.0900	6.1000	0.0	0.0	4.0000	0.0
I	2.	12.0000	2.0000	600.0000	9.0500	9.0100	6.1100	6.0700	0.0	0.0	7.0000	0.0
I	1.	14.0000	2.0000	600.0000	9.0200	8.0300	7.1100	6.0800	1.0000	1.0000	11.0000	0.0
I	3.	17.0000	17.0000	600.0000	7.1100	50.0000	1.0000	1.0000	10.0000	13.0000	7.0000	0.1000
	1.0000	0.0	0.0	0.0	0.0	0.0	0.0	0.0	0.0	0.0	0.0
I	4.	20.0000	12.0000	600.0000	9.0200	50.0000	0.9167	1.0000	10.0000	15.0000	7.0000	0.1000
	1.0000	0.0	0.0	0.0	0.0	0.0	0.0	0.0	0.0	0.0	0.0
I	5.	23.0000	9.0000	600.0000	6.0800	50.0000	0.6670	1.0000	8.0000	14.0000	7.0000	0.1000
	1.0000	0.0	0.0	0.0	0.0	0.0	0.0	0.0	0.0	0.0	0.0
I	6.	25.0000	7.0000	600.0000	8.0300	50.0000	0.7500	0.5000	10.0000	9.0000	7.0000	0.1000
	1.0000	0.0	0.0	0.0	0.0	0.0	0.0	0.0	0.0	0.0	0.0
I	2.	34.0000	2.0000	200.0000	9.0200	8.0500	7.0700	6.0600	1.0000	0.0	15.0000	0.0
I	1.	36.0000	2.0000	400.0000	9.0200	8.0000	7.1000	6.0800	1.0000	0.0	3.0000	0.0
I	2.	38.0000	2.0000	800.0000	9.0400	8.0300	7.0500	6.0800	0.0	0.0	17.0000	0.0
I	3.	39.0000	3.0000	1000.0000	8.0800	30.0000	1.0000	2.0000	8.0000	14.0000	11.0000	0.1000
	0.0	0.0	0.0	0.0	0.0	0.0	0.0	0.0	0.0	0.0	0.0
I	1.	42.0000	1.0000	1000.0000	9.0400	9.0300	8.0200	7.1100	0.0	1.0000	2.0000	0.0
I	2.	43.0000	0.5000	1000.0000	8.1100	8.0900	8.0700	8.0500	0.0	0.0	2.0000	0.0
I	2.	43.5000	0.5000	1000.0000	8.1100	8.0900	8.0700	8.0500	1.0000	0.0	3.0000	0.0
I	1.	44.0000	1.0000	1200.0000	9.0500	9.0200	8.0100	8.0000	1.0000	0.0	7.0000	0.0
I	3.	48.0000	16.0000	800.0000	9.0200	100.0000	0.9167	2.0000	12.0000	16.0000	7.0000	0.5000
	1.0000	0.0	0.0	0.0	0.0	0.0	0.0	0.0	0.0	0.0	0.0
I	4.	52.0000	8.0000	800.0000	9.0500	50.0000	0.6667	1.0000	12.0000	13.0000	7.0000	0.5000
	0.0	0.0	0.0	0.0	0.0	0.0	0.0	0.0	0.0	0.0	0.0
I	5.	52.0000	8.0000	800.0000	8.0100	50.0000	0.7500	1.0000	11.0000	13.0000	7.0000	0.5000
	0.0	0.0	0.0	0.0	0.0	0.0	0.0	0.0	0.0	0.0	0.0
I	6.	52.0000	8.0000	800.0000	8.0300	50.0000	0.8333	1.0000	7.0000	13.0000	7.0000	0.5000
	0.0	0.0	0.0	0.0	0.0	0.0	0.0	0.0	0.0	0.0	0.0
I	1.	61.0000	1.0000	1200.0000	9.0400	8.0100	7.0900	6.1000	1.0000	1.0000	4.0000	0.0
I	2.	61.0000	1.0000	1200.0000	9.0400	8.0100	7.0900	6.1000	0.0	1.0000	2.0000	0.0
I	1.	62.0000	0.5000	1200.0000	9.0500	9.0100	6.1100	6.0700	0.0	1.0000	3.0000	0.0
I	2.	62.0000	0.5000	1200.0000	9.0500	9.0100	6.1100	6.0700	1.0000	0.0	3.0000	0.0
I	1.	62.5000	1.5000	1500.0000	9.0200	8.0300	7.1100	6.0800	1.0000	1.0000	10.0000	0.0
I	2.	62.5000	1.5000	1500.0000	9.0200	8.0300	7.1100	6.0800	0.0	0.0	5.0000	0.0
I	4.	62.5000	1.5000	1000.0000	8.0300	15.0000	0.9167	1.0000	10.0000	16.0000	-1.0000	0.0100
	1.0000	0.0	0.0	0.0	0.0	0.0	0.0	0.0	0.0	0.0	0.0
I	5.	62.5000	1.5000	1000.0000	7.1100	15.0000	0.7500	1.0000	10.0000	13.0000	-1.0000	0.0100
	1.0000	0.0	0.0	0.0	0.0	0.0	0.0	0.0	0.0	0.0	0.0
I	6.	62.5000	1.5000	1000.0000	6.0800	15.0000	0.8333	1.0000	10.0000	13.0000	-1.0000	0.0100
	1.0000	0.0	0.0	0.0	0.0	0.0	0.0	0.0	0.0	0.0	0.0
F	0.	66.0000	0.0	0.0	0.0	0.0	0.0	0.0	0.0	0.0	0.0

END OF SCORE.   PASS TWO EXECUTION TIME WAS   5.59   SECONDS.

BEGINNING OF PERFORMANCE

Function No. 1 has been generated at time 0.0, and produces the cycle shown below.

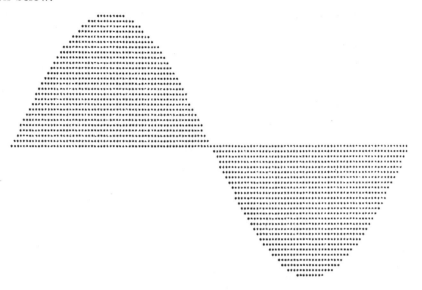

Function No. 2 has been generated at time 0.0, and produces the cycle shown below.

Function No. 3 has been generated at time 0.0, and produces the cycle shown below.

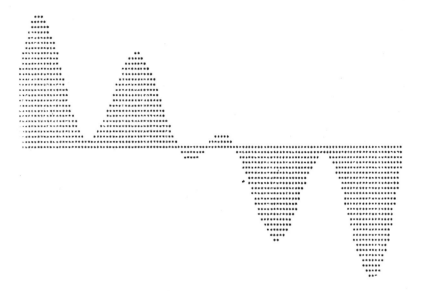

Function No. 4 has been generated at time 0.0, and produces the cycle shown below.

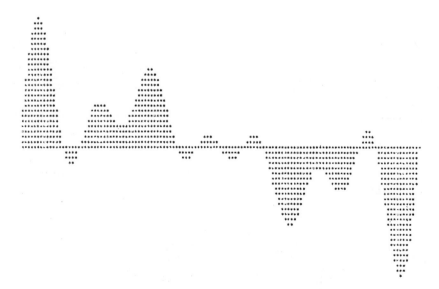

Function No. 5 has been generated at time 0.0, and produces the cycle shown below.

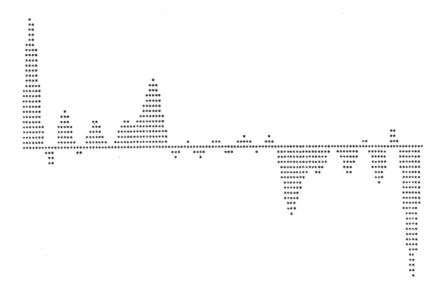

Function No. 6 has been generated at time 0.0, and produces the cycle shown below.

Function No. 7 has been generated at time 0.0, and produces the cycle shown below.

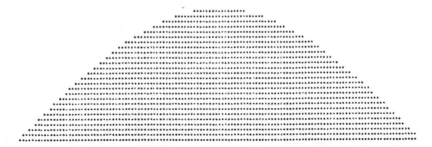

Function No. 8 has been generated at time 0.0, and produces the cycle shown below.

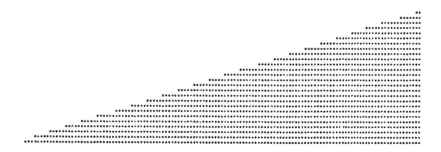

Function No. 9 has been generated at time 0.0, and produces the cycle shown below.

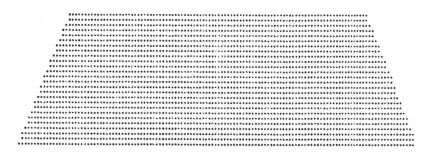

Function No. 10 has been generated at time 0.0, and produces the cycle shown below.

Function No. 11 has been generated at time 0.0, and produces the cycle shown below.

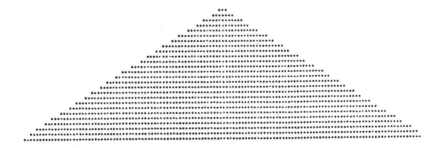

Function No. 12 has been generated at time 0.0, and produces the cycle shown below.

Function No. 13 has been generated at time 0.0, and produces the cycle shown below.

Function No. 14 has been generated at time 0.0, and produces the cycle shown below.

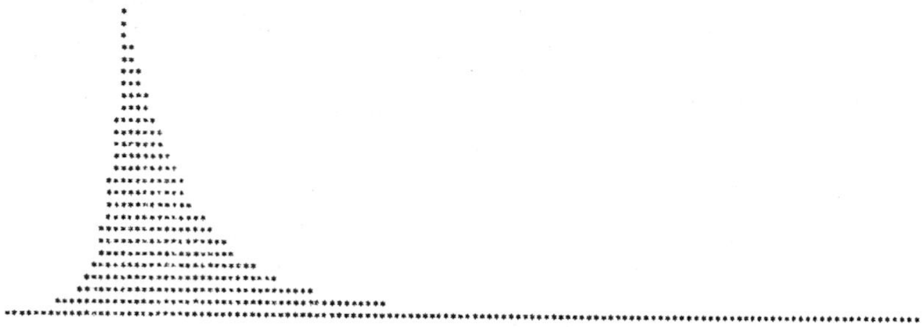

Function No. 15 has been generated at time 0.0, and produces the cycle shown below.

Function No. 16 has been generated at time 0.0, and produces the cycle shown below.

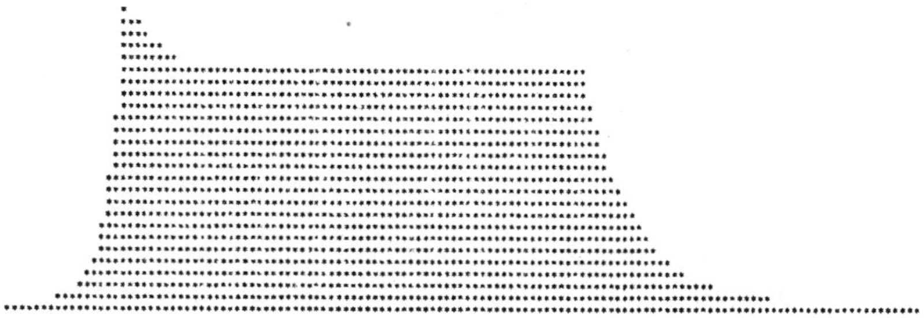

Function No. 17 has been generated at time 0.0, and produces the cycle shown below.

Function No. 18 has been generated at time 0.0, and produces the cycle shown below.

```
T     0.0   ...   2.0000              TT    2.0000         M        0.0           0.0
EXECUTION TIME FOR SECTION NO.   1  WAS    1  MINUTES AND  25.96  SECONDS.
                   MAXIMUM AMPLITUDE PER CHANNEL:                   0.0           0.0



SECTION NO.   2
T     0.0   ...   2.0000              TT    4.0000         M       629.08        721.36
T     2.0000 ...  6.0000              TT    8.0000         M        0.0           0.0
EXECUTION TIME FOR SECTION NO.   2  WAS    1  MINUTES AND  44.73  SECONDS.
                   MAXIMUM AMPLITUDE PER CHANNEL:                  629.08        721.36

SECTION NO.   3
T     0.0   ...  10.0000              TT   18.0000         M       996.74       1875.97
T    10.0000 ... 12.0000              TT   20.0000         M      1101.76       1282.73
T    12.0000 ... 14.0000              TT   22.0000         M      1489.26       1748.29
T    14.0000 ... 16.0000              TT   24.0000         M      1491.47       1896.93
T    16.0000 ... 17.0000              TT   25.0000         M        0.0           0.0
T    17.0000 ... 20.0000              TT   28.0000         M       384.47        891.86
T    20.0000 ... 23.0000              TT   31.0000         M       724.95       1295.25
T    23.0000 ... 25.0000              TT   33.0000         M       824.55       1670.97
T    25.0000 ... 32.0000              TT   40.0000         M      1259.34       2518.28
T    32.0000 ... 34.0000              TT   42.0000         M       388.89        982.23
T    34.0000 ... 36.0000              TT   44.0000         M       468.37        520.10
T    36.0000 ... 38.0000              TT   46.0000         M       627.99        748.96
T    38.0000 ... 39.0000              TT   47.0000         M      1936.57       1229.15
T    39.0000 ... 40.0000              TT   48.0000         M      2185.83       1440.47
T    40.0000 ... 42.0000              TT   50.0000         M       939.25       1724.95
T    42.0000 ... 43.0000              TT   51.0000         M      2724.45       2270.04
T    43.0000 ... 43.5000              TT   51.5000         M      3274.98       1959.03
T    43.5000 ... 44.0000              TT   52.0000         M      1496.79       2144.38
T    44.0000 ... 45.0000              TT   53.0000         M      2346.14       2383.66
T    45.0000 ... 48.0000              TT   56.0000         M        0.0           0.0
T    48.0000 ... 52.0000              TT   60.0000         M       764.85       1559.27
T    52.0000 ... 60.0000              TT   68.0000         M      1281.42       3001.08
T    60.0000 ... 61.0000              TT   69.0000         M       764.69       1559.63
T    61.0000 ... 62.0000              TT   70.0000         M      3684.38       3141.72
T    62.0000 ... 62.5000              TT   70.5000         M      3561.55       3473.81
T    62.5000 ... 64.0000              TT   72.0000         M      4965.10       5960.23
T    64.0000 ... 66.0000              TT   74.0000         M        0.0           0.0
EXECUTION TIME FOR SECTION NO.   3  WAS   43  MINUTES AND  50.93  SECONDS.
                   MAXIMUM AMPLITUDE PER CHANNEL:                 4965.10       5960.23

END OF PERFORMANCE.  PASS THREE EXECUTION TIME WAS    47  MINUTES AND   1.69  SECONDS.
                   MAXIMUM AMPLITUDE PER CHANNEL:                 4965.10       5960.23

OVERALL PEAK AMPLITUDE WAS 0.59602344E 04

   395 RECORDS WRITTEN ON INTERMEDIATE TAPE.
```

THE TOTAL STUDIO—TODAY AND THE FUTURE

Today's studio should contain facilities for both digital control of an analog synthesizer and computer sound synthesis. If a system similar to that described in the first section of this chapter were built, this system would also be sufficient to convert digital tapes to sound. The digital tapes would have to be generated on a large computer in another installation since it is unlikely that a small computing system that could control a synthesizer would also be able to run one of the large and complicated sound-generating programs.[4] In a university environment, the digital tape could be generated at the university's computation center. The only condition would be that the tape drive of the "music" system would have to be compatible with a tape drive at the main installation. At most computer centers, this method of converting digital tapes is much more practical than one that connects DACs directly to a large com-

---

[4] This situation is changing as witness a moderate sound synthesis program mounted at MIT on a PDP-11 computer and the MOM (MUSIC-ON-MINI) System at Princeton University using a small Hewlett-Packard computer.

puting system. If the subordinate system could be connected directly to the main computer, a limited type of almost "real-time" operation could be developed to allow more flexible experimentation. This would also be possible, without such connection, if the music-control computer possessed enough speed and storage to run a limited version of a sound-generation program.

Computer technology and its associated electronic technologies are changing rapidly. The growth of the "mini-computer" industry in the last five years is but one example of this. Another is the development of "hardware" (electronic components) that allows a more direct kind of digital control in music; we might call this "digital control of digital devices." For example, digital oscillators capable of a variety of wave-shapes are now being marketed at fairly low prices. Even special-purpose equipment such as digital reverberation units are appearing. Developments such as these are leading to hybrid systems in which the distinctions between digital and analog components are becoming blurred.

Technological developments are also speeding up the execution of computer sound synthesis programs. Each generation of new "maxi-computers" makes possible faster cycle times and more efficient operating systems. One can now purchase special-purpose hardware that speeds calculations done in computer sound synthesis; this can result in a dramatic decrease in the execution time of music programs.

Furthermore, it is now conceivable to build totally digital systems that operate in real-time. The new system of Peter Zinovieff and SYNTHI VCS Industries is a step in that direction. It uses a PDP-8 computer to control a large bank of digital oscillators, each of which contains a stored function to be sampled. A much more elaborate system is being designed by Barry Vercoe at the Massachusetts Institute of Technology. As presently envisioned, this amounts almost to a "hardware" version of MUSIC360.

A complete system should also be equipped with several ADCs. These can be used for many purposes, the most obvious being the analysis and modification of "real" sounds. One drawback of synthesizers and computer-generated-sound sytems has been that they do not lend themselves very well to "concrete" applications. But a system that includes ADCs can accept any type of sounds from the real world, mix and modify these sounds by using a sound synthesis program, and "generate" a "concrete" piece.

FINAL COMMENTS

It is always tempting to say that given enough money, all the technical problems of electronic music would disappear. There is a measure of truth in this. But it is even more true that these problems will not disappear totally until musicians trained in physics, engineering, and computing, and scientists trained in music work together in a complementary fashion. To this end, today's electronic music composer should not shrink from involving himself in all aspects of the design and operation of an electronic music studio. He should find that this involvement heightens his awareness of musical possibilities and makes likely a much more imaginative use of electronic facilities.

It is also tempting to say that one does not really need to know about computers and programming to run a sound synthesis job. This is true only if a consultant is available who does understand these things. Though most computer centers have many people who know about computers and programming, they do not often have programmers who are willing to learn a complicated program such as MUSIC360 just for the convenience of a user. Thus, for many of us it is absolutely necessary to understand the basics of computer organization and to know exactly how a particular sound synthesis program works.

These observations should not discourage the beginner in the field. Rather, they should indicate that he is entering a music in which he is the composer in a much larger sense than he ever was before. That his new opportunities and responsibilities require new and larger knowledge is natural and highly desirable.

6

Live-Electronic Music

GORDON MUMMA

This book begins and ends with an account of the speculations, technological innovations, and occasional bold inspiration that mark the history of electronic music. But the opening and closing chapters are in fact very different histories. Otto Luening looks back from the vantage point of a man who has personally witnessed the march of electronic technology from a point near its beginnings; he is a traditionally schooled composer who has gradually absorbed elements of this technology into an already-formed set of compositional attitudes and skills. For Gordon Mumma, on the other hand, electronic technology has always been present, the object of an absorbing curiosity and interest.

In a sense Mumma's history resumes where Luening's leaves off, examining the developments in electronic music before 1950, not so much as extensions of still earlier technological precedents but, rather, as aspects of the economic and social history of the period. From this viewpoint he considers various kinds of live performance with electronic media; surveys collaborative performance groups and special "heroes" of engineering; and explores in detail the influence of the new technology on pop, folk, rock, and jazz music as instruments are modified and the recording studio makes radical transformations of the original recorded sound. In the last section of the chapter, he discusses the extension of electronic technology into other live-performance arts, which involve sound sculpture, television, lasers, biophysics, and multimedia.

Gordon Mumma, one of the organizers of the ONCE Festival, is a composer and performing musician with the Merce Cunningham Dance Company and the Sonic Arts Union. He has been a consulting engineer for several electronic music studios, and has designed equipment for numerous live-electronic music applications. He has been a lecturer in residence at the University of Illinois, Brandeis University, the State University College of New York at Buffalo, and the Universities of California at Berkeley and Santa Cruz. His articles on contemporary music and electronic music have been published in several languages. His music is published by BMI Canada and has been recorded by Advance, CBS France, Mainstream, and Odyssey records.

INTRODUCTION

The history of electronic music begins with live-electronic music. The events of that history closely parallel, and are often dependent upon, the history of science and technology. Social and economic factors are often of critical importance. During the nineteenth century science and technology, and particularly the concept of electricity, were first applied on a broad scale to industry and commerce. In the second half of that century electrical science was applied to communications: as a result, the telegraph, the telephone, magnetic recording, and motion pictures were born.

The telegraph and telephone are means of immediate communication of information. Magnetic recording and motion pictures are means of delayed communication; they store information that is to be communicated later. For various social, economic, and technological reasons, the technology of immediate communication developed more rapidly than that of delayed communication. Though a patent for magnetic recording was issued to Valdemar Poulsen in 1898, this device was not generally used until the late '40s, following its technological development by the Germans just previous to the Second World War.

It is a common premise that electronic music became a reality because the magnetic tape recorder allowed a composer to work directly with stored sound. This premise thus places the beginnings of electronic music after the Second World War. But from 1885 on, patents for electrical and electronic music apparatus were issused at an accelerating rate. Much of this apparatus was to be used for live musical performance. Thus, we more rightfully place the beginnings of live-electronic music, at the latest, at the end of the nineteenth century.

LIVE-ELECTRONIC MUSIC BEFORE 1950

Technological, Economic, and Social History

One of the earliest electrical music instruments was patented in 1885 by Ernst Lorenz. It was an electromagnetic resonator controlled by a vibrating metal bar and a hammer. The principle is similar to that used in several present-day electronic pianos, and is related to various recent techniques of filtering and envelope control. However, before the turn of the century two other names are more important: William Duddell, an English physicist, and Thaddeus Cahill, an American lawyer.

Duddell's contributions were both theoretical and practical. In 1899 he demonstrated the transmission of sound by means of carbon arc lamps, and performed these "singing arcs" by means of oscillating circuits controlled from a keyboard. The significance of the "singing arcs" was that it enabled more than one person at a time to hear electrically produced music. The moving-coil loudspeaker, though patented one year earlier, was not developed for general use until 1926. Before that time the usual way of listening to electrically produced music was by telephone receivers. In 1900 Duddell formulated a theory for the negative-resistance oscillator, which was applied years later to neon bulbs and vacuum tubes in various electronic music instruments.

The musical use of the telephone brings us to the incredible Thaddeus Cahill. In the fifteen years between 1892 and 1907, Cahill designed, patented, and built a musical apparatus that, in certain respects, remains unsurpassed more than a half-century later. This apparatus, called the Telharmonium, was an electronic music synthesizer that could be performed live over the telephone system. The Telharmonium cost nearly a quarter-million dollars (in pre-First World War currency), weighed about 200 tons, and occupied the entire basement and first floor of a building at 39th St. and Broadway in New York City. It also set a precedent of sorts for a present-day requirement of live-electronic music instruments: portability. At one time in its existence the Telharmonium was transported in thirty railroad freight cars from Holyoke, Massachusetts to New York City, where it was installed in its Broadway home, called "Telharmonic Hall, the First Central Plant of the New York Electric Music Company." For its time the Telharmonium was an unusual technological achievement. Consider the fact that electronic amplification did not exist until Lee De Forest invented the "audion," a triode vacuum tube, in 1906, and that vacuum-tube amplification was not commercially feasible until after the First World War.

In the process of controlling sound electronically, there are many inherent losses in amplitude. Since amplification was not available to Cahill at that time he had to use other means of overcoming this problem. He overcame the amplitude losses of the system by building alternators that produced more than 10,000 watts, used these as his sound generators, and mixed his sounds with enormous multi-tapped transformers. Remarkably, he achieved many of the basic electronic music procedures used today—sustained oscillation, frequency control and filtering, envelope shaping, and mixing—by the use of a single phenomenon: inductive reactance. He built synchronized alternators with such accuracy that his Telharmonium could be performed with a variety of intonation systems besides that of equal temperament. Cahill's interest in intonation was part of an exploration from which he devised a system for the objective measurement of sound that was a predecessor of information theory. The Telharmonium had a frequency range of nearly seven octaves, almost twice as much as the best acoustic recordings of the time. The Telharmonium was a multiple-keyboard instrument, usually played by two performers, "four-hands." The performers presented a repertory of the respectable music of the day (Bach, Chopin, Gounod, Grieg, Rossini, etc.) on regularly scheduled programs. One could visit Telharmonic Hall to hear these programs or subscribe to a telephone circuit to hear them elsewhere. The New York Electric Music Co. was a predecessor of Muzak.

Besides representing a technological state-of-the-art, Cahill's Telharmonium was an economic and social product of its time. The scale of financial investment required was representative of capital expansiveness in the United

States at the turn of the century. Cahill's idea seemed like a good investment for many reasons, not the least of which was the detail and comprehensiveness of his patents. His creative contemporaries may have had equal scientific and artistic imagination, but few had Cahill's legal experience in securing patents.

The years from 1907 to 1919 saw very little electronic music activity. But the telephone industry was hard at work on technological development, particularly the process of electronic amplification.

In 1920 the Russian Leon Termen introduced his "Theremin" in Leningrad. The Theremin relied entirely upon sustained oscillations achieved by a vacuum-tube beat-frequency oscillator. This instrument is not performed from a keyboard, but, rather, is controlled by the indigenous interaction of human-body capacitance with the instrument itself. For several decades the Theremin was performed world-wide by a number of virtuosos, and is still used today in its updated transistorized versions.

Several other live-electronic music instruments were invented in the '20s, among them Jörg Mager's "Sphärophon," Maurice Martenot's "Ondes Martenot," René Bertrand's "Dynamophone," and Friedrich Trautwein's "Trautonium." The "Trautonium" was unusual because of its use of subtractive synthesis for sound production; it is still used in Germany in modified versions. The "Ondes Martenot," introduced in Paris in 1928, became the most widely known. Some of these instruments employed a moving-coil loudspeaker, and were thus freed from the use of telephone audition in traditional concert situations. The electronic music instruments of the '20s were not necessarily considered commercially feasible for mass production by their inventors—this despite the public enthusiasm, particularly in the late '20s, for the new products of affluence: radios, electrical recordings, appliances, and automobiles.

However, one man—Laurens Hammond—was definitely interested in commerce. Just before the Wall Street disaster of 1929 Hammond established, in Evanston, Illinois, a company to build electric organs. The Hammond organs of the '30s were remarkable instruments. They were attractive because by electronic means, they achieved in a smaller package at much less cost something of the effect of the glamorous pipe organs. To the purist the Hammond organ was a disgrace. But enough buyers were found during the economically precarious '30s to enable Hammond to stay in business, patent several basic procedures, and establish his instrument as a household word.

In certain technical and musical respects the Hammond organ is still a very interesting electronic organ. The purists were right: it didn't sound like a pipe organ. But the unique drawbar system of additive timbre synthesis (fundamentally an efficient extension of Thaddeus Cahill's Telharmonium) places the Hammond organ in the category of live-electronic music synthesizers. Among other achievements, Hammond accomplished stable intonation (a constant problem for electronic music instruments of that time) by another practical extension of a Cahill principle, synchronized electromechanical sound generators. Hammond also patented a procedure of electromechanical reverberation that used the helical torsion of a coiled spring, which is widely used today in many electronic music applications.

By the late '30s Hammond had competition, including the English Compton Organ, the Canadian Robb Wave Organ, and the "Bourne Electric Pipe Organ." In spite of an economic depression, the electronic organ had become the first widely used electronic music instrument, and it held a firm position in the "leisure market."

Among other technical achievements of the '30s were the first demonstration of television transmissions and several important developments in magnetic recording. The first of the latter was the discovery of alternating current (AC) bias, a procedure that mixes a supersonic current with the audio signal during recording. AC bias helps to minimize distortions that are inherent in the magnetic recording process. Following a German prototype of magnetic tape demonstrated by Fritz Pfleumer in 1927, I.G. Farbenindustrie (part of the cartel that included the BASF firm) developed the first practical oxide-coated plastic tape in 1932. In conjunction with the German industrial cartel AEG, the prototypical magnetic tape recorder called the "Magnetophon" was introduced at the 1935 Berlin Radio Fair. At the BASF Ludwigshafen factory in 1936, the first magnetic tape recording of a symphony orchestra was made; the London Philharmonic Orchestra performing Mozart. Other kinds of magnetic tape recording were being developed at the same time, including the "Blattnerphone" and the Marconi-Stille recorders, both of which were being produced by the late '30s. These two machines used solid steel tape of 3- to 6-mm. width. A reel of tape for the Marconi-Stille machine weighted about 35 lbs. and ran at nearly 60 inches per second. Splices were made by soldering. With the disruption of the Second World War, the artistic implications of magnetic tape were not explored again until the '50s.

Artistic Activity

Of all the live-electronic music instruments introduced by 1935, the "Ondes Martenot" has the distinction of having had a repertory of original music composed for it. Ultimately, it is the repertory of music composed for an instrument that establishes its most secure place in history. In the '30s several well-known composers experimented with the Ondes Martenot; these included Paul Hindemith, Darius Milhaud, Ernst Toch, and Edgard Varèse. One composer, Olivier Messiaen, composed an expansive piece, *Fête des Belles Eaux* (1937), for an ensemble of six Ondes Martenots, which is so musically innovative that it has achieved the status of a major work. (In the same year Percy Grainger composed a geometrically graphic score for an ensemble of four Theremins.) More recently, the Ondes Martenot has been championed by young performers such as Arlette Sibon-Simonovic, who has introduced new works by John Cage, Jose-Maria Mestres-Quadreny, and Bernard Parmegiani.

The future of electronic music was the subject of considerable discussion during the first half of this century. In 1907 the esteemed composer and pianist Feruccio Busoni mentioned electronic music in his "Sketch for a new esthetic of music," making specific reference to Cahill's Telharmonium. Edgard Varèse wrote and spoke about electronic music, and from 1916 on made repeated, though unsuccessful attempts to organize collaborative efforts. In the '30s Joseph Schillinger, Leopold Stokowski, Carlos Chavez, J. Murray Barbour, and John Cage added their writings and efforts to the subject.

In 1939 John Cage composed the first of a series of live-performance works called "Imaginary Landscapes," which were to be performed with conventional instruments and electronic devices. While working in Seattle, Cage experimented with the electronic equipment of the recording studio at the Cornish School, and composed a part for *Imaginary Landscape No. 1* that required disc recordings to be performed on a variable-speed record player. In 1941 Cage moved to Chicago, where he conducted further experiments at CBS in preparation for a collaborative radio broadcast with the poet Kenneth Patchen. In the *Imaginary Landscape No. 2, Credo in Us,* and *Imaginary Landscape No. 3* —all composed in 1942—Cage employed the performing of radio, electric buzzers, amplified marimbula and wire coil, audio oscillators, and variable-speed disc recordings. *Imaginary Landscape No. 3* was introduced to New York audiences at a Museum of Modern Art concert on February 7, 1943.

The impact of the Second World War on the creative arts was brutal; it left as a monument for posterity the spectacle of a fifteen-year gap in the historical continuity of European music. Many creative artists became refugees, thus adding to their usual struggles for survival the problems of new languages and customs in adopted lands. In an era of instantaneous communication, the dissemination of new music and ideas had become extremely difficult. The remarkable last works of Webern and Schönberg, and in particular the most innovative music of John Cage and the young Pierre Boulez, were refracted through this gap to meet their audiences as much as fifteen years later. Technology was directed toward war, with the ironical effect of accelerating innovation while restricting application. With an occasional exception, the momentum of interest in electronic music was suspended until the future. Two years after Cage's *Imaginary Landscapes* of 1942, Percy Grainger and Burnett Cross constructed an instrument of eight synchronized oscillators for the composition of "free music."

It was a few years after the war ended before experimental work resumed. In Paris in the late '40s Pierre Schaeffer and Pierre Henry began their experiments with disc recorders at the French Radio, and Paul Boisselet composed a series of live-performance works for instruments, tape recorders, and oscillators. In 1949 the German engineer Harald Bode built the electronic Melochord, and Oskar Sala modified the Trautonium and its original live-performance function—the result was the Mixtur-Trautonium, which was used to compose film soundtracks. The musical instrument firm of Hohner began producing various popular electronic musical instruments in Trossingen. In Canada, engineer Hugh Le Caine, working for the National Research Council, began in 1948 a long career designing electronic music instruments. Between 1945 and 1950 the tape recorder was introduced to the United States, the first production units being modeled after the German war booty "Magnetophon."

The appearance of the tape recorder engaged virtually the entire attention of the American composers interested in electronic music, with Louis and Bebe Barron beginning their tape experimentation in 1948.

LIVE-ELECTRONIC MUSIC SINCE 1950

The general availability of the tape recorder a few years after the Second World War stimulated a rapid increase in electronic music activity from 1950 on. Magnetic tape was the first storage medium for sound which was reasonably editable: it could be accurately cut and spliced. During the '50s most composers treated magnetic tape in a manner analogous to that of filmmakers working with film. As with film, tape music was "composed" largely through editing. Until 1960 there were very few exceptions to the use of tape as a studio medium, though it was a vastly more relevant use than is usually implied in the term "canned" music. These exceptions began to appear in the late '50s and increased rapidly throughout the '60s. Some composers used taped sound in live concert with instruments or voices. Others explored the use of tape in innovative performance situations without referring to traditional music; or they developed real-time studio techniques that were in themselves live performances, using tape only to record the result for distribution.

More significantly, some composers discarded the tape medium as a musical premise and explored the use of electronic devices, separately and in conjunction with acoustic instruments, as a basis for live-performance. Finally, digital computers became increasingly valuable tools for musical composition and sound synthesis, and by 1970 were variously applied as live-performance instruments.

Live Performance of Instruments with Tape

Composers that use magnetic tape continuously experiment with ways to present their work to audiences. Broadcast and recording are successful because they allow the audience to determine for themselves the formality (or informality) of how they listen. Playing tapes for audiences in the concert hall is another matter. The concert audience has strong traditional expectations. Audiences expect to see as well as hear a performance, and loudspeakers aren't much to look at.

Furthermore, many composers who work with tape still compose for conventional instruments and have specific ideas on how to combine the media. One of the first combined works has become a classic. Edgard Varèse's remarkable *Déserts* (1949–52) alternates between conventional instruments and taped sounds, producing the effect of a monumental sound sculpture. However, by the mid '50s two collaborative compositions by Otto Luening and Vladimir Ussachevsky had become better known. Their *Rhapsodic Variations* (1953–54) and *A Poem in Cycles and Bells* (1954) had reached the American public through broadcast and recording.

The Luening-Ussachevsky works were composed in New York City. Parts of the Varèse *Déserts* were done in Paris, where before 1955 other works for instruments and tape had been composed by Paul Boisselet, Pierre Henry, Andre Hodier, Darius Milhaud, and Pierre Schaeffer. From 1955 to 1960 the repertory for instruments and tape was increased by works from Belgium (Louis de Meester, Henri Pousseur), England (Roberto Gerhard), Germany (Mauricio Kagel, Karlheinz Stockhausen), Italy (Luciano Berio, John Cage, Luigi Nono), the Netherlands (Henk Badings), Japan (Kuniharu Akiyama, Shin Ichi Matsushita, Makato Moroi, Joji Yuasa), and the United States (Richard Maxfield, John Herbert McDowell, Gordon Mumma, Robert Sheff, Morton Subotnick). In the '60s works for this medium came from Argentina, Australia, Austria, Brazil, Canada, Czechoslovakia, Denmark, Finland, Greece, Iceland, Israel, Mexico, Poland, Spain, Sweden, and Yugoslavia as well.

The sounds composed on tape had many acoustic and electronic sources. A few composers, however, were more interested in electronic synthesis than in tape composition. For Milton Babbitt magnetic tape was primarily a way of storing the music that he had composed with the RCA Mark II Synthesizer. Babbitt also synthesized music that was stored on tape but was intended to be heard in live performance. His *Vision and Prayer* (1961) and *Philomel* (1964), both for soprano and synthesized sounds, are examples.

The ways of combining instruments with tape are diverse, and the methods of coordination are particularly interesting. In Luciano Berio's *Differences* (1958–60) and Mauricio Kagel's *Transicion II* (1958–59), the tape and instrumental sounds occur in ensemble. Being derived from the instruments themselves, the tape sounds at times like a natural extension of the live instruments. Mario Davidovsky, in his *Three Synchronisms* (1963–65), and Roberto Gerhard, in his orchestral *Collages* (1960), use taped sounds of electronic origin as well, and contrast is very specific.

Except for sophisticated experimental tape machines, where specific coordination is required, musicians must follow the tempo established on the tape. Some composers have invented special notation for the tape-stored sound and have added it to the musical notation of the instrumental parts. Over reasonably short durations, even with complex tape sounds, instrumentalists have found it practical to learn the tape "by ear," so that in Davidovsky's *Synchronisms,* for example, very strict timing is achieved. Another synchronizing procedure uses a special track of multi-channel tape for cues that the instrumentalist hears through headphones. An early example is Ramon Sender's *Desert Ambulance* (1964) for amplified accordion, stereo tape, and light projection. Sender used a special three-channel tape: two channels contained the stereo sounds heard by the audience, and the third, heard only by the accordionist, contained pitches, timing cues, and spoken instructions. In the *Lyric Variations for Violin and Computer* (1968) composer J. K. Randall synthesized the tape sounds with an IBM 7094 computer, and also had the computer produce a metronome tape heard only by the violinist.

Many live instrument-tape compositions do not require precise synchronization. Indeed, some composers are interested in having the tape and live sounds occur quite independently of each other. A classic example is John

Cage's *Aria with Fontana Mix* (1958). Finally, some works such as Barney Childs' *Interbalances VI* (1964) require the performers to prepare the tape from sounds and synchronization of their own making.

Performed tape

From a collaborative tape-music project established in 1951 by Earle Brown, John Cage, Morton Feldman, David Tudor, and Christian Wolff (with the technical assistance of Louis and Bebe Barron), Cage composed his *Williams Mix* (1952) for eight tracks of tape. The work has a score that constitutes a pattern for cutting and splicing the tapes and that establishes an early premise for treating tape music as a non-fixed medium. Working at the Studio di Fonologia Musicali in Milan in 1958, Cage composed *Fontana Mix* for four tracks of tape. *Fontana Mix* has a score that is used in live performance to modify and distribute the sounds in space. In Cage's *Rozart Mix* (1965), the performers, who may include members of the audience, supply tapes of sounds that are spliced into loops during performance for playing on a large ensemble of tape recorders. Other unusual applications of tape-loops include Alvin Lucier's *The Only Talking Machine of its Kind in the World,* and Daniel Lentz's *Rice, Wax, and Narrative.* In both works very long loops are used; in Lentz's piece the performers are encircled, and in Lucier's the entire audience is encircled.

Robert Ashley's classic, *The Fourth of July* (1960), a tape composition for theater as well as concert presentation, was made in a studio of the composer's own design, which allowed for considerable real-time performance on the equipment. The multi-channel tape of Ashley's *Public Opinion Descends Upon the Demonstrators* (1961) is performed live according to the interaction between a notated score and the audience response. The remarkable work of Richard Maxfield was composed on magnetic tape by his own live-performance studio techniques. Maxfield's *Night Music* (1960), *Amazing Grace* (1960), and *Piano Concert for David Tudor* (1961) have been belatedly recognized, and their technical and musical procedures are now widely imitated.

Employing all sorts of innovative studio procedures, Pauline Oliveros composed in 1966 a series of real-time stereophonic tape compositions, of which *I of IV* is best known. At the same time, Terry Riley developed a live, polyphonic, solo-performance interaction among tape recorders, soprano saxophone, and electric organ, from which compositions such as *Rainbow in Curved Air* (1968) and *Poppy Nogood and the Phantom Band* (1966) were produced.

On commission from NHK in Tokyo in 1966, Karlheinz Stockhausen began his *Solo für Melodieinstrument mit Rückkopplung.* Though open-structured, the form of this work requires precisely fixed time delays achieved by means of a magnetic tape feedback loop. The precision necessary for these time delays was not efficiently achieved until a few years later when a special mechanism of adjustable playback heads was constructed.

Perhaps the most unusual use of magnetic tape as a live-performance medium has been achieved by Jon Hassell in his works *MAP/1* and *MAP/2* (1969). Hassell composed these works on large sheets of magnetic tape. The performers select from the stored sounds by moving hand-held playback heads across the magnetized oxide surface of these sheets. Because of the large size of this "tape," the composer duplicates the tape by a special process of magnetic contact printing.

Live-Electronic Music without Tape
(Amplified Small Sounds, Performed Electronic Equipment)

Electronic amplification had been used in music before the Second World War to make traditional instruments louder and to develop electronic instruments; it was also used by John Cage in his *Imaginary Landscapes*. Cage's use of amplification was prophetic because it was a special sense of magnification. That is, instead of amplifying sounds that were simply not quite loud enough, he experimented with sounds of such small magnitude that without amplification they were practically inaudible. Electronically magnified, these micro-sounds revealed a whole new world of sound resources. At the studio of the French Radio in Paris, this direction was continued in 1952 by Jean Louis Brau in his *Concerto de Janvier,* made directly with microphone effects. But the live-performance implications of this work were missed by the French Radio experimentalists, who continued to work with magnetic tape and disk manipulations.

Following eight years of innovative work with the "prepared piano," Cage resumed composing for live-electronic means with the *Imaginary Landscape No. 4* (1951) for 12 radios with 24 performers. This work and the *Radio Music* (1952), *Speech* (1955), and *Music Walk* (1958) that followed, was an exploration of the radio receiver as a live-performance instrument. After composing *Imaginary Landscape No. 3* in 1942, Cage did not return to the use of microphones until his *Winter Music* and *Variations II* of the late '50s. These two compositions were developed by David Tudor as works for amplified piano. For *Winter Music,* the piano was performed from the keyboard and made ultra-loud; *Variations II* was an exploration with contact microphones that raised the micro-sounds from inside the piano to concert audibility.

In 1957 the members of the *Manifestations: Light and Sound* productions in Ann Arbor began live performances of amplified small sounds, tape music, and light projection. In 1960 John Cage composed the *Music for Amplified Toy Pianos,* which used contact microphones, and the classic *Cartridge Music,* which used phonograph cartridges. These four Cage works were performed widely, particularly by David Tudor and the composer, and were a considerable stimulus to experimentation in live-electronic music. Live performance with amplified small sounds aided by the development of new live-performance electronic equipment, became an important activity during the '60s. It gradually attracted the attention of many who, philosophically committed to the tape medium, had previously dismissed live-performance electronic music as an unworthy endeavor.

Only a few other composers worked with live-electronic music before 1960.

In Ankara, Bulent Arel composed his *Music for String Quartet and Oscillator* in 1957, and in New York, Dick Higgins composed *Graphis 24* (1958), a score for controlling theremins and feedback. In New York, Joe Jones created a marvelous menagerie of electrical, electronic, and mechanical instruments that on occasion could be heard performing by themselves in the lobbies of modern music concert halls.

Between 1960 and 1965 most live-electronic music activity occurred in the United States. It was nourished not only because of a spirited experimental milieu, but also because the benefits of solid-state electronic technology were most accessible in the United States. The Americans who composed for live-electronic performance during these years included Robert Ashley, Philip Corner, Max Deutsch, John Eaton, Alvin Lucier, Gordon Mumma, Max Neuhaus, David Tudor, and La Monte Young. Outside the United States, similar work was done by Takahisa Kosugi in Japan, Gil Wolman in France, Karlheinz Stockhausen in Germany, and Giuseppe Chiari in Italy. From 1966 through 1970 compositions of live-electronic music multiplied rapidly, the majority of activity still in the United States. Live-electronic music compositions were occasionally issued on commercial recordings, and were performed widely enough in concert to establish a sense of repertory for the growing audiences interested in new music

In the repertory of live-electronic music the continuing work of John Cage assumes large proportions. In 1961 Cage composed *Music for Carillon No. 4,* and in 1967, *Music for Carillon No. 5,* thereby completing a series of pieces for electronic carillon that he began in 1952. *Atlas Eclipticalis* (1961–62) is a work for large ensemble with variable electronic modification. *Rozart Mix* (1965) is a participation piece with a large ensemble of performed tape loops. *HPSCHD* (1969), a collaboration with composer Lejaren Hiller, combines fifty-one computer-synthesized tapes with seven electronic and amplified harpsichords in live performance. The series of *Variations* numbered from I to VIII, begun by John Cage in 1958 and completed in 1968, hold far-reaching implications. By various elegant innovations in graphic notation, the composer specified the circumstances and outlined the procedures for each of the *Variations.* These *Variations* are plans for societies of activity, not necessarily limited to musical activity, and as good plans should, they allow for the updating of electronic and other means to achieve their ends.

Closely associated with John Cage, David Tudor has been responsible for much of the technological and performance reification of these works. Paralleling his activities as the major performer of innovative piano music in the '50s, Tudor devoted much of his time in the '60s to proselytizing and to performing and nourishing the live-electronic music of other composers. In the wake of this incredible activity and dedication to others' work, the imposing figure of David Tudor as a composer appeared with his *Fluorescent Sound* (1964), *Bandoneon !* (1966) and *Rainforest* (1968).

Electronic modification of electronically generated sound and electronic modification of acoustically generated sound are the two most common procedures of live-electronic music. The first of these is the basis of commercial electronic music synthesizers. The second is applied by Tudor in his *Fluorescent Sound,* in which he electronically amplified and distributed the mechanical resonances of the fluorescent light fixtures of Stockholm's Moderna Museet on September 13, 1964. *Bandoneon !* (Bandoneon factorial) was a "combine" of programmed audio circuits, moving loudspeakers, TV images, and lighting, activated by the acoustic signals of an Argentine Bandoneon. For this work Tudor developed special "instrumental loudspeakers" with which he exploited the unique resonant characteristics of sounding physical materials. This concept of the loudspeaker as a musical instrument was further extended in the remarkable *Rainforest.* In this work, however, Tudor applied the second of the two basic concepts above in reverse: it is an example of acoustic modification of electronically generated sound.

The sounds of *Rainforest* are generated by sine and pulse oscillators, and are applied by special transducers to various resonant objects of wood, metal, and plastic. Each of the combinations of transducer and resonant object is an "instrumental loudspeaker" that adds and subtracts harmonics and occasionally creates complex intermodulations with the electronic oscillations. Further, attached to each "instrumental loudspeaker" is a small microphone that allows the acoustically modified sound to be further amplified and resonantly distributed by conventional loudspeakers throughout the performance space. Because the "instrumental loudspeakers" are affected by the sounds of the conventional loudspeakers, a recycling phenomenon takes place that makes the entire electronic-acoustic apparatus of *Rainforest* an ecologically balanced sound system. *Rainforest* is generally performed by two performers and an "orchestra" or "forest" of eight to twelve "instrumental loudspeakers" and four conventional loudspeakers. The performers articulate the electronic oscillators, distribute the oscillations to the "instrumental loudspeakers," and create combinations of "instrumental loudspeakers" that are heard from the conventional loudspeakers. The work has been widely performed by the Merce Cunningham Dance Company, by whom it was commissioned. Tudor has also produced *Rainforest* in an expanded concert version. One of these productions, at the "Chocorua 73" festival in New Hampshire, was implemented by a workshop of nearly twelve people who, collaborating with Tudor, built many new "instrumental loudspeakers" and extended the sound materials to include prepared sounds of non-electronic origin. The Chocorua 73 performance was presented in a large barn as a six-hour environment.

La Monte Young's amplified voices, traditional instruments, and sine-wave oscillators are performed with specific and carefully determined intonation, and are combined in ensembles with the mysterious projections of Marian Zazeela to create sonorous harmonic spectra that are extended in time to produce a music of epic proportions. Max Neuhaus, a virtuoso percussionist, has not only applied complex electronic amplification to the work of other composers—such as Earle Brown's *Four Systems* (1964), Sylvano Bussotti's *Coeur pour Batteur* (1965), and John Cage's *Fontana Mix-Feed* (1965)—but has also developed his own electronic works for public participation. Among these are *Public Supply* (1966), in which the public is invited to telephone a radio or TV station to have their voices immediately modified and combined in the transmission. In *Drive-in Music* (1967) a series of weather-sensing, low-power radio transmitters were installed along a road in Buffalo, N.Y., so that the commuting public heard the effects of climate and overlapping propagation on their automobile radios. In 1973 Neuhaus installed a more general access environment called *Walk Through* at the Jay Street–Borough Hall Station of the underground New York Transit System.

The live-electronic music of David Behrman has evolved from the technologically elementary (though musically difficult) use of acoustic feedback with conventional instruments in his *Wavetrain* (1966), to the notationally coordinated use of equalization and frequency shifting of instrumental sounds in his *Players with Circuits* (1967), to the technologically elaborate construction of an ensemble of electronic instruments for *Runthrough* (1968). *Runthrough* consists of oscillators, frequency shifters, voltage-controlled amplifiers, and a photo electric sound distribution matrix; it is performed by three or more players with miniature flashlights. Behrman designed the interacting circuit configuration of the piece so that the various actions of the players with their flashlights do not necessarily produce one-to-one musical correspondences. An ensemble situation is created in which the players must deal with elements of social stress as well as the technological and musical issues of *Runthrough*. For his ongoing work, *Homemade Synthesizer Music with Sliding Pitches,* Behrman has built a purely electronic synthesizer. By means of an interdependent configuration of voltage-controlled amplifiers, mixers, DC-level shifters, and thirty-two function generators, either live performance by human operators or automatic performance by the synthesizer alone is possible.

By virtue of their wide performance and acclaim (at least among audiences for new music), several other live-electronic works have become staples of the repertory. Robert Ashley's *The Wolfman* (1964)—for highly amplified human voice with tape accompaniment—and Salvatore Martirano's *L's G.A.* (1968)—performed by a gas-masked actor in an atmosphere modulated by helium, stereo tape, and film projection—have political as well as musical impact, and are unusually popular. Pauline Oliveros' contribution to this repertory is a series of apparently self-sustaining works for amplified apple boxes, including *Applebox* (1964), *Applebox Double* (1965), *Applebox Orchestra* (1966), and *Applebox Orchestra with Bottle Chorus* (1970). Roger Reynolds' widely performed *Ping* (1968) is a multi-media work, after a story by Samuel Beckett, for ring-modulated and electronically distributed instruments (multiphonic flute, motorized piano, harmonium, bowed cymbal, and tam-tam), magnetic tape, and projected images and calligraphy. Reynolds' *Traces* (1969), *Again* (1970), and the very complex *I/O* (1971)—for mimes, vocalists, instrumentalists, projections, and electronic modification and distribution—continue his work with the integration of acoustic and live-electronic procedures.

A significant aspect of the work of Behrman, Neuhaus, Martirano, and others such as David Rosenboom, Serge Tcherepnine and Stanley Lunetta is that these composers design and build their own electronic music instruments. Very few composers consider the creative design of electronic circuits as a requirement of their craft, though it is already clear that some of the most important innovations in electronic music have been contributed by electronically educated composers. An education in electronics is not mandatory in order to create live-electronic music, particularly since commercial synthesizers have been developed for use in live performance. John Eaton and Max Deutsch were involved early with the use of synthesizers as live-performance instruments. In 1965 Eaton composed and performed works with the Synket, a portable synthesizer developed by Paul Ketoff in Rome. The same year Deutsch composed in the United States two live-performance works that combined the Moog synthesizer with conventional instruments.

Outside the United States, live-electronic music activity had begun in Japan, where Takehisa Kosugi composed *Micro 1* (1961), a work for solo microphone. Beginning in 1967, Kosugi composed several poetic works with the generic titles *Manodharma* and *Eclipse,* which used both radio-frequency and audio-frequency electronics. Toshi Ichiyanagi composed a repertory of works for electronically modified Western and Japanese instruments, including *Space* (1966), *Situation* (1966), *Activities for Orchestra* (1967), and *Appearance* (1967). Ichiyanagi did not design his own equipment; instead he specified the electronic "instrumentation" and configuration of his pieces, much as a composer would enumerate the types and arrangement of conventional instruments for a piece, relying on the performers to supply the equipment and skill. In Italy, Domenico Guaccero introduced his *Improvvisazione 1962* in Rome; from 1964 through 1966 in Florence, Giuseppe Chiari composed a series of live-electronics works using contact microphones; and in 1966 Luigi Nono composed *A Floresta e Jovem e Cheia de Vida* for singers, instruments, and tape with electronic filters.

Of the German composers working with live-electronic music, Karlheinz Stockhausen has achieved much attention—particularly in Europe where most of his compositions are available on recordings—and his energetic efforts as a polemist are notorious. Stockhausen's large body of composition is diverse in style and idea; this is due to his expansive imagination as well as to his considerable facility to absorb the procedures of other composers' work into his own. In these and other respects his position in contemporary music is analogous to that of Maurice Bejart in ballet. Following *Kontakte* (1960) for percussion and magnetic tape, Stockhausen's next live-electronic works were *Microphonie I* (1964), for amplified and electronically filtered tam-tam; *Mixtur* (1964), for five instrumental ensembles with ring modulators; and *Microphonie II* (1965), for chorus, Hammond Organ, and ring modulator. These were followed by *Prozession* (1967), for amplified and filtered chamber ensemble; *Stimmung* (1968), for amplified singers; and *Aus den Sieben Tagen* (1968), for a variable ensemble with indeterminate electronic modification. Perhaps the most interesting of these works is *Aus den Sieben Tagen,* which, employing graphic and verbal notation, has evolved through performance into an attractively lyrical work of many hours duration, similar in scope to the earlier *Treatise* (1967), by the English composer Cornelius Cardew.

A younger German composer of promise is the violist Johannes Fritsch, who, independently of the usual state-radio resources, composed several works for instruments and live-electronic apparatus during the mid '60s. These include *Partita* (1965–66), for viola, contact microphone, tape, and equalization, and *Violectra I, II, and III* (1971–72), for Viola d'amore with EMS Synthi. Fritsch is a member of the independent German group "Feedback," organized in 1970, whose members also include Peter Eötvös, Rolf Gehlhaar, David Johnson, Mesias Maiguashca, John McGuire, and Michael von Biel. Several of the members of Feedback were associated with the live-performance ensemble at WDR (the West German Radio) during the years 1967–70, when many of Stockhausen's live-electronic works were recorded. They left the WDR ensemble following performances at EXPO 70 in Osaka because of growing ideological differences with Stockhausen.

A recent and unusual development of live-electronic music in the United States is exemplified by the works of Philip Glass and Steve Reich. Following a direction implied by the earlier work of LaMonte Young and Terry Riley, these composers have developed skilled performance ensembles that often combine acoustic instruments with electronic instruments used in rock music, such as the electric piano, combo organ, and electric harpsichord. Their compositions manifest a strong rhythmic and melodic basis, though the rather elegant style of the works is a fundamental departure from that of rock music.

Live Performance with Digital Computers

The digital computer is a configuration of logic modules to which is added an enlarged memory and various access and control functions. It is a general-purpose device that can be applied to specific problems by means of external programming. Logic modules are most commonly designed for specific functions in live-electronic music equipment, and are not externally programmable to any great extent. With integrated circuitry, logic modules can become relatively involved, as in the 16-bit digital computer/decoder used in Stanley Lunetta's *Moosack Machine*. Logic modules can, in fact, be designed with memory functions, and can be externally programmed. One reason digital computers have found limited use in live performance is their unportable size. Either the live performance must be taken to the computer, or it must be connected to a remote computer by a data-link. A common data-link is a telephone line, with the computer at one end and a teletype among the live performers at the other.

This procedure was used for my own work, *Conspiracy 8* (1970), which was performed live at the Guggenheim Museum in New York City, using a PDP–6 computer in Boston. Using a data-link, the remote computer received information about the performance, made decisions according to a basic program, and issued instructions to the performers. The computer participated as a decision-making member of the ensemble, and the ensemble accepted the sounds of its electronic decision-making—which were relayed to New York City by a second data-link—as a sonic contribution to the music.

For several years Salvatore Martirano has been working on a live-performance electronic music instrument derived from digital computer procedures. Early in his experimentation, he interconnected two portable digital-logic education modules and used them to articulate an ensemble of electronic oscillators. Though they contained no memory, direct access to the programmable functions of these machines allowed Martirano to treat them as live-performance instruments. During the course of his work he has performed with this continually evolving instrument. One of these performances had the bluntly descriptive title *Let's look at the back of my head for a while* (1970). The instrument has come to be known as the Sal-Mar Construction, and the performances that Martirano presents are literally state-of-the-art events.

With the recent advent of mini-computers—which include a memory capacity of several thousand words, cost only a few thousand dollars, and occupy only a few cubic feet of space—the digital computer is now a practical live-performance instrument. Edward Kobrin designed a logic-module interface that converts the digital output of his PDP–8 mini-computer into signals that operate voltage-controlled electronic-music modules. His instrument produces six voices simultaneously; each voice consists of a multi-waveform oscillator followed by three filters and an amplifier, all of which are voltage-controlled. The six voices of output are distributed around the performance area by the mini-computer through sixteen loudspeakers. Every aspect of Kobrin's instrument depends upon signals from his mini-computer. With a basic program and micro-routines stored in its memory, the mini-computer is performed live by choosing from the micro-routines. The complexity of the interactions, and the rates of speed with which they can be made, surpass any non-computerized live-electronic musical instrument.

A project with unusual live-performance implications is the digital-computer-controlled electronic music system being developed under the guidance of Jon Appleton at Dartmouth College. This system uses a large time-sharing computer with a satellite mini-computer. To the mini-computer is attached a rack of plug-in, digitally-controlled synthesizer modules. A library of new modules is under continuing development. The user (composer or performer) has access to the system by means of several teletype keyboard and cathode ray tube (CRT) displays, one of which is located right next to the mini-computer and synthesizer module rack in a Dartmouth music practice room. Access is remarkably easy. A single page of instructions enables the user to activate the system. All further questions are addressed through the teletype to the remote time-sharing computer, which displays its answers on the CRT. At this stage, the system functions as a teaching machine that develops the user's programming skills. The user can then compose a program, which is loaded into the mini-computer to operate the synthesizer. The results are heard immediately on loudspeakers in the practice room. Since all the instructions are in simple English, are displayed on a line-by-line basis on the CRT, and operate the synthesizer in real-time, the user can make rapid and exact changes in his work. When the user is through composing, an instruction can be typed by which the program returns from the mini-computer to storage in the time-sharing computer, ready to be called upon in the future. In the meantime, other persons can use the same practice-room computer satellite for their work. Among the intriguing possibilities of this system are ensemble performances that could be achieved by using several satellites at the same time; or collective or ongoing compositions and performances (perhaps even by an anonymous collective) could be achieved over considerable spans of space and time.

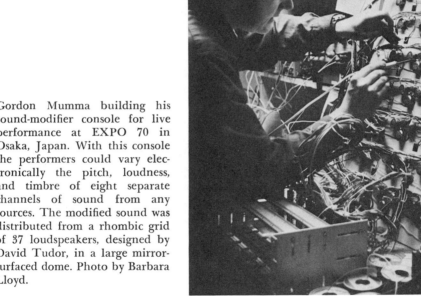

Gordon Mumma building his sound-modifier console for live performance at EXPO 70 in Osaka, Japan. With this console the performers could vary electronically the pitch, loudness, and timbre of eight separate channels of sound from any sources. The modified sound was distributed from a rhombic grid of 37 loudspeakers, designed by David Tudor, in a large mirror-surfaced dome. Photo by Barbara Lloyd.

Part of the *Moosack Machine* built by California composer Stanley Lunetta. This sound-sculpture combines electronic and acoustical sound-makers with light, temperature, and proximity sensors, all under the control of a digital logic system. Photo by Dennis Lunetta.

Violoncellist Charlotte Moorman performing on a video-sculpture musical instrument of artist Nam June Paik. Besides the three television screens which comprise the body of the instrument, the performer is wearing special glasses which support miniature television screens on each side of her head. Photo by Gordon Mumma, Bonino Gallery, New York, October, 1971.

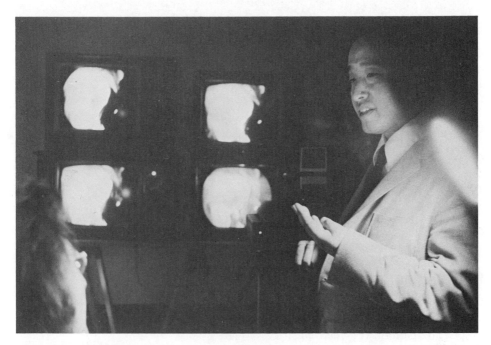

Korean-born video artist Nam June Paik discussing with John Lennon the operation of a video synthesizer designed in collaboration with Shuya Abe. The contours and colors of Lennon's image are modified live by the video synthesizer and presented in different aspects on the television screens in the background. Photo by Gordon Mumma, Bonino Gallery, New York, October, 1971.

David Rosenboom's New York Bio-Feedback Quartet during a performance in New York. The performer at the right has electrodes attached to his head by means of a headband. His electroencephalic signals are applied as control signals for the ARP synthesizers in the background. The performers are, left to right, David Rosenboom, Theodore Coons, Marge Hassell, and Jon Hassell. Photo by Gordon Mumma.

Left to right: Alvin Lucier, Wayne Slawson, and Gordon Mumma during preparation for a live-electronic music concert by the Sonic Arts Union at the Södra Theatre in Stockholm, Sweden, May, 1971. The electronic music equipment at the right is one of two mini-synthesizers used in the performance of Alvin Lucier's *The Duke of York*. Remote-control photograph by Gordon Mumma.

Gordon Mumma, in a performance of his *Hornpipe* (1967) at the Metropolitan Museum of Art, New York, in February, 1972. The electronic equipment attached to his belt is a special-purpose analog computer which analyzes and responds through loudspeakers to the resonances of the performance space which are actuated by the sounds of the French horn. Photo by Jumay Chu.

A dancer of the Merce Cunningham Dance Company, wearing a telemetry belt for the dance *TV Rerun*. The telemetry belt contains accelerometers which respond to the movements of the dancer, convert the accelerations into audio signals, and transmit them by UHF radio to electronic-music equipment in the orchestra pit. From these telemetered movements the sound score for the dance is generated live in performance and heard by the audience from loudspeakers. Photo by Gordon Mumma.

Left to right: David Borden, Linda Fisher, and Steve Drews, the members of Mother Mallard's Portable Masterpiece Company, performing live with an array of Moog synthesizers at the broadcast studios of WBAI in New York. Photo by Gordon Mumma.

David Tudor and John Cage in a simultaneous performance of Tudor's *Untitled* and Cage's *Mesostics* during its 1972 premiere for the European Broadcasting Union at Radio Bremen in Germany. John Cage alternates between the mixing console, at which he is seated, and the four microphones, where he stands while singing the vocal sections of *Mesostics*. Photo by Gordon Mumma.

David Tudor at the controls of his electronic-music equipment for *Untitled,* during its simultaneous performance with John Cage's *Mesostics.* Much of this equipment was built by David Tudor for his composition *Untitled.* Photo by Gordon Mumma.

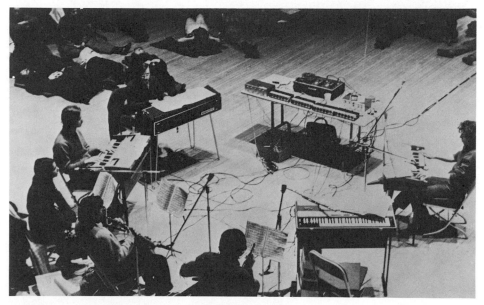

Philip Glass (far right) with his ensemble of live-electronic and conventional instruments, performing in New York, February, 1971. Photo by Cynthia Giruard.

Rolf Gehlhaar and Johannes Fritsch of the German group "Feedback" in a broadcast for Hessiche Rundfunk, Frankfurt, in 1971. Besides live-electronic music performances, Feedback also publishes scores and produces collaborative cybernetic environments. Photo by David Johnson.

Peter Eötvös, a member of the German group Feedback, preparing a Drehleier with a contact microphone for a 1972 performance in Darmstadt. The microphones are attached to a portable EMS synthesizer manufactured in England.

Interactions among Technological- and Artistic-Innovation Ensembles and Collaborative Groups

Because of the increasing complexity of technology and the greater facility of group performances (as well as a great attraction to working with multi-media), artists seem inclined to work in collaborative groups more so than in the past. The sharing of resources and ideas has made possible the survival of many artistic endeavors outside traditional institutions of support, and has thereby nourished an unusually roborant quality of creative freedom.

The Cunningham Dance Company is a particularly important collaborative ensemble because (like the Diaghilev Ballet in the earlier part of this century) the collaborations have been sustained over many years and have involved many exceptional creative artists. A list of the composers for the Cunningham Dance Company is a virtual cross section of contemporary music history. Moreover, because the Cunningham Dance Company has performed world-wide, its work has been more readily acknowledged and its influences immediate. Merce Cunningham was probably the first dancer to choreograph with electronic music. In 1952 he presented his "Collage I and II" with Pierre Schaeffer's *Symphonie pour un homme seul,* and in 1953, "Fragments" with Pierre Boulez's *Etude à un Son* and *Etude II.* The dances "Antic Meet" and "Aeon" (1958–61, both with music by John Cage), utilized live-electronic music procedures developed in collaboration with David Tudor. During this time Tudor also produced the spectacular live-electronic version of Cage's *Variations II* (1959). In *Variations V,* created for the French-American Festival at Lincoln Center in 1965, the dancers shared responsibility for the music with the musicians. Two interrelated systems of electronic sensors on the stage detected the movements of the dancers. These sensors were connected to electronic music equipment in the orchestra pit so that the dancers articulated the sound environment of the auditorium as well as the spatial environment of the stage. The decor included projected images by Stan Van der Beek and electronic-sound-producing stage props. The artistic and technological achievements of Cage's *Variations V* have made it a classic of collaborative multi-media.

The performance arts ensemble called the ONCE Group developed from the activities of the ONCE Festival in Ann Arbor, Michigan. Presented annually from 1960 through 1967, the ONCE Festival was a collaboration of architects, dancers, filmmakers, musicians, sculptors, and graphic and theater artists. A repertory of works was created, collaboratively as well as individually, which the ONCE Group presented on tour and for television. These works were artistically and technically experimental, and introduced many innovative live-electronic music procedures. An impetus for the ONCE Group was the multi-media Space Theatre activities that developed around the work of Milton Cohen in Ann Arbor from 1956 through 1964. Cohen established the Space Theatre for live performances of his unusual light-projection art, with the collaboration of architects Harold Borkin and Joseph Wehrer, filmmaker George Manupelli, and several composers. The best-known production of the Space Theatre was the hour-long *Teatro dello Spazio—luce e suono,* presented at the Venice Biennale in 1964. Besides the activities of the Ann Arbor performers, the ONCE Festival presented many contemporary live-performance artists from elsewhere. It was during the 1964 ONCE Festival that composers David Behrman and Alvin Lucier began their collaboration with Robert Ashley and myself, which led to the organization of the Sonic Arts Union in 1966.

The Sonic Arts Union is a repertory ensemble, working with multi-media on a "chamber-music" scale. Live-electronic music is the predominant activity of this group, which presents its work on performance tours divided about equally between the United States and Europe. Some of the works are collaborative, some are by other contemporary composers (such as Jacques Bekaert, George Cacioppo, and Pauline Oliveros), and some are composed by individuals in the group. The Sonic Arts Union has developed unusually sophisticated and diverse applications of electronic technology to musical performance, and since 1970 has extended its activities to radio broadcasts, television, and recordings.

Mother Mallard's Portable Masterpiece Co. uses studio synthesizers as live-performance instruments, and has developed virtuoso performance procedures for the real-time requirements of concert performance. The equipment of this ensemble consists of five studio-type electronic-music synthesizers mounted in portable cases. The ensemble performs in schools, colleges, and for recordings, presenting a repertory by David Borden, Steve Drews, and Linda Fisher. They also program improvisational situations that foster musical innovation. The ideas of Mother Mallard's Portable Masterpiece Co. have had considerable influence on a major manufacturer of synthesizers. The ensemble puts prototype equipment through rigorous field tests in live performance. They then return important data to the synthesizer designer, thus achieving a particularly beneficial relationship with technological innovation.

In Europe collaborative live-electronic music activity began in 1964 with the Gruppo di Improvvisazione Nuova Consonanza in Rome. This group was an international collaboration (as was the socially and artistically broader conspiracy called FLUXUS), and included the American composers Larry Austin, John Eaton, and William Smith, as well as the Europeans Mario Bertoncini, Aldo Clementi, Franco Evangelisti, Roland Kayn, and Ivan Vandor.

MEV, Musica Elettronica Viva, was organized in Rome in 1966 as a collaboration of mostly American musicians, including Frederic Rzewski, Allan Bryant, Alvin Curran, Jon Phetteplace, and Richard Teitelbaum. The first year of MEV activity consisted primarily of composed music. During 1967 MEV worked deliberately with improvisation, and by 1968 had abandoned formal musical and social structure entirely. Perhaps their most interesting contribution to live-performance procedures was the development of "Sound Pools," a concert situation that encouraged extensive audience participation. MEV maintained a strong precept: to make music with whatever means available. Because of this precept and the slower rate of technological innovation in Italy than in the United States, the MEV members developed general-purpose rather than specialized circuits for live-electronic music. One of these circuits was a photoresistor mixer designed by Frederic Rzewski, the principal of which has since been applied by composers outside of MEV. Richard Teitelbaum developed live-performance techniques that utilized individual components from the Moog Synthesizer rather than the standard studio configurations. MEV made extensive tours throughout Europe as well as a few performances in the United States. At times the "Sound Pool" concerts included several hundred performers, and the radical influence of the MEV group upon younger European musicians has been considerable.

Of the several British collaborations, AMM, which was formed in 1965, is the best known. Their precepts are similar to those of MEV, but the musical concerns of its early members (Cornelius Cardew, Lou Gare, Christopher Hobbs, Keith Rowe, and Eddie Prevost) seemed more social than technological. These concerns led to the eventual splintering of AMM and the formation of a large open-participation ensemble called the Scratch Orchestra, related in intent to the "Sound Pools" of MEV. Other British groups include "The Gentle Fire" (Richard Bernas, Hugh Davies, Graham Hearn, Stuart Jones, and Michael Robinson) and "Naked Software" (Hugh Davies, John Lifton, Anna Lockwood, Harvey Matusow, and Howard Rees). Both these groups are electroacoustic hybrids and are primarily concerned with experimental and improvisational performance practices. In Australia the innovative ensemble "Teletopa," which includes David Ahern, Roger Frampton and Peter Evans, has attracted considerable attention.

Primarily responsible for the performance of Stockhausen's live-electronic music is the group at the WDR in Cologne, which has included at various times Alfred Alings, Harald Boje, Peter Eötvös, Johannes Fritsch, Rolf Gehlhaar, and Aloys Kontarsky. These are musicians, primarily instrumentalists, whose performance skills extend to electronic modification of their instrumental sounds. In performances of his work, Stockhausen who generally operates filters and amplitude controls, tends to exercise ultimate decisions as to the outcome of the music.

In recent years an intensive collaborative activity in live-electronic music has occurred in northern California. These collaborations, which came after the activities of the San Francisco Tape Music Center in the early '60s, are not easily separated into groups. Rather, this activity is more a geographic phenomenon involving composers from Berkeley, Davis, Oakland, and the surrounding bay area.

A cooperative effort among musicians from the University of California at Davis and Mills College in Oakland was responsible for the First Festival of Live Electronic Music. Presented in December, 1967, the festival comprised concerts, panels, and seminars, and included the work of the "northern California group" of composers Larry Austin, Harold Budd, John Dinwiddie, Anthony Gnazzo, Stanley Lunetta, and John Mizelle, as well as guest composers from other parts of the United States and Japan. Subsequently, Stanley Lunetta became the prime mover of an ensemble called "AMRA ARMA," whose members also include Karl and Kurt Bischoff, Kenneth Horton, and Jeffrey Karl. With a large digital electronic mechanism designed by Lunetta and with substantial percussion resources, AMRA ARMA has developed a music of Nibelungen proportions and an energy level that is unusually high for California musicians.

A remarkable Japanese collaboration was the Cross Talk Intermedia festival, presented in Tokyo in February, 1969. Organized by Donald Albright, Kuniharu Akiyama, Roger Reynolds, and Joji Yuasa—who enlisted the support of the American Cultural Center in Tokyo and major Japanese industry—Cross Talk Intermedia was attended by capacity audiences in Kenzo Tange's Yoyogi Olympic games facility. The performances included live-electronic and multimedia works of Toshi Ichiyanagi, Takahiko Iimura, Takehisa Kosugi, Yori-Aki Matsudaira, Mieko Shiomi, Toru Takemitsu, and Joji Yuasa, as well as the participating Americans Robert Ashley, Salvatore Martirano, Gordon Mumma, Roger Reynolds, and Stan Van der Beek. If a prize were offered for the best-organized-most-complicated performance collaboration of the century, Cross Talk Intermedia, which smoothly presented six or seven artistically extravagant and logistically disparate works on each day, would be a prime candidate.

Certainly the largest performance collaboration was the ICES 1972 festival, which was presented in London and on a chartered British Rail "Music Train" between London and Edinburgh. ICES 1972 ran continuously in three different parts of London twelve hours a day for more than two weeks in August, 1972. It presented a cross section of live-electronic music from all over the world (excepting only Africa, Antarctica, and Greenland), including a spectrum from rock to academia, as well as dance, video, and conceptual possibilities.

Another kind of activity that is gathering momentum is the combined conference-seminar-workshop-performance format exemplified by projects such as DeBenneville Pines and Chocorua 73. The former was co-sponsored by radio stations KPFA and KPFK, Fluxus West, Source Magazine, and DeBenneville Pines, and was presented in late April, 1973 at a Unitarian Church camp in the San Bernadino Forest of California. Chocorua 73 was a three-week project at a farm-inn in the White Mountains of New Hampshire in June and July of 1973. In both projects a wide spectrum of new music was presented, with particular emphasis on the experimental. Like their predecessors, the ONCE Festival and the San Francisco Tape Music Center, they were also produced with remarkably small budgets independent of "establishment" institutions. Of special significance is the collaborative social and organizational nature of these projects, and the scope of their artistic, technological, and social concerns, which generally surpasses the more parochial "establishment" projects. These newer projects are inherently more inclusive and comprehensive.

Engineering Heroes

Like most endeavors, electronic music has its heroes. Besides certain illustrious composers and performers, there are the guiding spirits of glamorous or well-conceived festivals, such as Roger Reynolds of the spectacular Cross Talk Intermedia in Tokyo; Joel Chadabe, director of the annual festival in Albany; Hans Otte, who for years has directed the prestigious Pro Musica Nova in

Bremen; and Larry Austin, who with his California colleagues produced the historic First Festival of Live Electronic Music in 1967.

Then there are the pioneering inventors and engineers. Generally not composers themselves, they are instead creative artists of circuitry. Like the experimenting composers, their visionary work is often the target of disparaging opinion. Thaddeus Cahill, inventor of the Telharmonium, has become a formidable legend. Celebrated by many, though less well-known by name, is Earle Henry, inventor of the pinball machine and developer of the juke box. Leon Termen and Maurice Martenot are heroes of the infant electronic era between the two World Wars.

Present-day heroes include six "senior" names: Robert Moog and Donald Buchla of the United States, Hugh Le Caine of Canada, Paul Ketoff of Italy, Junosuke Okuyama of Japan, and Peter Zinovieff of England. The name of Robert Moog, who developed the first widely used electronic music synthesizers, has become a household word. Donald Buchla developed the "Electric Music Box," widely used in the western United States and becoming increasingly well-known elsewhere. Hugh Le Caine made early designs of voltage-controlled circuitry, and is responsible for much of the now classic equipment in the University of Toronto electronic music studio. Paul Ketoff designed and built the first portable synthesizer for live performance, which was widely used by John Eaton, and has designed many special-purpose circuits for other composers. Junosuke Okuyama is responsible for the original and remarkable circuits used not only by Japanese composers, but also by visitors to Japan fortunate to have made his acquaintance. Peter Zinovieff founded the firm of EMS, which has produced several generations of synthesizers, including the portable "VCS 3" or "Putney," the "Synthi 100"—which contains a small digital memory—and a more recent system incorporating computer control of both analog and digital devices.

Other engineering heroes in the United States include Dennis Colin and David Friend (who were involved in design innovations for the ARP synthesizers); Harald Bode, Carl Countryman, B. J. Losmandy, Thomas Oberheim, and William Ribbens (designers of special-purpose circuits); and James Beauchamp and James Seawright (designers of electronic-music studios). Outside the United States are the esteemed Marino Zuccheri of the Italian Radio in Milan, Fernando von Reichenbach of the Instituto Torcuato di Tella in Buenos Aires, and the English engineers David Cockerell and Ken Gale, who did the basic design work for Zinovieff's EMS Bournemouth firm. Recently, Ken Gale, with Gerry Rogers and Brian Hodgson, have established their own organization, Rogers Studio Equipments, and are developing a new synthesizer and environmental sound systems. A new generation of electronic engineers, not yet prominent, is already applying state-of-the-art technology to musical experiments.

Technology and Sociology in the Commerce of Live-Electronic Music

The largest audience for live-electronic music, the pop and rock audience, has a speaking familiarity with electronic-music technology. The hardware of this music has been relatively standardized by mass production, and the custom of most performers is to display it: instruments, wires, electronic devices, and lighting apparatus are strewn around the performance area, visible to everyone.

Among the commercially available electronic devices for musical instruments, amplification is fundamental. The minimal elements for musical instrument amplification are a microphone, amplifier, and loudspeaker. The performer has at least one electronic control—for the amount of amplification—which is generally called "volume" or "gain." It is a simple matter to add circuitry to control the "tone" of the amplified sound. Technically known as equalization, this involves the amplification of some groups of frequencies to a greater extent than others. The treble and bass controls of many amplifiers are an example of equalization.

Because solid-state electronics have made miniaturization of circuits feasible, musical instrument amplifiers often include several other sound-modifying circuits, each with controls that the performer can operate. Tremolo is widely employed. Sometimes erroneously called "vibrato," tremolo is a pulsing, periodic variation in the amount of amplification. Depending on the particular circuit, the rate of periodicity can be fixed or variable, and is generally pulsed in the range from four to fourteen times per second. With some circuits, the performer can also vary the amount of amplification change with a "depth" control. The difference between "tremolo" and "vibrato" is that tremolo is a variation of amplitude, whereas vibrato is a variation of frequency or "pitch." Some electronic organs have a true "vibrato" because it is economically feasible to vary the frequency of the electronically generated sound of an electric organ. Electronic variation of the pitch of acoustic instruments is also possible, but only with sophisticated circuitry that is presently too expensive to justify its use in commercial musical instrument amplifiers. Also, the difference in sound between tremolo and vibrato in many applications is not great enough to have created a demand by musicians for true electronic vibrato.

Reverberation is widely used in musical instrument amplifiers, and is technically interesting because it usually employs non-electronic components to achieve its effect. This effect is an apparent increase in the *space* in which the sound is heard. This is accomplished by making one or more time delays or echoes of the original sound, and mixing the delays with the original sound before final amplification. The performer can control the amount of mixing. The delays are usually measured in milliseconds. To achieve these delays purely by electronic means is extremely costly. Consider that sound travels in air at a speed of approximately $\frac{1}{5}$ mile per second. At this rate a perceptible echo can be heard at a reasonably small distance, and is measured at a few milliseconds. But after sound is converted to an electrical current, as in the musical instrument amplifier, it is travelling at almost the speed of light. This is approximately 186,000 miles per second, about 930,000 times faster than sound. To achieve even a few milliseconds of delay, an enormous amount of electronic circuitry is required. It is more efficient to convert the electrical currents back into a slower medium. The most common procedure is mechanical, by the use of vibrating coiled springs; or magnetic, by the use of loops of magnetic tape. The use of vibrating coiled springs is the oldest and most common form of electronic reverberation for musical instruments, having been patented in the '30s for the Hammond organ.

An entirely different means of reverberation, not yet in general use but likely to have a large future, is achieved by digital computer techniques. When sound vibrations are converted into analogous electric currents to be amplified and modified, it is an analog electronic process. By converting sounds into digital electronic form, it is possible to achieve time delays at considerably less expense than with analog electronics. Many electronic components are still required, but the state-of-the-art of digital electronic miniaturization by means of integrated circuits is much further developed because of its application in digital computers. As of the early '70s the expense is still not small enough to justify replacing vibrating coiled springs or tape loops in musical instrument amplifiers. But the demand for digital electronic time-delay equipment is enormous in many fields, and should stimulate the mass production of integrated circuitry that can be efficiently employed in music. Digital electronic circuitry for music has many uses beyond reverberation. It has already been experimentally applied to vibrato and equalization, and offers sound modification possibilities without precedent in analog electronic technology. It is a fairly safe prediction that digital electronics for live-electronic music will be a major development in the coming years.

With electronic control of volume, tone, tremolo, and reverberation—not to mention the musical instrument itself—the musician has become a very busy performer. All these means of control pose a human-engineering problem. Some of the electronic controls of the electric guitar are mounted directly on the instrument and some are on the musical instrument amplifier. Since the performer has only two hands, it has proven feasible to construct foot-operated switches and pedals. Furthermore, as new electronic music circuits are developed, it is often more efficient to use them as accessories rather than to build them into the already crowded musical instrument amplifier. Some of the accessory circuits are small enough to be built into the foot controls. The most common example is the "fuzz-tone," which is widely used with the electric guitar and bass. Technically quite simple, the fuzz-tone adds overtones to the original instrumental sound. These overtones are multiples of the original pitch and produce the effect of a cutting edge to the sound. Some fuzz-tone circuits include a treble boost, an extreme emphasis of the high frequencies. Generally the performer has one control of fuzz tone: to switch it on or off. Another example of foot-control is the "wah-wah." This is an application of equalization, a kind of tone-control circuit that sweeps a special filter through the amplified sound. The sweep of some wah-wah circuits can be controlled electronically as well as by the motion of the performer's foot. The electronically controlled wah-wah is varied periodically, much as is the tremolo, though sometimes at rates below one sweep per second.

A group of accessory circuits has been developed to modify the "amplitude-envelope" of musical instruments. Common among these is the "sustain," which is used mainly for the electric guitar and bass. The amplitude-envelope might be called the loudness-shape of these instruments. Similar to that of the piano, the amplitude-envelope of these electric instruments is characteristically very loud at the beginning, falls rapidly in loudness to some intermediate level, and then more gradually diminishes to inaudibility. The "sustain" is an automatic gain control, an electronically controlled amplifier. It is normally set at some intermediate level of amplification. When the extremely loud beginning of the guitar sound reaches the input of the sustain, the circuit automatically decreases its level of amplification, then increases it following the inverse of the guitar amplitude-envelope. The audible effect is much like the sustained sound of an electric organ. In its simplest form the performer has a single control of sustain, an on-off switch. Some sustain devices allow the performer to control aspects of the shape of the inverse amplitude-envelope.

Another accessory device called a "phaser" is quite subtle in its effect, and sometimes requires a stereo amplifier with two loudspeakers. The "phaser" achieves a change of phase. Phase change is a special application of time delay, but over a much shorter length of time. It is measured in degrees of a particular wavelength (rather than milliseconds, as in reverberation) and therefore depends on the frequency of the original sound. It is interesting that, psychoacoustically, we do not hear any difference in a sound that is shifted a fixed number of degrees in phase from itself. But we do hear an effect while the sound is being shifted. For example, if the sound stays at 0 degrees in one loudspeaker and changes gradually to 180 degrees in another loudspeaker, the effect is like a movement of that sound. But the listener is hard pressed to determine "what moved where." The effect seems to occur in the listener's head rather than in the performance space. The performer may have several controls for the phaser, including an on-off switch, a control for the number of degrees of shift, and a rate control for applying a periodic electronic phase shift. Phase changes are employed commonly in the studio processing of rock music recordings, where they are sometimes called "phasing" or "flanging." Under carefully controlled studio conditions, some incredible phasing effects have been achieved in stereophonic recordings.

Equalization, tremolo, reverberation, fuzz-tone, wah-wah, sustain, and phasing have been most widely used with the electric organ, guitar, and bass. They have been applied to amplified brass and woodwind instruments as well, but not as frequently. This is as much because of cultural reasons as of artistic traditions. Brass and woodwind instruments are not common in rock or country-western ensembles. As the country-western bands have gradually admitted electric guitars, they have occasionally amplified the violin. But the violin, woodwinds, and brass instruments carry the weight of classical European traditions much more heavily than the electric organ, guitar, or bass. Also, the performers of the traditional instruments have tended to be more conservative, except for a few pioneers in modern jazz and specialists in "serious" experimental music. Furthermore, innovation by the manufacturers of conventional instruments has not exactly been rampant. Electronic innovations notwithstanding, it is remarkable how little innovation in the use of plastics and special metals has occurred until very recently. Ornette Coleman's first use of a plastic saxophone was a scandal to traditional musicians. Plastic heads for drums were more easily accommodated because the artistic conservatism was outweighed by the practicality of marching bands being able to use such drums in the rain.

There are other cultural differences to consider. Electric guitarists, for example, tend to be young musicians in a culture premised on innovation, and in which originality is commercially viable. Modern jazz is an innovative culture, but, tragically, has achieved little commercial viability in the United States. Only an extremely well-established jazz figure such as Miles Davis is able to make electronic experimentation a commercial proposition. Classically trained musicians spend their formative years learning mostly old traditions, and whatever experimental inclinations existed in their youth tend to be severely repressed.

Except for the development of the electric piano, used mostly in rock and pop ensembles, the conventional mechanical piano has not seen a single important change in more than half a century. Only one major piano manufacturer, Baldwin, has done any fundamental research in acoustics and electronics. For many years this company has done sustained and important work, including the development of an electronic grand piano. The electric piano used in rock ensembles doesn't sound much like a piano and, like the electric guitar, is really a new instrument. Its prime advantages are that it is small and light enough to be portable, and that because of amplification it can match the loudness of the rock ensemble. Compact electric pianos have recently been installed in the lounge sections of transcontinental jetliners.

There is an exception to this conservatism with respect to woodwind and brass instruments. Several manufacturers have marketed an electronic device that enables the musician to add lower octaves to his sound. Technically, the device is a frequency divider, and is a relatively simple application of digital technology to analog electronics. A microphone is attached to the woodwind or brass instrument. Most often it is a miniature microphone that is attached to a modified mouthpiece in order to minimize the possibility of acoustic feedback. The commercial dividers are extremely compact, and are designed to be worn—attached to the clothing—by the musician. The specific details of the circuitry differ from one manufacturer to another, but the important similarity among all such devices is that the produced sounds of the lower octaves are purely electronic, and follow exactly the pitches performed by the woodwind or brass player.

Briefly, the instrumental sound is converted by the microphone to an electrical current, then modified from its original shape to a square wave of the same fundamental frequency as the instrumental pitch. This square wave is then applied to a divider circuit, several types of which are in use. A particularly reliable circuit called a "flip-flop" is widely used in digital computers and some types of electric organs. The output of the flip-flop is also a squarewave, but at exactly one-half the frequency of the input. One-half of any frequency is the next lower octave. To obtain the second lower octave, the output of the flip-flop is applied to a second flip-flop. This produces a division of the original instrumental pitch by four. Three flip-flops in a row will provide a third lower octave—a division by eight of the original instrumental pitch—and so on. Commercial dividers use, at most, three divider circuits. The outputs of each divider are available in parallel, so that by means of switches, the performer can choose any one or any combination of lower circuits. Finally, some lower-octave circuits include electronic filtering to shape the square-wave outputs so that they sound more like an acoustic instrumental sound. Because the musician varies his loudness when playing, automatic amplitude circuitry is sometimes included so that the dividers will function properly over a wide dynamic range. Except for more elaborate custom-built dividers—which can include division to intervals other than octave sub-multiples, and which will automatically produce an output amplitude proportional to the instrumentalist's dynamics—there are definite limitations on the commercial lower-octave accessories for woodwind and brass instruments. All of the above-mentioned electronic procedures have one feature in common: the pitch integrity of the original sound is preserved. Only amplitude, timbre, and time relationships are altered. Pitch relationships are changed only by divider circuits, and then only by exact sub-multiples that preserve traditional pitch relationships.

Performers of live-electronic music have also made use of circuits that modify pitch relationships, but mostly in the realm of "serious" experimental music. Modification of pitch relationships beyond the domain of the chromatic scale still presents the world of commercial music—even the most extreme innovators in rock music—with fundamental philosophic problems. These effects have been used in rock, but for incidental color rather than for the potential of their fundamentally new language. The device most often employed for changing pitch relationships is the balanced modulator. This instrument has various forms and names, including the ring modulator and the analog multiplier. In its simplest form it is a circuit with two inputs and one output. The original sound is applied to one input and a control signal is applied to the other input. The output is a multiplication of the two inputs, and depending on the characteristics of the control signal, consists of the arithmetical sums and differences of the two inputs. Considerable variation of the simple form of the circuit is possible. The sum and difference frequencies can be combined with the original sound, and the circuit can be unbalanced in various degrees. The control signal can derive from or depend upon the original sound or other instrumental pitches. At least one commercial accessory device of the balanced-modulator type, designed by Thomas Oberheim, has been marketed for live-performance electronic music, and several mini-synthesizers include this function.

Many complex circuit configurations of analog multipliers are possible. These enable the choice of either sum or difference frequencies, multiple multiplication with control signals in the radio-frequency spectrum, precise control of complex pitch relationships using parametric amplification, and other elaborate procedures. Besides the deterrent effect of musical conservatism, experimentation with these procedures has been limited by the relatively high cost of equipment. Integrated circuit technology is gradually reducing the cost to reasonable amounts.

Another live-performance electronic accessory, which is considerably more complicated, is the percussion generator. Known by names such as "sideman" and "bandbox," and historically related to the automated mechanical percussion of the nickelodeon, these accessories electronically synthesize sounds resembling the bass drum, tom-toms, bongos, woodblocks, cymbals, and the like. The performer has a choice of specific rhythms and tempi, which are also electronically generated. The percussion generator is commonly used as an accessory to the electric organ.

There are also several keyboard-operated electronic accessories for playing melodies with various timbres and inflections; these usually imitate traditional melodic instruments. One of the earliest, the Solovox, is often attached to the traditional piano. Recently the synthesizer firm of Tonus, Inc. introduced a keyboard-operated electronic melody-maker called the ARP Soloist, which updates the Solovox with numerous innovations, including portamento and diverse envelope and timbre control. More complicated are the mini-synthesizers. Though essentially able to produce only solo melodic lines, these instruments can be tuned to produce nontraditional scales. More significantly, the design premise of most mini-synthesizers is that they are live-performance instruments of electronic sound, not attempts to imitate acoustic instruments. At least one electric organ includes accessory functions that enable the performer to imitate the electronic sounds of the recently popular "switched-on" synthesized music!

The Chamberlain is probably the most unusual live-performance invention. It consists of a series of magnetic tape loops, with each loop actuated by a corresponding key on a traditional keyboard. The sounds to be heard from the Chamberlain can be from any source, and are recorded by the performer in advance. A dramatic example of the use of the Chamberlain is the introduction to Ramon Sender's *Desert Ambulance* (1964).

The skills applied by live performers with all these devices are evident not only in how they are used in a musical context, but also in how they are used in combination with one another. These many combinations represent the most promise for the further development of the musical capabilities of these accessories.

Extensions of Electronic Technology in various Live-Performance Arts

Throughout history creative artists have tinkered with technology and dabbled with multi-media. Da Vinci and Wagner are immediate examples. In the twentieth century the rapid increase of social mobility, technological affluence, and artistic innovation and communication have given the creative artist an irresistible access to multiple fields of endeavor. It is increasingly difficult to fit artists into traditional categories. It is no longer surprising to find that esteemed musicians invented the air brake, color photography film, and insurance actuarial procedures, nor that they hold patents in electronic design and in dye processes for synthetic fibers. It is not unusual to find people still in their early twenties who present their musical work in concert one week, and their papers in computer-science conferences or their films at international festivals the week after. What is to be said of a figure like John Cage, who is known to some as a composer, to others as a mycologist, a poet, or a graphic artist, or to still others as an influential writer on social and economic issues?

With few exceptions, the technological resources that have nourished multi-media performance are electronic in origin. This electronic feasibility is due to developments in solid-state physics ranging from the transistor to integrated circuitry. It is electronic *control,* of increasing complexity with decreasing cost, that has become artistically feasible. The logistics of multi-media production can be formidable, and may account for why multi-media projects are often collaborative efforts. But multi-media artists may also collaborate because they enjoy working on fundamental creative levels. Increasingly, they share the languages of various media, particularly the near-universal language of electronic technology.

Besides the new sources of sound, electronic control of audio has made possible entirely new ensemble forms, from musically interactive man-machine systems to complete automation. Applications of electronic control to video technology have expanded this medium from cinema to television, video recording, and laser projection. Electronic video control can be as simple as the synchronization of slide projectors, or as complex as the translation of sound into laser-projected images or the computer synthesis of color-television images. Finally, electronic control has given the artist a means of interrelating different media that in the past has been vastly too complicated to consider.

Sound Sculpture

Between the realms of live-electronic music and multi-media is the world of sound-producing sculpture. By slightly broadening this category, the earliest activities of this nature could include the electrically powered mechanical instruments of Luigi Russolo and the Milano Futuristi after the First World War and the incredible *Studies for Player Piano* composed in Mexico by Conlon Nancarrow. Between the Second World War and 1960 the first notable activities in sound-producing sculpture were those of Mauricio Kagel in Argentina, Jean Tinguely and the collaboration of Pierre Henry and Nicolas Schöffer in France, and Joe Jones in the United States. In 1953 Kagel made a sound and light score for a 120-foot tower of César Janello. Tinguely's mechanical sculptures of the '50s produced their own vigorous sounds without the aid of electronic amplification. In 1955 Pierre Henry made music for a 150-foot "cybernetic tower" by Nicolas Schöffer. Beginning in the late '50s, New York artist Joe Jones produced a veritable menagerie of ebullient sculptural soundmakers, which were electrically powered and controlled by switches, photocells, and various sensors.

After 1960, artists from many countries produced sound-sculpture. These include Belgium (Henri Pousseur), Canada (François Dallegret, Pierre Mercure), England (Roberto Gerhard, Daphne Oram), France (Takis, Marcel van Thienen), Japan (Kuniharu Akiyama, Toshi Ichiyanagi), the Netherlands (Peter Schat), Spain (Mestres Quadreny), Sweden (Öyvind Fahlström and Per-Olav Strömberg), and the United States (Milton Cohen, Walter De Maria and Le Monte Young, Robert Rauschenberg, James Seawright). The diversity of solid-state control devices that appeared during the '60s was a considerable stimulus to these creative artists of sound- and light-sculpture. The surge of activity in the kinetic sculpture of artists such as Seawright, and the programmed light performances of artists such as Cohen and Anthony Martin was nourished as well with by-products of the digital computer industry, including integrated logic-circuitry. The international phenomenon of the rock light-show discotheque followed closely the work of these artists.

A particularly interesting example of sound sculpture is the *Moosack Machine* of California composer Stanley Lunetta. The *Moosack Machine* produces, mixes, and processes sound and light activities completely on its own. Considering the interaction among its many elements, the probability of its repeating itself, even after many hours of continuous performance, seems incredibly small. The sounds of the *Moosack Machine* are produced by oscillators, the frequency and amplitude of which are controlled by a combination of light, temperature, and proximity sensors. The resultant sounds are mixed, modified, and articulated in conjunction with a logic system consisting of a 16-bit digital counter/decoder and a frequency-divider chain. Various moving parts, a transducer, and the lighting of the sculpture are also activated by the digital logic system. The motion, lighting, and temperature of the *Moosack Machine* and its environment are monitored by the same sensors that control the initial sound generation, thus completing the complex feedback loop of this self-sustained sculpture system. The design and character of the *Moosack Machine* is such that it is on that nebulous line between an automaton and an artificial intelligence. In this sense it is a candidate for the category of live-electronic music because it so closely mimics the attributes of live performance.

The "instrumental loudspeakers" of David Tudor's *Rainforest* (mentioned previously) also fit the category of sound sculpture. Many of the resonating materials are literally "found objects." Further, the sounds of *Rainforest* are very dependent upon the space in which they are heard. This use of the acoustical space as a significant factor in the electronic processing of the work suggests an extension of the category of "sound sculpture" to include "sound environment." Several other works belong here, including Pauline Oliveros' *In Memoriam Nicola Tesla, Cosmic Engineer* (1968), Alvin Lucier's *I am sitting in a room* (1970), and my own *Hornpipe* (1967).

Oliveros' *In Memoriam Nicola Tesla, Cosmic Engineer* was commissioned by the Merce Cunningham Dance Co. and has been widely performed with the evening-long dance *Canfield*. In her work Oliveros has the performers conduct an acoustical analysis of the performance space. For the closing section the space is subjected to a sea of low-frequency sounds which establish physically imposing standing waves and structural resonances in the building itself. Lucier's *I am sitting in a room* treats the natural resonances of the performance space as an acoustical filter. A spoken text is recorded, then immediately played back into the same space. That playback itself is recorded, and the second recording played back into the space. The process continues until the verbal intelligibility of the text has disappeared in the mysteriously abstracted resonances of the original speech rhythms. In my own work *Hornpipe* a solo hornist wears on his belt an electronic circuitry which analyzes the resonances of the space. This analysis is accomplished by a series of tunable, gated amplifiers which adjust their own resonances to complement those of the performance space. When sufficient resonance information has been gathered by each gated amplifier, the gate opens and the resonance of that particular amplifier is heard from loudspeakers. In the course of the performance the hornist learns the constellation of resonances for that particular space, and is able to deactivate the electronic circuitry by playing sounds which are out of the resonant constellation. Since the resonances are activated by the sounds which the hornist plays, both the electronic circuitry and the acoustical space are part of the ensemble of the work.

Television and Video Recording

Video technology—the translation of images into electrical and magnetic form for transmission, modification, and recording—requires considerably more sophisticated equipment than is usually encountered in audio technology. Compared to audio, the frequency spectrum (or bandwidth) of video is much wider (as much as 6 MHz) and requires the use of radio-frequency electronics. Video recording on magnetic tape, which has given creative artists access to television —much as magnetic audio recording made electronic music generally accessible —is quite different from audio recording, in which the magnetic translation of sound vibrations are recorded by a stationary recording head along the length of a moving magnetic tape. In video recording each image is scanned several hundred times, and each scan is recorded by a rotating recording head diagonally across the width of a moving magnetic tape. This complexity is necessary to achieve the greater bandwidth required for television signals. Besides having a head for the television signals, videotape has at least two other tracks: one for the audio signals and one for synchronizing signals. There are some similarities between video and audio recording. The camera is analogous to the microphone, the amplifiers are virtually the same except for differences in bandwidth and equalization, the recorders use magnetic tape that is stored on reels or cassettes, and the television screen is analogous to the loudspeaker. As with audio, video signals can be mixed, filtered, edited, and even "reverberated," though the specific equipment for these functions is different. The intensity of a video image is controlled in the same way as the amplitude of an audio signal. Of particular relevance to the creative artist is the fact that video images, like audio signals, can be electronically synthesized.

One of the most interesting aspects of video technology is the control of color. Though even more complicated than monochrome television, color has been particularly attractive to the artist, and to date the majority of video experimentation has been done with color synthesis. Technologically, color was an afterthought to television. For various reasons, color was not commercially feasible until the early '60s, some years after the basic monochrome standards had been established. Considerable ingenuity was required to design color television that was compatible with monochrome standards in the United States; this ingenuity, though, often consisted of not-so-satisfactory compromises. To complicate matters, different color systems have been established in other parts of the world. This, along with the already various international monochrome standards, numerous non-compatible video recording standards, substantial equipment expense, and the legal complications of television broadcasting, constitute forbidding aspects of the electronic video medium.

Yet even before the advent of portable video recorders in the late '60s, artists such as Nam June Paik, Eric Siegel, Stan Van der Beek, and John Cage had invaded television. Adventurous commercial stations, such as KQED in San Francisco and WGBH in Boston encouraged experimentation, and the state television systems of Europe and Japan did occasional work in this medium. Nam June Paik approached the problem of difficult access to commercial television with the premise that anything transmitted was useful material, and he treated the television receiver itself as a live-performance instrument. With an ensemble of receivers in view of the public, he moved around the sets with large magnets that modified and distorted the commercial images. Digging into the circuitry, he accomplished simple but effective electronic modifications, such as making negative images out of positive transmissions. He employed the television receiver as a sculptural device with cellist Charlotte Moorman, and encouraged audience participation in his use of closed-circuit television. Collaborating with engineer Shuya Abe, he developed an electronic-color synthesizer.

In 1960, at the age of 15, Eric Siegel was constructing his own television equipment; later, he built an Electronic Video Synthesizer, which has been used by many artists. Van der Beek has used television as an intermediate step in his process of filmmaking: synthesizing video images by computer and further modifying the images with film printing. In 1959 John Cage composed two short works, *Sounds of Venice* and *Water Walk*, scored for television studio facilities. In 1966 Cage's *Variations V* was produced at the Studio Hamburg of North German Television, with a score of composed parts for musicians, dancers, television cameramen, and video mixers.

Among the various electronic procedures used by television artists, debeaming (an attenuation of contrast with image retention) and image-mixing by "keying" are commonly used. Keying is a procedure whereby a television camera is adjusted to operate only above or below a specified level of luminosity. That camera then produces only a partial image of the original scene. When mixed with a second image, the missing section of the first image is replaced with the second image. When keying is used with color television it is called "chroma-keying," and is adjusted to color hue. The range of effects of keying is enormous, and the technique can be used for dramatic abstracting of images. It is curious that "audio-keying," which is analogous to video-keying, is also possible but has been used in very few electronic-music works. However, audio signals are commonly used to synthesize and modify television images.

Beginning in 1965 Lowell Cross composed a series of works in which television images were produced by audio deflection and modulation of the electron beam. One of the most interesting is *Musica Instrumentalis,* for color television, which is performed live by David Tudor on a stereophonic bandoneon. The score consists of color images that Tudor, by performing the bandoneon, attempts to reproduce on the television screen. Steven Beck has designed a live-performance electronic image synthesizer that uses both audio and video signals, and has produced several real-time video tapes in collaboration with composer Richard Felciano. Woody and Steina Vasulka perform live with a color synthesizer, which they often use with synthesized images from monochrome videotape, exploring the beautiful realm of color that lies just above the threshold of color perception.

The size of the television screen is limited by the practicalities of cathode-ray tube manufacture, and the general use of solid-state flat-screen developments is still some years in the future. Projection television has been used to fill large areas with image, though except for the Eidophor projection system, the image intensity has been less than satisfactory. To date, then, television has been an artistic medium of chamber-music scale.

Lasers

The electronic manipulation of images in large spaces first became practical in the '60s with the development of the laser. The laser is fundamentally different from any previous light-generating procedure in that it produces a beam of light that is coherent: the light energy is predominantly a single frequency. The laser most commonly used by artists—because of its low cost—is the helium-neon gas laser, which emits a deep red light beam of 6,328 Angstroms. The visible spectrum of light is roughly between 3,800 and 7,600 Angstroms. Lasers can be made with other gases, as well as with fluorides, tungstates, metallic oxides, and various semiconductors, to produce visible coherent light of other colors. The laser can be manipulated in two basic ways: beam deflection and intensity modulation. Beam deflection is accomplished in several ways; the most practical seems to be with a mirror-galvanometer, an electro-optical device in which a small mirror moves according to audio-frequency signals. If two mirror-galvanometers are used, one for the vertical axis and the other for the horizontal, the laser beam projects oscillographic images. Intensity modulation can be achieved by light-polarizing semiconductors.

Among the projects of artists who have used lasers in live performance, one of the most interesting was the *Video/Laser 1,* a collaboration of Lowell Cross, Carson Jeffries, and David Tudor, developed for the Pepsi-Cola Pavilion at EXPO 70 in Osaka. For *Video/Laser 1* a Krypton-ion laser that generated four colors (red, yellow, green, and blue) simultaneously was used. By modulating each of the four beams separately and by projecting them through various translucent materials, complex kinetic diffraction patterns were produced.

In Paris in October, 1972 the composer Iannis Xenakis, who had worked with Edgard Varèse and the architect Le Corbusier on the Philips Pavilion at Brussels in the late '50s, presented a stochastically determined light and sound spectacle called Polytope de Cluny. By means of program-control tapes, Xenakis synchronized musique concrète with a four-color matrix of rapidly articulated lasers and a constellation of several hundred strobe lights.

Artistic applications of holography, a three-dimensional image process that requires laser light, are just beginning. Present technology limits the viewing aperture of holographic images to approximately twelve square inches. Similarly small in area (as of the early '70s), other means of electro-visual display, such as light-emitting diodes and liquid crystals, are already being used in small calculators and digital time pieces. Along with holography, these phenomena hold fantastic possibilities for the visual arts of the future.

Astro-bio-geo-physical Application

With the development of ultra-sensitive electronic equipment during the past half century, much previously unknown astrophysical, biophysical, and geophysical activity has been detected. Geophysical activity had been experienced in the physical manifestations of tides, earthquakes, and tsunamis. But the accurate measurement of this activity, as well as of the formerly undetected microseisms, gravity waves, long-period resonance, and seismic propagation characteristics of the earth, were possible only with the development of low-noise, high-gain amplification and electronic transducers. Astrophysical activity was obvious from the visible light spectrum, but the greatest part of this activity—such as electromagnetic and cosmic radiation—was not revealed until the advent of specialized magnetic sensors, radio astronomy, and interplanetary exploration. Biophysical electrical activity became important with the use of sophisticated electronics in physiological and medical research.

In the '60s several composers began using these phenomena in their works, mostly for live-electronic music. The explorations of Alvin Lucier have been remarkable for their musical implications as well as their conceptual diversity. Lucier's *Music for Solo Performer 1965,* perhaps the earliest use of electroencephalic signals in live musical performance, amplifies the brainwave alpha currents of a solo performer. With practice, the performer learns to turn his alpha current on or off at will. Seated on stage, with electrodes attached to the occipital lobes of his head and to a neurological amplifier, the performer articulates with his alpha currents the sympathetic resonances of an ensemble of percussion instruments.

In December, 1970 composer David Rosenboom presented his *Ecology of the Skin,* in which the alpha, beta, and theta currents of several people were applied to control inputs of an electronic-music synthesizer. Not only were sounds heard from this synthesizer, but members of the audience could have their own private light show by applying phogene-stimulating electrodes to their temporal lobes. At the same time, in his *Corticalart* production at the Modern Art Museum of Paris, Pierre Henry wired his head into a sprawling arrangement of apparatus that purportedly modulated the color of a television set as well as producing sound.

In 1966 Alvin Lucier composed *Whistlers,* in which, with special VLF radios, the sounds of electromagnetic disturbances were received from the ionosphere and electronically processed by an ensemble of live performers. Later that year, at the 9 Evenings of Theater and Engineering in New York City, John Cage presented his *Variations VII,* the sounds of which were obtained live from wired and wireless communications sources. Also on the 9 Evenings performances, Lucinda Childs presented her *Vehicle,* a work using doppler sonar; Alex Hay presented his *Grass Field,* a work using amplified brain waves and muscle movements; and David Tudor presented his *Bandoneon!,* a "combine" of programmed audio circuits, moving loudspeakers, and instrumentally derived television images.

In 1967 Lucier presented his *Shelter,* in which environmental sound sensing, using the propagation characteristics of walls, floors, and ceilings, was achieved by amplifying the signals from special vibration transducers. This musical seismology makes use of man-made disturbances, though in twentieth-century urban life it is difficult to distinguish between man-made and geophysical microseismic activity. Other musical uses of geophysical phenomena include my own *Mographs* (1962–64), the sounds of which occur in time according to the wave-front arrivals of underground nuclear explosions; and Charles Dodge's *Earth's Magnetic Field* (1970), in which the succession of computer-synthesized sounds corresponds to the kp indexes of the magnetic activity of the Earth for the year 1961.

Lucier's *Vespers* (1968) uses pulsed, high-frequency sound for echo location, much as do (and in honor of) bats and other animal experts in acoustic orientation. In Gerald Shapiro's *The Second Piece* (1971), the audio modulations of infrared light beams are used by the performers for spatial orientation. These two works, along with Lucinda Childs' doppler-sonar *Vehicle,* are special examples of music derived from biophysical sources. They are *surrogate* electronic extensions of human biophysical capabilities, and are often modeled after other animal or artificial systems. One reason why surrogate biophysical systems are attractive is that a specific intention can be accomplished with greater convenience than is the case in directly monitoring a biophysical process. For example, my own piece, *BEAM,* performed in Tokyo in 1969, requires monitoring of the physical motion of the bow arms as well as the sounds of a violinist and violist. Originally, I planned to monitor directly the myoelectrical signals of the performers. These signals are pulses that change in rate according to the contraction and fatigue of the bow-arm muscles; they were to determine both the electronic modification of the instrumental sound and the digital display of the computer-controlled score. Because of the discomfort and unreliability of direct wiring to the muscles, a surrogate system of electronic position sensors was designed in the form of bow-arm sleeves that were comfortably worn by the performers. These sleeves generated variable-rate pulses similar to those of the muscles that they covered, and the original intention was fulfilled.

Some biophysical signals are relatively easy to obtain directly. Cardiac and respiratory sounds can be amplified from outside the chest. Pauline Oliveros has used amplified heartbeats in live performances of her *Valentine* (1968), for four card players, and in her ESP-oriented $\int \Psi * \Psi dT = 1$ (The Indefinite Integral of Psi Star Psi d Tau equals One), for heartbeat, Shakuhachi, and an ensemble of singers, actors, and instrumentalists. For the accompaniment to Merce Cunningham's *Loops* (1971), the heart and respiratory sounds of a solo dancer are transmitted by wireless and amplified in live performance.

Multi-Media

Using all sorts of spatial environments, multi-media can involve all the physical senses, and often transforms the audience from spectators to participants. The practice of multi-media is so widespread and is applied to so many performance circumstances that it is imperative here to focus primarily on the ways that *composers* have contributed to the art. Multi-media productions have received special attention at international expositions, particularly those at Brussels in 1958, Montreal in 1967, and Osaka in 1970. The Philips Pavilion at Brussels, in which Varèse's *Poème Electronique* was heard circulating through 425 loudspeakers, and the Pepsi-Cola Pavilion at Osaka, designed by a collaboration of several dozen avant-garde artists, are historic.

In the United States in 1957 (the year of preparation for the Philips Pavilion), the weekly *Vortex* performances at the Morrison Planetarium in San Francisco and the *Manifestations: Light and Sound* performances in Ann Arbor were pioneering events in the intermedia of electronic music and light projection. These performances were collaborations, *Vortex* being directed by Jordan Belson and Henry Jacobs, and *Manifestations* by Milton Cohen. In the following decade, at approximately three-year intervals, new multi-media collaborations were formed. 1960 saw the formation of the San Francisco Tape Music Center (Pauline Oliveros, Ramon Sender, Morton Subotnick, Terry Riley) and the activities of Tokyo's Group Ongaku and Sogetsu Art Center (Kuniharu Akiyama, Toshi Ichiyanagi, Joji Yuasa, Takahisa Kosugi, Chieko Shiomi, and others). 1963 was the beginning of the Los Angeles Experimental Music Workshop (composer Joseph Byrd and others), La Monte Young's Theatre of Eternal Music in New York, and, in Ann Arbor, the Space Theatre and the ONCE Group. 1966 witnessed the organization of USCO in New York (Gerd Stern, Stan Van Der Beek, Jud Yalkut, and others), Pulsa in New Haven, and the multi-media performances directed by Udo Kasemets at the Isaacs Gallery in Toronto. Throughout this decade parallel developments were occurring in theater, happenings, modern dance, and cinema. At the University of Illinois during the '60s, John Cage was involved in two multi-media extravaganzas. His *Music Circus* involved several hundred performers in a livestock pavilion. *HPSCHD,* a collaboration with Lejaren Hiller, Ronald Nameth, and a computer, was a five-hour performance with seven harpsichords and hundreds of tape recorders and projectors.

The beginnings of multi-media in South America were apparent after 1964 in the experimental music centers of Buenos Aires (at the Instituto Torcuato de Tella) and in Cordoba. In 1967 Jose Vicente Asuar composed his two-hour *Homenaje a Caracas* for four tracks of tape, thirty-eight projectors, fifty live performers, and a large metal structure. The Brazilian Jocy de Oliveira introduced her *Probabilistic Theatre I* in 1967, and her *Polinteracoes* in St. Louis in 1970.

The most remarkable of all multi-media collaborations was probably the Pepsi-Cola Pavilion for Expo 70 in Osaka. This project included many ideas distilled from previous multi-media activities, and significantly advanced both the art and technology by numerous innovations. The Expo 70 pavilion was remarkable for several reasons. It was an international collaboration of dozens of artists, as many engineers, and numerous industries, all coordinated by Experiments in Art and Technology, Inc. From several hundred proposals, the projects of twenty-eight artists and musicians were selected for presentation in the pavilion. The outside of the pavilion was a 120-foot-diameter geodesic dome of white plastic and steel, enshrouded by an ever-changing, artificially generated water-vapor cloud. The public plaza in front of the pavilion contained seven man-sized, sound-emitting floats, that moved slowly and changed direction when touched. A thirty-foot polar heliostat sculpture tracked the sun and reflected a ten-foot-diameter sunbeam from its elliptical mirror through the cloud onto the pavilion. The inside of the pavilion consisted of two large spaces, one black-walled and clam-shaped, the other a ninety-foot high hemispherical mirror dome. The sound and light environment of these spaces was achieved by an innovative audio and optical system consisting of state-of-the-art analog audio circuitry, with krypton-laser, tungston, quartz-iodide, and xenon lighting, all controlled by a specially designed digital computer programming facility.

The sound, light, and control systems, and their integration with the unique hemispherical acoustics and optics of the pavilion, were controlled from a movable console. On this console the lighting and sound had separate panels from which the intensities, colors, and directions of the lighting, pitches, loudness, timbre, and directions of the sound could be controlled by live performers. The sound-moving capabilities of the dome were achieved with a rhombic grid of thirty-seven loudspeakers surrounding the dome, and were designed to allow the movement of sounds from point, straight line, curved, and field types of sources. The speed of movement could vary from extremely slow to fast enough to lose the sense of motion. The sounds to be heard could be from any live, taped, or synthesized source, and up to thirty-two different inputs could be controlled at one time. Furthermore, it was possible to electronically modify these inputs by using eight channels of modification circuitry that could change the pitch, loudness, and timbre in a vast number of combinations. Another console panel contained digital circuitry that could be programmed to automatically control aspects of the light and sound. By their programming of this control panel, the performers could delegate any amount of the light and sound functions to the digital circuitry. Thus, at one extreme the pavilion could be entirely a live-performance instrument, and at the other, an automated environment. The most important design concept of the pavilion was that it was a live-performance, multi-media instrument. Between the extremes of manual and automatic control of so many aspects of environment, the artist could establish all sorts of sophisticated man-machine performance interactions.

As electronic technology continues to diversify, and as more physical phenomena become accessible, creative artists are likely to increase their exploration of new ways of relating human and other natural systems to artificial systems, for use in the live-performance arts.

Bibliography

INTRODUCTION

The selective bibliography is divided into three sections. The first lists other bibliographies for further reference, catalogues, instruction manuals, and those periodicals that either are devoted to electronic music or often contain articles on the subject. Special note should be made of Lowell M. Cross's *A Bibliography of Electronic Music,* which contains 1,562 entries prior to 1967.

The second section of the bibliography lists books that have been mentioned in the text, recommended by the authors of the chapters, or are thought to be useful by the editors. The same format is followed in the third section, which lists periodical articles.

I. Bibliographies, Catalogues, Periodicals

Bahler, Peter Benjamin, *Electronic and Computer Music: An Annotated Bibliography of Writings in English.* Unpublished M.A. dissertation. University of Rochester, 1966.

Bassart, Ann Phillips, *Serial Music: A Classified Bibliography of Writings on Twelve-Tone and Electronic Music.* Berkeley: University of California Press, 1961.

Cross, Lowell M., ed., *A Bibliography of Electronic Music.* Toronto: University of Toronto Press, 1967.

Davies, Hugh, ed, *International Electronic Music Catalogue.* Cambridge, Mass.: M.I.T. Press, 1967.

Electronic Music Reports, Vol. 1–4 (1969–71). Utrecht: Institute for Sonology. See also *Interface.*

Electronic Music Review, Vol. 1–7. Trumansburg, N.Y.: Independent Electronic Music Center. Ceased publication in 1969.

Electronic Musical Instruments, a Bibliography, 2nd ed. London: Tottenham Public Libraries and Museum, 1952.

Gravesaner Blätter. Mainz, Germany.

Henry, Otto. *A Preliminary Checklist: Books and Articles on Electronic Music*. New Orleans, La., 1966.

Interface. Vol. 1, No. 1 (April, 1972). Amsterdam: Swets and Zeitlinger, N.V. Incorporates *Electronic Music Reports*.

The Journal of the Acoustical Society of America. New York: American Institute of Physics (335 East 45th Street, 10017).

Journal of the Audio Engineering Society, New York (Lincoln Building, Room 929, 60 E. 42nd St., 10017).

Die Reihe. Vienna, Universal Editions. English translations published by Theodore Presser Company, Bryn Mawr, Pa. Vol. 1 devoted to electronic music.

Risset, J. C. *An Introductory Catalog of Computer Synthesized Sounds*. Murray Hill, N.J.: Bell Telephone Laboratories, 1970.

Schwann Record and Tape Guide. Boston: W. Schwann, Inc. Published monthly; contains a section on electronic music.

Source Magazine—Music of the Avant-Garde. Sacramento, Calif.

Synthesis. Minneapolis, Minn.: Sculley-Cutter Publishing, Inc. (1315 Fourth St., S. E.)

II. Books

Bachus, John, *The Acoustic Foundations of Music*. New York: Norton, 1969.

Beauchamp, N. W., and Von Foerster, eds., *Music by Computers*. New York: Wiley, 1969.

Beck, A. H. W., *Words and Waves*. New York: McGraw-Hill, 1967.

Beckwith, John, and Udo Kasemets, *The Modern Composer and His World*. Toronto: University of Toronto Press, 1961.

Békésy, G. von, *Experiments in Hearing*. New York: McGraw-Hill, 1960.

Benade, Arthur H., *Strings, Horns, and Harmony*. Garden City, N.Y.: Doubleday, 1960.

Beranek, Leo L., *Acoustics*. New York: McGraw-Hill, 1954.

Buban, Peter and M. L. Schmitt, *Understanding Electricity and Electronics*, New York: McGraw-Hill, 1969.

Busoni, Ferruccio, *Sketch of a New Aesthetic of Music*. New York: G. Schirmer, 1911.

Cage, John, *Notations*. New York: Something Else Press, Inc., 1969.

Coker, Cecil H, P. B. Denes, and E. N. Pinson, *Speech Synthesis*. Murray Hill, N.J.: Bell Telephone Laboratories, Inc., 1963.

Cope, David, *New Directions in Music—1950 to 1970*. Dubuque, Iowa: William C. Brown, 1970.

Crowhurst, Norman H., *Electronic Music Instruments*. Blue Ridge Summit, Pa.: TAB Books, 1971.

Dolan, Robert Emmett, *Music in Modern Media*. New York: G. Schirmer, 1967.

Douglas, Alan, *Electronic Music Production*. New York: Pitman Publishing Corp., 1973.

Dwyer, Terence, *Composing with Tape Recorders*. London: Oxford University Press, 1971.

Eaton, M. L., *Bio-Music*. Kansas City, Mo.: Orcus research, 1970.

———, *Electronic Music—A Handbook of Sound Synthesis and Control*. Kansas City: Orcus Research, 1969.

Eimert, Herbert, *Electronic Music*. Ottawa: National Research Council of Canada, Technical Translation TT–601, 1956.

Eimert, Herbert, Fritz Enkel, and Karlheinz Stockhausen, "Problems of electronic music notation." Ottawa: National Research Council of Canada, Technical Translation TT–612, 1956.

Enkel, Fritz, *The Technical Facilities of the Electronic Music Studio (of Cologne Broadcasting Station)*. Ottawa: National Research Council of Canada, Technical Translation TT–603, 1956.

Experiments in Art and Technology, Inc. (Klüver, Martin, and Rose, eds.), *Pavilion*. New York: Dutton, 1972.

Flanagan, J. L., *Speech Analysis Synthesis and Perception*. New York: Springer-Verlag, 1972.

Fletcher, H., *Speech and Hearing in Communication*. New York: Van Nostrand, 1953.

Fowler, Charles B., ed., *Electronic Music: Music Educators Journal*. Washington, D.C.: Music Educators National Conference, 1968.

Friend, David, Alan R. Pearlman, and Thomas D. Piggot, *Learning Music with Synthesizers*. Newton, Massachusetts: Hall Leonard Publishing Corporation, 1974.

Gamper, David E., *Preliminaries to Electronic Music Studio Design*. Thesis, University of California at San Diego, 1973.

Gulick, L., *Hearing, Physiology and Psychophysics*. New York: Oxford University Press, 1971.

Handel, Samuel, ed., *A Dictionary of Electronics*. Baltimore: Penguin, 1962.

Haynes, N. M., *Tape Editing and Splicing*. Flushing, N.Y.: Robin Industries, 1957.

Helmholtz, Hermann, *On The Sensations of Tone*, trans. A. J. Ellis. New York: Dover, 1954.

Hiller, Lejaren, *Music Composed with a Computer: An Historical Survey*. Illinois Technical Report No. 18. Urbana, Ill: University of Illinois School of Music, 1969.

Hiller, L. A., and L. M. Isaacson, *Experimental Music-Composition with an Electronic Computer*. New York: McGraw-Hill, 1959.

Howe, Hubert, *Buchla Manual*. Fullerton, Calif.: CBS Musical Instrument Research Department (1300 East Valencia Street, 92631).

———, *Music 7 Reference Manual*. New York: Queens College Press, 1970.

Hunt, F. V., *Electroacoustics*. Cambridge, Mass.: Harvard University Press, 1954.

Josephs, J. J., *The Physics of Musical Sound*. Princeton, N.J.: Van Nostrand 1967.

Judd, E. C., *Electronic Music and Music Concrete*. London: Neville Spearman, Ltd., 1961.

Karkoschka, Erhard, *Notation in New Music*. New York: Praeger, 1972.

Ladefoged, Peter. *Elements of Acoustic Phonetics*. Chicago: University of Chicago Press, 1962.

Lehiste, Ilse, ed., *Readings in Acoustic Phonetics*. Cambridge, Mass.: M.I.T. Press, 1967.

Levarie, Sigmund, and E. Levy, *Tone—A Study in Musical Acoustics*. Kent, Ohio: Kent State University Press, 1968.

Lincoln, Harry B., ed., *The Computer and Music*. Ithaca, N.Y.: Cornell University Press, 1970.

Lorentzen, Bengt, *An Introduction to Electronic Music*. Rockville Center, N.Y.: Belwin Mills Company, 1970.

Mathews, Max V., *Technology of Computer Music*. Cambridge, Mass.: M.I.T. Press, 1969.

Meyer-Eppler, Werner, *The Terminology of Electronic Music*. Ottawa: National Research Council of Canada, 1956.

Modugno, Anne, and Charles Palmer, *Tape Control in Electronic Music*. Talcottville, Conn.: Electronic Music Laboratories (P.O. Box H), 1970.

Moles, A. A., *Information Theory and Aesthetic Perception,* trans. Joel E. Cohen. Urbana, Ill.: University of Illinois Press, 1966.

Morse, Philip M., *Vibration and Sound*. New York: McGraw-Hill, 1948.

Nisbett, Alec., *The Technique of the Sound Studio*, 3rd ed. New York: Hastings House Publishers, 1972.

Olson, Harry F., *Music, Physics and Engineering*. New York: Dover, 1967.

Partch, Harry, *Genesis of a Music*. New York: Plenum Publishing Corp., 1970.

Pelligrino, Ronald, *An Electronic Studio Manual*. Columbus, Ohio: Ohio State University, College of the Arts, Publication No. 2, 1969.

Pierce, J. R., and E. E. David, Jr., *Man's World of Sound*. Garden City, N.Y.: Doubleday, 1958.

Prieberg, F. K., *Musica ex Machina*. Berlin: Verlag Ullstein, 1960.

———, *Musik des technischen Zeitalters*. Zürich: Atlantisverlag, 1956.

Reynolds, Roger, *Music—New Roles and Contexts*. New York: Praeger, 1974.

Schaeffer, Pierre, *A la recherche d'une musique concrète*. Paris: Editions du Seuil, 1952.

———, *Traité des objets musicaux*. Paris: Editions du Seuil, 1966.

Schwartz, Elliott, *Electronic Music: A Listener's Guide*. New York: Praeger, 1973.

Schwartz, Elliot, and Barney Childs, eds., *Contemporary Composers on Contemporary Music*. New York: Holt, Rinehart and Winston, 1967.

Sear, Walter, *The New World of Electronic Music*. New York: Alfred Publishers, 1972.

Skilling, H. H., *Electrical Engineering Circuits*. New York: Wiley, 1959.

Slonimsky, Nicolas, *Music Since 1900,* 4th ed. New York: Charles Scribner's Sons, 1971.

Stevens, Stanley S., ed., *Handbook of Experimental Psychology*. New York: Wiley, 1951.

Stevens, Stanley S., and H. Davis, *Hearing*. New York: Wiley, 1938.

Strange, Allen, *Electronic Music*. Dubuque, Iowa: William C. Brown, 1972.

Taylor, C. A., *The Physics of Musical Sounds*. New York: American Elsevier Publishing Company, Inc., 1965.

Trythall, Gilbert, *Principles and Practice of Electronic Music*. New York: Grosset & Dunlap, Inc., 1973.

University of Melbourne Faculty of Music, *The State of the Art of Electronic Music in Australia*. Seminar. n.p., Melbourne: Australian Council for the Arts; the Myer Foundation, August 9–13, 1971.

VanBergeijk, Wilhelm, A., *et al., Waves and the Ear*. Garden City, N.Y.: Doubleday, 1960.

Wells, Thomas, and Eric S. Vogel, *The Technique of Electronic Music*. Austin: University Stores, Inc., 1974. [© 1974 by Thomas Wells and Eric S. Vogel; available from University Stores, Inc., P.O. Box 7756, Austin, Texas, 78712.]

Winckel, Fritz, *Music, Sound and Sensation,* trans. T. Binkley. New York: Dover, 1967.

Youngblood, Gene, *Expanded Cinema*. New York: Dutton, 1970.

III. Periodical Articles

Appleton, Jon H., "Reevaluating the Principle of Expectation in Electronic Music," *Perspectives of New Music* VIII, No. 1, 106.

———, "Tone-Relation, Time-Displacement and Timbre," *The Music Review,* XXVII, No. 1, 54.

Babbitt, Milton, "An Introduction to the R.C.A. Synthesizer," *The Journal of Music Theory,* VIII (Winter, 1964), 251.

———, "Who Cares If You Listen?" *High Fidelity,* VIII (February, 1958), 38.

Backus, John, "Die Reihe—a Scientific Evaluation," *Perspectives of New Music,* I (Fall, 1962), 160.

Blaukopf *et al., Music and Technology*. Stockholm meeting, June 8–12, 1970, organized by UNESCO. Published by *La Revue Musicale,* Paris, 1971.

Carter, Elliott, and Vladimir Ussachevsky, "Reel vs. Real," *American Symphony Orchestra League Newsletter,* II (July, 1960), 8.

Chadabe, Joel, "New Approaches to Analog Studio Design," *Perspectives of New Music* VI, No. 1, 107.

Chowning, John, *"The Simulation of Moving Sound Sources,"* New York: Audio Engineering Society Reprint No. 726, 1970.

Ciamaga, Gustav. "Some Thoughts on the Teaching of Electronic Music," *The Yearbook of the Inter-American Institute for Musical Research,* III (1967), 69.

Cowell, Henry, "Composing with Tape," *Hi-Fi Music at Home,* II (January–February, 1956), 23.

Cross, Lowell, "Electronic Music, 1948–53," *Perspectives of New Music* VII, No. 1, 32.

Davies, Hugh, "A Discography of Electronic Music and Music Concrete," *Recorded Sound,* XIV (April, 1964), 205.

de la Vega, Aurelio, "Electronic Music, Tool of Creativity," *Music Journal,* XXIII (September, 1965), 52; (October, 1965), 61; and (November, 1965), 52.

————, "Regarding Electronic Music," *Tempo* LXXV (Winter, 1965–1966), 2.

Divilbiss, J. L., "The Real-Time Generation of Music with a Digital Computer," *Journal of Music Theory,* VIII, No. 1, 99.

Eimert, Herbert, "Elektronische Musik," *Die Musik in Geschichte und Gegenwart,* III. Kassel: Bärenreiter-Verlag, 1954.

"Electronic Music," in *The International Cyclopedia of Music and Musicians,* 9th ed. New York: Dodd, Mead 1964, p. 594.

Fennelly, Brian, "A Descriptive Language for the Analysis of Electronic Music," *Perspectives of New Music,* VI, No. 1, 79.

Forte, Alan, "Composing with Electrons in Cologne," *High Fidelity,* VI (October, 1956), 64.

Gerhard, Roberto, "Concrète and Electronic Sound Composition," *Music Libraries and Instruments.* London: Hinrichsen Edition, 1961, p. 30. Hinrichsen's Eleventh Yearbook.

Hiller, Lejaren A., Jr., "Acoustics and Electronic Music in the University Music Curriculum," *American Music Teacher,* XII (1963), 24.

Hiller, Lejaren A., Jr., "Electronic Music at the University of Illinois," *Journal of Music Theory* VII, No. 1, 99.

Howe, Hubert S., Jr., "Recent Recordings of Electronic Music," *Perspectives of New Music,* VII, 2, 178.

————, "Review of *Electronic Music: Systems, Techniques, and Controls,* by Allen Strange," *Perspectives of New Music,* XI, No. 2, 249.

————, "Review of *Music by Computers,* ed. by Beauchamp and von Foerster," *Perspectives of New Music,* VIII, No. 1, 151.

Hunkins, Arthur B., "First Creative Encounter with Electronic Music," *American Music Teacher,* XVI (1967), 29.

Ivey, Jean Eichelberger, "An Electronic Music Bookshelf," *College Music Symposium,* IX (Fall, 1969), 127.

Judd, F. C., "The Composition of Electronic Music," *Audio and Record Review,* I (November, 1961) 27.

Kelly, Warren E., "Tape Music Composition for Secondary School," *Music Educators Journal,* LII (June–July, 1966), 86.

Lawrence, H., "Music Criticism in the Electronic Age," *Audio,* XLIV (October, 1960), 78.

————, "Splitting the Tone," *Audio,* XLI (November, 1957), 78.

Le Caine, Hugh, "A Tape Recorder for Use in Electronic Music Studios and Related Equipment," *Journal of Music Theory,* VII, No. 1, 83.

Le Caine, Hugh, and Gustav Ciamaga, "A Preliminary Report on the Serial Sound Structure Generator," *Perspectives of New Music* VI, No. 1, 114.

Licklider, J. C. R., "Three Auditory Theories," in Sigmund Kock, ed., *Psychology: A Study of a Science*. New York: McGraw-Hill, 1959.

————, "Basic Correlates of the Auditory Stimulus," in S. S. Stevens, ed., *Handbook of Experimental Psychology*. New York: Wiley, 1951.

Luening, Otto, "Karlheinz Stockhausen," *Juilliard Review*, VI (Winter, 1958–59), 10.

————, "Some Random Remarks about Electronic Music," *Journal of Music Theory*, VIII (Spring, 1964), 89.

MacInnis, Donald, "Sound Synthesis by Computers: MUSICOL, a Program Written Entirely In Extended ALGOL," *Perspectives of New Music*, VII, No. 1, 66.

Marks, L. E., and A. W. Slawson, "Direct Test of the Power Function for Loudness," *Science*, CLIV (1966), 1036–37.

Mathews, M. V., F. R. Moore, and J. C. Risset, "Computers and Future Music," *Science*, CLXXXIII, No. 412 (January 25, 1974), 263–68.

Mumma, Gordon, "An Electronic Music Studio for the Independent Composer," *Journal of the Audio Engineering Society*, XII (July, 1964), 240.

"Musique Concrète," in *The International Cyclopedia of Music and Musicians*, 9th ed. New York: Dodd, Mead, 1964, p. 1432.

Perera, Ronald C., "The Three Part Academic Electronic Music Studio," *College Music Symposium* XI (Fall, 1971), 66.

Rabb, B., "Electronic Music is Valid!" *Music Journal*, XIX (October, 1961), 60.

Randall, J. K., "Three Lectures to Scientists," *Perspectives of New Music*, V, No. 2 (1967).

————, "A Report from Princeton," *Perspectives of New Music*, III, No. 2, 84.

Salzman, Eric, "Music from the Electronic Universe," *High Fidelity*, XIV (August, 1964), 54.

Schaeffer, Myron, "The Electronic Music Studio of the University of Toronto," *Journal of Music Theory*, VII, No. 1, 73.

Schuller, Gunther, "The New German Music for Radio," *Saturday Review*, XLV (January 13, 1962), 62.

Searle, Humphrey, "Concrete Music," in *Grove's Dictionary of Music and Musicians*, 5th ed., Vol. 9, Appendix 2. London and New York: MacMillan, 1954. Supplementary Volume, 1961. See also his article on "Electrophonic Music."

Seawright, James, "What is Electronic Music?" *Radio-Electronics*, XXXVI (June, 1965), 36.

Slawson, Wayne, "A Speech-Oriented Synthesizer of Computer Music," *Journal of Music Theory*, XIII, No. 1, 94.

————, "Vowel Quality and Musical Timbre as Functions of Spectrum Envelope and Fundamental Frequency," *Journal of the Acoustical Society of America*, XLIII (1968), 87–101.

Stevens, S. S., "Perceived Level of Noise by Mark VII and dB (E)," *Journal of the Acoustical Society of America*, LI (1972), 575–602.

————, "The Measurement of Loudness," *Journal of the Acoustical Society of America,* XXVII, No. 5 (September, 1955), 815.

Stravinsky, Igor, "Electronic Music," in *Memories and Commentaries.* Garden City, N.Y.: Doubleday, 1960, p. 94.

Subotnick, Morton, "The Use of the Buchla Synthesizer in Musical Composition," New York: Audio Engineering Society, Reprint 709, 1970.

Tenney, James C., "Sound-Generation by Means of a Digital Computer," *Journal of Music Theory,* VII, No. 1, 24.

Ussachevsky, Vladimir, "Music in the Tape Medium," *Juilliard Review,* VI (Spring, 1959), 8.

————, "Notes on A Piece for Tape Recorder," *Musical Quarterly,* XLVI (April, 1960), 202. Reprinted in Paul Henry Lang, ed., *Problems of Modern Music.* New York: Norton, 1962.

————, "The Process of Experimental Music," *Journal of the Audio Engineering Society,* VI (July, 1958), 202.

Weinland, John David, "An Electronic Music Primer," *Journal of Music Theory* XIII, No. 2, 250.

Winckel, Fritz, "The Psycho-Acoustical Analysis of Music as applied to Electronic Music," *Journal of Music Theory* VII, No. 2, 194.

Discography

INTRODUCTION

The selective discography includes works broadly representative of musique concrète, electronic music, and music for instruments or voices and electronic sounds. Compositions are listed alphabetically under composers' last names, except in cases where a group of three or more of a composer's works appear on one recording, in which event only the title of the *first* piece of the group is alphabetized. In the case of a collaboration, the work is listed under one of the composers' names, and each of the other contributors is cross-referenced to it (e.g., "USSACHEVSKY—See also LUENING and USSACHEVSKY"). Collaborative groups, such as AMM or MEV, are indexed both by the group name and by the names of individual members, where known.

Though an effort has been made to favor recordings on the major U.S. commercial labels, which are widely distributed, some recordings that the editors feel are important for this discography are available only on foreign labels or on relatively obscure domestic ones. To further assist the reader, an appendix to the discography lists the addresses of all record companies named and the addresses of three retail distributors through whom unusual or out-of-print recordings can be obtained by special order. When a work is known to have been recorded more than once, all the recordings have been listed in the hope that the reader will be able to find at least one of them in his area.

All discographies are ephemeral. Recordings are discontinued, or are re-released in different formats or on new labels; new and better versions appear of pieces that involve interpreters; monaural recordings are re-mastered as "stereo"; collections are made from collections. For the serious collector of electronic music on disc, two further publications are indispensable. The first is the monthly *Schwann* record catalog, which has a special section devoted to *current* recordings of electronic music. The *Schwann* catalog is issued by W. Schwann, Inc., 137 Newbury Street, Boston, Mass. 02116. The second publication is the *International Electronic Music Catalog*, compiled by Hugh Davies, which lists all known works of electronic music in the world through 1967, and which includes a thirty-three page discography. This publication is available from the M.I.T. Press, Massachusetts Institute of Technology, Cambridge, Mass.

AITKEN, ROBERT	*Noesis*	Folkways 33436
ALMURO, ANDRE	*Phonolite I and II*	Mouloudji/Festival EMZ 13514
AMM (Group) Cardew, Gare, Hobbs, Prevost, Rowe	*AMM Music*	Elektra (England) EUKS 7256
	Live Electronic Music Improvised	Mainstream MS 5002
ANHALT, ISTVAN	*Composition No. 4* (1962)	Allied Record 17
APPEL, KAREL	*Musique barbare*	Philips (Neth.) 99954 DL
APPLETON, JON	*Appleton Syntonic Menagerie*	Flying Dutchman FDS 103
	The World Music Theater of Jon Appleton	Folkways FTS 33437
APPLETON, JON and DON CHERRY	*Human Music*	Flying Dutchman FDS 121
AREL, BULENT	*Electronic Music No. 1* (1960); *Music for a Sacred Service: Prelude and Postlude* (1961)	Son Nova 1988
	Stereo Electronic Music No. 1	Columbia MS–6566
	Stereo Electronic Music No. 2	CRI S–268
ARTHUYS, PHILIPPE	*Boîte à musique*	DUC 8
ASHLEY, ROBERT	*Purposeful Lady Slow Afternoon*	Mainstream 5010
	The Wolfman	Source 4
	Untitled Mixes	ESP–DISK 1009
ASUAR, JOSE VINCENTE	*Divertimento*	Turnabout 34427
	Preludio "La Noche" (I)	JME ME–1–2
AUSTIN, LARRY	*Accidents*	Source 2
AVNI, TZVI	*Vocalise*	Turnabout 34004
BABBITT, MILTON	*Composition for Synthesizer* (1964)	Columbia MS–6566
	Ensembles for Synthesizer	Columbia MS–7051

	Philomel	Acoustic Research 0654083
	Vision and Prayer	CRI SD 216 CRI S–268
BADINGS, HENK	*Capriccio for Violin and Two Sound Tracks; Genese; Evolutions— Ballet Suite*	Epic BC 1118 Limelight 86055
BAKER, ROBERT	*See* HILLER and BAKER	
BARK, JAN	*Bar*	Phono Suecia PS2
BARONNET, JEAN	*See* DUFRÈNE and BARONNET	
BARRAQUE, JEAN	*Etude*	Barcley 89005
BAYLE, FRANÇOIS	*Espaces inhabitables*	Philips (Fr.) 836895 DSY
	L'Oiseau Chanteur	Candide CE 31025
	Vapeur	BAM LD 072 BAM 5072
BAZELON, IRWIN	*Chamber Concerto "Churchill Downs"*	CRI SD 287
BEATLES, The (Group) Harrison, McCartney, Lennon, Starr	*See* HARRISON	
BEAVER, PAUL, and BERNARD L. KRAUSE	*The Nonesuch Guide to Electronic Music*	Nonesuch HC–73018
BEHRMAN, DAVID	*Runthrough*	Mainstream 5010
	Wavetrain	Source 5
BERIO, LUCIANO	*Differences*	Mainstream 5004 Time S/8002
	Momenti	Philips 835 485/86 AY
	Momenti; Omaggio à Joyce	Limelight LS–86047
	Mutazioni	RAI (FONIT) (Milan) No number, included in "Elettronica," 1956 No. 3
	Thema (Omaggio à Joyce)	Turnabout TV–34177 Philips 835 485/86 AY
	Visage	Turnabout TV–34046S
BIELAWA, HERBERT	*Spectrum*	Cornell University 1

BLACHER, BORIS	*Impulsketten*	Wergo 60017 Mace S–9097
BODIN, LARS-GUNNAR	*Smoothing*	Sveriges Radio RELP 1102
	Winter-events	Sveriges Radio LPD 3
BOISSELET, PAUL	*Symphonie Rouge*	SFRP 30007
BONDON, JACQUES	*Kaleidoscope*	MHS 988
BORDEN, DAVID	*Variations on America by Charles Ives*	Cornell University 7
BOUCOURECHLIEV, ANDRE	*Texte I*	Philips 835 485/86 AY Mercury SR2–9123
	Texte II	BAM LD 071
BOULEZ, PIERRE	*Etude II (sur sept sons)*	Barcley 89005
BOZIC, DARIJAN	*Kriki*	Desto DC 6474–77
BRESS, HYMAN	*Fantasy, for violin, piano and electronic sounds*	Folkways FM 3355
BROWN, EARLE	*Four Systems (for four amplified cymbals*	Columbia MS–7139
	Times Five	BAM LD 072
BROWN, MARION, and ELLIOTT SCHWARTZ	*Soundways*	Bowdoin College Music Press No. 41746
BRÜN, HERBERT	*Anepigraphe*	Amadeo AVRS 5006
	Futility 1964	Heliodor HS–25047
BRUYNDONCKX, JAN	*Een Roos a Rose;* *Kleine Caroli;* *Ogenblik; Veronika;* *Vertigo Gli*	OU 28–29
BRUYNEL, TON	*Arc*	Donemus Audio- Visual Series 7172/1
	Collage Resonance II; *Reflexen; Relief*	EFC 2501
BRYANT, ALLEN	*See* MEV	
	Pitch Out	Source 2
BUDD, HAROLD	*Coeur D'Orr; Oak of Golden Dreams*	Advance 16
BUSSOTTI, SYLVANO	*Coeur pour batteur—Positively Yes*	Columbia MS–7139
CAGE, JOHN	*Aria with Fontana Mix*	Mainstream MS–5005

	Cartridge Music	Mainstream 5015 DGG 137009
	Fontana Mix (for Magnetic Tape alone)	Turnabout 34046S
	Fontana Mix-Feed	Columbia MS–7139
	Imaginary Landscape No. 1	Avakian 1
	Solos for Voice 2 (Electronic Realization by Gordon Mumma and David Tudor)	Odyssey 3216 0156
	Variations II	Columbia MS–7051 CBS France S–3461064 JME ME 2
	Variations III	DGG 139442 Wergo 60057
	Variations IV (excerpts)	Everest 3132
	Variations IV, Vol. 2	Everest 3230
	Williams Mix	Avakian 1
CAGE, JOHN and LEJAREN HILLER	*HPSCHD*	Nonesuch H–71224
CANTON, EDGARDO	*Voix Inouïes*	JME ME 1–2
CARDEW, CORNELIUS	*See* AMM	
CARLOS, WALTER	*Dialogues for Piano and Two Loudspeakers*	Turnabout 34004
	Sonic Seasonings	2-Columbia KG–31234
	Switched-On Bach	Columbia MS–7194
	Variations for Flute and Electronic Sound	Turnabout 34004
	Well-Tempered Synthesizer	Columbia MS–7286
CARSON, PHILIPPE	*Turmac*	BAM LD 072 BAM 5072
CASTIGLIONI, NICCOLO	*Divertimento*	Compagnia generale del Disco ESZ–3
CHARPENTIER, JACQUES	*Lalita*	MHS 821
CHERRY, DON	*See* APPLETON and CHERRY	
CHOPIN, HENRI	*Le Corps en Trois Parties; Nu; Décorché; Squelette*	OU 30
	L'énergie du Sommeil	OU 23–24

	La Fusée Interplanétaire	OU 26–27
	Indicatif I	OU 26–27
	Play Leap-Frog	Sveriges Radio RELP 1102
	Sol Air	OU 28–29
	Vibrespace	OU 20–21
CLEMENTI, ALDO	*Collage II*	Compagnia generale del Disco ESZ–3
COBBING, BOB	*As Easy*	Sveriges Radio RELP 1103
	Chamber Music	Sveriges Radio RELP 1049
CONSTANT, MARIUS	*Le joueur de flute*	Philips (Fr.) A76. 050R
COPE, DAVID	*K; Weeds*	Discant 1227
CURRAN, ALVIN	*See* MEV	
CZAJKOWSKI, MICHAEL	*People the Sky*	Vanguard C–10069
DAVIDOVSKY, MARIO	*Electronic Study No. 1*	Columbia MS–6566
	Electronic Study No. 2	Son Nova 3
	Electronic Study No. 3	Turnabout 34487
	Synchronism No. 1	Nonesuch 71289
	Synchronisms 1, 2 and 3	CRI S–204
	Synchronism No. 3	Opus One 6
	Synchronism No. 5	CRI S–268
	Synchronism No. 6	Turnabout 34487
DOBROWOLSKI, ANDRZEJ	*Muzyka na tasme magnetofonowa no. 1*	Muza Warsaw Fest 211
	Muzyka na tasme magnetofonowa i oboj solo	Muza Warsaw Fest 244
DOCKSTADER, TOD	*Drone; Water Music; Two Fragments from Apocalypse*	Owl ORLP–7
	Eight Electronic Pieces	Folkways FM 3434
	Luna Park; Apocalypse; Traveling Music	Owl ORLP–6
	Quatermass	Owl ORLP–8
	See also REICHERT and DOCKSTADER	
DODGE, CHARLES	*Changes*	Nonesuch 71245

	Earth's Magnetic Field	Nonesuch 71250
DONATONI, FRANCO	*Quartetto III*	Compagnia generale del Disco ESZ–3
DRUCKMAN, JACOB	*Animus I*	Turnabout TV–34177
	Animus II	CRI S–255
	Animus III, for clarinet and tape; Synapse; Valentine	Nonesuch 71253
DUBUFFET, JEAN	*Musical Experiences*	Finnadar 9002
DUCKWORTH, WILLIAM E.	*Gambit*	Capra 1201
DUFRÈNE, FRANÇOIS	*Batteries Vocales; Paix en Algérie; Ténu-tenu*	OU 23–24
	Paris-Stockholm	Sveriges Radio RELP 1049
	Tripticirythme	OU 28–29
DUFRÈNE, FRANÇOIS and JEAN BARONNET	*U 47*	Philips 835 485/86 AY Limelight LS–86047
EATON, JOHN	*Blind Man's Cry*	CRI S–296
	Concert Piece for Syn-ket and Symphony Orchestra	Turnabout 34428
	Electro-Vibrations	Decca 710165
	Mass	CRI S–296
	Microtonal Fantasy; Prelude to "Myshkin"; Repose of Rivers; Mirage; The Return; Piece for Solo Syn-Ket No. 3	Decca DL 710154
ECHARTE, PEDRO	*Treno*	JME ME 1–2
EIMERT, HERBERT	*Einführung in die Elek- tronische Musik (Intro- duction to Electronic Music)*	Wergo WER 60006
	Epitaph für Aikichi Kuboyama	Wergo WER 60014
	Etüde über Tongemische; Fünf Stücke; Glockenspiel	DGG LP 16132 DGG LPE 17242
	Sechs Studien	Wergo WER 60014

	Sélection I	Philips 835 485/86 AY Mercury SR 2–9123
EL-DABH, HALIM	*Leiyla and the Poet*	Columbia MS–6566
	Symphonies in Sonic Vibration—Spectrum No. 1	Folkways FX 6160
ENGLERT, GIUSEPPE	*Vagans animula*	DGG 139442
ERB, DONALD	*In No Strange Land; Reconnaissance*	Nonesuch 71223
ERICKSON, ROBERT	*Ricercar à 3*	Ars AN–1001
	Ricercar à 5	DGG 0654–084
FASSETT, JAMES	*Symphony of the Birds*	Ficker FR 1002
FERRARI, LUC	*Etude aux Accidents*	BAM LD 070
	Etude aux Sons Tendus	BAM LD 070
	Tautologos I	BAM LD 072 BAM 5072
	Tautologos II	BAM LD 071
	Tête et Queue du Dragon	Candide 31025
	Und so Weiter	Wergo WER 60046
	Visage V	Philips 835 485/86 AY Limelight LS–86047 Mercury SR2–9123
FONGAARD, BJÖRN	*Galaxy*	Limelight LS–86061
FRANKS, L. E.	*Fantasia (after Orlando Gibbons)*	Decca DL 79103
GABURO, KENNETH	*Antiphony III (Pearl-white moments); Antiphony IV (Poised); Exit Music I: The Wasting of Lucrecetzia; Exit Music II: Fat Millie's Lament*	Nonesuch 71199
	Lemon Drops; For Harry	Heliodor HS–25047
GARE, LOU	*See AMM*	
GASLINI, GIORGIO	*Corri, nella miniera si odono voci*	Voce del Padrone QELP 8086
GASSMANN, REMI, and OSKAR SALA	*Electronics: Music to the Ballet*	Westminister 8110
GERHARD, ROBERTO	*Collages*	Angel S 36558

GLASS, PHILIP	*Music with Changing Parts*	Chatham Square Productions
GLOBOKAR, VINKO	*Discours II*	DGG 137005
GLUSHANOK, PETER	*In Memoriam for my friend Henry Saia*	Turnabout 34427
GRAUER, VICTOR	*Inferno*	Folkways 33436
GRAYSON	*Live Electronic Music*	Orion 74142
GRUBER, HEINZ KARL	*Konjugationen*	Serenus Sep 2000
GRUPPO DI IMPROV-VISAZIONE NUOVA CONSIONANZA (Group)		RCA ITALIANA MILDS 20273 DGG 643541
GUTTMAN, NEWMAN	*Pitch Variations*	Decca DL 79103
GYSIN, BRION	*Calling All Reactive Agents*	OU 23–24
	I Am That I Am; Pistol Poem	OU 20–21
HAMBRAEUS, BENGT	*Constellations II for Organ Sounds* (1959)	Limelight LS 86052
HAMM, CHARLES	*Canto*	Heliodor HS 25047
HAMPTON, CALVIN	*Catch-Up; Triple Play*	Odyssey 3216 0162
HANSON, STEN	*Coucher et Souffler; Che*	Sveriges Radio RELP 1054
HARRISON, GEORGE	*Revolver* [*The Beatles*]	Capitol
	Sgt. Pepper's Lonely Hearts Club Band [*The Beatles*]	Capitol MAS 2653
	Strawberry Fields Forever [*The Beatles*]	Capitol
HEIDSIECK, BERNARD	*La Cage; La Convention Collective; L'exercice*	OU 26–27
	Ne restez pas debout	Sveriges Radio RELP 1054
	Poème-partition D4P	OU 20–21
	Poème-partition J	OU 23–24
	Poesie Action, Qui Je Suis?	Sveriges Radio RELP 1103
	Le Quatrième Plan	OU 23–24
HEINTZ, JAMES R.	*Fanfare and Raga for Bassoon and Tape*	Westminister 8129
HELLERMANN, WILLIAM	*Ariel*	Turnabout 34301S

HENDRIX, JIMI	*The Jimi Hendrix Experi-ence*	Reprise 6261
HENRY, PIERRE	*Entité*	Philips 835 485/86 AY Mercury SR 2–9123
	Mass for Today [with Colombier]; The Green Queen	Limelight LS–86065
	Variations for a Door and a Sigh	Limelight LS 86059
	Le voile d'Orphée	Supraphon DV 6221
	Le Voyage	Limelight LS 86049 Mercury SR 90482
	Orphée	Philips (Eur.) 835484 LY
HENRY, PIERRE and PIERRE SCHAEFFER	*Symphonie pour un homme seul*	London DTL 93121
	Bidule en Ut	DUC
HILLER, LEJAREN	*Avalanche; Computer Music; Suite for Two Pianos and Tape*	Heliodor 2549006
	Machine Music	Heliodor HS–25047
	Peroration	JME ME 102
HILLER, LEJAREN	*See also* CAGE *and* HILLER	
HILLER, LEJAREN and ROBERT BAKER	*Computer Cantata*	Heliodor HS 25053
HOBBS, CHRISTOPHER	*See* AMM	
HODELL, ÅKE	*U.S.S. Pacific Ocean*	Sveriges Radio RELP 1049
HODIER, ANDRE	*Jazz et Jazz*	Fontana 680 208 ML
ICHIYANAGI, TOSHI	*Extended Voices*	Odyssey 3216 0156
ISHII, MAKI	*Hamon-Ripples*	Nippon Victor SJU 1515
IVEY, JEAN EICHELBERGER	*Pinball*	Folkways 33436
JACOBS, HENRY	*Chan; Electronic Kabuki Mambo; Logos; Rhythm Study No. 8*	Folkways 6301
	Sonata for Loudspeakers	Folkways FX 6160

JANSON, ALFRED	*Canon* (for Chamber Orchestra and Tape)	Limelight LS–86061
JOHNSON, BENGT EMIL	*2/1967 (while); 2/1967 (medan)*	Sveriges Radio RELP 1054
JOHNSTON, BEN	*Casta Bertram*	Nonesuch H–71237
KAGEL, MAURICIO	*Acoustica*	2–DGG 2707059
	Transición I	Philips 835 485/86 AY Mercury SR2–9123
	Transición II	Mainstream 5003
KARKOFF	*Landschaft aus Schreien, Op. 86*	Phono Suecia PS2
KIRCHNER, LEON	*Quartet No. 3 for Strings and Tape*	Columbia MS–7284
KLAUSMEYER, PETER	*Cambrian Sea*	Turnabout 34427
KLINTBERG, BENGT	*Calls*	Sveriges Radio RELP 1054
KNIGHT, MORRIS	*After Guernica; Refractions for Clarinet and Tape; Origin of Prophecy; Luminescences*	Golden Crest S–4092
KOENIG, GOTTFRIED MICHAEL	*Funktion Gelb*	Wergo WER 324
	Funktion Gruen	DGG 137011
	Klangfiguren II	DGG LP 16134
	Terminus II	DGG 137011
KOMOROUS, RUDOLF	*Nahrobek Malevicuv*	Supraphon DV 6221
KORTE, KARL	*Remembrances*	Nonesuch 71289
KOTONSKI, WLODZIMIERZ	*Etiuda*	Muza Warsaw Fest 200
KRAUSE, BERNARD L.	*See* BEAVER and KRAUSE	
KŘENEK, ERNST	*Quintona*	JME ME 1–2
	Spiritus Intelligentiae	DGG LP 16134
KUBICZEK, WALTER	*Ein Stadtbummel, Fox für Subharcord und Tanzorchester*	Eterna 720205
KUPFERMAN, MEYER	*Superflute*	Nonesuch 71289

KURTH, ADDY	*Der faule Zauberer*	Eterna 720205
KYROU, MIREILLE	*Etude I*	Philips 835 487 AY
LAABAN, ILMA	*Ciels Inamputables; In the Snow of Revolution*	Sveriges Radio RELP 1103
	Stentorian Groan	Sveriges Radio RELP 1054
LANZA, ALCIDES	*Plectros II*	JME ME 1–2
LeCAINE, HUGH	*Dripsody*	Folkways 33436
LEEDY, DOUGLAS	*Entropical Paradise (6 Sonic Environments)*	3-Seraphim S–6060
LEWIN, DAVID	*Study No. 1; Study No. 2*	Decca DL 79103
LEWIN-RICHTER, ANDRES	*Study No. 1*	Turnabout 34004
LIGETI, GYORGY	*Artikulation*	Philips 835 485/86 AY Wergo 60059 Mercury SR2–9123
LOCKWOOD, ANNA, and HARVEY MATUSOW	*End*	Sveriges Radio RELP 1102
LONGFELLOW, GORDON	*Notes on the History of the World*	Folkways 6301
LOUGHBOROUGH, WILLIAM	*For the Big Horn*	Folkways 6301
LUCIER, ALVIN	*I Am Sitting in a Room*	Source 7
	North American Time Capsule	Odyssey 3216 0156 CBS France S 3461066
	Vespers	Mainstream 5010
LUENING, OTTO		
	Fantasy in Space; Inven- tion on 12 Notes; Legend; Low Speed; Lyric Scene; Moonflight	Desto 6466
	Fantasy in Space	Folkways FX 6160
	Gargoyles	Columbia MS–6566
	In the Beginning, from Theatre Piece No. 2	CRI S–268

	Synthesis for Orchestra and Electronic Sound	CRI 219 USD
LUENING, OTTO, and VLADIMIR USSACHEVSKY	*Concerted Piece for Tape Recorder and Orchestra*	CRI S–227
	Incantation	Desto 6466
	A Poem in Cycles and Bells; Suite from King Lear	CRI 112
	Rhapsodic Variations for Tape Recorder and Orchestra	Louisville 545–5
LUNDSTEN, RALPH	*EMS NR 1*	Sveriges Radio RELP 5023
	Energy for Biological Computer; Suite for Electronic Tape	Odeon E 061–34052
LUNDSTEN, RALPH, and LEO NILSSON	*Jo, Nä, Oj; Flygande tefat*	Sveriges Radio RELP 5023
	Kalejdoskop; Aloha Arita	Sveriges Radio LPD 1
LUNETTA, STANLEY	*Moosack Machine*	Source 8
MACHE, FRANÇOIS-BERNARD	*Prélude*	Philips 835 487 AY
	Terre de Feu	BAM LD 072
	Terre de feu, 2nd version	Candide 31025
	Volumes	BAM LD 071
MacINNIS, DONALD	*Collide-a-Scope*	Golden Crest S–4085
MADERNA, BRUNO	*Continuo*	Philips 835 485/86 AY Limelight LS–86047
	Notturno	RAI (FONIT) (Milan) No number, included in "Elettronica," 1956, No. 3
MAGNE, MICHEL	*Self-Service*	Paris 313001
MALEC, IVO	*Dahovi*	Candide 31025
	Reflets	BAM LD 072 BAM 5072
	Tutti	Philips (Fr.) 836894 DSY
MALOVEC, JOSEF	*Orthogenesis*	Turnabout 34301S

	Vyhybka	Supraphon DV 6221
MARDEROSIAN, ARDASH	*Fantasia for Organ and Tape*	Westminister 8129
MAREN, ROGER	*Natural Pipes*	Folkways FX 6160
MARTIRANO, SALVATORE	*L's G.A.*	Polydor 245001
	Underworld	Heliodor HS–25047
MATHEWS, MAX V.	*Bicycle Built for Two; Frère Jacques; Joy to the World; Numerology; The Second Law; Three Against Four (May Carol II)*	Decca DL 79103
	Masquerades; Slider; Swansong	Decca 710180
MATUSOW, HARVEY	*See* LOCKWOOD and MATUSOW	
MAXFIELD, RICHARD	*Night Music*	Odyssey 3216 0160
	Pastoral Symphony; Bacchanale; Piano Concert for David Tudor; Amazing Grace	Advance S–8
MAYUZUMI, TOSHIRO	*Campanology*	Nippon Victor SJU 1515
	Electronic Music for the Opening Show of the Tokyo Olympic Games 1964	King Record Company SKK 122
	Mandare	Nippon Victor SJX 1004
MAZUREK, BOHDEN	*Bozzetti*	Turnabout 34301
MELLNÄS, ARNE	*Conglomerat*	Sveriges Radio LPD 3
	Far Out	Sveriges Radio RELP 1103
	Intensity 5/6 for tape	EMICSDS–1088
MERCURE, PIERRE	*Tetachromie*	Columbia MS–6763
MESSIAEN, OLIVIER	*Fêtes des Belles Eaux*	Erato LDE 3202; Musical Heritage Society 821
MEV	*See* MUSICA ELETTRONICA VIVA	

MEYERS, EMERSON	*Rhythmus; Excitement; In Memoriam for Soprano and Tape; Chez Dentiste; Moonlight Sound Pictures; Intervals I*	Westminister 8129
MIMAROGLU, ILHAN	*Agony (Visual Study 4 after Arzhile Gorky)*	Turnabout 34046
	Music for Jean Dubuffet's Coucou Bazaar	Finnadar 9003
	Piano Music for Performer and Composer; 6 Preludes for Magnetic Tape: Nos. I, II, XI, IX, VI, XII	Turnabout 34177
	Sing me a Song of Songmy	Atlantic S–1576
	Tombeau d'Edgar Poe; Intermezzo; Bowery Bum	Turnabout 34004
	Wings of the Delirious Demon and other electronic works	Finnadar 9001
MIYOSHI, AKIRA	*Ondine*	Time 2058
MON, FRANZ	*Blaiberg Funeral*	Sveriges Radio RELP 1103
MOORE, RAYMOND	*Trip Through the Milky Way*	Turnabout 34427
MOREL, FRANÇOIS	*Voix de 8 poètes du Canada*	Folkways FL 9905
MOROI, MAKOTO	*Shosanke*	Nippon Victor SJX 1004
MORTHENSON, JAN	*Epsilon Eridani*	Sveriges Radio LPD 3
	Neutron Star	Phono Suecia PS 2
MOTHERS OF INVENTION, The (Group)	*See* ZAPPA	
MUMMA, GORDON	*The Dresden Interleaf 13 February 1945*	JME ME–102
	Horn	Aspen 4
	Hornpipe	Mainstream 5010
	Mesa	Odyssey 3216 0158 CBS France S 3461065
	Music for the Venezia Space Theatre	Advance FGR–5

MUSICA ELETTRONICA VIVA (MEV) (Group)	*Live Electronic Music Improvised*	Mainstream MS 5002
Bryant, Curran, Rzewski, Teitelbaum, Vander		
	The Sound Pool	BYG 529 326 (actuel 26)
NIKOLAIS, ALWIN	*Choreosonic Music of the New Dance Theatre of Alwin Nikolais*	Hanover HM 5005
NILSSON, LEO	*Aurora*	Sveriges Radio RELP 5023
	That Experiment HZS	Odeon EO61–34052
	See also LUNDSTEN and NILSSON	
NONESUCH GUIDE TO ELECTRONIC MUSIC		2-Nonesuch HC–73018
NONO, LUIGI	*La Fabrica Illuminata*	Wergo WER 60038
	Ricorda cosa ti hanno fatto in Auschwitz	Wergo WER 60038
NORDHEIM, ARNE	*Epitaffio (for Orchestra and Tape); Response I (for two Percussion Groups and Tape)*	Limelight LS–86061
NOVAK, LADISLAV	*Les Miroirs Aux Allouettes*	Sveriges Radio RELP 1102
NUOVA CONSONANZA GRUPPA	*Credo*	DGG 137007
	Improvisations	RCA Italiana MILDS 20243
OLIVEROS, PAULINE	*I of IV*	Odyssey 3216 0160
OLNICK, HARVEY	*See* WALTER, SCHAEFFER, and OLNICK	
PARMEGIANI, BERNARD	*Bidule en Re; Capture ephemère; Violostres*	Philips (Fr.) 836889 DSY
	Danse	Candide CE 31025
PENDERECKI, KRZYSZTOF	*Psalmus 1961*	Supraphon DV 6221
PERSSON	*Proteinimperialism*	Wergo 60047
PFEIFFER, JOHN	*Electronomusic*	Victor VICS–1371
PHILIPPOT, MICHEL	*Ambiance I*	BAM LD 070
	Ambiance II	BAM LD 071

	Etude III	Candide 31025
PIERCE, JOHN R.	*Beat Canon; Five Against Seven; Melodie; Molto Amoroso; Stochatta; Variations in Timbre and Attack*	Decca DL 79103
	Eight-Tone Canon	Decca 710180
PONGRACZ, ZOLTAN	*Phonothese*	DGG 137011
POUSSEUR, HENRI	*Electre*	Universal Edition UE 13500
	Jeu de Miroirs de Votre Faust	Wergo WER 60026
	Rimes pour Différentes Sources Sonores	Victor VICS–1239
	Scambi	Philips 835 485/86 AY Mercury SR2–9123
	Trois visages de Liège	Columbia MS–7051
POWELL, MEL	*Events, M; Improvisation; Second Electronic Setting; 2 Prayer Settings*	CRI S–227
	Electronic Setting I	Son-Nova S–1
PREVOST, EDDIE	*See* AMM	
RAAIJMAKERS, DICK	*Contrasts*	Epic BC 1118
RABE, FOLKE	*Was??*	Wergo 60056
RANDALL, JAMES K.	*Lyric Variations for Violin and Computer*	Vanguard C–10057
	Quartets in Pairs; Quartersines; Mudgett (monologues by a mass murderer)	Nonesuch 71245
REA, JOHN	*Synergetic Sonorities*	Allied 16
REIBEL, GUY	*See* SCHAEFFER, P. and REIBEL	
REICH, STEVE	*Come Out*	Odyssey 3216 0160
	Four Organs	Shandar 10005
	It's Gonna Rain	Columbia MS–7265
	Phase Patterns	Shandar 10005
	Violin Phase	Columbia MS–7265

REICHERT, JAMES, and TODD DOCKSTADER	*Omniphony*	Owl ORLP–11
REYNOLDS, ROGER	*Ping; Traces*	CRI SD 285
RIEDL, JOSEF ANTON	*Daniel-Henry Kahnweiler-Erzähltes Leben*	DGG 18738–9
	Zwei Studien für elektronische Klänge	Supraphon DV 6221
RIEHN, RAINER	*Chants de Maldoror*	DGG 137011
RILEY, TERRY	*Dorian Reeds*	Mass Art M–131
	Poppy Nogood and the Phantom Band; Rainbow in Curved Air	Columbia MS 7315
	Untitled Organ	Mass Art M–131
RISSET, JEAN-CLAUDE	*Computer Suite from "Little Boy"*	Decca 710180
	Mutations I	Turnabout 34427
ROBB, JOHN DONALD	*Collage*	Folkways 33436
	Electronic Music from Razor Blades to Moog	Asch 3438
ROBINSON, RICHARD ALLAN	*Ambience*	Turnabout 34427
ROWE, KEITH	*See AMM*	
RUDIN, ANDREW	*Tragoedia*	Nonesuch 71198
RUDNIK, EUGENIUSZ	*Dixi*	Turnabout 34301
RZEWSKI, FREDERICK	*See MEV*	
SAHL, MICHAEL	*Mitzvah for the Dead*	Vanguard C–10057
	Tropes on the Salve Regina	Lyrichord 7210
SALA, OSKAR	*Five Improvisations*	Westminister 8110
	See also GASSMAN, REMI, and SALA	
SALZMAN, ERIC	*The Nude Paper Sermon*	Nonesuch H–71231
SAUGUET, HENRI	*Trois Aspects Sentimentaux*	BAM LD 070
SCHAEFFER, MYRON	*Dance 4:3*	Folkways 33436
	See also WALTER, SCHAEFFER, and OLNICK	
SCHAEFFER, PIERRE	*Etude aux Allures*	BAM LD 070

	Etude aux Objects	Philips 835 487 AY
	Etude aux Sons Animés	BAM LD 070
	Flute Mexicaine; Etude aux torniquets; Le voile d'Orphée; Etude aux chemins de fer; Etude pathétique	DUC 8
	Objets liés	Candide 31025
	See HENRY and SCHAEFFER	
SCHAEFFER, PIERRE, and GUY REIBEL	*Solfège de L'objet Sonore (musical illustrations with spoken text)*	Editions du Seuil O.R.T.F. SR 2
SCHWARTZ, ELLIOTT	*Aria No. 4*	Advance FGR–7
	Interruptions	Advance FGR–11
	(*See also* BROWN, MARION and SCHWARTZ)	
SHEPARD, R. N.	*Ascending; Descending*	Decca 710180
SHIBATA, MINAO	*Improvisation*	Nippon Victor SJX 1004
SHIELDS, ALICE	*Transformation of Ani*	CRI S–268
SIKORSKI, TOMASZ	*Antyfony*	Muza Warsaw Fest 212
SLAWSON, A. WAYNE	*Wishful Thinking About Winter*	Decca 710180
SMILEY, PRIL	*Eclipse*	Turnabout 34301S
	Kolyosa	CRI S–268
SONIC ARTS UNION (Group)		Mainstream 5010
	See separate listings under ASHLEY, BEHRMAN, LUCIER and MUMMA	
SPEETH, SHERIDAN D.	*Theme and Variations*	Decca DL 79103
STEPHEN, VAL T.	*Fireworks; The Orgasmic Opus*	Folkways 33436
STOCKHAUSEN, KARLHEINZ	*Aus den Sieben Tagen*	Harmonia Mundi 30899M
	Gesang der Jünglinge	DGG 138811
	Hymnen	2-DGG 2707039 DGG 139421/2

	Kontakte	DGG 138811 Candide 31022 Vox 678011 Wergo 60009
	Kurzwellen	2-DGG 2707045
	Mantra	DGG 2530208
	Mikrophonie I; *Mikrophonie II*	Columbia MS–7355
	Mixtur	DGG 137012
	Momente	Nonesuch H–71157 Wergo 60024
	Opus 1970	DGG 139461
	Prozession	Candide 31001 Vox 678011
	Solo	DGG 137005
	Spiral	Wergo SHZW 903 BL DGG 2561109
	Studie I	DGG 16133
	Studie II	DGG LPEM 19322 DGG 16133
	Telemusik	DGG 137012
STRANG, GERALD	*Composition No. 4*	JME ME 1–2
STRANGE, ALLEN	*Two X Two*	Capra 1201
SUBOTNICK, MORTON	*Sidewinder*	Columbia M–30683
	Silver Apples of the Moon	Nonesuch H–71174
	Touch	Columbia MS–7316
	The Wild Bull	Nonesuch H–71208

SWICKARD, RALPH	*Sermons of Saint Francis,*
	   for narrator and tape;
	   Hymn of Creation, for
	   narrator and tape
		Orion 7021

SYNTHI AND THE
   COMPOSER
	Demonstration record for
	   EMS London with ex-
	   cerpts of works by
	   Birtwistle, Zinovieff,
	   Cary, Derbyshire, and
	   Whitman	

TAKEMITSU, TORU	*Eurydice-La Mort; Relief* *Statique*	Universal Recording (Japan) ALP 1009

	Sky Horse and Death	Nippon Victor SJU 1515
	Vocalism Ai (Love); Water Music	Victor VICS 1334
TALCOTT, DAVID	*Loop Number 3; Trilogy*	Folkways 6301
TANNENBAUM, ELIAS	*Movements; Contrasts; Blue Fantasy; For the "Bird"*	Desto 7130
	Improvisations and Patterns for Brass Quintet and Tape	Decca DL 79103
TAYLOR, KEITH	*Lumière, for Synthesized and Concrete Sound*	Varese 81001
TEITELBAUM, RICHARD	*See* MEV	
TENNEY, JAMES	*Noise Study*	Decca DL 79103
	Stochastic Quartet	Decca 710180
THIENEN, MARCEL VAN	*La relantie*	BAM LD 037
TOGNI, CAMILLO	*Recitativo*	Compagnia generale del Disco ESZ–3
TOYAMA, MICHIKO	*Aoi-no-Ue; Waka*	Folkways FW 8881
TRYTHALL, GILBERT	*Entropy*	Golden Crest S–4085
USSACHEVSKY, VLADIMIR	*Computer Piece No. 1; Two Sketches for a Computer Piece*	CRI S–268
	Creation-Prologue	Columbia MS–6566
	Metamorphosis (1957); Linear Contrasts (1958); Improvisation No. 4711 (1958)	Son Nova 3
	Piece for Tape Recorder	CRI 112
	Sonic Contours	Desto 6466
	Sonic Contours; Transposition; Reverberation; Composition; Underwater Waltz	Folkways FX 6160
	Wireless Fantasy	CRI S–227
	Of Wood and Brass	CRI S–227
	See also LUENING and USSACHEVSKY	
VAGGIONE, HORACIO	*Sonata IV*	JME ME 1–2
VANDELLE, ROMUALD	*Crucifixion (extracts)*	BAM LD 071

VANDOR, IVAN	*See* MEV	
VARÈSE, EDGARD	*Déserts*	Columbia MS 6362 Angel S–36786 CRI S–268
	Poème Electronique	Columbia MS–6146
VERCOE, BARRY	*Synthesism*	Nonesuch H–71245
VLAD, ROMAN	*Ricercare elettronica*	Compagnia general del Disco ESZ–3
VORTEX (Group)	*See* separate listings under JACOBS, LONGFELLOW, LOUGHBOROUGH, and TALCOTT	Folkways FX 6301
WALTER, ARNOLD, MYRON SCHAEFFER, and HARVEY OLNICK	*Summer Idyll*	Folkways 33436
WEHDING, HANS HENDRIK	*Concertino*	Eterna 720205
WHITE, RUTH	*Flowers of Evil*	Limelight 86066
	Pinions	Limelight LS 86058
	Seven Trumps from the Tarot Cards	Limelight LS 86058
	Short Circuits	Angel S–36042
WHITTENBERG, CHARLES	*Electronic Study No. 2, with contra-bass*	Advance FGR–1
WILSON, GALEN	*Applications*	Capra 1201
WILSON, GEORGE B.	*Exigencies*	CRI S–271
WILSON, OLLY	*Cetus*	Turnabout 34301
WISZNIEWSKI, ZBIGNIEW	*3 Postludia electrone*	Muza Warsaw Fest 211
WOLFF, CHRISTIAN	*Burdocks*	Wergo 60063
	For 1, 2, or 3 People	Odyssey 3216 0158 CBS France S 3461065
WUORINEN, CHARLES	*Time's Encomium*	Nonesuch H–71225

XENAKIS, IANNIS	*Analogique A and B*	Philips 835 487 AY
	Bohor I; Orient-Occident III; Diamorphoses II; Concret P-H II	Nonesuch H–71246
	Concret P.H.	Philips 835 487 AY
	Diamorphoses	BAM LD 070
	Orient-Occident	Philips 835 485/86 AY Limelight LS 86047 Mercury SR2–9123
YOUNG, La MONTE	*31 VII 69 10:26–10:49 PM 23 VIII 64 2:50: 45– 3:11 AM*	Edition X
YUASA, JOJI	*Projection esemplastic*	Nippon Victor SJU 1515
ZAJDA, EDWARD M.	*Study No. 10; In March for Ann; Points; Magnificent Desolation; Study No. 3*	Ars 1006
ZAPPA, FRANK	*Lumpy Gravy*	Verve 6–8741
ZELJENKA, ILJA	*Studio 0, 3*	Supraphon DV 6221
ZIMMERMANN, BERND ALOYS	*Tratto*	Wergo 60031 Heliodor 2549005

Appendix

Record labels, abbreviations, and addresses:

Acoustic Research
    Acoustic Research Inc.
    24 Thorndike St.
    Cambridge, Mass. 02141

Advance
    Advance Recordings Inc.
    7443 Calle Sinaloa
    Tucson, Arizona 85710

Allied Records
    P.O. Box 517
    104 Doncaster Avenue
    Willowdale, Ontario
    Canada

Amadeo (AVRS)
    Apon Record Company, Inc.
    P.O. Box 3087
    Long Island City, N.Y. 11103

Angel
    Capital Records Inc.
    1750 N. Vine St.
    Hollywood, California 90028

Ars Nova
    Ars Antiqua Recordings (Ars)
    P.O. Box 7048, S.E.
    Washington, D.C. 20032

Asch

Pioneer Recording Sales Inc.
701 7th Avenue
New York, New York 10036

Aspen

Roaring Fork Press Inc.
107 Waverly Place
New York, New York 10011

Atlantic

Atlantic Recording Corp.
1841 Broadway
New York, N.Y. 10023

Avakian

c/o Mr. George Avakian
Avakian Brothers
10 West 33rd St.
New York, N.Y. 10001

Barclay

143 Av. de Neuilly
Neuilly-sur-Seine
France

Bôite à Musique (BAM)

Disc'AZ
32 Rue François 1
Paris VIII, France

Bowdoin College Music Press

Bowdoin College
Brunswick, Maine 04011

BYG

Promodisc (Société)
20 Rue Louis-Philippe
92 Neuilly-sur-Seine, France

Candide

Vox Productions Inc.
211 East 43rd Street
New York, N.Y. 10017

Capitol

Capitol Records Inc.
1750 N. Vine St.
Hollywood, California 90028

Capra
> Capra Records
> 1908 Perry Ave.
> Redondo Beach, California 90278

CBS France
> CBS Disques
> 3 Rue Freycinet
> Paris XVI, France

Chatham Square Productions
> Available from Bykert Gallery
> 24 E. 81st St.
> New York, N.Y. 10028

Columbia
> CBS Records
> 51 West 52nd St.
> New York, N.Y. 10019

Compagnia Generale del Disco (ESZ)
> Corso Europa 5
> 20122 Milan
> Italy

Composers Recordings, Inc. (CRI)
> 170 West 74th St.
> New York, N.Y. 10023

Cornell University
> 159 Sapsucker Woods Road
> Ithaca, New York 14850

Decca
> MCA Records Inc.
> 100 Universal City Plaza
> Universal City, California 91608

Desto
> Desto Records
> Loch Road
> Franklin Lakes, New Jersey 07417

Deutsche Grammophon Gesellschaft (DGG)
> Polydor Inc.
> 1700 Broadway
> New York, N.Y. 10019

Discant
(no address available)

Donemus
Jacob Obrechtstraat 51
Amsterdam-Z
Holland

Ducretet-Thomson (DUC)
Pathe-Marconi
19 Rue Lord Byron
Paris 8, France

Editions du Seuil
O.R.T.F.
Centre Bourdan
5 Av. du Recteur Poincare
Paris XVI, France

Edition X
Available from Heiner Freidrich,
Klingsorstrasse a3
D–8000 München 81
West Germany

Elektra (England)
Kinney Recording Group Ltd.
69 New Oxford St.
London W.C. I, England

EMI
P.O. Box 27053
Stockholm 102 51
Sweden

Epic
CBS Records
51 West 52nd Street
New York, N.Y. 10019

Erato
Erato (Disques)
60 Rue de la Chaussée d'Antin
Paris VIII, France

ESP–Disk
ESP–Disk Ltd.
5 Riverside Drive
New York, N.Y. 10023

Eterna
> Leipzigerstr. 26
> Berlin 102
> DDR (East Germany)

Europese Fonoclub (EFC)
> 262 Singel
> Amsterdam, Netherlands

Everest
> Everest Recording Group
> 10920 Wilshire Blvd.
> Los Angeles, California 90024

Ficker (FR)
> Ficker Record Co.
> Old Greenwich, Connecticut

Finnadar
> (no address available)

Flying Dutchman
> Flying Dutchman Productions Ltd.
> 1841 Broadway
> New York, N.Y. 10023

Folkways
> Folkways/Scholastic Recordings
> 43 West 61st Street
> New York, N.Y. 10023

Fontana
> Mercury Recording Corp.
> 35 East Wacker Drive
> Chicago, Ill. 60601

Golden Crest
> Golden Crest Records Inc.
> 220 Broadway
> Huntington Station, L.I.
> New York 11746

Hanover
> c/o Alwin Nikolais
> 344 West 36th St.
> New York, N.Y. 10018

Harmonia Mundi
>   Apon Record Co. Inc.
>   P.O. Box 3087
>   Long Island City, N.Y. 11103

Heliodor
>   Polydor Inc.
>   1700 Broadway
>   New York, N.Y. 10019

Jornadas de Musica Experimental (JME)
>   (no address available)

Kama-Sutra
>   Buddah/Kama-Sutra Records, Inc.
>   1650 Broadway
>   New York, N.Y. 10019

King Record Company
>   King Record Co. Ltd.
>   2-12-13 Otowa-cho
>   Bunkyo-ku
>   Tokyo, Japan

Limelight
>   Mercury Recording Corp.
>   35 East Wacker Drive
>   Chicago, Ill. 60601

Louisville
>   Louisville Philharmonic Society
>   830 South Fourth St.
>   Louisville, Ky. 40203

Lyrichord
>   141 Perry Street
>   New York, N.Y. 10014

Mace
>   Scepter Records Inc.
>   254 W. 54th Street
>   New York, N.Y. 10019

Mainstream
>   Mainstream Records, Inc.
>   1700 Broadway
>   New York, N.Y. 10019

Mass Art
    246 Grand St.
    New York, N.Y.

Mouloudji/Festival (EMZ)
    3 Rue de Gramont
    Paris 2, France

Musical Heritage Society (MHS)
    1991 Broadway
    New York, N.Y. 10023

Muza Warsaw
    Polskie Nagrania
    Dluga 5
    Warsaw, Poland

Nonesuch
    Elektra Corp.
    15 Columbus Circle
    New York, N.Y. 10023

Odéon
    Pathe–Marconi
    19 Rue Lord Byron
    Paris 8, France

Odyssey
    CBS Records
    51 West 52nd St.
    New York, N.Y. 10019

Opus One
    212 Lafayette St.
    New York, N.Y. 10012

Orion
    Orion Records
    Box 24332
    Los Angeles, Calif. 90024

Ou
    c/o Henry Chopin
    9 Rue des Mesanges
    Sceaux (Seine), France

Owl

Owl Records
1229 University Ave.
Boulder, Colorado 80302

Paris

Président
30 Rue Pierre Sémard
Paris 9, France

Philips

Mercury Recording Corp.
35 East Wacker Drive
Chicago, Illinois 60601

Phono Suecia

STIM
Tegnerlunden 3
Stockholm, Sweden

Polydor

Polydor Inc.
1700 Broadway
New York, N.Y. 10019

RAI (Fonit)

Fonit–Cetra SpA
Via Bertola 34
10122 Turin, Italy

RCA Italiana

RCA SpA
Via Tiburtina Km. 12
00131 Rome, Italy

Reprise

Warner Bros. Records Inc.
4000 Warner Blvd.
Burbank, California 91505

Seraphim

Capitol Records Inc.
1750 N. Vine Street
Hollywood, California 90028

Serenus Record Editions

414 E. 75th Street
New York, N.Y. 10021

Shandar
>   101 Boulevard Malesherbes
>   Paris VIII, France

Société Française de Productions Phonographiques (SFP)
>   131 Rue du Cherche-midi
>   Paris XV, France

Son Nova
>   Wayne Record Corp.
>   160 East 48th Street
>   New York, N.Y. 10017

Source
>   2101 22nd St.
>   Sacramento, California 95818

Supraphon Records
>   Palackeho 1
>   Nove Mesto
>   Prague 1, Czechoslovakia

Sveriges Radio
>   S–105 10 Stockholm
>   Sweden

Time
>   Mainstream Records Inc.
>   1700 Broadway
>   New York, N.Y. 10019

Turnabout
>   Vox Productions Inc.
>   211 East 43rd St.
>   New York, N.Y. 10017

Universal Corp. of Japan, Ltd.
>   1-17-8 Uchikanda
>   Chiyoda-ku
>   Tokyo, Japan

Universal Editions
>   Karlsplatz 6
>   Vienna, Austria

Vanguard
>   Vanguard Recording Society Inc.
>   71 West 23rd St.
>   New York, N.Y. 10010

Varese
(no address available)

Verve
MGM Records
7165 Sunset Blvd.
Hollywood, California 90046

Victor
RCA Records
1133 Avenue of the Americas
New York, N.Y. 10036

Voce del Padrone (QELP)
EMI Italiana SpA
Piazza Cavour 1
20121 Milan,
Italy

Vox
Vox Productions Inc.
211 East 43rd St.
New York, N.Y. 10017

Wergo
Wergo Schallplattenverlag
Postfach 1103
(757) Baden–Baden
West Germany

Westminister
ABC
Dunhill Records
8255 Beverly Blvd.
Los Angeles, California 90048

Retail Distributors

Blackwells
Broad Street
Oxford, England

Discophile Inc.
26 West 8th St.
New York, N.Y. 10011

FNAC Diffusion
6 Blvd. du Sebastopol
Paris 4, France

Index